Rural Society and Economic Change in County Durham

Rural Society and Economic Change in County Durham

Recession and Recovery, c.1400–1640

A.T. Brown

THE BOYDELL PRESS

First published 2015
The Boydell Press, Woodbridge

ISBN 978 1 78327 075 0

The Boydell Press is an imprint of Boydell & Brewer Ltd
PO Box 9, Woodbridge, Suffolk IP12 3DF, UK
and of Boydell & Brewer Inc.
668 Mt Hope Avenue, Rochester, NY 14620–2731, USA
website: www.boydellandbrewer.com

A catalogue record for this book is available from the British Library

In loving memory of my grandad Tom Brown

This publication has been made possible by a grant from the
Scouloudi Foundation in association with the
Institute of Historical Research

Contents

Figures

Tables

Maps

Acknowledgements

The production of this book has incurred many debts along the way, most notably to my PhD supervisors, Ben Dodds and Adrian Green, for their tireless support and constant encouragement at every stage of the process. They have endured endless emails and discussions about the following topics, proving sources of information and help far beyond what could reasonably be expected. I would also like to thank numerous members of Durham University for their advice and helpful comments on various aspects of this work, including Chris Brooks, Christian Liddy, Andy Wood, Andy Burn, Lindsay Varner and Sue Trees. I owe a debt of gratitude to the staff of Durham University's Archives and Special Collections, especially Michael Stansfield, Francis Gotto and Andrew Gray, for their endless patience and knowledgeable help in locating numerous sources of information. Similarly, I owe Caroline Palmer, editorial director at Boydell & Brewer, Sarah Bryce and Nick Bingham, many thanks for their gracious help throughout the publication process. I would further like to thank the organisers and participants who have provided helpful comments on aspects of this book given as papers at the annual conferences of the Economic History Society, Social History Society, and the Fifteenth-Century conference, as well as the Economic and Social History of the Pre-modern World seminar series at the Institute of Historical Research, and the Cambridge Medieval Economic and Social History seminars. I have received help and advice from many colleagues over the course of the last six years, not least from members of the Economic History Society, who have always proven to be encouraging and supportive.

In particular, I would like to thank John Hatcher and Richard Britnell, my doctoral examiners, as well as Chris Briggs and Adrian Green for reading through parts of the early manuscript and making numerous suggestions which have greatly improved the book. I especially owe a debt of gratitude to Steve Rigby, Ben Dodds and Richard Hoyle for reading through the entire manuscript and making a comprehensive range of excellent suggestions which have improved what follows immeasurably. Of course, any errors or deficiencies, of which there are no doubt many, remain my own. This research would not have been possible without a 1+3 studentship from the Economic and Social Research Council to fund my postgraduate studies at Durham University, as well as the EHS Postan Fellowship at the Institute of Historical Research, which provided the opportunity to expand and develop several lines of thought, and finally the Addison Wheeler Fellowship at Durham University which has provided the time to finish researching and writing this work up. My thanks are also owed to the Scouloudi Foundation Publications Award at the Institute of Historical Research for a grant in aid of publication. In addition to the above people, I'd like to thank

Rob Doherty, Christian Schneider, Philippa Haughton, Nicki Kindersley, Ben Pope, Poppy Cullen, Reetta Humalajoki, Anna Jones, Mike Cressey, Lauren Working, Kathleen Reynolds and Barbara Gribling for tolerating endless discussions on the topic of medieval peasants and copyhold tenure. Finally, I would like to thank my parents, Alan and Sue Brown, my sister Gemma Simpson, and the rest of my family, without whose constant support this book would never have reached fruition.

Abbreviations

AA	*Archaeologia Aeliana*
AgHR	*Agricultural History Review*
AHEW	*The Agrarian History of England and Wales*
AHR	*The American Historical Review*
BIHR	*Bulletin of the Institute of Historical Research*
CCB	Church Commission Deposit of Durham Bishopric
DCM	Durham Cathedral Muniments
DKR	'Durham Records: Cursitor's Records: Inquisitions Post Mortem', in *The Forty-Fourth Annual Report of the Deputy Keeper of the Public Records* (London, 1883) and *The Forty-Fifth Annual Report of the Deputy Keeper of the Public Records* (London, 1885)
DPRI	Durham Probate Records, Durham University Library
DUL, ASC	Durham University Library, Archives and Special Collections
EcHR	*Economic History Review*
HJ	*Historical Journal*
IPM	Inquisition Post Mortem
JEcH	*Journal of Economic History*
JIH	*Journal of Interdisciplinary History*
JMH	*Journal of Medieval History*
MH	*Midland History*
NH	*Northern History*
P&P	*Past and Present*
SHC	Surrey History Centre
TNA	The National Archives, London

Introduction

In 1597, Richard Bellasis wrote his will which detailed extensive bequests to his extended family, with each of his many nieces and nephews receiving between £100 and £200, as well as £100 being put aside for mending the highways of county Durham. Unlike many testators, he was not anticipating that these substantial bequests would be financed by the sale of his personal goods or from mortgaging his property but instead expected them to be made from the gold and silver he had sequestered around his home at Morton, a list of which was included with his will. Running to a total of over £2,000, this list included £800 walled away to the west side 'of the litell darke staire that goeth downe out of my bedde chamber'; a small stash 'put underfote, under the boordes'; further money 'laide within the bottom of the table chair'; some £400 in 'eight severall lether bagges' in the presser in his study; and a further £64 'thrust into an old lether shoe that lieth upon the upper floore of the said presser'.[1] Only his servant, Margaret Lambert, knew of these large stores of gold and silver throughout his home, having helped him hide them, and perhaps this explains the very generous bequest of £100 she was to receive on his death. Richard Bellasis was no mere hoarder, however, having already purchased the manors of Ludworth, Haswell and Owton in county Durham. In the fifteenth century the Bellasis family had been little more than members of the minor gentry, owning the single manor of Henknoll near Bishop Auckland, which was valued at £5 in 1409, but by the time of the lay subsidy of 1624, William Bellasis was one of the highest appraised individuals in the county. How did families like the Bellasises not only survive the difficulties of the mid-fifteenth-century recession, but actually come to prosper during the high levels of inflation in the sixteenth century? In the fifteenth century, rural society experienced one of the worst recessions in documented English history which was followed by a century of population growth and high levels of inflation, but what were the effects of these economic changes on the social structure of the English countryside?

This book seeks to answer these questions by exploring the effects of recession and inflation on rural society in county Durham, a region characterised by a high concentration of ecclesiastical landownership and the precocious development of large-scale coal production. It traces the fortunes of different types of estates and landholders in county Durham between the late fourteenth and early seventeenth centuries, showing the degree to which patterns of landholding fixed in the period of recession and low

1 DPRI/1/1599/B6/3–4. See chapter 4 for a more extensive discussion of Richard Bellasis.

population levels of the fifteenth century affected the distribution of profits between different types of lords and tenants in the sixteenth and early seventeenth centuries. This book is broadly divided into three sections: the first two chapters explore the divergent development of the two major ecclesiastical estates in Durham; the next three chapters analyse the changing distribution of landed power amongst the laity of the palatinate; and the final two chapters explore how these changes in rural society affected the opportunities and challenges facing Durham tenants, with the gradual stratification of landed society and the emergence of the yeomanry as a social group. As such, it addresses the causes and consequences of agrarian capitalism in the sixteenth century and the relationship between these economic changes and the social structure of late medieval and early modern England. It shows that estate management and institutional constraints were crucial factors in the transformation of the English countryside, often creating a degree of path dependency which affected decision-making and economic opportunities for landlords and tenants alike into the early seventeenth century.

There has been considerable debate about the mechanisms of change in agrarian societies between those who, broadly speaking, favour changes in demography, commercialisation or class relations as explanatory factors of change.[2] In primarily agrarian societies demography has traditionally been seen as the most fundamental factor influencing the demand for land, labour and food, thus affecting, although by no means straightforwardly determining, levels of rent, wages and prices respectively. As such, changes in demography have been seen as vital in producing structural transformations of pre-industrial societies, often as fluctuations in population size push the supply or demand of resources to a crisis point.[3] M. M. Postan was a primary advocate of this neo-Malthusian approach to the agrarian history of medieval Europe, arguing that population growth outstripped economic expansion between 1000 and 1300. Thus for Postan, medieval society was pushed towards a crisis point by population growth as more marginal agricultural land was cultivated, producing a steady decline in yields.[4] This interpretation of population growth in the thirteenth century has come under criticism in recent decades, most notably from

2 See John Hatcher and Mark Bailey, *Modelling the Middle Ages: the History and Theory of England's Economic Development* (Oxford, 2001), pp. 1–20; see also the essays in Rodney Hilton et al., *The Transition from Feudalism to Capitalism* (London, 1976); T. H. Aston and C. H. E. Philpin (eds.), *The Brenner Debate: Agrarian Class Structure and Economic Development in Pre-Industrial Europe* (Cambridge, 1987); C. Dyer, P. Coss and C. Wickham (eds.), *Rodney Hilton's Middle Ages: An Exploration of Historical Themes* (Oxford, 2007).

3 For a survey of this literature see Hatcher and Bailey, *Modelling the Middle Ages*, pp. 21–65; Mark Bailey, 'Demographic Decline in Late Medieval England: Some Thoughts on Recent Research', *EcHR*, 49 (1996), pp. 1–19; M. M. Postan, 'Some Economic Evidence of Declining Population in the Later Middle Ages', *EcHR*, 2 (1950), pp. 221–46.

4 M. M. Postan, 'The Economic Foundations of Medieval Society', in M. M. Postan, *Essays on Medieval Agriculture and General Problems of the Medieval Economy* (Cambridge, 1973), pp. 3–27 and his 'Medieval Agrarian Society in its Prime: England', in M. M. Postan (ed.), *The Cambridge*

Bruce Campbell and Mark Overton, whose work has shown that medieval society may well have followed a Boserupian rather than a Malthusian model of agricultural growth.[5] They have found that 'in the late-thirteenth and early-fourteenth centuries, and again in the late-sixteenth and early-seventeenth centuries, yields did not fall as population grew: on the contrary, they rose', arguing that land responds far more generously to additional inputs of labour than has traditionally been assumed.[6]

Whether or not historians would now agree with Postan's argument that the Great Famine of 1315–17 was an inevitable Malthusian check, many still advocate the primacy of demographic change in creating economic and social transformations of agrarian societies. Most notably, demography has taken centre stage in much of the historiography of pre-industrial England thanks to the efforts of the Cambridge Group for the History of Population and Social Structure, and rightly so, for it clearly played a very important role in the transformation of rural society.[7] The Black Death, for example, was more than just a catalyst for processes already underway and had profound effects on rural society, standing 'unchallenged as the greatest disaster in documented human history, claiming the lives of up to half the population of Europe in just a handful of years'.[8] After the price crash of the 1370s there was at least a century of population stagnation or decline which affected all sections of rural society and, although the inflation of the sixteenth century was partially caused by debasement of the coinage, it is clear that many of the problems faced by rural society in this century were caused by rapid demographic growth.[9] Rentier landlords strug-

Economic History of Europe, Vol. 1: The Agrarian Life of the Middle Ages (Cambridge, 1966), pp. 548–70.

5 Bruce M. S. Campbell, 'The Agrarian Problem in the Early Fourteenth Century', *P&P*, 188 (2005), pp. 3–70; Bruce M. S. Campbell and Mark Overton, 'A New Perspective on Medieval and Early Modern Agriculture: Six Centuries of Norfolk Farming, c.1250–c.1850', *P&P*, 141 (1993), pp. 38–105; Ester Boserup, *The Conditions of Agricultural Growth: the Economics of Agrarian Change Under Population Pressure* (London, 1965); for Malthus, see *An Essay on the Principle of Population*, first published in 1798.

6 Campbell and Overton, 'A New Perspective', p. 41.

7 For the work of the Cambridge Group, see for example: E. A. Wrigley and R. S. Schofield, *The Population History of England, 1541–1871: A Reconstruction* (London, 1981); E. A. Wrigley, R. S. Davies, J. E. Oeppen and R. S. Schofield, *English Population History from Family Reconstitution, 1580–1837* (Cambridge, 1997); Lloyd Bonfield, Richard Smith, Keith Wrightson (eds.), *The World We Have Gained: Histories of Population and Social Structure* (Oxford, 1986).

8 Phillipp Schofield, 'Tenurial Developments and the Availability of Customary Land in a Later Medieval Community', *EcHR*, 49 (1996), p. 250. Quotation from Mark Bailey, 'Introduction' in Mark Bailey and S. H. Rigby (eds.), *Town and Countryside in the Age of the Black Death: Essays in Honour of John Hatcher* (Turnhout, 2012), p. 20.

9 For an overview of these economic and social changes, see for example: M. M. Postan, *The Medieval Economy and Society: Economic History of Britain, 1100–1500* (London, 1972); Richard Britnell, *Britain and Ireland, 1050–1530: Economy and Society* (Oxford, 2004); Christopher Dyer, *An Age of Transition? Economy and Society in England in the Later Middle Ages* (Oxford, 2005); Keith Wrightson, *Earthly Necessities: Economic Lives in Early Modern Britain, 1470–1750* (New Haven, 2000); Andy Wood, *The Memory of the People: Custom and Popular Senses of the Past in*

gled to increase their rents to keep pace with inflation, often leaving the aristocracy and larger landowners at an economic disadvantage compared to the lesser gentry who still worked their own lands. Moreover, the consolidated holdings created during the fifteenth century did not break apart as population increased, which produced a large rural landless population: some people were forced to carve out cottage holdings on the waste, others worked as wage labourers on the farms of their more fortunate neighbours or in the burgeoning cities, and still others roamed the roads of early modern England in search of work.[10]

Overall movements in demography were therefore important in producing the conditions for change in rural society during this period, but alone they cannot explain the direction or nature of that change. Why, for example, did population increase in the thirteenth century lead to a fragmentation of peasant holdings whereas a similar growth in the sixteenth century led to the engrossment of holdings by a wealthy yeomanry who were employing wage labour from the rural poor? Demographic factors were a key dynamic in the creation of various socio-economic trends, but how rural society adapted to them was not a linear or predictable process. Of course, this is widely acknowledged by historical demographers and often embraced by them, but the demographic model became so pervasive in the historiography of this period that in many works it seemed as though population fluctuations were *the* determinant of change in pre-industrial societies.[11] For example, in his introduction to Tawney's *Agrarian Problem*, Lawrence Stone described how 'population pressure has replaced the wicked enclosing or rack-renting landlord as the *diabolus ex machina*'.[12]

Alternatively, the extent of commercialisation has been seen as fundamental in producing economic growth. Nearly a century ago, Henri Pirenne put forward his thesis that long-distance mercantile trade and the evolution of cities created economic growth in medieval Europe between the eleventh and thirteenth centuries.[13] Robert Lopez drew on this work to advocate a Commercial Revolution which preceded the better-known Industrial Revolution. Through the growth of various businesses

Early Modern England (Cambridge, 2013); C. G. A. Clay, *Economic Expansion and Social Change: England 1500–1700*, 2 vols. (Cambridge, 1984).

10 See for example Henry French and R. W. Hoyle, *The Character of English Rural Society: Earls Colne, 1550–1750* (Manchester, 2007); David Palliser, 'Tawney's Century: Brave New World or Malthusian Trap?', *EcHR*, 35 (1982), pp. 339–53; R. H. Tawney, *The Agrarian Problem in the Sixteenth Century* (London, 1912); Jane Whittle, *The Development of Agrarian Capitalism: Land and Labour in Norfolk, 1440–1580* (Oxford, 2000); Keith Wrightson and David Levine, *Poverty and Piety in an English Village: Terling, 1525–1700* (Oxford, 1995).

11 For a survey of this research, see Hatcher and Bailey, *Modelling the Middle Ages*, pp. 21–65; D. B. Grigg, *Population Growth and Agrarian Change: An Historical Perspective* (Cambridge, 1980).

12 Lawrence Stone's introduction to the Harper Torchbooks version of R. H. Tawney, *The Agrarian Problem in the Sixteenth Century* (New York, 1967), p. xi.

13 Henri Pirenne, *Medieval Cities: Their Origins and the Revival of Trade* (Princeton, 1925). For a summary of this research, see J. Masschaele, 'Economic Take-Off and the Rise of Markets', in Carol Lansing and Edward D. English (eds.), *A Companion to the Medieval World* (Chichester, 2009), pp. 89–110.

and institutions, international banking, credit exchanges and debt enforcements were increasingly possible across medieval Europe. Acknowledging the importance of demographic growth, Lopez went on to demonstrate how the medieval economy experienced a commercial revolution between the tenth and the fourteenth centuries, in which an 'underdeveloped society succeeded in developing itself, mostly by its own efforts': 'even as demographic growth was a prime motor of agricultural progress, so agricultural progress was an essential prerequisite of the Commercial Revolution'.[14] James Masschaele and John Langdon have tried to combine these factors to show that there was a 'powerful conjunction between entrepreneurial activity and population growth, and that the former tended to lead the latter' in medieval England.[15]

The extent of commercialisation in medieval society has received significant attention in recent decades and has been the focus of much of the work of Richard Britnell, Bruce Campbell, Christopher Dyer, David Stone and Ben Dodds.[16] Rather than focusing upon international trade, this research has shown that commercialisation penetrated deeply into the medieval English economy, affecting not only how merchants and towns operated but also how peasants responded to market opportunities. As a result, Dyer has advocated that some features of a 'consumer society' can be traced back to the fourteenth century, if not earlier. These include, for example, the concept of economic investment and improvement; the notion of moral improvement in relation to charity; the growth in self-confidence and independence amongst peasants; and the widespread ownership of consumer items.[17] Growing market penetration saw the increasing commercialisation of land, labour, food and services, all of which helped pave the way for the development of agrarian capitalism. However, there are limitations on how far market penetration can be used as an explanatory factor, not least its potentially circular nature: there were more markets therefore peasants became more market-oriented, which in turn produced more markets and thus a greater market-orientation. There are, for example, many societies which have

14 Robert Lopez, *The Commercial Revolution of the Middle Ages, 950–1350* (Englewood Cliffs, 1971), preface and p. 56.

15 J. Langdon and J. Masschaele, 'Commercial Activity and Population Growth in Medieval England', *P&P*, 190 (2006), p. 36.

16 David Stone, *Decision-Making in Medieval Agriculture* (Oxford, 2005), pp. 3–44; Christopher Dyer, *Making a Living in the Middle Ages: The People of Britain, 850–1520* (London, 2002), pp. 155–86; Britnell, *Britain and Ireland*, pp. 158–222; Ben Dodds, *Peasants and Production in the Medieval North-East: the Evidence from Tithes, 1270–1536* (Woodbridge, 2007), pp. 132–61; Also see the essays in Richard Britnell and Bruce M. S. Campbell (eds.), *A Commercialising Economy : England 1086 to c.1300* (Manchester, 1995). For a survey of the importance of this research, see Mark Bailey, 'The Commercialisation of the English Economy, 1086–1500', *JMH*, 24 (1998), pp. 297–311. Eric Schneider has recently questioned the price responsiveness of seigniorial agriculture, Eric B. Schneider, 'Prices and Production: Agricultural Supply Response in Fourteenth-Century England', *EcHR*, 67 (2014), pp. 66–91.

17 Dyer, *An Age of Transition?*, pp. 242–6.

markets, money and commodities but do not develop agrarian capitalism, and so the key issue is why this happened in the specific case of England across this period.

The third school of thought to which historians have traditionally ascribed is the historical materialism of Marxism, with Marx arguing that 'in the social production of their existence, men inevitably enter into definite relations which are independent of their will, namely relations of production appropriate to a given stage in the development of their material forces of production'.[18] The leading Marxist historian of the middle ages Rodney Hilton maintained throughout his career that the 'conflict between landlords and peasants, however muted or however intense, over the appropriation of surplus product of the peasant holding, was a prime mover in the evolution of medieval society'.[19] There have been many historians since Marx who have emphasised the primacy of social relations who might not consider themselves Marxist in political terms but whose work has often been inspired by historical materialism.[20] For example, though R. H. Tawney was not a Marxist, Jane Whittle has recently noted that his focus upon landlord and tenant relations and, in particular, the expropriation of the peasantry during the sixteenth century highlighted exactly those issues which Marx chose to emphasise. In Marx's words, the 'great feudal lords created an incomparably larger proletariat by the forcible driving of the peasantry from the land', a claim which Tawney would not have refuted.[21]

Most notably Robert Brenner followed in Marx's footsteps in arguing that it is the surplus-extraction relationship that defines the fundamental classes in a society, and that it was changes in this relationship which were the key mechanism in producing much broader transformations in society.[22] In particular, he highlighted problems with the demography model by his comparisons with Eastern Europe, showing how the same exogenous impact could have different social and economic effects. He sought to explain why serfdom came crashing down in Western Europe at the same time as it was being reimposed in Eastern Europe, despite these societies having

18 Karl Marx, 'Preface' to *A Contribution to the Critique of Political Economy* (1859). For other important Marxist thinkers, see: A. V. Chayanov, *The Theory of Peasant Economy* (ed.) Daniel Thorner et al. (Madison, 1986); Maurice Dobb, *Studies in the Development of Capitalism* (London, 1946); E.A. Kosminsky, *Studies in the Agrarian History of England in the Thirteenth Century* (ed.) by R. H. Hilton, trans. by Ruth Kisch (Oxford, 1956); R. H. Hilton, *The Decline of Serfdom in Medieval England* (London, 1969); and Eric Hobsbawm, *How to Change the World: Tales of Marx and Marxism* (London, 2011).

19 R. H. Hilton, *Class Conflict and the Crisis of Feudalism* (London, 1985), p. 9.

20 S. H. Rigby, 'Historical Materialism: Social Structure and Social Change in the Middle Ages', *Journal of Medieval and Early Modern Studies*, 34 (2004), p. 498.

21 Karl Marx, *Capital*, quoted in Jane Whittle, 'Introduction: Tawney's *Agrarian Problem* Revisited', in Jane Whittle (ed.), *Landlords and Tenants in Britain, 1440–1660: Tawney's Agrarian Problem Revisited* (Woodbridge, 2013), p. 1.

22 Robert Brenner, 'Agrarian Class Structure and Economic Development in Pre-Industrial Europe', in T. H. Aston and C. H. E. Philpin (eds.), *The Brenner Debate: Agrarian Class Structure and Economic Development in Pre-Industrial Europe* (Cambridge, 1987), pp. 10–12.

endured similar demographic decline.[23] His argument has often been questioned, not only because of the historical accuracy of his observations but also because of their theoretical underpinning in which he asserted that class relations were of primary importance.[24] However, his critique of the demography model is significant because it highlighted the importance of other factors which could radically affect how rural society adapted to the challenge of demographic change. As Steve Rigby has noted, there are essentially two Brenners:

> the 'strong' version illegitimately ascribes a causal primacy to class structure and even denies that demographic change was a genuine 'cause' of economic change on the grounds that different socio-economic outcomes resulted from similar demographic trends: the 'dilute' version impressively demonstrates that demographic trends acquire their significance for long-term economic change only in connection with specific forms of class structure.[25]

More recently, Rigby, followed by John Hatcher and Mark Bailey, has advocated the pluralism of causes in creating economic change. Using Mill's emphasis upon 'the whole of the contingencies of every description', Rigby has questioned the professional compulsion to establish a hierarchy of causes which would permit the ultimate or primary cause to be identified.[26] Similarly, Hatcher and Bailey have noted the 'recurrent streaks of superficiality and foolishness' in many of these causation debates: 'how can it be thought essential to minimise the role of demographic factors simply because one believes in the power of property relations?'[27] It was the combination of demographic changes, increasing commercialisation and changes in class relations which, when taken together, help to explain economic change in this period. Thus perceived differences between these schools of explanatory thought lie in the importance they place on individual causes, often reflecting differences between the purposes of individual historians rather than necessarily disputes over the events themselves.

In more recent years, economists have sought ways of modelling unpredictable and non-economic influences in the long-term evolution of societies. This has led to the development of path-dependency theory and new institutional economics, which have become important concepts in the social and political sciences: both offering some important challenges to neoclassical economics. Path dependency has

23 Ibid., pp. 10–64.

24 See the essays in Aston and Philpin (eds.), *The Brenner Debate*. See also, S. H. Rigby, *English Society in the Later Middle Ages: Class, Status and Gender* (Basingstoke, 1995); and Mark Bailey, *The Decline of Serfdom in Late Medieval England: From Bondage to Freedom* (Woodbridge, 2014), pp. 3–15.

25 S. H. Rigby, 'Historical Causation: Is One Thing More Important Than Another?', *History*, 80 (1995), p. 239.

26 Ibid., p. 233.

27 Hatcher and Bailey, *Modelling the Middle Ages*, p. 238.

especially been evoked to explain the adoption of certain technologies despite more efficient alternatives often existing. For example, Paul David argued that the universal adoption of the QWERTY keyboard showed the importance of historical accidents and the power of institutional constraints, despite the fact that other layouts were demonstrably more efficient and ergonomic.[28] Similarly, the width of 60 per cent of world railways today was developed from the width of waggonways used in the coal industry in north-eastern England, and, despite being regarded as narrower than optimal by many modern engineers, has never been replaced, displaying nearly two centuries of path dependency.[29]

In many ways, path dependence is very familiar to historians and has often been reduced to the metaphorical and vague sentiment that 'history matters' – that what's gone before will affect what will come – but at its most powerful path dependence 'may help explain why some countries succeed and others do not.'[30] Scott Page has argued that this theory has three related causes: increasing returns, meaning that the more a choice is made the greater its benefits (although this is in fact debatable since there are many instances of inefficiencies being introduced into economies in this fashion); self-reinforcement, in which taking an action sets in place complementary forces that encourage that choice to be sustained; and lock-in, which means that one choice becomes better than any other because a sufficient number of people have already made that choice and it becomes difficult to overturn it.[31] In path-dependency theory, decisions taken under past conditions remain fundamentally important long after those economic conditions have changed. As Paul Pierson has argued, the complexities of historical contingency mean that:

> specific patterns of timing and sequence matter; starting from similar conditions a range of social outcomes is often possible; large consequences may result from relatively small or contingent events; and particular courses of action, once introduced, can be virtually impossible to reverse.[32]

Given the long-term nature of landownership, tenure and agricultural production in rural societies, this theoretical framework has considerable implications for the study of medieval and early modern England.

28 P. A. David, 'Clio and the Economics of QWERTY', *American Economic Review*, 75 (1985), pp. 332–7. See also, for example, W. Brian Arthur, 'Competing Technologies, Increasing Returns, and Lock-In by Historical Events', *Economic Journal*, 99 (1989), pp. 116–31.

29 Douglas J. Puffert, 'Path Dependence, Network Form, and Technological Change', in Timothy W. Guinnane, William A. Sundstrom, and Warren Whatley (eds.), *History Matters: Essays on Economic Growth, Technology, and Demographic Change* (Stanford, 2004), pp. 63–94.

30 William Easterly, *The Elusive Quest for Growth: Economists' Adventures and Misadventures in the Tropics* (Cambridge, 2001).

31 Scott E. Page, 'Path Dependency', *Quarterly Journal of Political Science*, 1 (2006), p. 89.

32 Paul Pierson, *Politics in Time: History, Institutions and Social Analysis* (Princeton, 2004), pp. 18–19.

The revival of institutional economics has complemented many of the above theories, questioning the idea of evolutionary economic theory by showing how many economies have levels of inefficiency which survive in the long term.[33] In this respect, Douglass North has argued that 'institutional change shapes the way societies evolve through time and hence is the key to understanding historical change'.[34] Although we should be careful about describing institutional factors as 'the key' to understanding economic development, it is clear that institutional constraints play a considerable role in affecting how societies respond to changes in demography, commercialisation and class relations. The way organisations and institutions interact with formal and informal constraints, therefore, often helps to explain why some societies experience economic growth and others experience long-term stagnation. To put this in the present context, the relationship between landlords and tenants had reached an equilibrium based upon economic conditions in the fifteenth century which was fundamentally altered by population growth, inflation and commercial expansion in the sixteenth century. Individual landowners and groups of tenants sought to renegotiate that equilibrium, whether through law, custom or riot, but their ability to do so was often constrained by the previous arrangements in place, with many of the conflicts in rural society arising from these landlord–tenant relations. There are limitations to path dependency as a theory for economic development, not least its potentially deterministic approach to history and the seeming inevitability of events, but given the relative inflexibility of agrarian tenures in this period it has the potential to help explain the success or failure of economic groups in society. As we will see, the decisions taken during the depth of the mid-fifteenth-century recession, or indeed those not taken, continued to have an impact upon rural society for generations to come, long after those economic conditions were no longer prevalent.

It has often been recognised that there are many structural differences in agrarian societies which help to produce, accelerate or inhibit change. Joan Thirsk and William Hoskins, for example, highlighted the importance of understanding regional variations in agrarian history, for they often influenced, amongst other things, the extent of manorialisation, the population density, the market opportunities and above all the type of agriculture practised in an area.[35] Estates and seigniorial lordship also

33 For a brief overview of new institutional economics see: Douglass C. North, *Institutions, Institutional Change and Economic Performance* (Cambridge, 1991); Ronald Coase, 'The Nature of the Firm', *Economica*, 4 (1937), pp. 386–405; Ronald Coase, 'The Problem of Social Cost', *Journal of Law and Economics*, 3 (1960), pp. 1–44; Thrainn Eggertsson, *Economic Behaviour and Institutions* (Cambridge, 1990); and Paul Milgrom et al., 'The Role of Institutions in the Revival of Trade: the Law Merchant, Private Judges, and the Champagne Fairs', *Economics and Politics*, 2 (1990), pp. 1–23. For the evolutionary economics North was criticising, see: Armen Alchian, 'Uncertainty, Evolution and Economic Theory', *Journal of Political Economy*, 58 (1950), pp. 211–21.

34 North, *Institutions, Institutional Change*, p. 3.

35 Joan Thirsk, 'The Farming Regions of England', in J. Thirsk (ed.), *The Agrarian History of England and Wales, Vol. 4: 1500–1640* (Cambridge, 1967), pp. 1–112; W. G. Hoskins, 'Regional Farming in England', *AgHR*, 2 (1954), pp. 3–11.

provided structural constraints upon landowners and tenants in this period that were as real and as important as the weather, soil conditions, market opportunities or indeed population movements. Placing a village within the institutional context of the estate it was a constituent part of is as important as placing it within a geological topography. As will be seen, the monks of Durham Cathedral Priory and the bishops of Durham faced the same demographic crisis in the late fourteenth century, but how the two institutions reacted differed greatly, creating long-term structural differences between their estates which had significant consequences for their sixteenth-century counterparts. These differences had profound effects upon their tenants, providing them with entirely different opportunities and challenges in both centuries. It was this same path dependence which posed such problems for rentier landlords after their withdrawal from direct-demesne agriculture in the late fourteenth and early fifteenth centuries. Many of their successors ran into difficulties in the sixteenth century and were forced to sell off their ancestral estates piecemeal, often to their own tenants who were increasingly benefiting from rising agricultural prices.[36] Estates and institutional constraints played a significant role in the economic development of rural society in this period and had long-term consequences by affecting the real incomes of landowners and their tenants alike.[37]

The Problems of Periodisation

The ability of historians to explore the changes in English society across this period has been hindered by the division of the profession into medieval and early modern specialisms, usually split at the end of the fifteenth century. Although this division has often been disparaged, it has persisted with extraordinary tenacity, not only in the historiography, but also in research projects and undergraduate courses studying this period. Margaret Yates summarised this division as:

> A historical fault line of seismic proportions [which] lies at the end of the fifteenth century. It has been re-enforced by the institutional and academic divisions within the discipline into 'periods' of history as medieval, early modern, and modern, which have led to segregation into specialisms and a fragmentation of research into chronologically discrete agendas.[38]

36 See the introduction to chapter 2 for a more in-depth discussion of path-dependency, rent and tenure.

37 Phillipp Schofield has discussed the 'ways in which lords served as "filters" for the range of exogenous influences' which affected rural society, but since the 1970s when there was a flurry of institutional studies across the country, there has been a relative paucity of work focusing upon estate management and institutional constraints, Phillipp Schofield, *Peasants and Community in Medieval England, 1200–1500* (Basingstoke, 2003), p. 35.

38 Margaret Yates, *Town and Countryside in Western Berkshire, c.1327–c.1600: Social and Economic Change* (Woodbridge, 2007), p. 1.

We need to bridge the gulf between these specialisms as this division is particularly detrimental for our understanding of such a key transitional period: many of the challenges and opportunities people faced in the sixteenth century had their origin in the fourteenth century, whilst many of the seeds of change planted in the earlier period did not reach fruition until the late sixteenth century.

Richard Britnell has argued that:

> The period 1471–1529 is often seen as an epilogue to the middle ages, or a prologue to the early modern period, for reasons that have more to do with the way in which historians specialise than with any intrinsic characteristics of these particular years.[39]

This conceptual division not only hinders our ability to trace developments across this period but it has also directly affected our interpretations of rural society. Interdisciplinary approaches have become commonplace in new research projects, and yet, despite our willingness to break down some traditional boundaries by engaging with the work of neighbouring disciplines, there is still a remarkable reluctance to demolish the artificial walls we have erected through the process of periodisation. Occasionally we peer over them, sometimes we even take a few bricks down and surreptitiously rebuild them elsewhere, but these walls have proven surprisingly enduring despite criticism. Thus disagreements abound surrounding the timing, extent and mechanisms of change, much akin to two neighbours arguing over a boundary dispute.[40]

The division between the medieval and early modern periods is not just a matter of arbitrary professional preferences because there are myriad practical problems with crossing this divide which have been imposed upon historians by the sources themselves, with a complete discontinuity in the sources used by economic and social historians from the fourteenth to the early seventeenth centuries. Parish registers and probate inventories form the predominant sources for the early modern period, whilst the records of feudal estates have offered a fertile ground for medievalists. This change has naturally had an impact upon the effectiveness with which historians of each period can engage with certain debates. Early modernists, for example, have focused upon detailed demographic studies, upon the living standards of the poor and upon household economics. There have been numerous admirable studies of these topics by medievalists, but the lack of adequate sources has plagued such

39 R. H. Britnell, *The Closing of the Middle Ages? England, 1471–1529* (Cambridge, 1997), p. 1.

40 For example, the end point of Dyer's *An Age of Transition?* is not necessarily the starting point of Wrightson's *Earthly Necessities*, two of the best explorations of the medieval and early modern economy respectively. This relates to, amongst other themes, the level of commercialisation in society; the economic rationality and individualism of everyday people; improving living standards and social ambition; the rise of the yeomanry and commercial farming; and even the development of the European marriage pattern.

attempts. We need only compare the work on demography by E. A. Wrigley and R. S. Schofield using parish registers with Hatcher's attempts to estimate life expectancies of monks in the fifteenth century or with Campbell's estimates of total population based upon the amount of land under cultivation: the former obviously benefit from the availability of sources which are more appropriate for such investigations.[41] Although medievalists traditionally bemoan their lack of sources, there are in fact some areas in which their knowledge far exceeds that of early modernists as, for example, in the abundance of data on yields in the early fourteenth century compared to the lack thereof in the latter period: a lack which obliged Overton to use probate inventories as an indirect source for calculating yields in the sixteenth and seventeenth centuries.[42]

This period is made even more difficult to study by the scarcity of surviving sources concerning agricultural progress from the late fourteenth to the mid-sixteenth century, a lack which has been widely commented upon. In his summary of agricultural sources in 1955, Rodney Hilton wrote that:

> the agrarian history of England between the rising of 1381 and the Dissolution of the Monasteries is much more obscure than it ought to be. The fact seems to be that historians have been nurtured in the manorial documentation of the great estates, and when these sources fail, as a result of the almost universal leasing of manors to farmers, they have found nothing to replace them. Consequently, bibliographies of English history of the fifteenth century contain little more than a sprinkling of inadequate and out-of-date material on agrarian conditions.[43]

He concluded that here lies 'one of the most formidable gaps in our knowledge of English rural life'. Although there has been much work on this period in the intervening decades Campbell and Overton still remarked in the 1990s on this relative paucity of investigation:

> the most marked dichotomy in the historiography of this six hundred year period is between interpretations of the medieval and early modern periods. Between them lie the fifteenth and early sixteenth centuries; *a murky, ill-documented and under-researched period.*[44]

41 Wrigley and Schofield, *The Population History of England*; John Hatcher, Alan Piper, David Stone, 'Monastic Mortality: Durham Priory, 1395–1529', *EcHR*, 59 (2006), pp. 667–87; Bruce M. S. Campbell, *English Seigniorial Agriculture, 1250–1450* (Cambridge, 2000).

42 See for example the medieval debate on yields: Postan, 'Medieval Agrarian Society in its Prime: England', pp. 548–59; J. Z. Titow, *Winchester Yields: a Study in Medieval Agricultural Productivity* (Cambridge, 1972); Bruce M. S. Campbell, 'Arable Productivity in Medieval England: Some Evidence from Norfolk', *JEcH*, 43 (1983), pp. 379–404; Mark Overton, 'Estimating Crop Yields from Probate Inventories: An Example from East Anglia, 1585–1735', *JEcH*, 39 (1979), pp. 363–78.

43 R. H. Hilton, 'The Content and Sources of English Agrarian History before 1500', *AgHR*, 3 (1955), p. 6.

44 Campbell and Overton, 'A New Perspective', pp. 47–8. My italics.

It is a problem which has been compounded by contemporary events themselves, for socio-economic trends separate the fifteenth and sixteenth centuries as surely as do our own conceptions of the past, with rural society in the late-sixteenth century facing significantly different problems to their counterparts of the mid-fifteenth century. The fifteenth century is typically characterised as a period of economic stagnation or recession, with low prices, low rents and high wages, providing agricultural producers and landowners with a whole host of difficult decisions.[45] Did tenants retreat from the market into subsistence agriculture because of low prices and high wages despite generally having enlarged their holdings? How did landlords manage to retain their tenants when land was now so abundantly available?[46] The population of England was between 4 million and 6 million on the eve of the Black Death; it was reduced to just 2.5 million by 1377, and may have fallen to around 2 million by the end of the fifteenth century.[47] By comparison, the population grew to around 3 million by 1560, reaching 4 million by 1600 and was over 5 million by the time of the English Civil War.[48] This rapid recovery brought with it a whole plethora of different problems, not least a high demand for food which increasingly outstripped supply, with a resultant increase in grain prices. Although there was a general rise in inflation, partially exacerbated by Henry VIII's debasement of the coinage, it is generally thought that food prices, especially grain prices, rose more steeply than those for other goods.[49] Hoskins, for example, found that the average price of wheat increased from between 4s and 5s per quarter in the last two decades of the fifteenth century

45 See for example: M. M. Postan, 'The Fifteenth Century', *EcHR*, 9 (1939), pp. 160–7; John Hatcher, *Plague, Population and the English Economy, 1348–1530* (London, 1977); for a dissenting view, see A. R. Bridbury, *Economic Growth: England in the Later Middle Ages* (Westport, 1983).

46 For some of the problems facing landlords after the Black Death, see Christopher Dyer, *Lords and Peasants in a Changing Society: The Estates of the Bishopric of Worcester, 680–1540* (Cambridge, 1980); and his 'A Redistribution of Incomes in Fifteenth-Century England', *P&P*, 39 (1968), pp. 11–33.

47 For an estimated figure of pre-plague population of 6 million see Postan, 'Medieval Agrarian Society in its Prime: England', pp. 549–632 and R. M. Smith, 'Human Resources', in G. Astill and A. Grant (eds.), *The Countryside of Medieval England* (Oxford, 1988), pp. 188–212; for a lower estimate of around 4.7 million, see Campbell, *English Seigniorial Agriculture*; for mortality rate estimates in the fifteenth century see: Hatcher, *Plague, Population and the English Economy*; John Hatcher, 'Mortality in the Fifteenth Century: Some New Evidence', *EcHR*, 39 (1986), pp. 19–38; R. M. Smith, 'Measuring Adult Mortality in an Age of Plague: England, 1349–1540', in Bailey and Rigby (eds.), *Town and Countryside in the Age of the Black Death*, pp. 43–85; for a European estimate see Josiah C. Russell, 'Population in Europe', in Carlo M. Cipolla, (ed.), *The Fontana Economic History of Europe, Vol. 1: The Middle Ages* (Glasgow, 1972), pp. 25–71.

48 See for example: Bruce M. S. Campbell, 'The Population of Early Tudor England: A Re-evaluation of the 1522 Muster Returns and 1524 and 1525 Lay Subsidies', *Journal of Historical Geography*, 7 (1981), pp. 145–54; Wrigley and Schofield, *The Population History of England*; J. Cornwall, 'English Population in the Early Sixteenth Century', *EcHR*, 23 (1970), pp. 32–44.

49 For a European perspective, see: F. Braudel and F. Spooner, 'Prices in Europe from 1450 to 1750', in E. E. Rich and C. H. Wilson (eds.), *The Cambridge Economic History of Europe, IV: the Economy of Expanding Europe in the Sixteenth and Seventeenth Centuries* (Cambridge, 1967), pp. 378–486.

to consistently over 30s in the 1610s: a six-fold increase in just over a century.[50] Similarly, Harrison recorded an increase in his index of the moving average of all grain prices from around 100 in the second half of the fifteenth century to over 700 by the 1620s.[51] Meanwhile, wages rose but did not keep pace with agricultural prices, producing a decline in real wages over the course of the century, although the extent of this has been questioned.[52] There is still much debate about the course of rents, with custom and tenure often making rent increases difficult, but there was certainly increasing pressure on landed resources, especially after the general engrossment of holdings across the fifteenth century. As a result of these changes, there were more opportunities for agricultural producers to profit during the sixteenth century, but there were also many hidden dangers.

Nonetheless, while there are undoubtedly many valid reasons for viewing these two centuries separately rather than comparatively, the period needs to be analysed as a whole because changes wrought across these centuries were vitally important in the development of agrarian capitalism. Agrarian capitalism involved the transition from a 'rural, peasant society based on subsistence-oriented agriculture to a market-dependent economy in which agriculture is productive enough to support a large non-agricultural population employed in industry and services.'[53] The period from the Black Death to the English Civil War is a key part of this development because it saw the de facto end of serfdom in the late fourteenth century, large-scale engrossment of holdings amongst peasants in the fifteenth century and the emergence of widespread landlessness in the sixteenth century.[54] In this context, Marx and his followers have placed particular emphasis upon the shift from the extra-economic coercion of serfdom to the more purely economic relations of wage labour. Two of the most important changes in the transition from feudalism to capitalism debate were the end of serfdom and the expropriation of peasants from the land, but it is here that Marxism is particularly weak because it struggles to explain why this transition took centuries to fulfil.[55]

50 W. G. Hoskins, 'Harvest Fluctuations and English Economic History, 1480–1619', *AgHR*, 12 (1964), p. 31.

51 C. J. Harrison, 'Grain Price Analysis and Harvest Qualities, 1465–1634', *AgHR*, 19 (1971), pp. 147–51.

52 E. H. Phelps Brown and S. V. Hopkins, 'Seven Centuries of the Prices of Consumables, Compared with Builders' Wage-Rates', *Economica*, 23 (1956), pp. 301–4; John Hatcher, 'Unreal Wages: Long-Run Living Standards and the "Golden Age" of the Fifteenth Century', in Ben Dodds and Christian Liddy (eds.), *Commercial Activity, Markets and Entrepreneurs in the Middle Ages: Essays in Honour of Richard Britnell* (Woodbridge, 2011), pp. 1–24.

53 Whittle, *Agrarian Capitalism*, p. 1.

54 See Mark Bailey's recent book on serfdom which tackles many of the problems related to tenurial development in this period, *The Decline of Serfdom in Late Medieval England*.

55 S. R. Epstein, 'Rodney Hilton, Marxism and the Transition from Feudalism to Capitalism', in C. Dyer, P. Coss and C. Wickham (eds.), *Rodney Hilton's Middle Ages: An Exploration of Historical Themes* (Oxford, 2007), pp. 248–69; see, for example, Dobb, *Studies in the Development*

There is still much debate over the exact timing, nature and mechanisms of these changes, however, as well as the importance of these two centuries as a 'transitional' period between feudalism and capitalism. Cicely Howell, for example, argued that by the second half of the fifteenth century a 'modern society' had emerged and that our discussion of the early modern period must begin with a prelude, 1440–1520, in which 'we must view a modern society through the perhaps distorting medium of medieval archival practice'.[56] Margaret Yates similarly placed this transition at a very early stage and disagreed that there were any 'rapid and revolutionary changes in the fifteenth and sixteenth centuries', arguing that 'by 1400 the process of change that would shape the economy and society of the future was already under way', whilst the 'fifteenth century saw little that was decisive or unprecedented'. [57] She concluded that although the pace of change would escalate in the second half of the sixteenth century, we are unable to identify a specific moment that constitutes a break with the past and the end of the middle ages, but it is undeniable that fundamental change had occurred by 1600 through a discontinuous process which continues to this day.[58] Change after 1400 was, therefore, an organic process: evolutionary rather than revolutionary. The economic and social history of England saw a gradual shift towards a capitalist economy in this period but there were also many continuities from the middle ages, with Richard Britnell describing the economic history of the century 1450–1550 as one of 'exceptionally gradual and unremarkable change in England'.[59]

Rather than see this period as one of transition during 'which the so-called medieval development was completed and the great Tudor achievement prepared', Postan famously characterised the fifteenth century as 'an age of recession, arrested economic development and declining national income'.[60] Likewise, Hatcher observed that 'tales of falling land rents, of retreating cultivation, of dilapidated holdings, and often also of chronic insolvency, pervade the rural history of the fifteenth century'.[61] In his essay on the mid-century slump he went on to identify the depth of the recession across agriculture, trade and industry from the 1430s to the 1470s.[62] His work has also cast doubt on there being significant population recovery by the end of the fifteenth century,

of Capitalism; Hilton, *The Decline of Serfdom*; R. H. Hilton et al., *The Transition from Feudalism to Capitalism* (London, 1976); and Rigby, 'Historical Materialism', pp. 473–522.

56 Cicely Howell, *Land, Family, and Inheritance in Transition: Kibworth Harcourt, 1280–1700* (Cambridge, 1983), p. 58.

57 Yates, *Town and Countryside*, p. 23.

58 Ibid., p. 23.

59 R. H. Britnell, 'The English Economy and the Government, 1450–1550', in John Watts (ed.), *The End of the Middle Ages? England in the Fifteenth and Sixteenth Centuries* (Stroud, 1998), p. 116.

60 Postan, 'Fifteenth Century', p. 160.

61 John Hatcher, *Rural Economy and Society in the Duchy of Cornwall, 1300–1500* (Cambridge, 1970), p. 148.

62 John Hatcher, 'The Great Slump of the Mid-Fifteenth Century', in R. H. Britnell and John Hatcher (eds.), *Progress and Problems in Medieval England: Essays in Honour of Edward Miller* (Cambridge, 1996), pp. 237–72.

with the life expectancy of various monastic communities throughout England plummeting in the last few decades of the century.[63] Campbell also characterised the later middle ages as a period of contraction in which a protracted process of rationalisation and restructuring was underway after the relative achievements of the twelfth and thirteenth centuries.[64] The post-Black Death economy could, therefore, be said to have undergone a process of retrenchment and retreat after the high degree of commercialisation achieved during the thirteenth century. Christopher Dyer has similarly agreed that many of these processes began before the Black Death but he has gone on to argue that rural society underwent an important restructuring in the fifteenth century with a vital stratification of landholding that led to the emergence of the yeomanry as a social group.[65] He has particularly emphasised the role played by demesne lessees as an emergent group of farmers who worked on a much larger scale than their peasant neighbours, and who were often the forerunners of the commercial farmers who feature so prominently in the literature of the late sixteenth century.[66]

By contrast, many early modernists have placed the challenges of the sixteenth century at the forefront of debates surrounding socio-economic change in this period, with R. H. Tawney, Hugh Trevor-Roper, Lawrence Stone and Christopher Hill arguing that the century before the English Civil War was particularly tumultuous as they sought the origins of that conflict in the changes rural society was undergoing.[67] These historians emphasised that there was a revolutionary change in the distribution of landed power during the sixteenth century as each section of rural society struggled to come to terms with a century of demographic growth and rapid inflation, although they disagreed over who were the main beneficiaries of these changes. Tawney, and more recently Brenner, argued that the period 1540–1640 was particularly significant for the transformation of rural society as landlords sought to increase their incomes by evicting copyhold tenants, converting their lands to leasehold tenure and subsequently rack-renting their lands.[68] Stone, by comparison,

63 Hatcher et al., 'Monastic Mortality', pp. 667–87.

64 Bruce M. S. Campbell, 'England: Land and People', in S. H. Rigby (ed.), *A Companion to Britain in the Later Middle Ages* (Oxford, 2003), pp. 3–25.

65 Dyer, *An Age of Transition?*, pp. 194–200. See also, for example: P. C. Maddern, 'Social mobility', in R. Horrox and W. M. Ormrod (eds.), *A Social History of England 1200–1500* (Cambridge, 2006), pp. 113–33; R. Almond and A. J. Pollard, 'The Yeomanry of Robin Hood and Social Terminology in Fifteenth-Century England', *P&P*, 170 (2001), pp. 52–77.

66 Christopher Dyer, 'Were there any Capitalists in Fifteenth-Century England', in Jennifer Kermode (ed.), *Enterprise and Individuals in Fifteenth-Century England* (Gloucester, 1991), pp. 1–24.

67 Lawrence Stone, *The Crisis of the Aristocracy, 1558–1641* (Oxford, 1965); R. H. Tawney, 'The Rise of the Gentry, 1558–1640', *EcHR*, 11 (1941), pp. 1–38; H. R. Trevor-Roper, *The Gentry, 1540–1640* (Cambridge, 1953). Christopher Hill, *Puritanism and Revolution: Studies in Interpretation of the English Revolution of the Seventeenth Century* (London, 1958).

68 Tawney, *The Agrarian Problem in the Sixteenth Century*, pp. 177–260. For recent views on Tawney, see the essays in Whittle (ed.), *Landlords and Tenants in Britain*, and J. P. Bowen and A. T. Brown (eds.), *Custom and Commercialisation in English Rural Society: Revisiting Postan and Tawney* (Hatfield, forthcoming).

pointed to a particularly severe period of sales by the aristocracy from 1585 to 1606, 'during which time the net losses were so alarming that one may reasonably talk about a financial crisis of the aristocracy, which was arrested soon after the death of Queen Elizabeth', whilst Tawney similarly concluded that 'to say that many noble families, though not they alone, encountered in the two generations before the Civil War a financial crisis is probably not an over-statement'.[69] These historians saw fundamental changes in the relative distribution of landed resources amongst the aristocracy and gentry in the second half of the sixteenth century, which was greatly in favour of the latter at the former's expense. Trevor-Roper questioned the universal rise and fall of these social groups, preferring to think of these conflicts as between the 'court' gentry who had access to Crown patronage and the 'country' or 'mere' gentry who retired to their estates in relative poverty.[70] In contrast, Hill argued that the gentry were a social group who had a diverse range of economic interests, and so we would be better analysing the sixteenth century through the economic categories of rentier landlords and agricultural producers.[71]

Since then, early modernists have focused more upon topics like the importance of village life, the county community and the landscape, but the conflict arising from the relationship between landlords and tenants has remained an important area of research. This has produced a considerable emphasis upon the strength of customary tenures, the importance of the commons and the changes brought about by enclosure. Richard Hoyle, for example, has demonstrated the regional diversity between copyholds of inheritance and copyholds for life, as well as the importance of tenant-right, a customary tenure in northern England.[72] Much of this more recent research has been conducted through micro-histories of the parish in early modern England, with historians like Andy Wood using this technique to show the level of negotiation which occurred between landlords and tenants over issues like custom, or the work of Keith Wrightson and Steve Hindle in highlighting the everyday politics of sixteenth-century village life.[73] This research has increasingly revealed the complexity of the relationship between landowners and their tenants with, for example, John Broad showing the role the Verneys and Claydons had in changing the village communities on their estate over the seventeenth and eighteenth centuries.[74] Much of this litera-

69 Stone, *Crisis of the Aristocracy*, pp. 72–3; Tawney, 'Rise of the Gentry', p. 10.

70 Trevor-Roper, *The Gentry*, pp. 26–7.

71 Hill, *Puritanism and Revolution*, p. 8.

72 R. W. Hoyle, 'Lords, Tenants, and Tenant-Right in the Sixteenth Century: Four Studies', *NH*, 20 (1984), pp. 38–63, and his 'Tenure and the Land Market in Early Modern England: or a Late Contribution to the Brenner Debate', *EcHR*, 43 (1990), pp. 1–20.

73 Andy Wood, *The Politics of Social Conflict: The Peak Country, 1520–1770* (Cambridge, 1999); Steve Hindle, *On the Parish? The Micro-Politics of Poor Relief in Rural England, c.1550–1750* (Oxford, 2004); David Levine and Keith Wrightson, *The Making of an Industrial Society: Whickham, 1560–1765* (Oxford, 1991); Wrightson and Levine, *Poverty and Piety*.

74 John Broad, *Transforming English Rural Society: the Verneys and the Claydons, 1600–1820* (Cambridge, 2004).

ture arises out of these older historiographical debates over the rise of the gentry and crisis of the aristocracy because at the heart of many of the conflicts in rural society during the sixteenth century lie disputes between rentier landlords and agricultural producers over who was to gain from the unearned increment of inflation: producing in turn this emphasis upon tenure and custom amongst contemporaries and historians alike. The withdrawal from the direct-demesne management of land in the fourteenth and early fifteenth centuries was of long-term importance because it divorced the ownership of land from its use, and so rentier landlords struggled to access the profits of their lands in the sixteenth century. As an economic group, most of these families had a restricted income, but as a social group their expenditure continued to rise, creating financial challenges which many families found insurmountable.

Many of these historiographical disagreements stem from identifying particular changes in rural society as being more important than others, whilst regional variations have confused the picture still further. In his insistence that the proletarian nature of the agricultural workforce was of fundamental importance, Leigh Shaw-Taylor, for example, has placed the date for these developments much later than the current study, but he acknowledged that:

> given the extent of commercialisation during the medieval period a high degree of commercialisation seems probable even for family farms throughout the early modern period. If being commercially oriented were a sufficient definition of a capitalist farm then we would probably have to push the description of English agriculture as 'capitalist' a good deal further back than will be suggested here.[75]

Likewise, Robert Allen found engrossment across the seventeenth century in the south midlands but identified the eighteenth century as the critical period. However, he did not investigate the same phenomenon across the fifteenth century – a period Outhwaite has called '*the* period of engrossment'– and so can provide no real conclusions about its importance with regard to earlier developments.[76] Despite the importance of industry and urban settlement in the medieval period, early modernists have argued that the pace of change quickened in the sixteenth century, with these sections of society increasingly driving the national economy of England.[77] As this book will show, the fifteenth and sixteenth centuries should not be studied in isolation, and

75 Leigh Shaw-Taylor, 'The Rise of Agrarian Capitalism and the Decline of Family Farming in England', *EcHR*, 65 (2012), pp. 5–6.

76 Robert Allen, *Enclosure and the Yeoman: The Agricultural Development of the South Midlands, 1450–1850* (Oxford, 1992); R. B. Outhwaite, 'Progress and Backwardness in English Agriculture, 1500–1650', *EcHR*, 39 (1986), pp. 1–18.

77 See for example: E. A. Wrigley, 'Urban Growth and Agricultural Change: England and the Continent in the Early Modern Period', *JIH*, 15 (1985), pp. 683–728; Langdon and Masschaele, 'Commercial Activity and Population Growth', pp. 35–82; John Hatcher, *The History of the British Coal Industry, Vol. 1: Before 1700: Towards the Age of Coal* (Oxford, 1993); J. U. Nef, *The Rise of the*

indeed cannot be studied thus, because decisions taken by rural society during the fifteenth-century recession had a direct impact upon the ability of their successors to adapt to the inflation of the sixteenth century.[78] The disputes between rentier landlords and agricultural producers, for example, often revolved around forms of land tenure, which, as Whittle has commented, 'were the most significant legacy of the manorial system to the sixteenth century and beyond'.[79]

The Durham Region

This book charts the effects of the fifteenth-century recession on rural society between the River Tyne and the River Tees in north-east England and explores how landed society responded to this period of stagnant population, low prices, low rents and high wages.[80] It then analyses the long-term consequences of these responses by exploring how they affected the ability of their sixteenth-century counterparts to respond to high levels of inflation. This focus upon landed society has meant that labourers, and those who possessed relatively little land, have largely been excluded, although they obviously formed an important group in rural society which will be explored partially in the final chapter. The county palatine of Durham was an area of northern England ruled by the prince-bishops of Durham who retained both spiritual and temporal jurisdiction there throughout this period, although many of these privileges were slowly eroded from the sixteenth century onwards.[81]

British Coal Industry, 2 vols. (London: 1932); John Hatcher, *English Tin Production and Trade Before 1550* (Oxford, 1973).

78 See especially chapter 2 which emphasises the long-term implications of many of the changes wrought during the fifteenth-century recession upon the ecclesiastical estates of Durham.

79 Whittle, *Agrarian Capitalism*, p. 64.

80 There is a considerable corpus of work on the north-east of England during this period. The most important includes, for constitutional history: G. T. Lapsley, *The County Palatine of Durham: a Study in Constitutional History* (London, 1900); for political history: A. J. Pollard, *North-Eastern England During the Wars of the Roses: Lay Society, War, and Politics, 1450–1500* (Oxford, 1990); Christian Liddy, *The Bishopric of Durham in the Late Middle Ages: Lordship, Community and the Cult of St Cuthbert* (Woodbridge, 2008); Mervyn James, *Family, Lineage, and Civil Society: A Study of Society, Politics and Mentality in the Durham Region, 1500–1640* (Oxford, 1974); and Diana Newton, *North-East England, 1569–1625: Governance, Culture and Identity* (Woodbridge, 2006); for economic and social history: Christine Newman, *Late Medieval Northallerton: A Small Market Town and its Hinterland, 1470–1540* (Stamford, 1999); Ben Dodds, *Peasants and Production in the Medieval North-East: The Evidence from Tithes, 1270–1536* (Woodbridge, 2007); and Levine and Wrightson, *The Making of an Industrial Society*; and for the history of Durham Priory: R. B. Dobson, *Durham Priory, 1400–1450* (Cambridge, 1973); Peter Larson, *Conflict and Compromise in the Late Medieval Countryside, 1349–1400* (New York, 2006).

81 Including land in Norham and Islandshire in the very north of England, surrounding Berwick upon Tweed, and Bedlingtonshire in Northumberland. This book focuses upon the land between the River Tyne and River Tees, although the receivers of Norham and Islandshire often accounted to the receiver generals of the bishops of Durham under the category of 'foreign receipts'.

Map 1. The Palatinate of Durham in England.

There were three medieval palatinates in England: Durham, Chester and Lancaster, though Durham retained its independence the longest. The bishops of Durham held many royal powers within the palatinate for much of this period; it was, after all, the bishop's peace rather than the king's peace which was upheld there, whilst the bishop possessed his own exchequer and chancery.[82] There were repeated efforts

[82] For more on the constitutional history of the palatinate, see Lapsley, *The County Palatine of Durham*.

to constrain the powers of the prince-bishops of Durham, especially in the sixteenth century, culminating in the Act of Resumption in 1536 which deprived the bishops of their rights to pardon offences. A more serious threat to the bishops of Durham came in 1551 when Bishop Tunstall was arrested and the see of Durham was divided into the two dioceses of Durham and Newcastle, and the palatinate abolished.[83] This was quickly reversed upon the accession of Mary and, although the bishop did not receive the forfeited lands of the rebels of the Rising of the North in 1569 as he would have once expected to, the palatinate continued in existence in a diminished form until 1836.

Although the 'armed' nature of Durham society might be questioned in this period, the region was still a frontier between England and Scotland, and remained distant from royal government. This could at times render the bishops of Durham, the supreme ecclesiastical and lay power in the palatinate, relatively helpless to direct the course of events. During the Pilgrimage of Grace in 1536, for example, Bishop Tunstall fled north to his castle at Norham rather than heading south, and remained there, waiting to see how events played out. Similarly, before the Rising of 1569 Bishop Pilkington was approached by Dean Whittingham who, according to his biographer, asked him to rally his tenants and Whittingham would 'cause all the tenants of the church [i.e. cathedral] to join likewise with them, which would be a means to awe the collecting rebels, and be a stay and refuge for many', but Pilkington refused.[84] The wars with Scotland, moreover, gave many Durham families the opportunity for advancement, not least the Nevilles, but they were also important to the tenants of the region, many of whom had the requirement to perform border service written into their tenures in the sixteenth century.[85] As such, many tenants were protected from rent increases because the Crown and the aristocratic families of the region needed a strong tenantry to form the backbone of their armies. After 1603, when James VI of Scotland became king of England, this rationale was removed as were many of the favourable terms by which Durham tenants held land.

Durham was chosen as the research area not only because of its high concentration of ecclesiastical landownership, which enables an in-depth study of two neighbouring landlords and their tenants, but also because of the precocious local development of the coal industry. It has been argued that the north-east of England did not follow national trends in this period, partly because of a delayed recovery from the fifteenth-

83 James, *Family, Lineage, and Civil Society*, p. 49.

84 Ibid., p. 148. This could be a later fiction by either Whittingham or his biographer, for if he genuinely believed that the church tenants, many of whom retained Catholic sympathies and had at best an ambivalent relationship with their Protestant dean, would follow him rather than their traditional military leaders, the Nevilles, then he was to be sadly disappointed when many of the cathedral's tenants rose with the last earl of Westmorland in 1569. For the biography of Whittingham see Mary Anne Everett Green (ed.), 'Life of Mr. William Whittingham, dean of Durham', *Miscellany VI*, Camden First Series, 104 (1871), p. 24.

85 For tenant-right, see for example, Hoyle, 'Lords, Tenants, and Tenant-Right', pp. 38–63.

century recession, but also because of the early boom of the coal industry during the second half of the sixteenth century. For example, A. J. Pollard concluded that:

> the fifteenth century after 1440 was a bleak era in the economic history of the north-east. Parts of southern England grew in wealth in the last decades of the century, while the north-east stood still. In this context the plight of the north-east was even more grave; for during the second half of the fifteenth century the gap between prospering and expanding southern districts and a stagnant north-east widened. The north-east was experiencing relative as well as absolute decline.[86]

Christine Newman similarly found depressed rents for Northallerton in North Yorkshire throughout the period 1470–1540, whilst Ben Dodds' work on production levels from tithe data found few signs of increased output, with levels stagnating right through until the 1530s.[87] Existing studies, therefore, suggest that Durham was experiencing a prolonged agricultural recession, but in this same period Britnell has highlighted the success of the bishops' coal mines at Railey, an entirely landlocked group of mines near Bishop Auckland which were dependent on local sales.[88] Was this industrial sector of the rural economy able to promote recovery from the mid-century recession, and how was local demand sufficient to encourage such precocious levels of output from the Railey coal mines? Certainly, the take-off of the coal industry on Tyneside from the mid-sixteenth century has come to dominate the historiography of the north-east of England, with a rapid expansion in all aspects of this industry, resulting in a tenfold increase in exports from the 1570s.[89] The north-east of England is thus thought to have undergone an 'early industrial revolution' in the seventeenth century.[90] How far did the economy of the Durham region stagnate behind the rest of England in the fifteenth century and what was the impact of the coal industry on rural society in the sixteenth and early seventeenth centuries?

The county of Durham was also chosen because of the geographical and geological diversity present in such a relatively small area. Map 2 clearly shows this diversity, including the two lowland zones concentrated in the Tyne and Wear valleys to the north and the fertile Tees lowlands to the south-east respectively. These areas were fertile zones, characterised by earlier settlement, open fields and heavily manorialised nucleated villages focused predominantly on arable agriculture.[91] It was in these

86 Pollard, *North-Eastern England*, pp. 78–80.

87 Newman, *Late Medieval Northallerton*, pp. 70–80; Dodds, *Peasants and Production*, p. 101.

88 R. H. Britnell, 'The Coal Industry in the Later Middle Ages: The Bishop of Durham's Estates', in M. Bailey and S. H. Rigby (eds.), *Town and Countryside in the Age of the Black Death: Essays in Honour of John Hatcher* (Turnhout, 2012), pp. 447–50.

89 Hatcher, *British Coal Industry*, p. 78.

90 Nef, *Rise of the British Coal Industry*, vol. 1, p. 165; Levine and Wrightson, *The Making of an Industrial Society*, p. ix.

91 Dodds, *Peasants and Production*, pp. 32–5. H. M. Dunsford and S. J. Harris, 'Colonisation of the Wasteland in County Durham', *EcHR*, 56 (2003), p. 37.

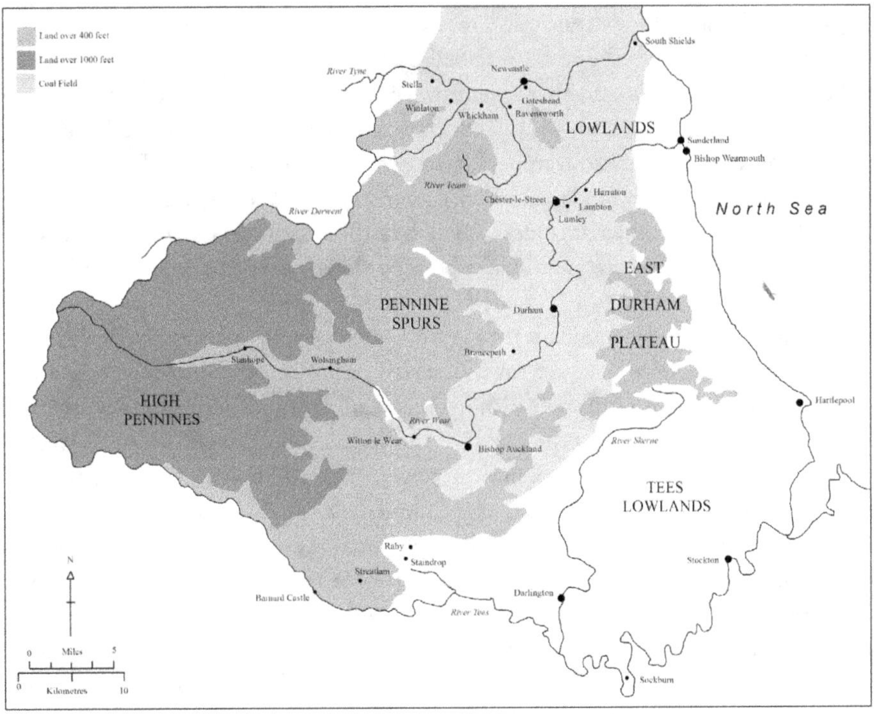

Map 2. The Main Coal Field and Profile of Land in County Durham.
Source: John Hatcher, *The History of the British Coal Industry, Vol. 1: Before 1700: Towards the Age of Coal* (Oxford, 1993), p. 71; H. M. Dunsford and S. J. Harris, 'Colonisation of the Wasteland in County Durham', *EcHR* 56 (2003), p. 37.

zones, and the East Durham Plateau region, that the majority of the ecclesiastical manors were located, as well as many of the wealthiest agricultural manors of the laity. As will be discussed in chapter 6, the cathedral's tenants of Harton to the north and Cowpen Bewley to the south-east focused primarily upon arable cultivation and, by the sixteenth century, they had acquired engrossed holdings also capable of maintaining modest numbers of livestock. Dodds found that yields on these manors were comparable with those further south, whilst the cropping systems never approached a monoculture of oats as in some districts in the north-west of England.[92]

By comparison, the west of the county was characterised by more extensive pastoral farming, and it was in the high Pennine region that the bishops had their extensive parks and forests at Wolsingham and Stanhope. The Pennine spurs were also where later reclamations from the waste took place in the thirteenth century, producing numerous manors which were little more than moorland farms but whose owners were considered members of the parish gentry of the fourteenth century. 'On

92 Dodds, *Peasants and Production*, pp. 32–5; Campbell, *English Seigniorial Agriculture*, pp. 249–302.

the whole,' Christian Liddy concluded, 'estates in the north and west, compared to the south and east of the bishopric, contained only small arable demesnes.'[93] However, as he went on to point out, there were other valuable resources available to these landowners than arable land: woodland, pasturage for livestock, and perhaps most importantly, coal. This precious mineral resource which penetrated the Pennine spurs and Tyne and Wear lowlands provided the gentry of these regions with an alternative supplement to their incomes and it was these same lands which Newcastle merchants coveted the most and could be seen slowly acquiring from the fifteenth century onwards.

Durham was, and remained throughout this period, a predominantly rural county, with the primary market towns centred upon the north road, passing from Darlington in the south, through Bishop Auckland, Durham, Chester-le-Street and finally reaching Newcastle to the north of the region. There were also small weekly markets at Barnard Castle and Staindrop to the south-west of the county, Stockton and Hartlepool in the south-east, and Sunderland on the mouth of the River Wear. These were predominantly small village markets, with the likes of Stockton possessing a population of only around 400 people in the fifteenth century, whilst Staindrop provided a forum for the craftsmen of the Neville's lordship of Raby.[94] The only major urban centre in the region, and certainly the most important in England north of York, was Newcastle, situated on the River Tyne. In 1300, the population of Newcastle was around 7,000–8,000, and it was one of the most important towns in medieval England after London, Bristol and York, but the Black Death and subsequent outbreaks of disease reduced the population to around 3,000 people by 1400.[95] The commercialising effect of having a large town in the region was therefore relatively limited in the fifteenth century, but the growth of Newcastle in the sixteenth and early seventeenth centuries, from some 7,000–8,000 in 1563 to 13,000 in 1666, meant that it exerted a considerable commercial pull on the surrounding countryside.[96] This was in terms of providing both a ready market for the grain and livestock needed to provision the town and the inward migration needed to sustain such population growth given that, for example, the 1636 plague outbreak alone killed at least 5,600 people.[97]

93 Liddy, *The Bishopric of Durham*, p. 46 and p. 53.

94 For the population of Stockton see T. Lomas, 'Land and People in South-East Durham in the Later Middle Ages' (Teesside Doctoral Thesis, 1976), p. 183; D. S. Reid, *The Durham Crown Lordships in the Sixteenth and Seventeenth Centuries and the Aftermath* (Durham, 1990), p. 16.

95 A. F. Butcher, 'Rent, Population and Economic Change in Late-Medieval Newcastle,' *NH*, 14 (1978), pp. 66–77.

96 Keith Wrightson, *Ralph Tailor's Summer: A Scrivener, his City and the Plague* (London, 2011); Diana Newton and A. J. Pollard, 'Introduction,' in Diana Newton and A. J. Pollard (eds.), *Newcastle and Gateshead Before 1700* (Chichester, 2009), pp. xix–xxv.

97 Keith Wrightson, '"That Lamentable Time": Catastrophe and Community in the Great Newcastle Plague of 1636,' in D. Newton and A. J. Pollard (eds.), *Newcastle and Gateshead Before 1700* (Chichester, 2009), pp. 241–64.

At the start of the sixteenth century, Durham rural society was dominated by the estates of the bishops of Durham and Durham Cathedral Priory, whose large and concentrated estates between the Tyne and Tees accounted for some £2,500–£3,000 and £1,500–£2,000 per annum respectively. These lands were generally found in the most fertile regions of the south-east of the county which, along with another significant group of manors to the north of the county around the mouths of the Tyne and Wear rivers, formed the bulk of their estate. Next came the earl of Westmorland, the largest lay landowner in terms of income, influence and importance in the region, whose estate contained some forty-five manors, predominately focused upon the upland and wooded regions of Brancepeth to the west of Durham and Raby to the south-west of Bishop Auckland, although with some significant outlying manors, especially around Elwick near Hartlepool.[98] The other resident peer in the county was lord Lumley, whose lands in Durham and Yorkshire placed him above the upper gentry of the Bowes of Streatlam, the Eures of Witton-le-Wear, the Hiltons of Hylton castle and the Conyers of Sockburn. This group was formed of the traditional ruling families of the palatinate, some of whom could trace their lineage back to the twelfth-century '*barones et fideles Sancti Cuthberti*'.[99] Below these families came significant gentry families like the Claxtons, Tempests, Salvins, Blakistons and Lambtons, and below them a group of lesser or parish gentry like the Bellasises, Millots and Billinghams, some of whom had little more claim to gentility than rich yeomen farmers in the region, especially the smaller gentry families who scratched a living on the moorland farms to the west of the county.

This was a rural society, therefore, heavily dominated by a high concentration of ecclesiastical landownership, a resident aristocracy whose primary focus was upon the region and a group of knightly families who dominated local office and landholding. But this had not always been the case in Durham and, as will be seen, was in many ways a direct product of the economic and social conditions of the late fourteenth and fifteenth centuries. It was in this period of low prices and high wages that many of the lesser gentry struggled, often providing the stimulus for the acquisitions that these knightly families were able to make and thus consolidate their position in the region. Moreover, this was a concentration of landownership which was not to survive the challenges of the sixteenth century, with a redistribution of landed wealth in the region primarily aided by the long leases of many ecclesiastical manors, the dissolution of the subordinate cells of Durham priory, the forfeiture and eventual sale of the Neville lands, and the sale of much of the Lumleys' Durham estate. The 1624 lay subsidy reveals the extent of these changes, with the likes of Henry Hilton being joined by some of the lesser gentry like William Bellasis and Ralph Featherstonhaugh amongst the highest-appraised individuals listed, as well as a significant

98 James, *Family, Lineage, and Civil Society*, pp. 10–11.

99 W. Aird, *St Cuthbert and the Normans: the Church of Durham, 1071–1153* (Woodbridge, 1998), pp. 209–13; Liddy, *The Bishopric of Durham*, pp. 58–9.

group of Newcastle coal merchants including Henry Anderson, Thomas Liddell, Thomas Riddell and Robert Brandling appearing in the north of the county.[100]

This book explores the transformation of landed society in Durham from the late fourteenth century to the early seventeenth century in broadly three sections. Chapters 1 and 2 explore the responses of the two main ecclesiastical landowners in Durham to the depopulation of the countryside after the Black Death and to the fifteenth-century recession, as well as the long-term consequences of these decisions for their sixteenth-century counterparts. Chapters 3, 4 and 5 explore the balance of landownership amongst the aristocracy and gentry of the Durham palatinate, including the influx of 'new wealth' created by the take-off of the coal industry. The final two chapters explore how the long-term development of these estates created institutional constraints upon the tenantry of the region that affected their gradual differentiation into yeomen, smallholders and wage labourers. The combination of the fifteenth and sixteenth centuries is especially important because often how individuals, families and institutions responded to the fifteenth-century recession had long-term consequences which directly influenced their descendants' abilities to respond to the inflation of the sixteenth century.

Despite the general problems of discontinuity in the sources for economic and social history, the records of Durham's ecclesiastical estates provide a rare opportunity to study developments on the estates of the two largest landowners between the River Tyne and the River Tees in considerable detail. The importance of Durham Priory's archives hardly needs to be emphasised, containing as they do some of the 'longest non-government accounts ever produced in medieval England'.[101] Because of the profusion of records created, and importantly, retained, by these institutions it is possible to trace the rental incomes of these ecclesiastical estates across both centuries, and thus gain a much greater understanding of the economic fluctuations of the period. It quickly becomes apparent that the fifteenth century was not one of continual or unrelenting recession but one of sub-periods, with the hardship of the 1430s, the mid-century depths of the 1450s and '60s, and the renewed problems of the 1480s emerging particularly prominently.[102] Overall these two centuries were particularly problematic for rentier landlords because the difficulties of collecting rents during the fifteenth-century recession were matched by the problems of trying to increase those rents in the sixteenth century in order to compensate for inflation. Neither was an easy task but, as will become clear, the two estates responded differently to the former, which greatly affected their successors' ability to respond to the latter.

The second section of this book is composed of three chapters which explore the laity, whose experiences provide a different response to that of ecclesiastical land-

100 DUL, ASC, Mickleton and Spearman Manuscript 7, ff. 26–47.

101 Dobson, *Durham Priory*, p. 260.

102 As pointed out and discussed in Hatcher, 'The Great Slump', pp. 237–40.

owners to the recession. Given that one of the primary characteristics of ecclesiastical institutions was their inability to sell or alienate land, these chapters go on to investigate the balance of landownership amongst the laity in order to explore the wider accumulation of manors by certain sections of society. Through the use of Inquisitions Post Mortem, accounts, wills and probate inventories, this study analyses how the laity struggled with the fifteenth-century recession and the inflation of the sixteenth century, charting those who survived and exploring why others did not. How far did the inflation and burgeoning coal industry of the sixteenth century provide opportunities or challenges for the Durham gentry, and how much of a hindrance was posed to some of their number by their adherence to Catholicism? This section engages with long-standing debates surrounding the rise of the gentry and crisis of the aristocracy in the sixteenth century, with Durham forming an important case study after the downfall of the Nevilles for their part in the Rising of the North, as well as the economic opportunities arising from the coal industry for both members of the gentry and Newcastle merchants. How far, for example, does the traditional account of the gentrification of merchants explain the settlement of many Newcastle coal merchants in the Durham countryside from the late sixteenth century onwards? These chapters explore how far social status was the defining feature of these changes or whether our analysis of conflict in the sixteenth century should focus more on land usage and economic occupation with a 'rise of agricultural producers' and a 'crisis of rentier landlords'.

The final section of this book is composed of two chapters exploring how the transformations of the ecclesiastical estates of Durham affected their tenants. These chapters especially explore the impact of the divergent development of the two ecclesiastical estates upon their tenants, questioning how far estate management and institutional constraints shaped the opportunities and challenges tenants faced in this period. During the fifteenth century the monks and tenants of Durham Priory reorganised their holdings, which was to have long-term consequences for their successors as it led to the gradual transformation of bond tenants with fragmented smallholdings into a modest yeomanry possessing consolidated holdings of between 50 and 150 acres on 21-year leases. By comparison, the bishops of Durham did not implement any kind of uniform redistribution of land on their estate, which resulted in several families accumulating much larger holdings than many of their neighbours, producing a much greater degree of stratification of landholding than on the dean and chapter's estate. This also enabled smallholders to persist in much greater number as these holdings were still financially viable because of their copyhold tenure and stagnant rents.[103] The tenure by which land was held in medieval

103 There were numerous types of tenure which evolved from medieval customary tenures: copyholds for life, which were granted to named tenants; copyholds of inheritance, which as their name suggests conveyed an inheritable interest in the land; tenant-right, which was a northern customary tenure that provided security of tenure if upheld in court; and leasehold land, which could be held

and early modern England was of fundamental importance to landlords and tenants alike, often determining who benefited from rising agricultural prices.[104] As will be seen, if we were to choose examples of Durham villages at random in the early seventeenth century we would find significant differences in the tenure, rents and size of holdings between a village on the dean and chapter's estate and its counterparts on the bishops' estate.

The Durham region is thus significant for a number of reasons. The county featured a high concentration of lordship, both ecclesiastical and lay, allowing for a study of how this institutional context affected economic and social change across the medieval and early modern periods. This is especially the case for the two ecclesiastical estates, whose excellent records allow for an exploration of how neighbouring, often contiguous, estates could diverge under very similar economic pressures, creating a path dependency which affected both their successors and their tenants. Along with the Nevilles and Lumleys, this amounted to the presence of a powerful resident aristocracy in the county, but this concentration of landownership did not survive the sixteenth century, allowing for a re-evaluation of some long-standing historical disputes. But Durham was more than this, becoming as it did the first industrial region in the country by the seventeenth century. This early industrialisation allows for a study of how capital was invested in the coal industry by the yeomanry and gentry of the region, facilitating the rise of successful rural families, but also the context in which mercantile wealth was diverted back into the countryside. As a result of this symbiotic relationship, the social, economic and political status of Newcastle merchants takes on a new dimension, challenging the traditional narrative of the gentrification of mercantile wealth. Moreover, an exploration of the tenants of the region sheds light on the development of agrarian capitalism and social mobility further down the social scale, demonstrating the effect that estate management and institutional constraints could have on the accumulation of wealth and the emergence of a rural elite.

for years or for lives, but which was generally considered to be the most commercial form of tenure, with little or no inheritable right.

104 J. Whittle, 'Tenure and Landholding in England, 1440–1580: A Crucial Period for the Development of Agrarian Capitalism?', in Bas van Bavel and Peter Hoppenbrouwers (eds.), *Landholding and Land Transfer in the North Seas Area* (Turnhout, 2004), pp. 237–49.

1

Ecclesiastical Responses to the Fifteenth-Century Recession

The fifteenth century has traditionally been described as an 'age of recession, arrested economic development and declining national income', with a decrease in land rents, the area under cultivation and overall levels of production.[1] Mark Bailey has described the years from 1430 to 1465 as witnessing 'one of the most sustained and severe agricultural depressions in documented English history', whilst John Hatcher has shown that this recession spread across agriculture, trade and industry.[2] Continuing demographic stagnation, a shortage of silver bullion, a collapse in foreign trade, and bad harvests in the 1430s all contributed towards this recession, whose effects were felt across England.[3] In exploring the financial difficulties of the bishops of Worcester during the fifteenth century, Christopher Dyer noted that:

> the most convincing argument is that the main economic trends of the early/mid-fifteenth century were against magnates, as rents, which formed the bulk of their revenues, declined. However, it has been maintained that skilful management could stabilise or even increase estate revenues.[4]

The first of these two points has become something of an orthodoxy, but could estates which were managed efficiently avoid the recession entirely? Was efficient and skilful management sufficient to achieve this success in the Durham region or was the early

1 Postan, 'Fifteenth Century', p. 161; Hatcher, *Rural Economy and Society*, p. 148.

2 Mark Bailey, 'Rural Society', in R. Horrox (ed.), *Fifteenth-Century Attitudes* (Cambridge, 1994), p. 153; Hatcher, 'The Great Slump', pp. 237–72.

3 Important works on the fifteenth-century recession include, Postan, 'Fifteenth Century', pp. 160–7; and Hatcher, *Plague, Population and the English Economy*; for a more optimistic view, see Bridbury, *Economic Growth*; for an urban perspective, see R. B. Dobson, 'Urban Decline in Late Medieval England', *Transactions of the Royal Historical Society*, 5th series, 27 (1977), pp. 1–22; P. J. P. Goldberg, 'Mortality and Economic Change in the Diocese of York, 1390–1514', *NH*, 24 (1988), pp. 38–55; and S. H. Rigby, 'Urban Population in Late Medieval England: the Evidence of the Lay Subsidies', *EcHR*, 63 (2010), pp. 393–417; for a prospering textile industry, see J. N. Hare, *A Prospering Society: Wiltshire in the Later Middle Ages* (Hatfield, 2011); for landlord–tenant relations in the fifteenth century see Dyer, *Lords and Peasants*; and Dyer, 'A Redistribution of Incomes'; for the silver bullion shortage, see Martin Allen, 'Silver Production and the Money Supply in England and Wales, 1086–c.1500', *EcHR*, 64 (2011), pp. 114–31.

4 Dyer, *Lords and Peasants*, p. 153.

development of the coal industry capable of providing the region with sufficient stimulus to lessen the effects of the agricultural recession in the north-east of England?

One of the most significant developments between the fourteenth and sixteenth centuries was the large-scale leasing out of land by the majority of landowners, who had thus become rentier landlords by the latter period with relatively little direct interest in the land they owned. In the intervening centuries, and most prominently in the fifty-year period between 1370 and 1420, medieval lords withdrew from the direct exploitation of their demesnes, preferring to lease them to gentlemen, yeomen, husbandmen and merchants.[5] Although there was some regional variation to this withdrawal and not all lords stopped working their own demesnes entirely, there was a remarkable trend for large landowners in England to withdraw almost wholesale from direct-demesne production in these years.[6] With this withdrawal from direct agricultural production, much of the recovery from the depths of the mid-fifteenth-century recession took the form of the efficient collection of rents and arrears.

Dyer's study of the estates of the bishops of Worcester, for example, found tales of 'great decay and falling down of the buildings of tenants for lack of repair'. The bishops' rent collection improved in the second half of the fifteenth century, however, with '1486 marking a turning point in the history of arrears on the estate' through an 'orgy of administrative activity'; after this date, arrears remained at a relatively low level, less even than in the late fourteenth and early fifteenth centuries.[7] There are many other estates with a similar tale of recovery by the last few decades of the fifteenth century through a concerted effort in improving their efficiency. Du Boulay's study of the estates of the archbishops of Canterbury revealed an increase in revenues on the majority of the Kentish estates after 1490, with there being a 'moderate burden of arrears up until the 1480s or 1490s, but after this arrears declined and often died away altogether, and the payments of money, always fairly steady, rose gently to a correspondingly high plateau'.[8] There was a similar improvement in the collection of

5 Du Boulay found that the archbishop of Canterbury was slower in leasing out his demesne than his cathedral monastery in F. R. H. Du Boulay, 'Who were Farming the English Demesnes at the End of the Middle Ages?', *EcHR*, 17 (1965), pp. 445–6; Mate has shown the indecision between direct-demesne management and leasing on the estates of the prior of Christ Church, Canterbury in M. Mate,'The Farming out of Manors: a New Look at the Evidence from Canterbury Cathedral Priory', *JMH*, 9 (1983), pp. 331–43; Halcrow and Lomas disagreed over the transition from high farming to leasing on the estates of Durham Priory in E. M. Halcrow, 'The Decline of Demesne Farming on the Estates of Durham Cathedral Priory', *EcHR*, 7 (1955), pp. 345–56 and R. A. Lomas, 'The Priory of Durham and its Demesnes in the Fourteenth and Fifteenth Centuries', *EcHR*, 31 (1978), pp. 339–53.

6 Hare pointed to an important distinction between lay and ecclesiastical responses: by 1400 there were only three out of twenty-five documented lay manors involved in direct production, whereas only six of thirty-one ecclesiastical manors had been leased out by this date in Wiltshire, J. N. Hare, 'The Demesne Lessees of Fifteenth-Century Wiltshire', *AgHR*, 29 (1981), pp. 1–15.

7 Dyer, *Lords and Peasants*, p. 165 and p. 185.

8 F. R. H. Du Boulay, 'A Rentier Economy in the Later Middle Ages: The Archbishopric of Canterbury', *EcHR*, 16 (1964), pp. 435–6.

arrears for the lordship of Newport, not only showing a broadly similar chronology of recovery, but also an improvement in collecting arrears achieved by the end of the fifteenth century which outstripped that experienced by the lords' early fifteenth-century predecessors.[9]

How badly did the north-east of England suffer from the fifteenth-century recession and was the region's recovery delayed compared to the rest of the country?[10] Dyer concluded that revenues fell by around 20 per cent in southern and midland England, but were reduced by a third in the north-east.[11] Pollard has argued further that there was little recovery in the regional economy, especially after the harvest failures of the 1430s which hit the north-east harder than much of the country.[12] He went on to explain that 'the north-east was experiencing relative as well as absolute decline' because other regions of the country 'came out of recession earlier than the north-east, and began to enjoy the fruits of sustained economic resurgence from the 1470s'.[13] It is argued here that there actually were signs of recovery from this date on some estates in the north-east but that this was far from universal, for although it seems unlikely that the efficiency of a landowner could enable them to completely avoid such a pervasive recession in this period, it was the acumen and initiative of estate managers that enabled some landowners to recover earlier than their neighbours. Furthermore, if the coal trade was still in its infancy in the fifteenth century, it was at least capable of providing landlords with a cushion against some of the worst ravages of the agricultural recession. This chapter will show that the road to recovery from the fifteenth-century recession could take decidedly different paths, even amongst neighbouring estates, which was to have long-term consequences for landlords and tenants alike.

9 Arrears increased from £46 14s at the start of the fifteenth century to £229 10s in 1434/35, staying high in the 1450s until they dropped to just over £60 in 1465/66 and were £23 1s in 1497/98, T. B. Pugh (ed.), *The Marcher Lordships of South Wales, 1415–1536: Select Documents* (Cardiff, 1963), p. 182.

10 The income of Canterbury Cathedral Priory declined from £2,202 in 1419/20 to £1,757 by 1469, Dyer, *Making a Living*, p. 337; the income of the Suffolk manor of Staverton declined from £59 in 1400 to £40 by the 1470s, Mark Bailey, *Medieval Suffolk: an Economic and Social History, 1200–1500* (Woodbridge, 2007), p. 208; the income of Leicester Abbey declined from £268 19s 9d in 1408 to £229 9s 4d in 1477, R. H. Hilton, *The Economic Development of Some Leicestershire Estates in the Fourteenth and Fifteenth Centuries* (London, 1947), p. 86. By comparison, Bean argued that the income of the Percy's Northumberland estates showed a 'decline of over a half in the value of the demesne lands in the first half of the fifteenth century', J. M. W. Bean, *The Estates of the Percy Family, 1416–1537* (London, 1958), pp. 30–1.

11 Dyer, *Making a Living*, p. 337.

12 See the Introduction for an outline of the historical literature on Durham in the fifteenth century. A. J. Pollard, 'The North-Eastern Economy and the Agrarian Crisis of 1438–40', *NH*, 25 (1989), pp. 88–105.

13 Pollard, *North-Eastern England*, pp. 78–80.

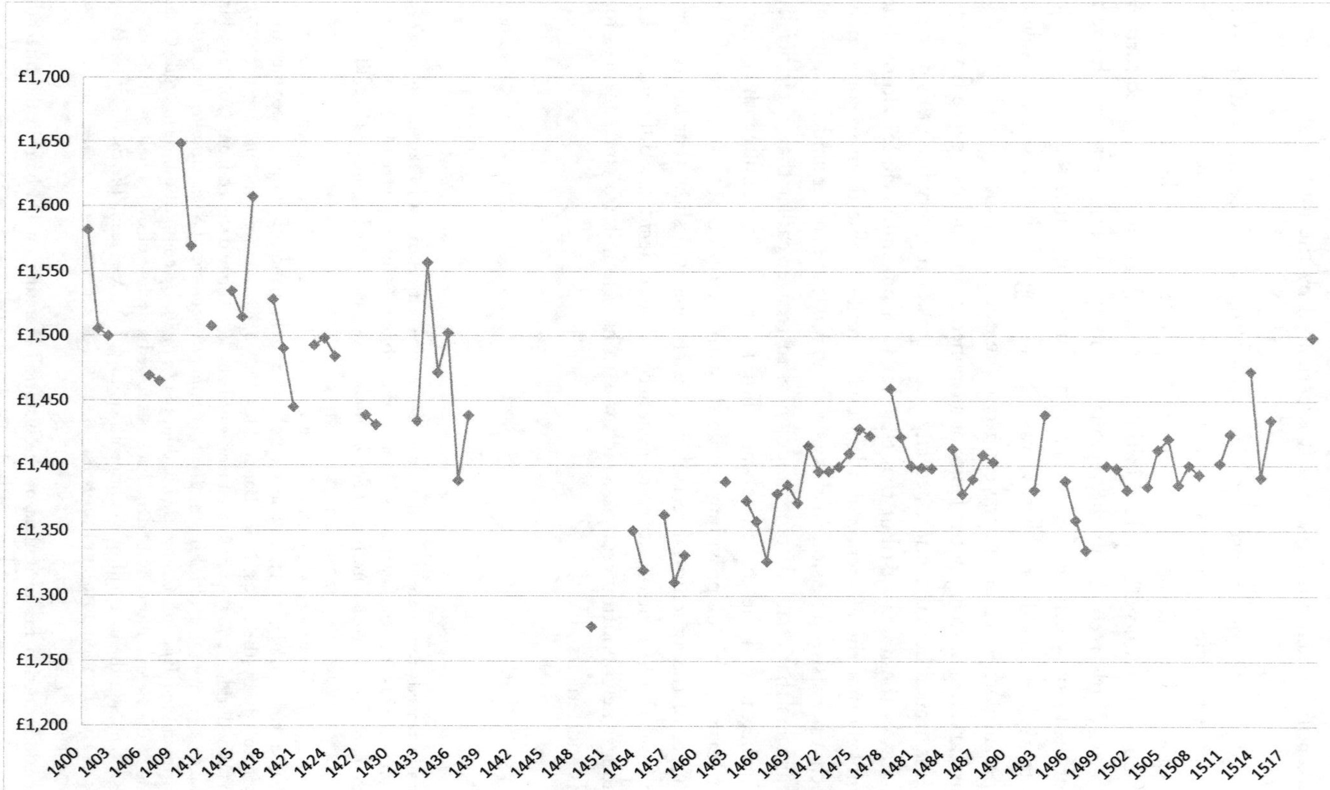

Figure 1. Total Potential Revenue of the Bursars of Durham Cathedral Priory, 1400–1520.
Source: DCM, Bursar's Accounts, 1400/01–1519/20.

Durham Cathedral Priory

Durham Cathedral Priory was one of the wealthiest landowners in the palatinate, second only to the bishops of Durham, with its income being divided between its eight obediences. In the fifteenth century the bursar's office, which was responsible for the general provisioning of the Durham monks, could expect an income of around £1,400, with the other obedientiaries possessing much smaller incomes to carry out their more specialised roles, approximately as follows: the hostillar, £170; the almoner, £100; the chamberlain, £100; the sacrist, £80; the commoner, £90; the feretrar, £30; and the terrar, £20.[14] The bursar thus accounted for approximately three-quarters of the priory's revenue, and as such his accounts represent much of the priory's financial position. He collected rents from villages spread across the counties of Durham, Northumberland and Yorkshire, but the vast majority were between the two rivers, the Tyne and the Tees. These included a high concentration of villages close to the River Tyne, such as Harton, Monkton, Heworth, Willington, Westoe, Wallsend and South Shields, and a similar concentration in the fertile south-east of the county, including Billingham, Wolviston, Newton Bewley and Cowpen Bewley.[15] The bursar also collected rents from numerous tenements in the urban boroughs of Newcastle, Sunderland, Hartlepool and Durham, but these formed a very small proportion of overall receipts, perhaps as little as 5 per cent, and so the majority of the rental income came from agricultural property in the Durham region.[16]

Although they did not report for all of the priory's income, it is the bursars' accounts which are used here as the yardstick for the cathedral's economic prosperity, for if the bursars were struggling to collect rents then the whole monastery felt its effects. Unlike on the bishops' estate, which will be explored later in this chapter, there was no major redistribution in the bursars' income during this period.[17] The bursars' overall income fell from around £1,600 at the start of the fifteenth century to its lowest figure of £1,276 in 1450, and although recovery did happen in the second half of the fifteenth century, this still only brought the bursars' income to £1,498, falling short of levels a century earlier.[18]

14 Dobson, *Durham Priory*, pp. 253–4.

15 Durham Priory also maintained an arable home farm throughout the fifteenth century at Elvet Hall, R. A. Lomas, 'A Northern Farm at the End of the Middle Ages', *NH*, 18 (1982), pp. 26–53.

16 R. A. Lomas and A. J. Piper (eds.), *Durham Cathedral Priory Rentals, Vol. I: Bursar's Rentals*, Surtees Society, 198 (1989), pp. 129–99.

17 An approximate breakdown of the composition of this income in 1450 shows that £937 came from landed rents, £272 from tithe collection and £65 from other receipts, whilst in 1536 this was as follows: £1,067 from rents for landholdings, £290 from tithe receipts and £98 from other receipts. See below for a comparison to the bishops of Durham, pp. 51–3.

18 DCM, Bursar's Accounts, 1449/50 and 1519/20. All data produced from Durham Cathedral Muniments by permission of the Chapter of Durham Cathedral.

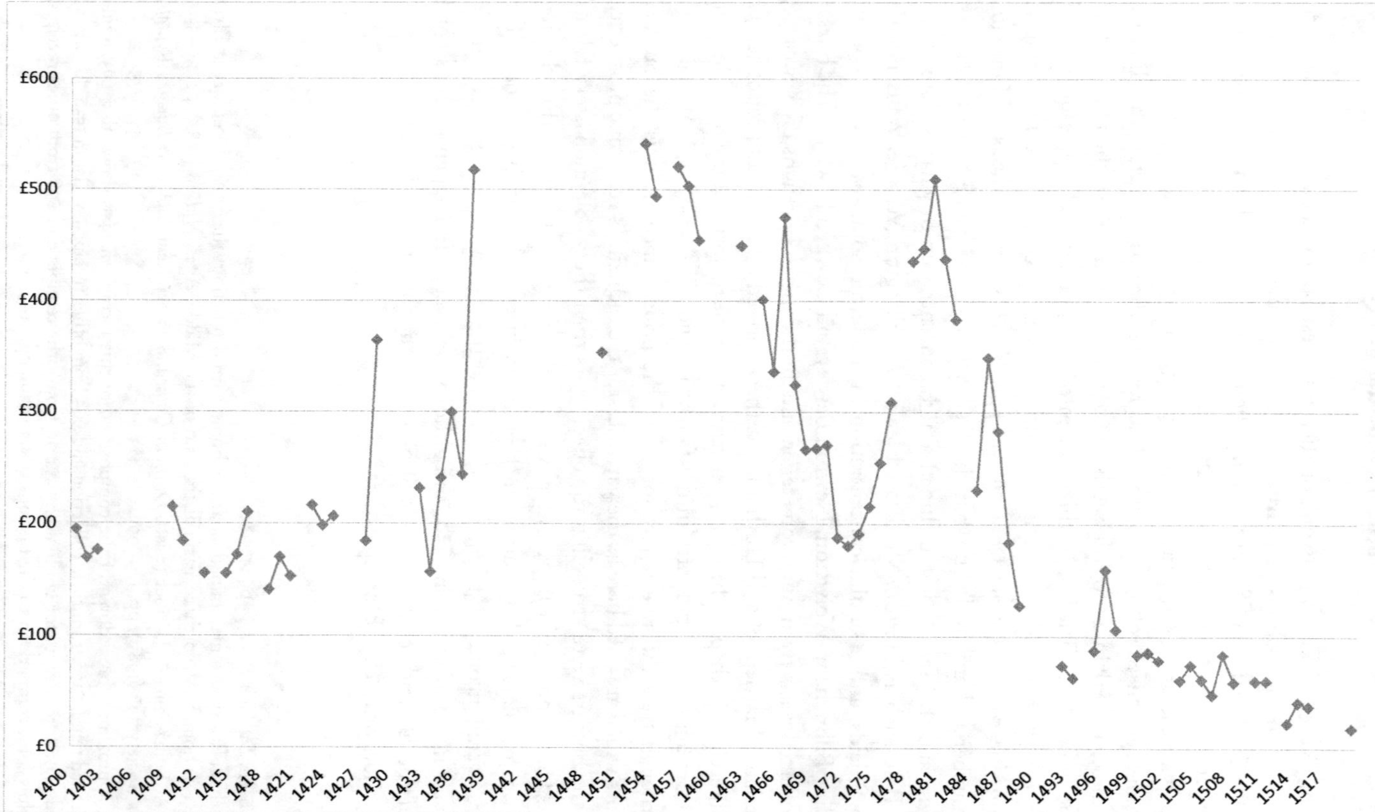

Figure 2. Sum of Arrears, Waste and Decay for the Current Accounting Year for the Bursars of Durham Priory, 1400–1520.
Source: DCM, Bursar's Accounts, 1400/01–1519/20.

Figure 1 shows the gradual decline in revenues in the first half of the fifteenth century, with a complete stagnation in the second half of the century. However, this only tells part of the story of the priory's financial struggles: these figures represent only what the bursars could expect to receive if all their land was occupied and every single tenant paid their rent on time and in full, a situation unlikely to happen in the fifteenth century.[19] The bursars' real net income is to be found at the end of the account rolls where the arrears, waste and decay are totalled. Waste was the medieval accounting term for lost income through vacant holdings, whilst decay represented the income lost because of rents which had been temporarily reduced but which the bursar hoped would return their full value in the future. These were both structural and potentially long-lasting problems for a landowner, but a more transient obstacle to fully collecting all rental income was arrears. Whereas waste and decay were potentially permanent reductions in net income and often represented long-term problems, arrears tended to be temporary and thus reflected short-term fluctuations in the economy of the region, being especially sensitive to harvest failures or outbreaks of disease. These combined deductions were not static or continual problems for the bursars of Durham Priory but reflect the complex chronology of economic trends in the fifteenth century as shown in Figure 2.

When these losses from permanent reductions and late payments are taken away from the potential annual income of the bursars of Durham Priory a radically different image of the fifteenth century is revealed, as shown in Figure 3. The full depth of the mid-fifteenth-century recession is revealed, as is an initial phase of recovery in the late 1460s and early 1470s, with a renewed crisis in the 1480s, before eventual recovery to levels even slightly higher than those at the start of the century.[20]

The financial history of Durham Priory confirms the view that the years from 1430 to 1465 were particularly difficult for landowners.[21] The 1430s witnessed some of the worst harvest failures of the fifteenth century and Thomas Lawson, who was appointed as bursar 'in the absence of a more suitable candidate', later fled after being accused of hiding debts worth £1,210 'concealed from the prior and convent'.[22] This led to an administrative experiment whereby the bursars' lands and responsibilities were divided into three roughly equal amounts: the first retained by the bursar, the second given to the cellarer and the third to the granator. However, it is far from clear that this radical new division of labour actually improved the collection of arrears: although the bursar's income had been reduced to approximately £500, he was still experiencing arrears consistently over £100 up until 1445 when the new administra-

19 For a more in-depth discussion of priory's response to the fifteenth-century recession, see A. T. Brown, 'Surviving the Mid-Fifteenth-Century Recession: Durham Cathedral Priory, 1400–1520', *NH*, 47 (2010), pp. 209–31.

20 DCM, Bursar's Accounts, 1400/01–1519/20.

21 Bailey, 'Rural Society', p. 153. See also Hatcher, 'The Great Slump', pp. 237–72.

22 Dobson, *Durham Priory*, pp. 285–6.

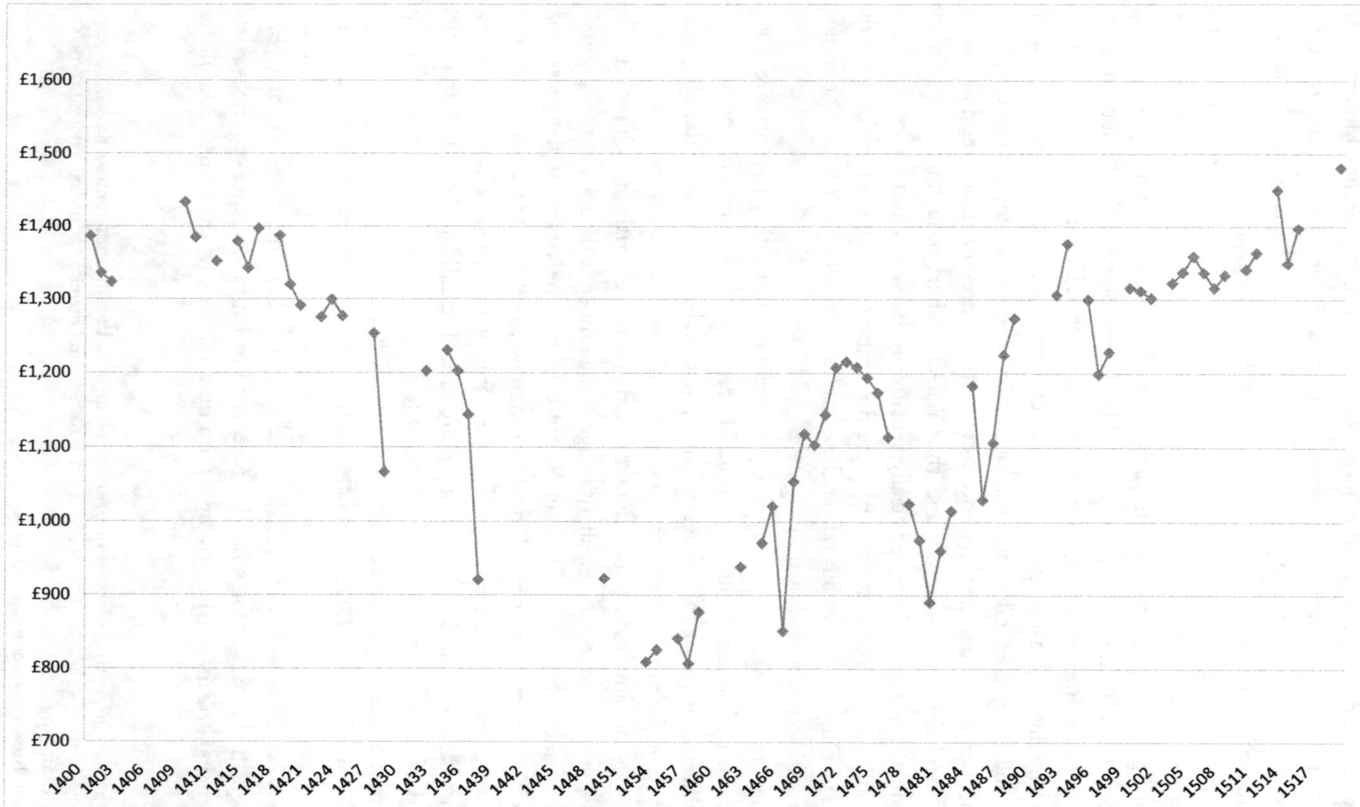

Figure 3. Total Income Less Annual Arrears, Waste and Decay for the Bursars of Durham Priory, 1400–1520.
Source: DCM, Bursar's Accounts, 1400/01–1519/20.

tive arrangement came to an end.[23] In 1446, Prior Ebbchester described the state of the monastery as nearing collapse, whilst several of the priory's manorial farmers were ruined by the agrarian depression.[24] By the middle of the fifteenth century the bursars' income reflects Ebbchester's pessimism, with the total expected receipts reaching their lowest in the priory's history, a meagre £1,276 in 1449/50.[25] The true depth of the recession is even more visible in the annual deductions, with arrears totalling £444 in 1453/54, whilst waste often reached £40 and decay averaged over £50 for the 1450s.[26] Bad arrears were also accumulating rapidly so that, although cumulative arrears were only £452 in 1449/50, they had reached £1,949 by 1462/63, most of which the bursar would never be able to recoup.[27]

The first signs of recovery from this pervasive recession can be seen in the late 1460s and early 1470s. Arrears were initially brought under control, so that by 1472/73 they were down to £119, a level still higher than average arrears before Lawson's disastrous occupation of the office, but much more manageable than two decades before.[28] Decay in the accounts gradually decreased to £45 by 1475/76, a figure nearly half that of 1406/07, and waste dropped to a record low of £7.[29] Unfortunately for the priory, these levels were not maintained in the decade to follow as high mortality and bad harvests were to wreak havoc once more on the bursars' income. After such promising recovery, the successive shock of renewed plague outbreaks in 1479/80 and the second worst harvests of the fifteenth century in 1480–82 increased annual arrears to the sum of £454 in 1480/1.[30] Despite this financial nightmare, the bursars' account rolls show the tenacity of the monks in this period as waste and decay did not appreciably rise, and so their major concern was with late payment rather than no payment at all. After the crisis of the early 1480s, the bursars' income recovered quickly and decisively as Table 1 demonstrates. By 1520, the last full surviving bursar's account, arrears, waste and decay had been reduced to unprecedentedly low levels: waste was reduced to £5, decay to £6 and arrears were around £5 during the 1510s.[31] This improved collection of rents was significantly better even than the bursars managed in the early fifteenth century, with the sum of all arrears, waste and decay averaging over £150 in the 1410s and 1420s, whereas it never went above £100 in the early sixteenth century.[32]

23 DCM, Bursar's Accounts, 1438/39–1444/45.

24 Dobson, *Durham Priory*, pp. 286–7.

25 DCM, Bursar's Account, 1449/50.

26 DCM, Bursar's Accounts, 1449/50–1458/59.

27 See below for a further discussion of arrears, pp. 38–43.

28 DCM, Bursar's Account, 1472/73.

29 DCM, Bursar's Accounts, 1406/07 and 1475/76.

30 DCM, Bursar's Accounts, 1478/79–1481/82; Pollard, *North-Eastern England*, p. 47.

31 DCM, Bursar's Accounts, 1485/86–1519/20.

32 DCM, Bursar's Accounts, 1400/01–1419/20 and 1485/86–1519/20.

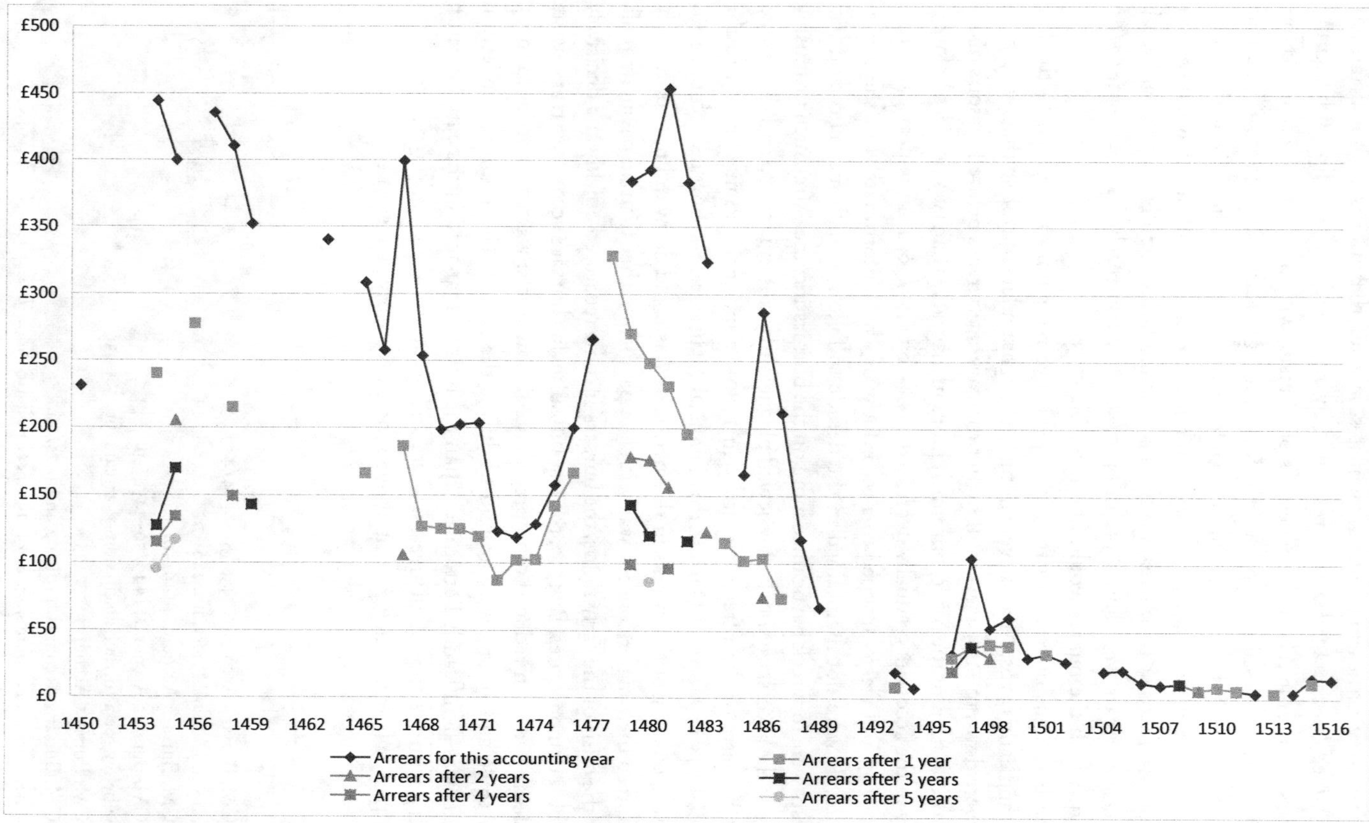

Figure 4. The Collection of Arrears by the Bursars of Durham Priory, 1450–1520.
Source: DCM, Bursar's Accounts, 1450/51–1519/20.

Table 1. Annual Income, Arrears, Waste and Decay of the Bursars of Durham Priory, 1400–1520

	1400/01	1437/38	1453/54	1471/72	1480/81	1493/94	1519/20
Expected Income	£1,581	£1,438	£1,350	£1,395	£1,400	£1,439	£1,499
Annual Arrears	£92	£487	£445	£123	£454	£8	£7
Waste	£40	£14	£45	£13	£11	£5	£5
Decay	£63	£16	£51	£51	£45	£50	£6

Source: DCM, Bursar's Accounts, 1400/01–1519/20.

Arrears were clearly a major problem for landowners in this period, especially during the mid-fifteenth-century recession. In the 1450s and again in the 1480s, arrears for a single accounting year could reach as high as £450, around one-third of the bursars' total expected income. But how much of this amount could the bursar expect to recoup in years to come? Fortunately, when accounts survive from consecutive years this can be estimated because the accounts often include arrears from the previous year. Occasionally this method was used to keep track of arrears for several years and so we can see how the bursar slowly managed to claw back his income in the second half of the fifteenth century.

Figure 4 shows that the bursars were quite efficient at reducing arrears, and within five years had often succeeded in cutting them down to one-fifth of the original figure. The bursar thus managed to recoup just under £320 of the high arrears in 1479/80, so that the original arrears of nearly £400 were reduced to £86 within five years.[33] This reinforces the idea of the tenacity of the monks of Durham Priory in this period: during the 1480s, despite renewed outbreaks of plague, the sweating sickness and the second worst harvests of the century, waste and decay did not appreciably increase, whilst arrears, although initially crippling, were gradually recouped so that only a fifth of late payments would eventually have to be written off. Any hope of collecting outstanding arrears seems to have ended after five years and these amounts accumulated on the accounts until they were simply cancelled as uncollectable. Although harvest failures posed many difficulties for tenants in the fifteenth century it appears that they were able to pass at least some of these financial problems onto landlords by withholding their rents for several years until harvests improved. Within five years most tenants had repaid these arrears: they were not withholding their rents as an ideological stand against the rapaciousness of a medieval landlord, but were simply unable to pay on time because of the succession of poor harvests.[34]

A comparison of average grain prices in the region with levels of arrears, waste and decay reveals just how dependent the bursars' rent collection process could be

33 DCM, Bursar's Account, 1479/80.

34 For the problems of collecting rents in the fifteenth century, see Dyer's 'A Redistribution of Incomes', pp. 11–33.

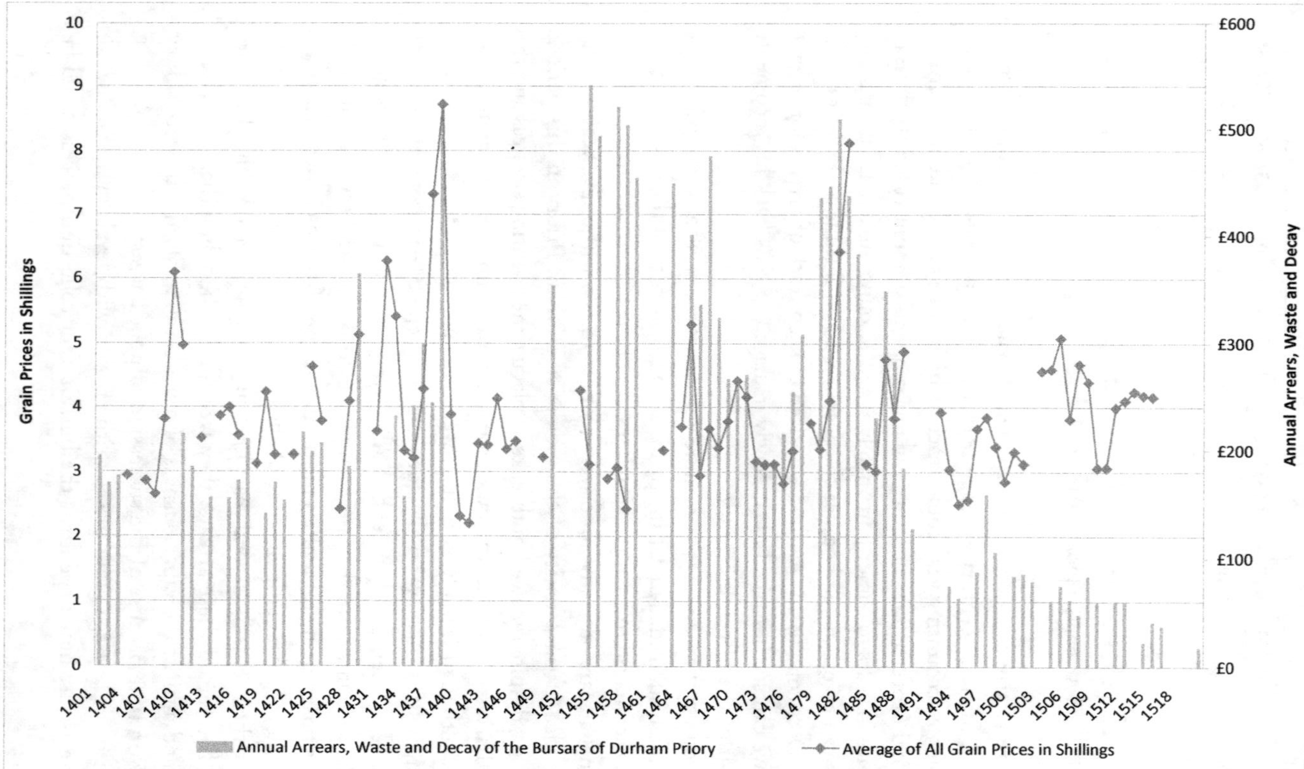

Figure 5. Average of All Grain Prices Compared to the Sum of Arrears, Waste and Decay for the Bursars of Durham Priory, 1400–1520.

Sources: DCM, Bursar's Accounts, 1400/01–1519/20; A. T. Brown, 'Surviving the Mid-Fifteenth-Century Recession: Durham Cathedral Priory, 1400–1520', *NH*, 47 (2010), pp. 209–31; Ben Dodds, Elizabeth Gemmill and Phillipp Schofield, 'Durham Grain Prices, 1278–1515', *AA*, 39 (2010), pp. 307–27.

on the success of the harvest.[35] The two worst periods of harvest failure, when the average price of all grains roughly doubled, coincided with two of the highest levels of arrears, waste and decay – in 1438–40 and 1480–82 (Figure 5). However, there are two distinct periods when the losses of Durham Priory do not correlate so well with grain prices: the mid-fifteenth-century recession and the recovery underway from the 1490s onwards. In these periods, arrears, waste and decay seem to be acting independently of the quality of harvests, with the bursar struggling to collect rents in the 1450s and 1460s far beyond what should have been the case if the success of the harvest was the only factor, whilst the recovery from the 1490s is better than any improvement in harvest qualities alone would account for.

The endless struggle landlords faced against accumulating permanent arrears can be seen in the bad debts increasing on the bursars' accounts. It is impossible to reconstruct the amount of income lost to permanent arrears on an annual basis accurately because temporary arrears were constantly being added to this total. However, once long-term arrears were written off, it is possible to produce an approximation of yearly losses for the period those arrears covered (Figure 6). Thus, between 1450 and 1463 permanent arrears rose by £1,500, an annual increase of around £115.[36] This meant that in a typical year during this same period the bursar was permanently losing over £200 to waste, decay and bad arrears, whilst having to wait for several years before he managed to recoup the further £300 worth of arrears that accumulated on an annual basis. By comparison, between 1465 and 1475, permanent arrears increased at the much slower pace of around £20 per year, clearly supporting the earlier impression that this was a period of recovery from the depths of the mid-century recession.[37] Cumulative arrears then leapt to their record height of £3,089 in 1479/80, primarily due to the rapid increase in temporary arrears as a result of the poor harvests and plague outbreaks of these years.[38] At this stage £1,500 worth of bad arrears were written off; the remaining arrears stabilised for several years, after which the bursar cancelled a further £1,500 worth of bad arrears at the end of the 1480s. By the 1510s, permanent arrears were increasing by as little as £5 a year, which, when added to the £11 lost in waste and decay, meant that the bursar was only losing approximately 1 per cent of his annual income: a clear testament to the improvement in rent collection made by successive bursars of Durham Priory.[39]

The increasing efficiency of the monks of Durham Priory greatly helps to explain how they were able to reduce arrears, waste and decay by over £500 at the same time as improving rents by £130 during the fifteenth century, which is tradition-

35 Ben Dodds, Elizabeth Gemmill, and Phillipp Schofield, 'Durham Grain Prices, 1278–1515', *AA*, 39 (2010), pp. 307–27.

36 DCM, Bursar's Accounts, 1449/50–1462/63.

37 DCM, Bursar's Accounts, 1464/65–1474/75.

38 DCM, Bursar's Accounts, 1479/80.

39 DCM, Bursar's Accounts, 1509/10–1519/20.

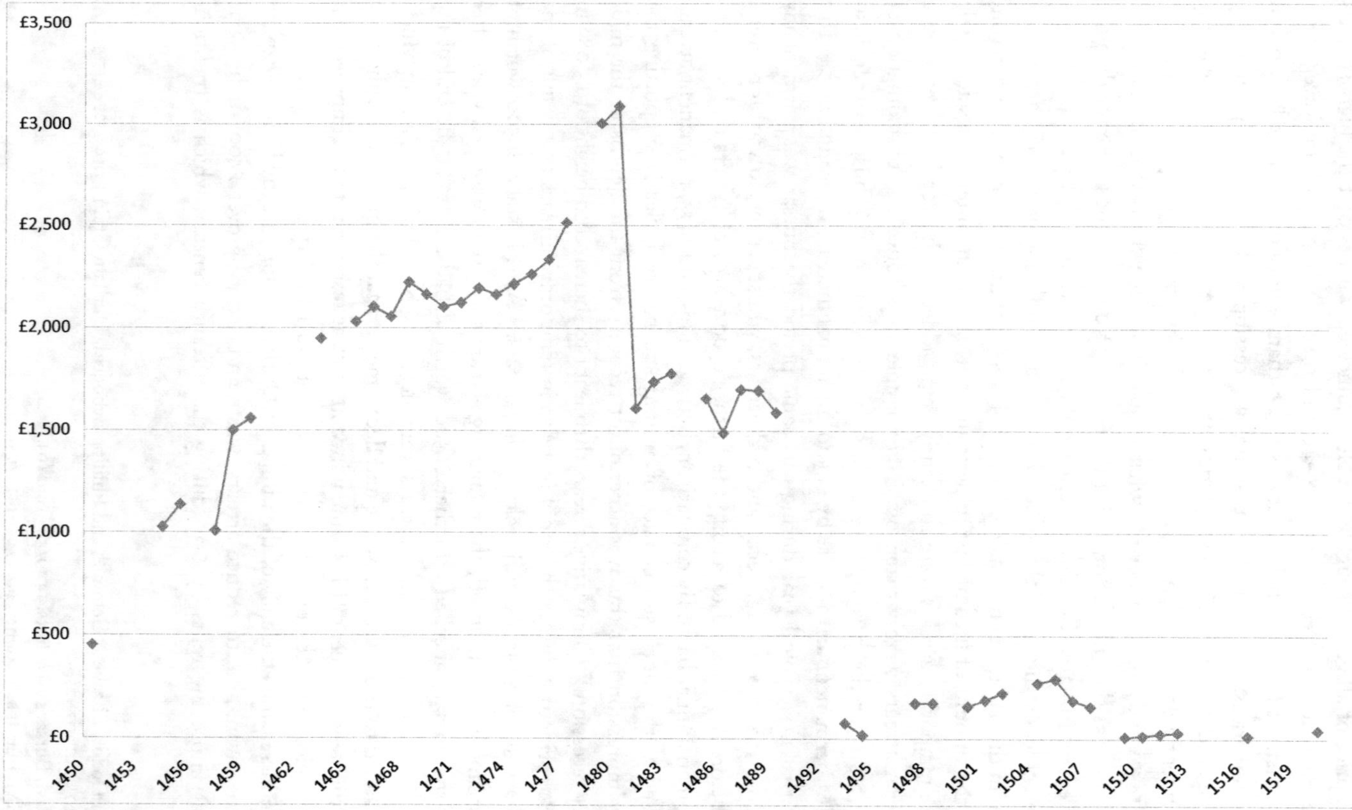

Figure 6: Cumulative Arrears in the Account Rolls of the Bursars of Durham Priory, 1450–1520.
Source: DCM, Bursar's Accounts, 1450/51–1519/20.

ally described as a golden age for labourers and tenants.[40] In 1436/37, the Durham monks expressed alarm at the decline in their spiritual income.[41] The monks not only analysed their economic position over the past century, but went on to give suggestions as to why their income had declined since the thirteenth century, blaming the loss of Scottish parishes and explaining how garb tithes had declined as land was put to pasture and frequent outbreaks of pestilence led to many places becoming waste.[42] This awareness of their own declining economic position played a large part in the monks' search for a more efficient system of rent collection in the face of continued recession later in the century.

It was at this time that the bursars' office was divided in a major administrative experiment that sought not only to spread the responsibility of the bursar but also to improve efficiency and eradicate the arrears which had accumulated under Lawson. Although this experiment was ultimately a failure, it is representative of the resourcefulness of the monks of Durham Priory and it is likely that this adaptability explains the transformation that the bursars' rent book underwent in this period, changing from a rental which merely listed what rent each tenant owed to one of the most detailed lists of rent payment imaginable. In the fourteenth century, the procedure was to place a mark by a tenant's name when they had paid, but this developed at some point in the fifteenth century into a detailed account of how tenants met their rental obligations and where and when they did so, often including extra details such as in whose presence they paid. It is unclear exactly when this new style of rent book came into use, with the book of 1495/96 being the first surviving example, but it might have been used from the mid-century onwards.[43] As the tenants met their obligations, new entries were recorded underneath their names, a typical entry looking like this:

> + From John Calvert per annum 73s. 10d.
>
> Whereof he paid at the court of Pittington 6s; he paid in 8 quarters of wheat 32s; in 8 quarters of barley 24s; in 4 quarters of oats 5s; in 4 chickens 12d.[44]

40 J. Rogers, *Six Centuries of Work and Wages: The History of English Labour* (London, 1906), p. 326.

41 Broadly speaking, the medieval Church derived income from two main types of source: temporalities, which included rent and feudal dues from agricultural and urban tenants; and spiritualities, which generally consisted of tithes and offerings to the Church.

42 Ben Dodds, 'Durham Priory Tithes and the Black Death between the Tyne and Tees', *NH*, 39 (2002), pp. 23–4.

43 After a gap in the records of almost a century, the 1495/96 rent book is the 'earliest example of this type of document to survive', though it was foreshadowed by a similar document for the communar's office for 1454 and the Bursar's Receipts Book for 1432, Lomas and Piper (eds.), *Durham Priory Rentals*, pp. 8–9 and pp. 129–32.

44 Lomas and Piper (eds.), *Durham Priory Rentals*, p. 156; DCM, Bursar's Books, G–M. The '+' denotes that John Calvert had outstanding payments. For a discussion of the rents paid in kind, see A. T. Brown, 'A Money Economy? Provisioning Durham Cathedral across the Dissolution, 1350–1600', in J. P. Bowen and A. T. Brown (eds.), *Custom and Commercialisation in English Rural Society: Revisiting Postan and Tawney* (Hatfield, forthcoming).

Such a detailed description would have proven invaluable in improving the efficiency of rent collection: tenants prone to late payment could be targeted by the itinerant rent collectors, whilst those still owing could be identified more easily and pressured into paying. One of the clearest changes from earlier rentals is that the two-payment system in evidence in the fourteenth century appears to have disintegrated, if indeed it was ever that simple in reality.[45] The new style of rent book allowed for a greater flexibility in recording rent payments, to represent the fact that tenants were paying on a more ad hoc basis than earlier rentals would suggest. As in the above example of John Calvert, tenants often paid in multiple transactions throughout the year, instead of the two traditional collection days in earlier rent books, whilst the monks could be quite tenacious in tracking down tenants who still owed rent, as when John Oxenhird paid 8s of his rent in Monkton 'at the plough in the presence of the Master of Jarrow'.[46]

Further management changes took place in this period which also show the adaptability of the priory so that 'by the middle of the fifteenth century the structure of the estate was completely altered'.[47] The most prominent of these changes was the process of syndication: as the fifteenth century progressed tenures were renegotiated so that whole townships were leased to groups of tenants. Gone were the myriad rental obligations due in the fourteenth century, leaving all of the land and tenements of a region, except freeholds, divided into equal shares amongst the remaining tenants. Around 1360, with few exceptions, tenants were granted their holdings for life, but by the mid-fifteenth century this form of tenancy had given way completely to the short lease. Syndication replaced the confused state of landholding, where tenants could owe ad hoc amounts of rent for holdings of unequal size and number that were often spread throughout the region, with a uniformity which must have increased the bursars' efficiency. As Richard Lomas has argued, the 'number of syndics was the same as the previous number of tenants, and was between two, as at South Pittington, and thirteen, as at Billingham and Ferryhill'. He concluded that the 'creation of syndicates is less easy to explain, especially as they appear to have done no more than neaten ragged arrangements'.[48] As far as can be discerned, landholdings retained their integrity within these syndicates, which were an official recognition of the redistribution of land after the Black Death. For example, at Harton there were twenty-one bondlands before the Black Death which were consolidated by the remaining tenants so that each tenant had either two or three bondlands. When Harton was syndicated the remaining ten tenants each held a tenth of the total

45 Lomas and Piper (eds.), *Durham Priory Rentals*, pp. 129–32.

46 Ibid., p. 139.

47 Richard Lomas, 'Developments in Land Tenure on the Prior of Durham's Estate in the Later Middle Ages', *NH*, 13 (1977), p. 35.

48 Ibid., pp. 35 and 38.

township, which amounted to approximately two bondlands each; thus the process does appear to have neatened pre-existing arrangements.

A more detailed exploration of this process of syndication and its consequences for the priory's tenants is given in chapter 6 in relation to the rise of the Church leaseholder, but it remains unclear from the surviving sources where the demand for this engrossment and conversion of tenure originated.[49] Peter Larson has suggested that, 'although partly a seigniorial initiative, the tenants had much to gain by this change, as the new leases provided more flexibility in land management', while the monks gained from filling vacant land, making this an 'excellent example of lord–peasant consensus'.[50] Short leases began to replace grants for life from the 1360s, but as Lomas has shown, they formed little more than 10 per cent of total lettings before 1390; it was only in the following decade that they outnumbered grants for life.[51] He went on to argue that the chronology of syndication suggests 'the adoption of syndicates stemmed from local considerations as much as from central policy'.[52] This process of engrossment and conversion of tenure could have been at the behest of tenants and might help to explain why tenants were paying more of their rents on time, but given that this syndication of holdings slowly took place on all of the agricultural land belonging to Durham Priory, it seems likely that the monks had a guiding hand in these changes. This not only improved the process of rent collection but was of vital importance in the long-term tenurial development of their estate.

The conversion to leasehold tenure was most significant because it made the enlarged holdings created after the Black Death the typical unit of land on the priory's estate, and thus when population grew in the sixteenth century these holdings did not fragment into their pre-Black Death arrangements, but nor were they subsumed into larger farms.[53] This long-term history of leasing on the priory's estate is significant because several historians have argued that it was the newly created dean and chapter who imposed these leases upon their tenants, whereas in fact there was a much longer tradition of leasing customary land on the priory's estate. For example, Jean Morrin has recently noted that the chapter 'tried to grant commercial leases to the tenants they had inherited' from the suppressed priory because the 'Crown instructed the new Chapter to impose a 21-year lease on each agricultural property

49 See chapter 6 for the consequences of these changes for their tenants.

50 Larson, *Conflict and Compromise*, p. 167; Peter Larson, 'Rural Transformation in Northern England: Village Communities of Durham, 1340–1400', in B. Dodds and R. H. Britnell (eds.), *Agriculture and Rural Society After the Black Death: Common Themes and Regional Variations* (Hatfield, 2008), pp. 199–216.

51 Lomas, 'Developments in Land Tenure', p. 37.

52 Ibid., p. 37. The first syndicate was created at South Pittington in 1371 and the last was not created until 1524 at Cowpen Bewley. However, with this final syndication, it meant that all agricultural land belonging to the Durham monks had been converted to leasehold tenure before the dissolution.

53 See chapter 6 for more details of this.

at the same fixed annual rent previously charged by Durham Priory'.[54] During the fifteenth century, when the monks were more focused upon retaining their tenants rather than on increasing rents, this conversion of tenure was not a source of conflict and may even have been welcomed by their tenants. As will be seen in chapter 2, however, the inflation and population increase of the sixteenth century brought the issue of tenure to the forefront of the dean and chapter's relationship with their tenants, especially in the 1560s and 1570s.[55]

The improvement in rent collection achieved by Durham Priory could have been the result of a general improvement in the region which benefited landowners, but there are few signs of this in the current literature on the north-east of England. On the contrary, as will be seen below, the rental income of the bishops of Durham actually declined across this period, whilst there are other indicators of weak recovery in the region. Ben Dodds, for example, found no discernible increase in arable production from the 1480s onwards, and there are no signs of resurgence in urbanisation or trade in the region: quite the reverse is generally believed to have occurred, with Newcastle and York losing out to London.[56] The only section of the regional economy to have noticeably increased was the mining industry, but this was still in its infancy and could not have stimulated enough demand to account for such large improvements in rent collection.[57] In a period and region where land was relatively abundant, the priory may well have experienced difficulties with particularly truculent tenants who sought to take advantage of the monks' weakened economic position. As Dyer pointed out, how else can we explain the many examples of tenants paying absolutely none of their rents, something which is also in evidence at Durham?[58] Some tenants may well have used rent payment as a bargaining position, falling into arrears for several years and then promising to make amends if the monks paid for some repairs on their land or reduced their overall rent. For an earlier period, Larson has suggested that the 'bursar had little hope of generating and then sustaining economic

54 Jean Morrin, 'The Transfer to Leasehold on Durham Cathedral Estate, 1541–1626', in Jane Whittle (ed.), *Landlords and Tenants in Britain, 1440–1660: Tawney's Agrarian Problem Revisited* (Woodbridge, 2013), p. 117.

55 See chapter 2 for the history of the dean and chapter's estate in the sixteenth and early-seventeenth centuries, pp. 76–91.

56 Dodds, *Peasants and Production*, p. 101; Pollard, *North-Eastern England*, pp. 78–80; Goldberg, 'Mortality and Economic Change', pp. 38–55; D. M. Palliser, *Medieval York, 600–1540* (Oxford, 2014), pp. 240–93; Jennifer Kermode, 'Merchants, Overseas Trade, and Urban Decline: York, Beverley and Hull, c.1380–1500', *NH*, 23 (1987), pp. 51–73; Pamela Nightingale, 'The Rise and Decline of Medieval York: A Reassessment', *P&P*, 206 (2010), pp. 3–42.

57 See coal mining later in this chapter. For an overview of the coal industry in the north-east of England, see: Nef, *Rise of the British Coal Industry*, vol. 1, pp. 24–41 and pp. 165–89; J. B. Blake, 'The Medieval Coal Trade of North-East England: Some Fourteenth Century Evidence', *NH*, 2 (1967), pp. 1–26; Hatcher, *British Coal Industry*, pp. 70–96; Britnell, 'The Coal Industry', pp. 439–72.

58 Dyer, *Lords and Peasants*, p. 183.

recovery with a recalcitrant peasantry'.[59] It is possible, therefore, that tenants became more cooperative as the fifteenth century progressed, perhaps because the monks of Durham Priory became more responsive to their tenants' needs. Although this is perennially difficult to prove, it seems unlikely that the priory could have forced a higher percentage of rent payments unless the tenants themselves were more compliant.

Durham Priory experienced real recovery from the 1470s onwards, so that by the turn of the century the priory was in a much stronger economic position than it had been at the end of the fourteenth century. Successive bursars showed a remarkable degree of flexibility in adapting their style of rent collection, and the recording thereof, to reflect the complexity and ad hoc nature of tenant payments. The process of syndication likely improved the efficiency of rent collection as well, not only easing the job expected of rent collectors, but also recognising tenant accumulation. The mid-century recession was indeed a dark period in the economic history of Durham Priory, and the period from c.1430 until the 1460s should rightly be seen as amongst the most challenging in its financial history. However, by the 1470s recovery was well underway and, despite further crises in the 1480s, the priory emerged from the fifteenth century in a strong and stable economic position. Successive bursars were thus able to reduce arrears, waste and decay from a combined total of £540 in 1453/54 to a meagre £18 by 1519/20 at the same time as increasing overall rents by £130: a truly remarkable feat.[60]

The fifteenth century was not necessarily a period of ceaseless decline, but should be seen as a period of 'new beginnings' for landowners, who experimented and adapted to the difficulties of the economic situation, showing 'a readiness to spend and to innovate', whilst displaying considerable financial acumen.[61] Given the complexity of collecting hundreds of such disparate rents, often in kind rather than cash, Durham Priory showed a remarkable adaptability and ingenuity in improving rent collection to the degree that successive bursars managed.[62] A more cautionary tale could be told in which the bursars' income was still much lower than it had been in the fourteenth century, but we should not fall into the trap that so many contemporaries did: to compare the bursars' income with pre-Black Death levels, or indeed even with those of the 1370s, is unrealistic and unfair. Successive bursars had stopped the rot that had set in on their lands and improved the position of the office so that by the end of the fifteenth century the economic fortunes of the priory looked healthier than they had for over a hundred years. The priory faced serious financial problems in this

59 Larson, *Conflict and Compromise*, p. 143.

60 DCM, Bursar's Accounts, 1453/54–1519/20.

61 J. N. Hare, 'The Monks as Landlords: The Leasing of the Monastic Demesnes in Southern England', in C. Barron and C. Harper-Bill (eds.), *The Church in Pre-Reformation Society: Essays in Honour of F. R. H. Du Boulay* (Woodbridge, 1985), p. 90.

62 See chapter 6 below and also Brown, 'A Money Economy?'.

period, but the financial acumen of the Durham monks enabled them to overcome this challenge, intensifying their rent collection process and ultimately recovering from the recession. The gradual process of converting land to enlarged leasehold plots was to have long-term consequences for both the dean and chapter and their tenants in the sixteenth and seventeenth centuries because once this had been done, it was difficult to reverse.[63] By contrast, the recovery on the neighbouring estate of the bishops of Durham took a decidedly different course.

The Bishops of Durham

R. L. Storey concluded that Thomas Langley, bishop of Durham, 'was one of the five richest landowners in England', with an estimated income of between £3,000 and £4,000 at the start of the fifteenth century: only the duke of York, the earl of Warwick and the sees of Winchester and Canterbury possessed comparable incomes.[64] However, it is the geographical concentration of this income which was almost unique in the medieval countryside, with the receiver general of the Durham exchequer accounting for around £2,500–£3,000 in revenue from between the Tyne and the Tees alone. This was comprised of the rental income of lands in the four wards of the shire – Darlington, Chester, Easington and Stockton – as well as various ancillary incomes like the perquisites of the halmote court, the Durham mint and, importantly, the master forester who was responsible for the bishopric's parks and coal mines.[65] Some other substantial sources of income did not reach these annual accounts, the most significant being the bishop's Yorkshire estates in Allertonshire and Howdenshire, as well as the liberty of Crayke, which in total increased the income of the see by a further £500.[66] The geographical concentration of these two ecclesiastical estates in the Durham region allows for a detailed study of how two relatively compact and often contiguous estates responded in contrasting ways to the successive pressures of recession and inflation.

The income of the receiver general underwent a substantial decline from the 1430s to the 1460s, which supports Pollard's conclusion that the agrarian crisis of

63 See chapter 2 for the consequences for the dean and chapter of Durham Cathedral and chapter 6 for the consequences of this reorganisation of holdings for their tenants.

64 R. L. Storey, *Thomas Langley and the Bishopric of Durham, 1406–1437* (London, 1961), p. 68.

65 DUL, ASC, Receiver General's Accounts: CCB B/1/1–CCB B/12/139. All data produced from Archives and Special Collections by permission of Durham University Library. For the Durham mint, see Martin Allen, *The Durham Mint*, British Numismatic Society Special Publication, 4 (London, 2003).

66 DUL, ASC, Allerton Receiver's Accounts: CCB B/84/1–CCB B/90/124; DUL, ASC, Howden Receiver's Accounts: CCB B/93/1a–CCB B/101/142. Unfortunately, the accounts of the receivers of these outlying estates do not survive in sufficient quantity before the sixteenth century to be included in this analysis.

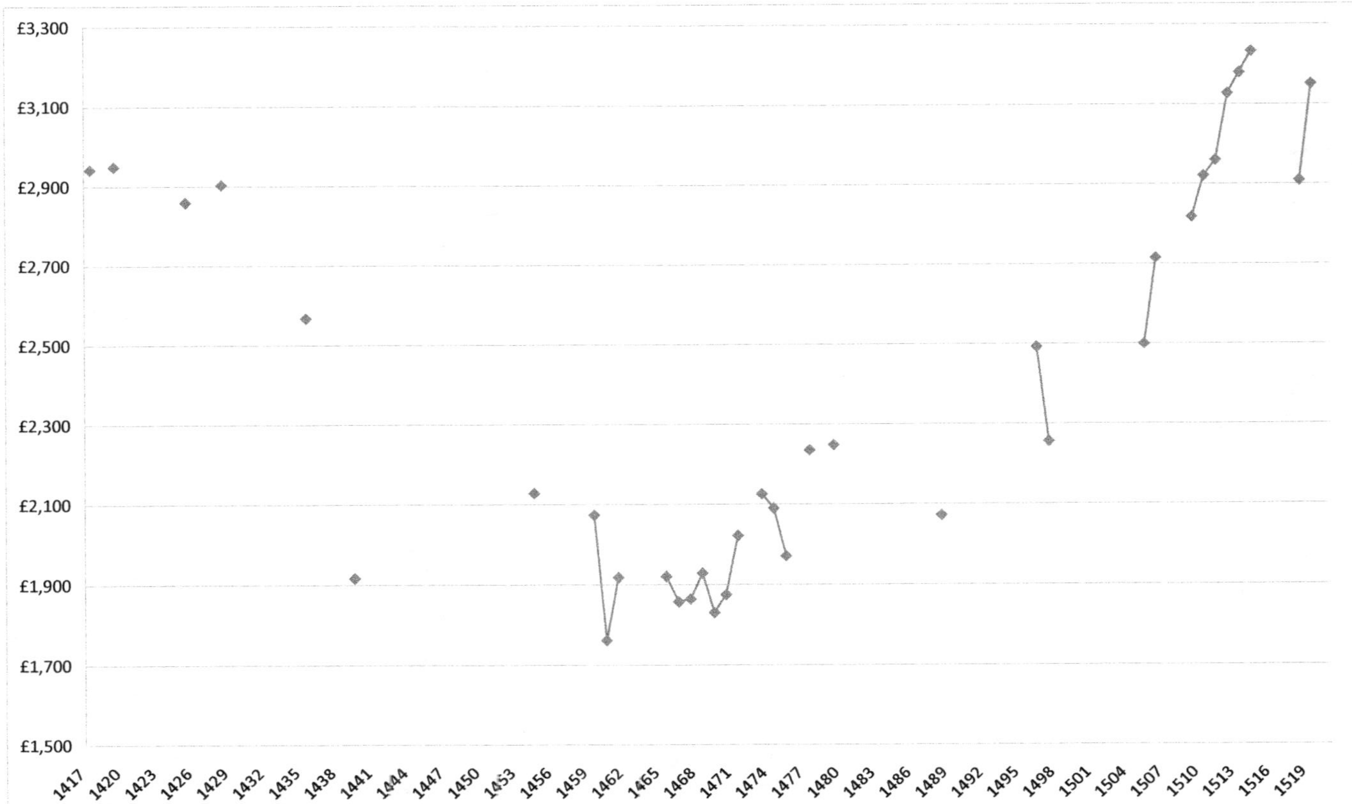

Figure 7. Total Income of the Receiver Generals of the Bishops of Durham, 1417–1520.
Source: DUL, ASC, Receiver General's Accounts, CCB B/1/1–CCB B/1/10.

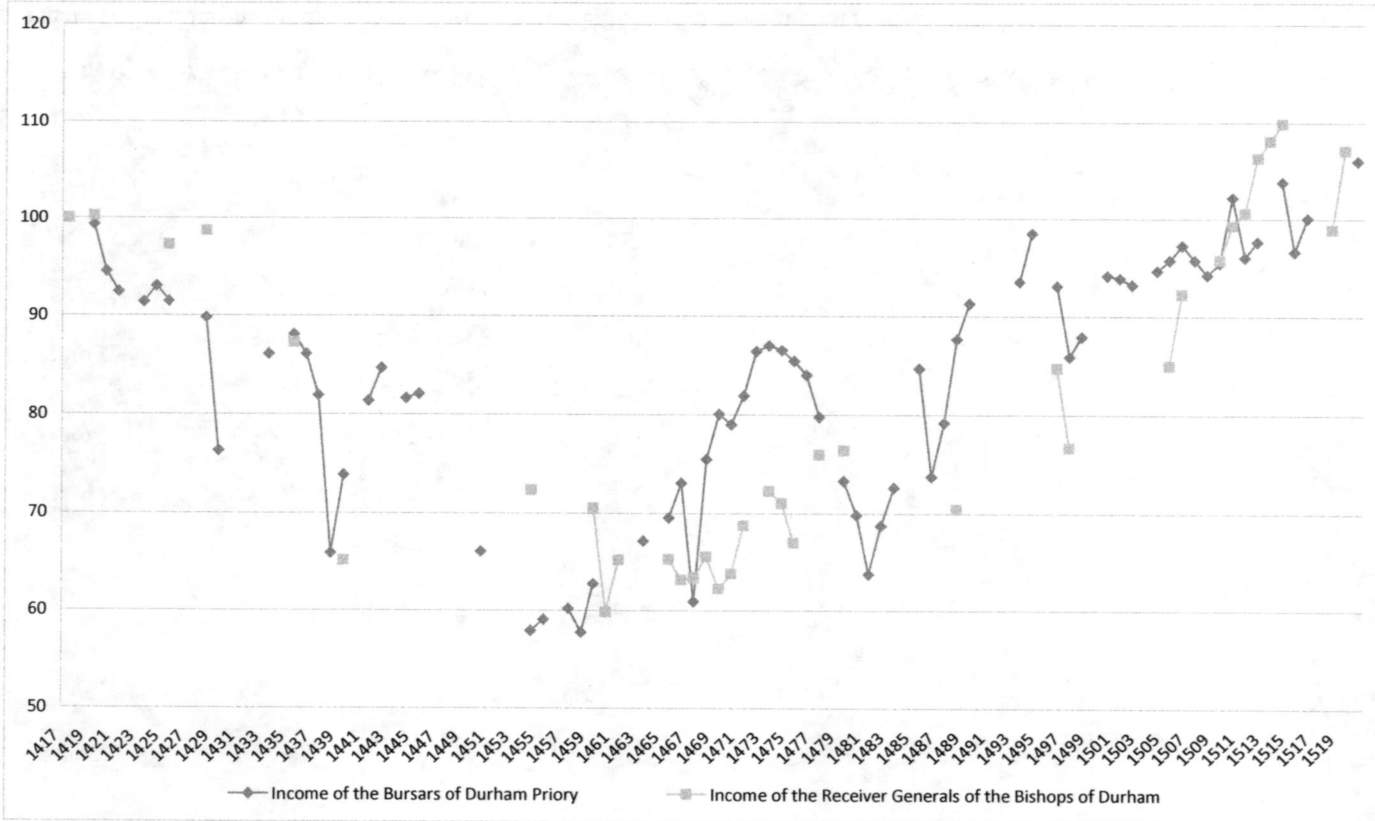

Figure 8. Index of the Incomes of the Bursars of Durham Priory and the Receiver Generals of the Bishops of Durham, 1417–1520.
Sources: DCM, Bursar's Accounts, 1400/01–1519/20; DUL, ASC, Receiver General's Accounts, CCB B/1/1–CCB B/1/10.

the 1430s hit the north-east of England particularly hard and plunged the bishopric into decades of economic hardship as Figure 7 shows.[67]

The depth of the mid-fifteenth-century recession was certainly a bleak period for the bishop, with the receiver general's income being reduced by around 40 per cent from £2,900 in 1417 to just over £1,700 by the 1450s – a decline which closely mirrors that of the bursars of Durham Cathedral Priory outlined above.[68] As Figure 8 shows, the incomes of both estates were hit hard by the bad harvests of the 1430s, reaching a nadir in the 1450s and 1460s at approximately 60 per cent of their previous levels. However, recovery was underway by the 1470s, and although this was interrupted by the bad harvests and pestilence of the early 1480s, both of their incomes recovered to levels which bettered their early fifteenth-century achievements.

Yet, despite the chronological synchronicity of these recoveries they were in fact achieved through quite different means. The monks of Durham Cathedral Priory focused upon the collection of arrears and so managed to increase the income they actually collected even though rents on their lands did not increase markedly.[69] By comparison, the bishops of Durham diversified their sources of income, with a noticeable increase in receipts from the bishopric's forests, parks and coal mines. Unlike the bursars of Durham Priory, the bishops' rental income from agricultural sources was still substantially below its early fifteenth-century level at the end of the century. The bishops' income had undergone a significant transformation in the fifteenth century with the rental income of the four Durham wards down by over £450, whereas the income collected by the master forester increased by a similar amount, more by design than coincidence.[70] Figure 9 shows this change in the composition of the receiver general's income. In the face of continued low revenues the monks intensified their rent collection process, whereas the bishops appear to have sought other sources of revenue to bolster their ailing rent rolls.

A more detailed breakdown is given in Table 2, which clearly shows how the rental income of each ward suffered dramatically across this period. In 1416/17, the four wards together accounted for an income of over £2,300, but by 1459/60 this had been reduced to just £1,461, and although recovery is clearly visible, this income was still only £1,800 by the early sixteenth century.[71] In complete contrast, the receipts of the master of forests and mines had more than quadrupled in the intervening

67 Pollard, *North-Eastern England*, pp. 78–80.

68 DUL, ASC, Receiver General's Accounts, CCB B/1/1–CCB B/1/10.

69 See earlier section in this chapter, p. 39.

70 DUL, ASC, Receiver General's Accounts, CCB B/1/1–CCB B/6/69.

71 DUL, ASC, Receiver General's Account, CCB B/1/1. Part of the reason for this rapid decline was that some land which had previously been accounted for under the four wards of the palatinate seems to have been transferred to the bailiff's responsibility. However, even if this is taken into consideration, the rental income was still significantly lower than it had been at the start of the century.

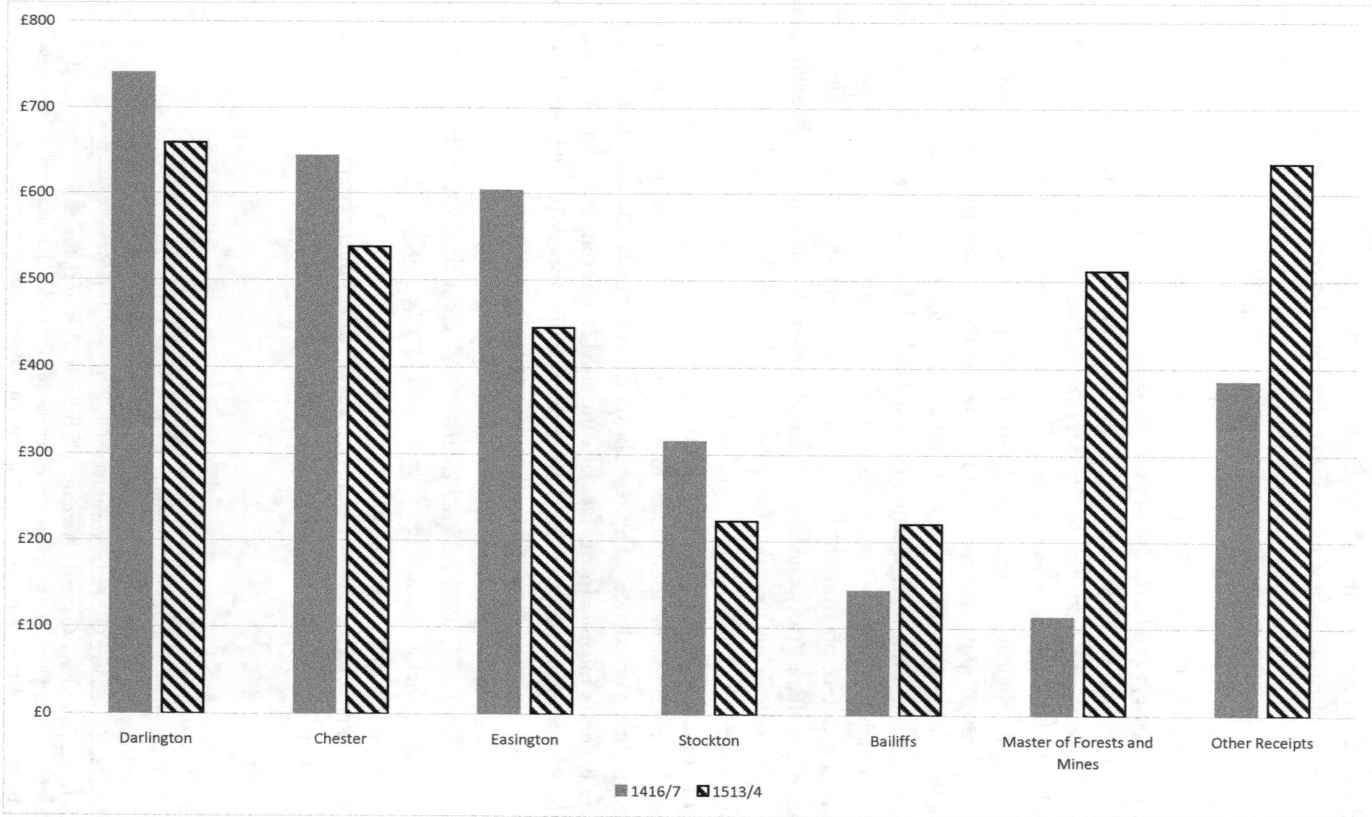

Figure 9. The Changing Composition of the Income of the Receiver Generals of the Bishops of Durham in 1416/17 and 1513/14. Source: DUL, ASC, Receiver General's Accounts, CCB B/1/1–CCB B/6/69.

period, declining from £112 in 1416/17 to £74 in 1459/60 but leading the recovery in the receiver general's accounts to a new high of £511 in 1513/14.[72]

Table 2. Breakdown of the Income of the Receiver Generals of the Bishops of Durham, 1416/17–1529/30

	1416/17	1459/60	1478/79	1513/14	1529/30
Darlington Ward	£739	£433	£574	£659	£661
Chester Ward	£643	£399	£442	£537	£508
Easington Ward	£603	£412	£413	£444	£402
Stockton Ward	£315	£217	£212	£223	£227
Bailiffs	£142	£85	£197	£220	£217
Master of Forests and Mines	£112	£74	£271	£511	£468
Other Receipts	£384	£138	£135	£636*	£288
Total	£2,942	£1,761	£2,247	£3,233	£2,774

Source: DUL, ASC, Receiver General's Accounts, CCB B/1/1–CCB B/1/10.

* This account year was boosted by high receipts from the escheator and foreign receipts, especially from Norham and Islandshire, but these were not sustained levels into the sixteenth century. The escheator's office reported for £216 6s 4d whilst foreign receipts were £242 18s 4d in 1513/14: DUL, ASC, Receiver General's Accounts, CCB B/4/45 and DUL, ASC, Escheator's Account, CCB B/41/10.

The administration of the bishop of Durham's agricultural land diverged significantly from that of the monks of Durham Priory in the late fourteenth and fifteenth centuries. The former continued to grant holdings of customary land for life, whereas by the early fifteenth century the monks had introduced short leases of generally between three and nine years on the majority of their estate.[73] Similarly, the monks allowed entry fines to lapse so that by 1420 they had ceased to be exacted on the majority of the priory's estate, whereas the bishopric continued to charge fines throughout, although the extent of this fluctuated across the course of the fifteenth century.[74] The status quo, therefore, was the order of the day on much of the agricultural land of the bishops of Durham. These differences had significant long-term consequences for both estates because they led to the survival of copyhold tenure on much of the bishop of Durham's estate whereas the monks had clearly introduced leases on the majority of their estate.[75]

72 DUL, ASC, Receiver General's Accounts, CCB B/1/1–CCB B/1/10.

73 Larson, *Conflict and Compromise*, p. 235.

74 Lomas, 'Land and People in South-East Durham', pp. 142–4.

75 See chapter 2 for a more detailed discussion of the bishops' copyhold lands and the long-term consequences this had for both estates. Chapters 6 and 7 explore the consequences for the tenants of these two estates.

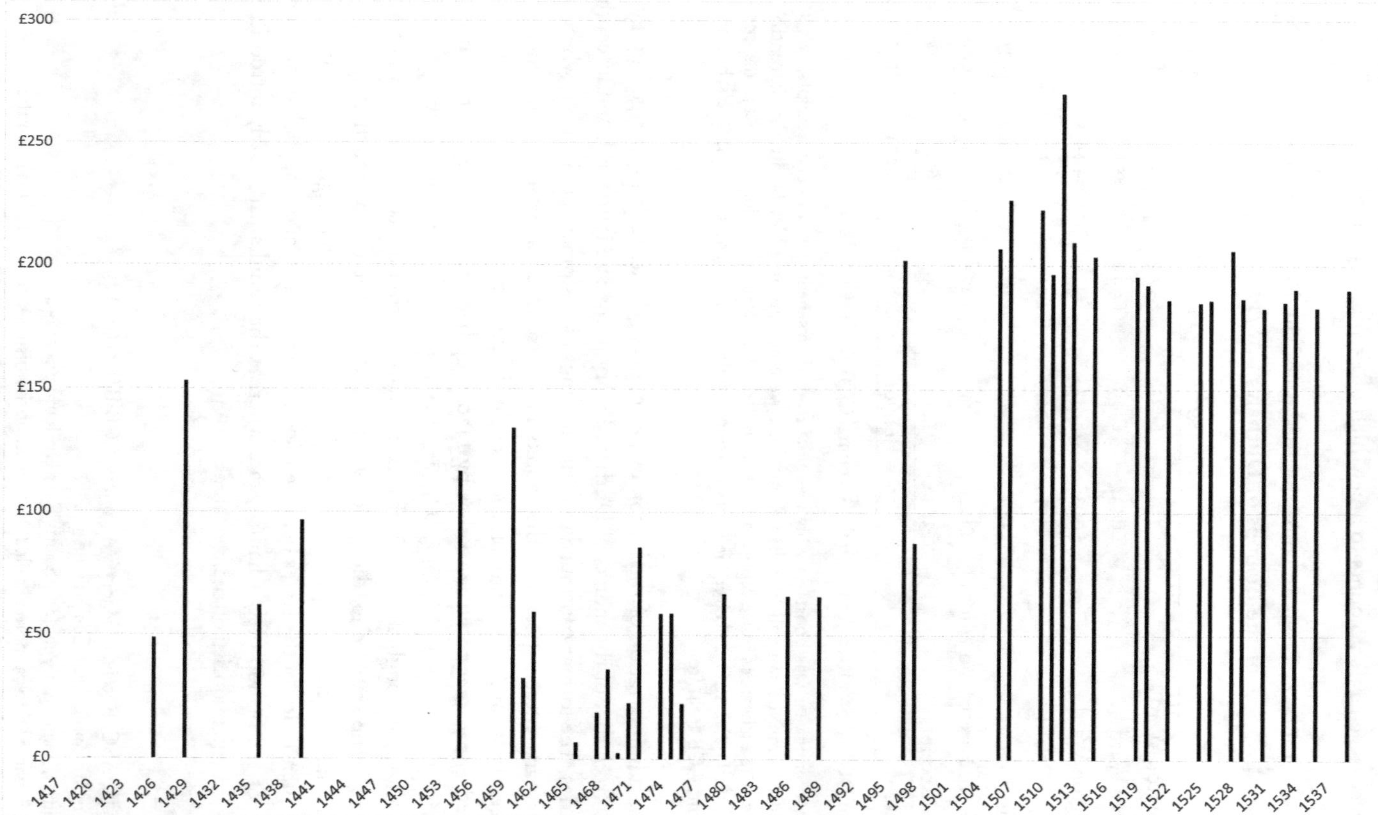

Figure 10. Receipts of the Master Forester Less the Receipts from Coal Mines, 1417–1537.
Source: DUL, ASC, Receiver General's Accounts, CCB B/1/1–CCB B/12/139.

One of the reasons for the resurgence in the income of the master of forests and mines was a change in the exploitation of the bishopric's parks and forests.[76] Linda Drury has shown how the bishops of Durham slowly leased out land in their upland forests and parks in the fifteenth century as they no longer hunted in Weardale Forest or Stanhope Park. In 1381, for example, there were 936 cattle and 258 horses in the Weardale Forest but by 1515 there were only 91 cattle and 589 sheep divided between the forest and the park.[77] This decline in hunting and the direct management of their livestock went alongside the leasing out of the land to tenants. Two meadows were initially let for grazing, with ten houses built after 1406, which fell to individual tenants from the 1440s onwards. By the time of Bishop Booth's translation to York in 1476, the park was 'in the hands of about twenty graziers, some of whom had doubtless begun to till the soil'.[78] Several accounts of the master forester survive for the late fifteenth century, one of which covers the two years 1484–86 and shows the numerous sources of income he was responsible for, varying from fixed ancient rents to the sale of 662 hens, the pannage of pigs and the sale of wood, wax and honey.[79] However, the primary source of income came from tenants with holdings at farm in the High Forest of Weardale, Stanhope Park, Wolsingham Park, Bedburn Park, Evenwood Park, Birtley Park and Auckland Park.[80] His discharge section was particularly extensive, including £6 13s 4d for his own wages, £20 8s 6d for the decay of farmed-out shielings in the High Forest and a further 106s 8d for the decay of Wolsingham Park. The upkeep of the walls and enclosures, hay-making for deer and allowances to tenants for work on their holdings cost a further £14 12s 7d, as well as £14 which was granted by Richard III as fees to retainers from the rents of Stanhope Park. Despite these expenses, George, Lord Lumley, still accounted for over £70 worth of profit to the receiver general for the period covered by this account.[81]

76 The accounts of the stockman of the bishops of Durham show that they still possessed some livestock in the 1470s, but an increasingly large amount of their income (£69 6s 8d in 1469/70) was coming from the sales of herbage. In 1469/70, the stockman held 4 bulls; 90 cattle and oxen; 60 cows; 102 bullocks of 3 years old; 52 stirks of 2 years old; 12 heifers of 2 years old; 6 this year's calves; 4 rams; 169 wethers; 152 ewes; 25 hogs; no lambs. DUL, ASC, Instaurer's Accounts, CCB B/81/5.

77 Linda Drury, 'More Stout than Wise: Tenant Right in Weardale in the Tudor Period', in D. Marcombe (ed.), *The Last Principality: Politics, Religion and Society in the Bishopric of Durham, 1494–1660* (Nottingham, 1987), pp. 71–100.

78 Linda Drury,'Early settlement in Stanhope Park, Weardale, *c.* 1406–79', *AA*, 5th series, 4 (1976), pp. 139–49.

79 DUL, ASC, Master Forester's Account, CCB B/83/4; translated online here: <http://reed.dur.ac.uk/xtf/view?docId=ead/ccb/ccfina1.xml&toc.id=#qxj-18017> (accessed 4 January 2013).

80 The High Forest of Weardale owed £82 6s 8d, and the herbage of various parks farmed out included: Stanhope Park, £66 4s 3d; Wolsingham Park, £26 13s 4d; Bedburn Park, 40s; Evenwood Park, £14; Birtley Park, 30s; and Auckland Park, £13 6s 8d. DUL, ASC, Master Forester's Account, CCB B/83/4.

81 Other than Muggleswick (which in c.1310 had 904 wethers and 122 cattle), Durham Priory did not possess upland equivalents to Weardale Forest and Stanhope Park and so the monks did not

The financial success of the master forester, especially from the end of the fifteenth century onwards, can be seen in Figure 10.

Coal Mining in the Fifteenth Century

The bishops thus began to look to other sources of income to bolster their ailing rent rolls and, naturally enough, their gaze quickly turned to their ample coal reserves being, as they were, the most productive and financially rewarding in England in the middle ages.[82] Coal mines became increasingly important to the bishops' overall income in this period because they began to yield more during the fifteenth century at a time when their other sources of income were in decline, and came to form as much as 10 per cent of the bishops' total revenue from within the palatinate.[83] This income, moreover, was the net revenue that the bishops received from their lessees rather than the gross receipts from coal sales, and so the bishops faced neither the expenses of winning the coal nor of transporting it, both of which could be exorbitantly high.[84] These revenues came from two primary groups of coal mines which had drastically varying fortunes in this period: the Tyneside mines at Whickham and Gateshead, which were to become so important from the mid-sixteenth century onwards with their easy access to water transportation, and a group of landlocked mines around Railey near Bishop Auckland. By the start of the sixteenth century successive bishops of Durham could consistently rely on an annual income from coal mines of around £250, and in good years this could top £300.[85]

As Richard Britnell has shown from the receiver generals' accounts, the success of the Railey mines was the primary cause for such buoyancy in coal receipts during the fifteenth century (Figure 11).[86] The regularity of income here shows the financial benefits of leasing out these coal mines. On the few occasions when revenues fell below average it was because the bishops held these mines in hand, as for example in 1460/61: the only time revenues fell below £50 in the fifteenth century. The other

have the same opportunities to exploit these assets. R. H. Britnell (ed.), *Durham Priory Manorial Accounts, 1277–1310*, Surtees Society, 218 (2014), pp. lii–lvii.

82 Hatcher, *British Coal Industry*, p. 72. For the history of coal mining in the north-east of England, see Nef, *Rise of the British Coal Industry*, vol. 1, pp. 24–41 and pp. 165–189; Blake, 'The Medieval Coal Trade', pp. 1–26; Hatcher, *British Coal Industry*, pp. 70–96; Britnell, 'The Coal Industry', pp. 439–72.

83 DUL, ASC, Receiver General's Accounts, CCB B/1/1–CCB B/12/139.

84 See below for a discussion of expenses in coal mining incurred by Durham Priory and Finchale Priory, pp. 63–8.

85 DUL, ASC, Receiver General's Accounts, CCB B/1/1–CCB B/6/69.

86 Britnell, 'The Coal Industry', pp. 447–50. Much of the following pages use the same clerk of mines accounts and receiver general accounts which Richard Britnell used in his article on the bishops' coal industry. There is remarkably little other surviving evidence about coal mining in this period for the bishops of Durham.

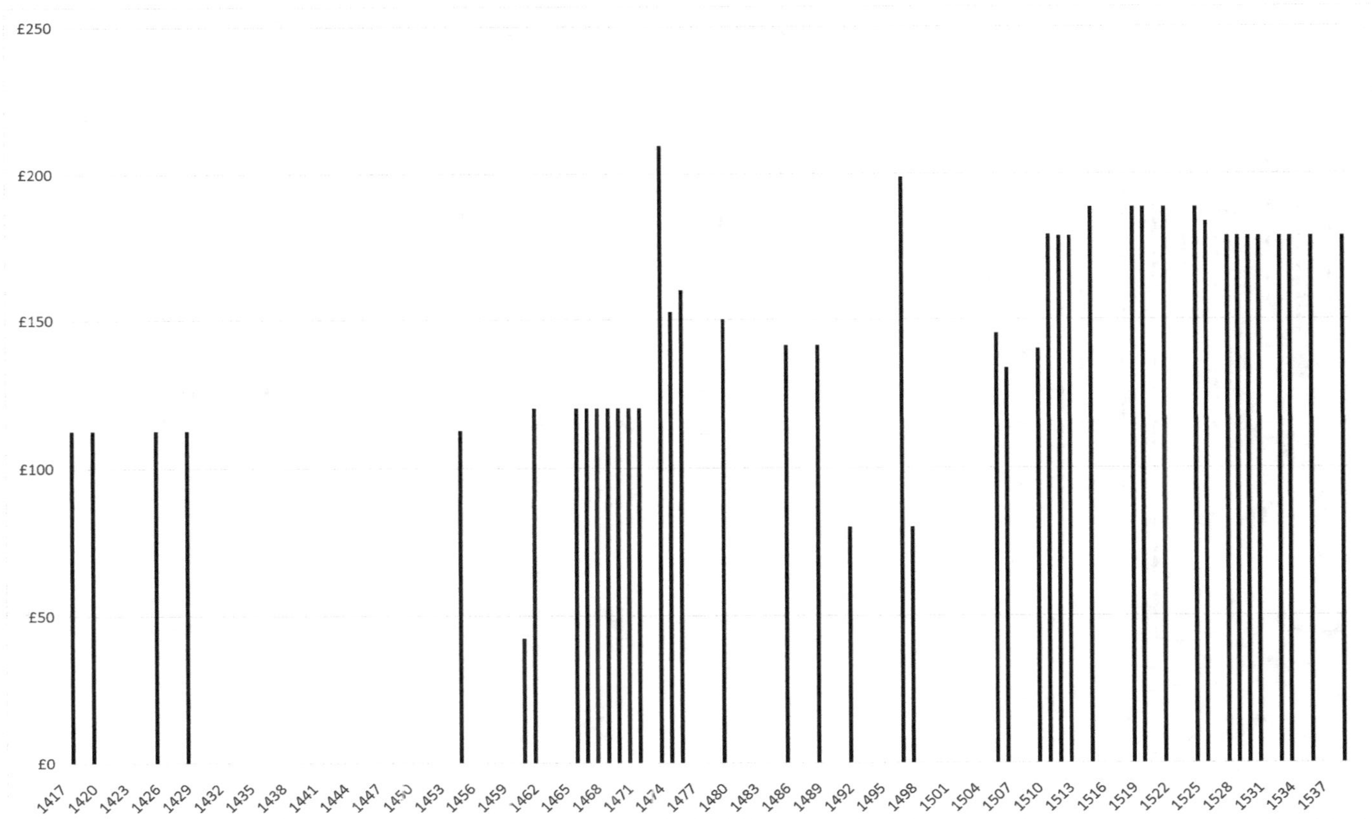

Figure 11. Receipts from the Bishops' Railey Mines, 1417–1537.
Source: DUL, ASC, Receiver General's Accounts, CCB B/1/1–CCB B/6/69.

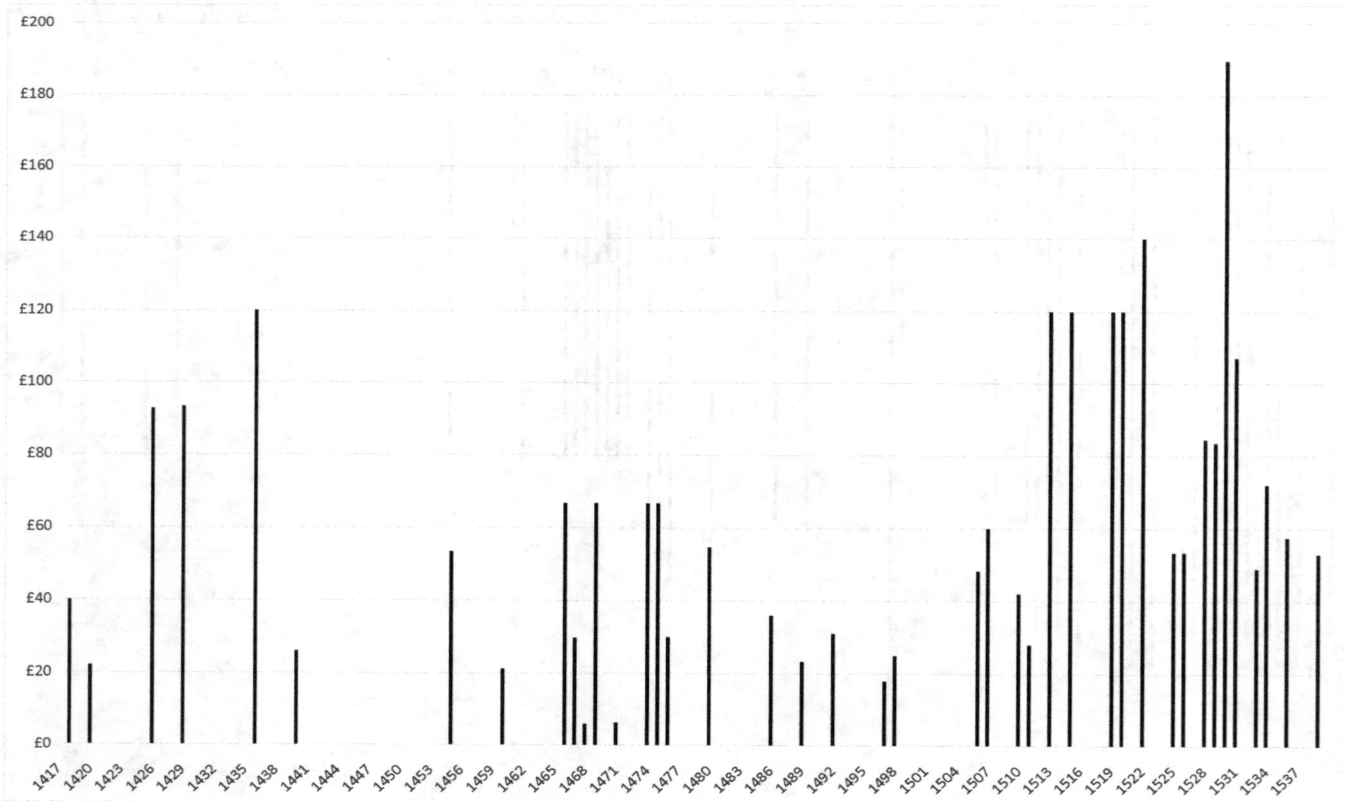

Figure 12. Receipts from the Bishops' Whickham and Gateshead Mines, 1417–1537.
Source: DUL, ASC, Receiver General's Accounts, CCB B/1/1–CCB B/6/69.

primary coal mines of Whickham and Gateshead did not yield significant profits during much of the fifteenth century because their success was heavily dependent on export sales (Figure 12). Not only were the prospects for trade bleak during much of this period, but the bishops also faced competition from lay landowners with their own coal mines near the river.[87] The Tyneside mines appear to have been hit much harder by the mid-century slump than the Railey group of mines, with several of the pits going completely out of production. However, their recovery was underway by the sixteenth century, and although this improvement in receipts was delayed, the income from these mines could be double that achieved during the middle of the century, if somewhat sporadic compared to the Railey mines.[88]

Unfortunately, because the bishops' coal mines were usually leased out there are few detailed accounts which reveal the daily operations of these mines, although occasionally they were kept in hand for a year, offering a brief glance into their operations.[89] For example, after Sir William Eure's lease of the mines lapsed in 1459, the Railey mines were not leased out immediately but were kept in the bishop's hands, and so we have a rare view of their production schedule. John Baker, the manager of the Railey coal mines from 14 June to 25 December 1460, won 2,601 chaldrons of coal and sold 2,315 chaldrons for £78 16s 5d.[90] He paid the workforce 5d each per day: three hewers for winning 300 corves of coal per day; three barrowmen for taking the coal from where it was hewn to the foot of the pit shaft; and four drawers for pulling the coal from the foot of the shaft to the bank – in total, £23 2s 6d. Other expenses included the purchase of necessary materials: 79s 2d for 760lbs of candles; 9s for three ropes of forty-one fathoms; 27s for a dozen corves; and a further 6s 10d for shovels, a wheelbarrow, a bushel measure and a windshield for the pit mouth. There were also necessary expenses for repairs which reveal the nature of coal mining in the fifteenth century, including the mending of the old roof at the pit, the underground wall and ironwork, the water sinking tub and the high road by the pit, as well as mending two wheelbarrow ways underground which had become obstructed by earth and stone. The total expenditure came to £30 17s 1d, with the manager reporting for gross receipts from coal sales of £78 16s 5d, and thus the Railey mines produced a net profit of £47 19s 5d with a further 286 unsold chaldrons of coal in just half a year's worth of activity.

87 For the grant of wayleaves to lay landowners for permission to take coal across the bishops' lands, see Britnell, 'The Coal Industry', pp. 445–6; and DUL, ASC, Receiver General's Accounts, CCB B/1/1–CCB B/6/69. See also the purchases of coal-bearing land by the Newcastle merchant Roger Thornton in the fifteenth century in chapters 3 and 5 below, pp. 119–21 and 177–9.

88 DUL, ASC, Receiver General's Accounts, CCB B/1/1–CCB B/6/69.

89 DUL, ASC, Clerk of Mines Accounts, CCB B/79/1–CCB B/79/12.

90 The following taken from DUL, ASC, Clerk of Mines Account, CCB B/79/4; translated and online at: <http://reed.dur.ac.uk/xtf/view?docId=ead/ccb/ccfina1.xml&toc.id=#qxj-17373> (accessed 23 August, 2013).

There are signs, however, that even the successful mines at Railey were suffering from a slump in demand during the mid-fifteenth century, with the two accounts covering 1460 both showing a considerable surplus of coal being produced which remained unsold at the pithead, perhaps helping to explain why the Eures let the lease of Railey lapse in 1459 after having held it since at least 1416. Table 3 shows that the approver had a considerable surplus of 1,537 chaldrons already on hand at the start of April, but during the course of the two months that the mine was operating this overall surplus increased to 1,981 chaldrons. The coal mines actually made a loss over this short period, with expenses of £22 18s but receipts of only £17 13s 7d, primarily because of the production of 444 chaldrons of unsold coal.[91] The generation of this surplus was not a unique occurrence and, despite better sales during the half-year period covered by the succeeding account, the overall surplus of coal at the Railey mines increased to some 2,267 chaldrons (Table 4).[92]

Table 3. Coal Production and Sales at the Railey Mines, 2 April–1 June 1460

Received from former approver: 1,537 chaldrons
Coal won during this period: 1,171 chaldrons, 3 quarters, 1 bushel
Coal sold during this period: 727 chaldrons of coal, total: £17 13s 7d
After sales, surplus of: 1,981 chaldrons and 3 bushels

Source: DUL, ASC, Clerk of Mines Account, CCB B/79/3.

Table 4. Coal Production and Sales at the Railey Mines, 14 June–25 December 1460

Received from former approver: 1,981 chaldrons and 3 bushels
Coal won during this period: 2,601 chaldrons, 2 quarters, 2 bushels
Coal sold during this period: 2,315 chaldrons, 1½ quarters of coal, total: £78 16s 5d
After sales, surplus of: 2,267 chaldrons, 2 quarters and 2 bushels

Source: DUL, ASC, Clerk of Mines Account, CCB B/79/4.

It is possible that this is an artificial view of the mines because the manager was forced to produce his accounts for the bishop before he had been able to sell all coal produced in the same period. This seems unlikely, however, because much of this coal appears to be unsold for multiple accounts, even from the preceding winter, and was forming a clear stockpile at the pit. The growing surplus of coal at the Railey mines from several consecutive accounts in 1460 is hardly definitive proof of problems in

91 DUL, ASC, Clerk of Mines Account, CCB B/79/3.
92 DUL, ASC, Clerk of Mines Account, CCB B/79/4.

the industry, but it is certainly indicative of a slump in local demand for coal, especially as by the end of the year the mine had accumulated approximately six months' worth of coal just sitting at the pithead.

Who were the people purchasing this coal in such quantities from a landlocked mine and how were they able to afford it in the midst of the fifteenth-century recession? The Railey mines were located near the major residences of the bishops of Durham at Auckland and of the Eures of Witton-le-Wear, who were the major lessee of the mines for much of the fifteenth century. This led Pollard to argue that the 'exploitation of coal ... was undertaken in the mid-fifteenth century not to satisfy market demand, but to satisfy seigniorial consumption, and to preserve future supply'.[93] There is undoubtedly an element of truth in this but, as Britnell has shown from a schedule of sales at the Railey mines, at least some of this coal was going to fuel local demand with 'diversis hominibus patrie' purchasing coal by the wagonload at the pithead.[94] Between Christmas 1460 and 12 January 1461, 23¾ chaldrons and 7 bushels of coal were sold to twenty-five people scattered throughout the surrounding region of Stockton, Houghton-le-Side, West Auckland, St Helen Auckland, North Auckland, Woodhouse, Evenwood, Eldon, Coundon and Escomb with amounts varying from five loads costing 5d to eight wagonloads worth 6s 8d. As Britnell went on to show, these lists give no indications of industrial usage, and even though a Thomas Smythson of Escomb purchased a wagonload which could suggest usage in a blacksmith's, a William Gregge who was a chaplain purchased four wagonloads.[95] It is still unclear, however, how these individuals could afford to purchase such quantities of coal, especially if they were for domestic fuel rather than industrial usage, or indeed how this coal was being used at home. After all, 'fireplaces designed for the burning of wood were rarely well suited to the burning of coal', with a shift in domestic architecture to better incorporate the required ventilation for a coal fire across this period, so that 'by the second half of the sixteenth century there is clear evidence that standards of domestic comfort and heating were improving in many modest homes'.[96] Were these Durham tenants using this coal for household fuel and if so, what led them to incorporate coal into their daily lives at such a relatively early period and during the very depths of the mid-fifteenth-century recession?[97] Furthermore, if the ordinary expenses of coal mining often halved gross receipts, as suggested below, this meant that the lessee of Railey would have had to sell between £200 and £350 worth of coal annually simply to break even, representing a remarkable level of

93 Pollard, *North-Eastern England*, p. 76.

94 Britnell, 'The Coal Industry', p. 449.

95 Ibid., p. 449.

96 Hatcher, *British Coal Industry*, p. 409.

97 At present the answer to this question remains unclear. A combination of archaeological and archival research may well reveal that Durham tenants were embracing the use of coal as a domestic fuel earlier than tenants in other parts of the country.

demand from the local populace in the fifteenth century, even if much of this coal did indeed find its way into gentry and noble households.

Another glimpse of activity at these Railey mines is possible in the early sixteenth century and there are clear indications that coal sales were much better than during the 1460s, with receipts reaching over £275 per annum for the two surviving account years.[98] This improvement in the receipts from coal mines was not some serendipitous stroke of good fortune for the bishops of Durham: they consciously protected and promoted their coal interests, often through quite aggressive means if necessary. Britnell found that in the 1490s the bishop of Durham leased the mines of the earl of Westmorland for £22 a year either to take them out of production or to eliminate price competition, whilst in 1476/77 Richard of Gloucester organised on the bishop's behalf the blocking of a road near Escomb by which the earl of Westmorland conveyed coal from one of his pits.[99] Moreover, the bishops kept a close eye on all coal mines being opened in the region. For example, Finchale Priory's mine at Softley produced a consistent income of £6 13s 4d up until the 1410s when the pit went out of production.[100] Galloway attributed this failure of Softley to the large lease of the bishop's mines at Railey to Ralph Eure in the same period, the competition proving too great for the monks.[101] However, the monks of Finchale Priory tried to re-open their mine at Softley in the 1480s, which was soon noticed by the bishop of Durham: he agreed in 1487/88 to rent out the mine for 20s in order to take it out of production.[102] This is significant because the mine at Softley had not produced substantial coal receipts since the 1410s, with receipts of less than 10s for the few years prior to the bishop's intervention.[103] Clearly the bishops wanted to ensure that the monks did not begin coal production which could challenge their dominance of the market, but the fact that they sought to close such a relatively small mine reveals the keen watch which they kept on coal production in the region. Indeed, it is likely that this policy was crucial to the success of the Railey mines, given that they were landlocked and thus sales were completely dependent on their monopoly of local demand.[104] Whether this diversification of the bishops' income was part of a strategy implemented by a specific bishop or receiver general is unclear, but there was

98 Between 6 November 1502 and 11 November 1503 workers at the Railey mine won 8,031 chaldrons of coal and sold all of it for £205 12s. In the same period, the coal mine at Growbourne (which was normally leased with the Railey mine) produced a further 2,991 chaldrons for £76 11s: DUL, ASC, Clerk of Mines Account, CCB B/79/10. In the next year, they produced 8,815 chaldrons of coal, all of which was sold for £225 13s 4d, and at Growbourne a further £77 8s: DUL, ASC, Clerk of Mines Account, CCB/B/79/12.

99 Britnell, 'The Coal Industry', p. 448.

100 J. Raine (ed.), *Charters of Endowment, Inventories, and Account Rolls of the Priory of Finchale*, Surtees Society, 6 (1837), pp. lxxx–clxxxii.

101 R. L. Galloway, *Annals of Coal Mining and the Coal Trade*, vol. 1 (Newton Abbot, 1882), p. 72.

102 Raine (ed.), *The Priory of Finchale*, p. ccclxxxi.

103 Ibid., pp. ccclxxiv–ccclxxxi.

104 Britnell, 'The Coal Industry', pp. 445–55.

an increasing reliance on the receipts from coal and the herbage of parks which had clearly begun to affect decision-making to the extent that they can be seen aggressively blocking access to other coal mines or even buying out their competitors. It was this improvement in coal revenues, and the increase from forests and parks, which helped the bishops survive the mid-fifteenth-century recession and compensated for the decline in their rent rolls.

Although the survival of the bishops' records has enabled a fuller view of coal production on their lands than on most, there are other glimpses of the coal industry, especially in the records of the other ecclesiastical landowners in the region. Why did Durham Priory and Finchale Priory not exploit their coal assets in the same manner as the bishops of Durham? Was it a matter of scale and geographical location or was there a qualitative difference in the way these monks exploited their mineral resources? Unfortunately, the direct records of Durham Priory's mining activities only survive for the early fifteenth century and so it is much harder to evaluate its overall contribution to coal production in this period or the profitability of its operations. However, from these accounts it is clear that Durham Priory had an interest in coal mining at Rainton, Fery and Aldin Grange from at least the mid-fourteenth century onwards. The monks of Durham 'were not endowed with rich collieries', which were primarily located around the city of Durham and thus proved useful for fulfilling the household consumption needs of the monks.[105] By comparison, the Tyneside coal mines of the bishops of Durham were much better positioned for the Newcastle market and for export of coal from the region, whilst their mines at Railey had the advantage of being close to the bishop's palace at Bishop Auckland and near the home of the Eure family, who became their most prominent lessees. The more extensive seams in favourable locations which the bishops possessed no doubt proved important in their decision to exploit their coal reserves more commercially than the monks did, but the institutional context of these mines was similarly important; after all, the Railey coal mines were landlocked and so it was the acts of numerous bishops that ensured the success of these mines. Why, then, did the monks of Durham Priory not show the same entrepreneurial vigour in exploiting their coal assets that they showed in reorganising their landholdings?

The receipts of the coal mines of Durham Priory never achieved the equivalent levels of those of the bishops of Durham primarily because the mines seem to have been oriented more towards the household consumption of the cathedral itself: for example in 1442/43 the Aldin Grange coal mine accounted for receipts of £11 5s 7d, but with a further £10 2s 6d noted for 230 chaldrons of coal 'pro expensis domus'.[106] The levels of coal production at the priory's pits were presumably higher, therefore, than the receipts of sales alone would suggest because some of the coal was sent for the cathedral's consumption rather than sold. However, even if this is taken into

105 Hatcher, *British Coal Industry*, p. 75.

106 DCM, Coal Mines, 1442–43.

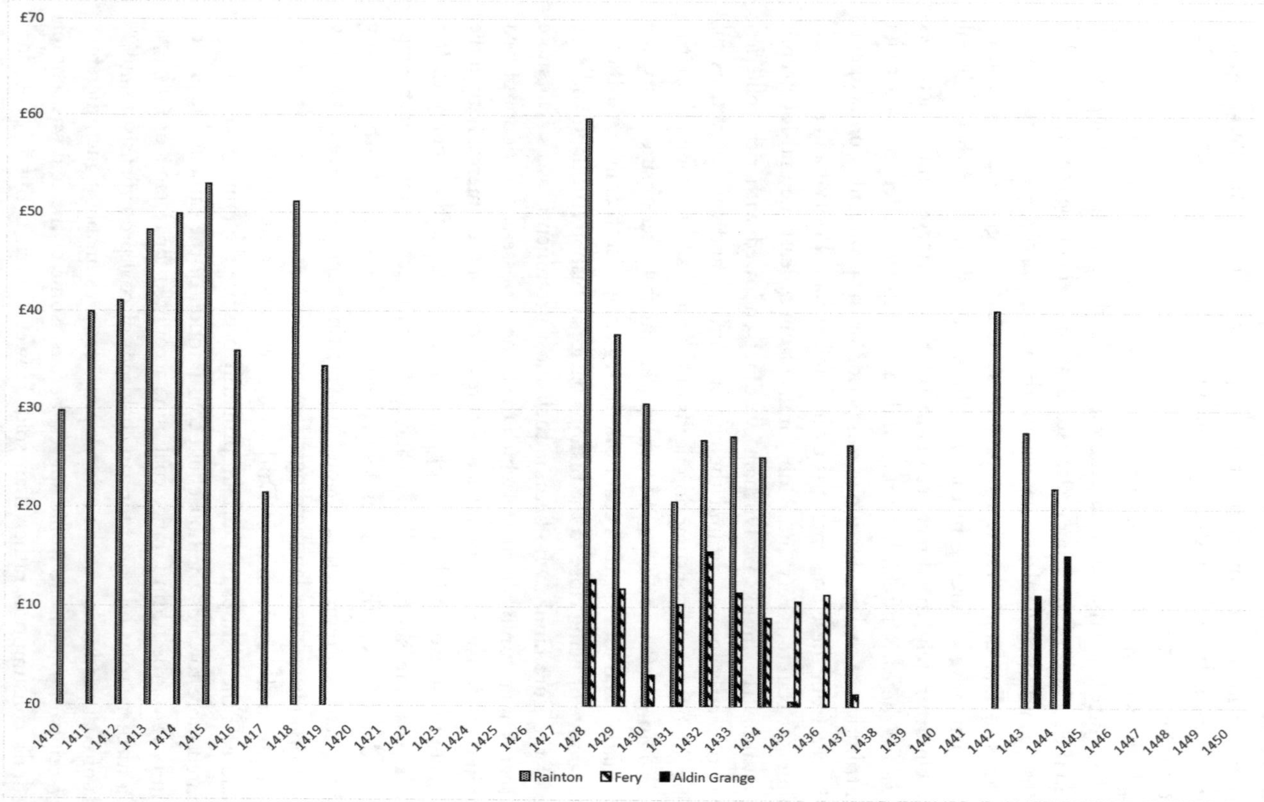

Figure 13. Receipts of Durham Cathedral Priory's Coal Mines, 1410–50.

Source: DCM, Coal Mines, 1409/10–1452/53 and J. T. Fowler, (ed.), *Extracts from the Account Rolls of the Abbey or Durham*, vol. 3, Surtees Society, 103 (1900), pp. 708–13.

consideration, it is clear that the priory's coal ventures never reached the same scale as those of the bishops of Durham. Moreover, the steady receipts from coal mines shown in Figure 13 are deceptive because these revenues were often gross receipts from sales rather than net profits, with the expenses of operating the coal mines sometimes equalling their potential revenues.

The mine accounts of the bishops of Durham and Finchale Priory make it clear that ordinary operating expenditure could represent half the gross receipts of the coal mines, but there were also one-off expenses which could completely eradicate any profits in that year.[107] Drainage and water damage were perennial problems for coal mining in this period, whilst sinking a new pit could represent a significant investment. The necessary expenses section of the bursars' account rolls is littered with expenditure on coal mines, including references to new pits, aqueducts and watergates.[108] These expenses were a constant burden for the monks of Durham Priory who seem to have kept the mines in hand for much of the period, with the bursar in 1536/37 excusing any rental receipts from the coal mines of Rainton because of this.[109] This unfortunately means that once the coal accounts cease in the mid-century there are few indicators of their productivity, although evidence from the early sixteenth century does not suggest any rapid take-off in production.[110] It seems likely that the monks kept the mines in hand in order to meet the household consumption of the cathedral itself rather than as a large-scale commercial venture. It is often thought that their coal mines were situated unfavourably compared to the Tyneside mines of the bishops of Durham, but given the success of the bishops' Railey mines the lack of access to water transportation was not necessarily a hindrance in this early period. It is more likely that the monks thought the expenses of coal mining could often outweigh its successes and that they only sought to produce enough to satisfy their own demand.

Finchale Priory was another ecclesiastical landowner whose accounts have survived in sufficient number to allow a view of their coal production across the fifteenth

107 See the examples of Finchale Priory below for the day-to-day running costs of coal mining in the medieval period. In 1434–35, for example, the Rainton coal mine only produced 10s 8d above the expenses in 'lucracione unius aqueductus': DCM, Coal Mines, 1434–35. For a more detailed view of the weekly operations of the monks' coal mines, see DCM, Bursar's Book F, esp. ff. 1, 17, 20–36v, 43v, and 47–9.

108 In 1351/52 'in via aquatica minere de Rainton novo facienda, £39 8s 2.5d'; in 1368/69 'in expensis factis pro uno Watergate pro minera de Rainton £8 17s 4d'; and again in 1375/76 'in expensis factis circa aqueductus carbonum de Rainton, £37 7s 2d'; whilst in 1397/98 they sank a new pit for coal at Aldin Grange which cost £14 5s 6d. DCM, Bursar's Accounts, 1351/52, 1368/69, 1375/76, 1397/98.

109 This was because:'nec de minera carbonum nichil, quia in manu domini': DCM, Bursar's Account, 1536/37. The monks appear to have only employed two hewers to work their Rainton mines, who worked on average three to four days a week between 3 May 1439 and 1 May 1440: DCM, Bursar's Book F, ff. 25r–27r.

110 Coal mines at Fery and Rainton were leased out at £20 during the sixteenth century: DCM, Dean and Chapter Registers, 1–15, 1541–1670. See also Brown, 'A Money Economy?'.

century, revealing many of the potential advantages and problems of directly working coal mines in this period. Finchale was a small Benedictine priory situated by the River Wear, some three miles away from Durham.[111] It possessed two primary coal mines in the fourteenth century at Softley and Lumley, opening up further coal mines in Baxter Wood and Coxhoe in the early fifteenth century, and finally another pit at Moorhouse Close in the second half of the fifteenth century which was to prove the priory's most financially rewarding endeavour. Unlike the bishops of Durham who possessed several core coal mines, Finchale Priory opened up numerous new mines, which often produced a short-lived but profitable decade of coal receipts before being abandoned. For example, in the 1360s and '70s the Lumley mines were particularly profitable but from then onwards rarely produced coal receipts worthy of mention.[112] Likewise the pit at Coxhoe was opened up in 1427/28, costing £60 for the construction of an aqueduct.[113] This represented a substantial outlay for the priory as its total income in the previous year was only £178. However, the coal mine was successful in the short term with the priory's total revenue increasing to nearly £200, almost solely because of the receipts of the Coxhoe mine over the next three years: £15, £54 and £24 per annum.[114] This was a short-lived venture for soon the mine appears to have been abandoned and is never mentioned again in the accounts. Perhaps the mine encountered further problems and the monks decided it was unwise to invest further money in repairing the pit, or the seam became much harder to mine; otherwise it would seem peculiar that they simply stopped production at such a previously profitable mine.

The mine at Softley produced a consistent and reliable return of £6 13s 4d up until the 1420s when the pit ceased making a profit.[115] As has been seen, the bishop soon closed this mine down when the monks showed signs of trying to reopen it in the second half of the fifteenth century.[116] The pit at Baxter Wood followed the same pattern as many of the priory's other mines, producing a relatively short-lived profit in the 1410s. Once again the monks had their pit bought out by a larger landowner, this time by Durham Cathedral Priory itself who purchased four acres of coal-bearing land in Baxter Wood for £40 in 1427/28.[117] However, the monks of Finchale Priory tried reopening a pit there in 1442/43 when they paid £26 5s 9d for

111 Finchale Priory was one of the richest dependencies of Durham Cathedral and would often house the Durham monks during periods of leave from the cathedral.

112 For example, the Lumley mine produced receipts of £12 14s 5d in 1364/65; £6 12s 11d in 1365/66; £8 in 1366/67; and 70s in 1367/68. Raine (ed.), *The Priory of Finchale*, pp. lv–cvi.

113 Ibid., p. cxcvii.

114 Ibid., pp. cxcix–ccvi.

115 Ibid., pp. i–clxxix.

116 The monks of Finchale Priory recorded that: '20s, receptis de scaccario domini Episcopi pro stacione putei carbonum minerae de Softley hoc anno' in 1488/89. Ibid., p. ccclxxxi.

117 Ibid., pp. cxcvi–cxcvii.

the construction of an aqueduct.[118] This was a high outlay for a coal mine which had barely produced any profits earlier in the century, especially as their total income was a mere £177 14s 6d whilst the overall sum of their expenses was well over £350. It was to prove a failure, with the receipts in the next year recording nothing above expenses, and the pit never again produced income equivalent to what it had generated before Durham Priory purchased some of this land in the 1420s.[119]

The most successful pit, however, was opened up in the 1450s at Moorhouse Close, which greatly bolstered the priory's ailing rent rolls during the particularly harsh decades of the 1450s and '60s, ensuring that its overall revenues were above £200. Once again these receipts are deceptive: they represent the gross revenues from the sale of coal at the pit rather than the net income that the monks actually received. During the 1460s, when the Moorhouse Close pit was at its most productive, their accounts bore a regular annual charge of approximately £10 per annum (Figure 14).[120] Thus the net income of the monks of Finchale Priory from coal mines was not as high as their accounts would make it appear; the cost of winning the coal often reduced their gross receipts to little more than half their value. These expenses, moreover, represented the ordinary expenditure involved in coal mining and there is no mention of constructing further aqueducts, which would almost certainly have doubled expenses. Coal mining could thus be a very speculative proposition in medieval England, even in the north-east where its precocious development was so remarkable. The regular expenses of the coal industry meant that net profits were often half those of gross receipts, whilst exceptional expenditure on repairing aqueducts could quite literally wash away profits.[121]

John Hare's study of the differences between the demesne agriculture of the bishops of Winchester and Winchester Cathedral Priory showed that there were 'subtle variations between the two estates that reflected both individual decisions by estate managers, and the contrasting demands of the two estates for cash or food'. He went on to describe how the priory's need to feed a static household may have encouraged a more conservative management, whereas the 'itinerant nature of the bishopric ... probably encouraged a greater emphasis on cash and the market'.[122] The differing needs of these two estates and their consequences were similar to those found at Durham, especially with regard to how the two ecclesiastical landowners approached their mineral resources. The bursars of Durham Priory kept their coal mines in hand for long periods, preferring to supply the consumption needs of a large group of monks rather than to commercially exploit them. By comparison, the bishops of

118 Ibid., p. ccxxxviii.

119 Ibid., p. ccxl.

120 Ibid., pp. cclxv–cccxix.

121 Whilst the costs of transporting coal, especially across land, could be exorbitantly expensive. See for example: Hatcher, *British Coal Industry*, pp. 459–82.

122 J. N. Hare, 'The Bishop and the Prior: Demesne Agriculture in Medieval Hampshire', *AgHR*, 54 (2006), pp. 211–12.

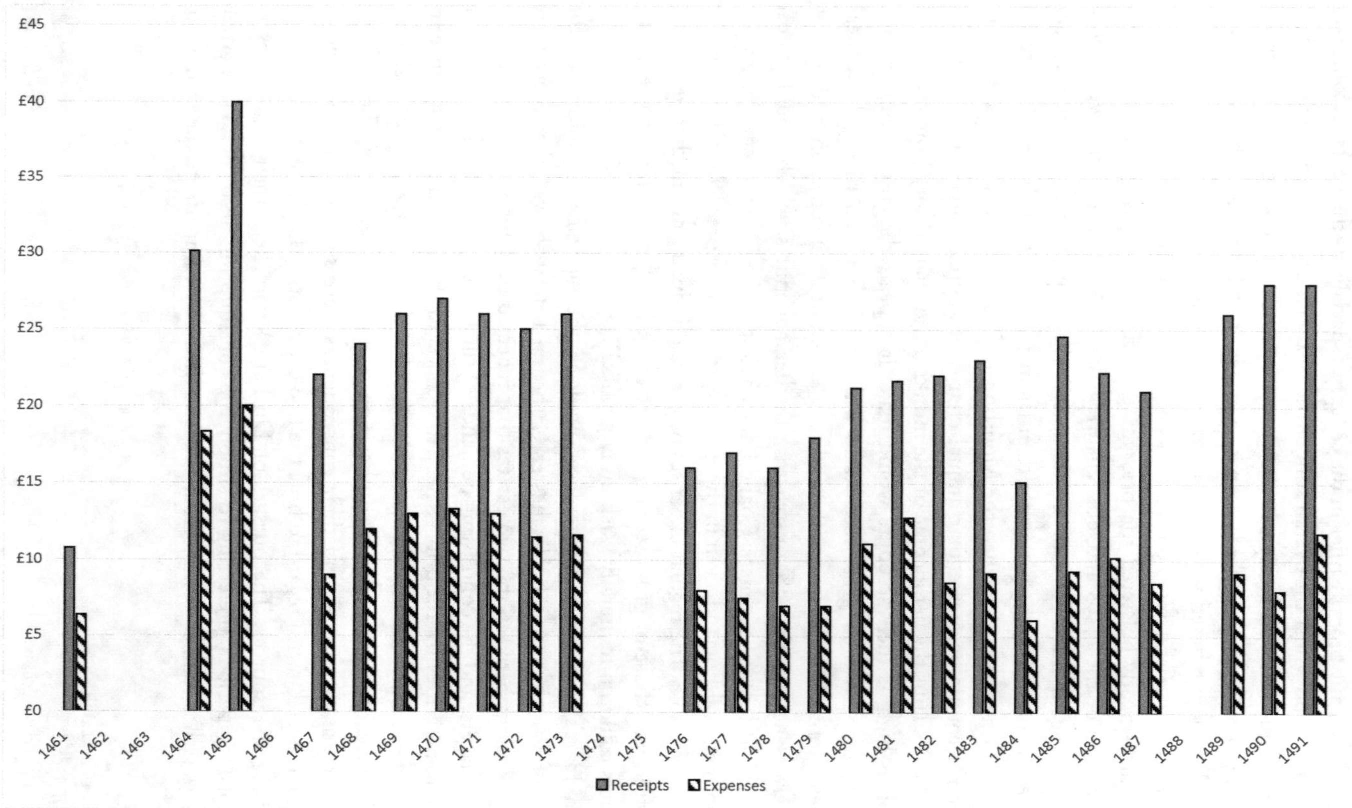

Figure 14. Receipts and Expenses of Finchale Priory's Coal Mine at Moorhouse Close, 1460–90.
Source: J. Raine (ed.), *Charters of Endowment, Inventories, and Account Rolls of the Priory of Finchale*, Surtees Society, 6 (1837).

Durham, who were itinerant both within the palatinate and nationally, preferred the flexibility of leasing out their coal mines with the provision for purchasing cheap coal from the lessee when it was required. Thus, it was the institutional context in which these mineral resources were found as much as their location which dictated how they were exploited, in a fashion akin to the way the differing household demands of the monks and bishops of Winchester affected their agrarian policies.

Conclusion

The two largest landowners in Durham faced substantial economic challenges in the fifteenth century, suffering similar falls in real income, but also experiencing a similar chronology to their recoveries. Although this overall improvement was roughly synchronous, it was achieved through fundamentally different methods: the monks of Durham Priory intensified their rent collection process, restructuring their estates and so improving the actual income they collected, whereas the bishops diversified their income, supplementing their ailing rent rolls with receipts from their forests, parks and coal mines. The major difference between the ecclesiastical estates of Durham across this period derives from changes made in the late fourteenth and fifteenth centuries, when the monks of Durham Priory were increasingly leasing out their lands and the bishops were not. As Larson concluded for the late fourteenth century, 'the major discernible difference between the two estates had to do with the tenure of customary land. On the bishopric, although the steward granted some leases, most holdings were held for life; on the priory, leases for a short length of time quickly became standard.'[123] The wholesale change of tenure on the priory's estate may have begun at the behest of its tenants in certain villages, but the complete transformation wrought in this period is highly suggestive of at least some managerial direction from the monks. But why did the bishops of Durham, a neighbouring landowner whose primary residence was within the same peninsula complex as Durham Cathedral, not follow suit? The answer remains unclear, but it does not lie in any inherent conservatism on the part of the bishops; given the sometimes aggressive protection of their coal interests, the bishops of Durham were clearly not unconcerned with financial matters in the palatinate. The answer lies more in their different management styles, with Larson, for example, finding much less conflict in townships on the bishops' estate than on the priory's lands because of their more hands-off approach: 'the bishopric stewards appear somewhat distant, largely content to let the communities regulate themselves', whereas the 'hand of the bursars was felt constantly' from injunctions for repairs to bylaws about stints and ploughing, while 'the tone continued to be paternalistic'.[124] These different management styles are

123 Larson, *Conflict and Compromise*, p. 235.

124 Ibid., pp. 225–40.

reflected in the physical presence that the monks of Durham Priory had in shaping village life on their estate and whose constant household requirements affected the exploitation of their mineral resources, whereas the peripatetic nature of the bishops of Durham seems to have produced a more hands-off approach. Although it has been argued that Bishop Hatfield tried to implement a 'feudal reaction' in the aftermath of the Black Death, later bishops appear to have retreated from this aggressive management style, preferring to use their mineral resources and parks to compensate for the decline in rental income.[125] These different responses were to have lasting implications for both estates when they faced the problems of inflation and population increase in the sixteenth century.[126]

How do the experiences of these two northern landowners compare with similar estates in other areas of the country? Broadly speaking the rural economy of England went through three sub-periods in the fifteenth century: a period of relative stagnation up until the bad harvests of the late 1430s; a deep and pervasive period of low rents, vacant holdings and high arrears from the late 1430s to the 1460s; and a period of recovery from the 1470s onwards, despite the bad harvests and recurrent outbreaks of disease during the 1480s.[127] There were regional variations in these trends, however, not least where industry played a role in the local economy as in Wiltshire and Cornwall. These regions of local industry and trade enjoyed a period of continued prosperity in the first third of the fifteenth century, but appear to have suffered from the mid-century recession regardless, primarily because these industries were also hit hard by the recession. Hare concluded that the Wiltshire evidence 'reinforces the idea of a great slump in the mid-fifteenth century, but suggests an important qualification[:] ... in Wiltshire the growth of the cloth industry generated high prosperity until about 1450'. [128] It was in the first phase of the fifteenth century, therefore, that the textile industry provided a respite to agricultural stagnation, especially in creating demand for land and resurgent profits in pastoral farming. In a similar fashion, Hatcher found that 'rents in south-east Cornwall soared to new peaks in the first half of the fifteenth century, boosted by a growing demand for agricultural produce from centres of industry and trade ... whilst in western Cornwall fluctuations in the output of tin were paralleled by fluctuations in rents'.[129] Thus two of the regions which were most buoyant in the first quarter of the fifteenth century owed their success to their regional industries.

125 R. H. Britnell, 'Feudal Reaction after the Black Death in the Palatinate of Durham', *P&P*, 128 (1990), pp. 28–47.

126 See chapter 2 for the sixteenth-century consequences of these developments, and chapters 6 and 7 for the impact upon their tenants.

127 Hatcher, 'The Great Slump', pp. 237–72.

128 Hare, *A Prospering Society*, p. 211.

129 Hatcher, *Rural Economy and Society*, p. 258.

The north-east of England has traditionally been described as a region of precocious industrial activity, but despite the coal industry being 'exceptional in the middle ages', it was insufficient to provide the regional economy with the levels of demand which were achieved either in Wiltshire or Cornwall, or indeed were to be provided by the coal industry in the north-east from the mid-sixteenth century onwards.[130] At this early stage in its history, coal production still employed relatively few people, with even the successful coal mine at Railey only employing three hewers, three barrowmen and four drawers, whilst there was no comparable workforce to the throngs of keelmen waiting to export coal from the region in the early modern period.[131] There were even signs that the coal industry suffered its own slump in the fifteenth century with slack demand at Railey in the 1460s and a complete collapse in the Tyneside mines for much of the century.[132] Although Pollard has highlighted the 'burgeoning prosperity' of cattle rearing in the Pennine Spurs of Upper Weardale and Stanhope Park during the second and third decades of the century, this 'was highly specialised' and made 'a comparatively small contribution to the gross product of the region'.[133] If anything the north-east region may well have gone into recession slightly earlier because of the impact of the poor harvests of the 1430s, with a 'spate of high mortality and failed harvests which culminated at the end of the decade in a major agrarian crisis', and led to high levels of arrears on Durham Priory's lands.[134]

The chronologies of recession and recovery on the estates of these two Durham landowners were similar to national trends despite the current belief that the north-east came out of recession later than the rest of the country.[135] An analysis of the arrears of Durham Cathedral Priory has shown that there was a marked improvement in the collection of rents from the 1470s onwards which is in line with national trends, whilst there was a similar improvement in the prospects of the coal industry during the last quarter of the fifteenth century. It seems to have been in the severity of the recession that the main difference between Durham and the rest of the country lies. It was not that the north-east recovered more slowly than other parts of the country, but that the recession had hit harder in the north and thus there was more to recover from.[136] Why this should be so is not immediately apparent. In his work on

130 Hatcher, *British Coal Industry*, p. 72.

131 DUL, ASC, Clerk of Mines Account, CCB B/79/4.

132 Ibid., CCB B/79/3–4.

133 Pollard, 'Agrarian Crisis of 1438–40', p. 92.

134 Ibid., p. 93.

135 Pollard, *North-Eastern England*, pp. 78–80.

136 The income the bursars of Durham Cathedral Priory annually collected had declined by some 43 per cent of its previous level by the 1450s, whilst the receiver generals of the bishops of Durham suffered a remarkably similar decline of some 42 per cent, from around £2,900 in 1417 to just over £1,700 by the 1450s: DCM, Bursar's Accounts, 1449/50 and 1519/20; DUL, ASC, Receiver General's Accounts, CCB B/1/1–CCB B/12/139. By comparison, Dyer concluded that revenues fell by around 20 per cent in southern and midland England, but were reduced by a third in the north-east. Dyer, *Making a Living*, p. 337.

the harvest failures of 1438–40, Pollard has suggested that this crisis was 'particularly severe in north-eastern England. The midlands and southern England, recent studies suggest, felt only a muted effect with no apparent lasting consequences', and thus this crisis was 'without doubt the major turning point in the economic fortunes of the north-east'.[137] Therefore on the eve of England's mid-century recession, the rural economy of the north-east could already be described as in the throes of a depression. The severity of the mid-fifteenth-century recession in the north-east of England is perhaps best explained by this combination of the long-term consequences of the agrarian crisis of the 1430s and the immediate impact of the mid-century recession. The decisions taken under these pressures, however, had longstanding repercussions for their successors in the sixteenth and early seventeenth centuries.

137 Pollard, 'Agrarian Crisis of 1438–40', p. 94.

2

Path Dependency on the Ecclesiastical Estates in the Sixteenth Century

During the fifteenth century landlords had adapted to a prolonged period of population decline and subsequently to low prices, low rents and high wages, but the sixteenth century posed entirely different problems.[1] It is not clear whether the population recovered because of lower mortality or increased fertility, but many of the problems of the sixteenth century were associated with rapid demographic growth from some 2 million people at the end of the fifteenth century to 3 million by 1560, increasing to over 4 million by 1600 and reaching 5.3 million by 1650.[2] The rise in inflation across the sixteenth century was partially caused by Henry VIII's debasement of the coinage and the influx of Spanish silver into Europe, but also by the rapid increase in population that led to higher prices, especially grain prices, which had increased some sixfold by the early seventeenth century.[3] The question of how far landowners and tenants were able to capitalise on this situation still remains controversial with much of the debate focusing on the ability of landlords to increase their rents in the face of inflation and how far their tenants were able to resist such incursions; this has resulted in considerable focus upon the strength of customary tenures.[4] An equally important question is how far the changes which rural society

1 For overviews of some of the problems facing rural society in the sixteenth century see Tawney, *The Agrarian Problem in the Sixteenth Century*; Clay, *Economic Expansion and Social Change*; Wrightson, *Earthly Necessities*; W. G. Hoskins, *The Midland Peasant: the Economic and Social History of a Leicestershire Village* (London, 1957); F. Heal and C. Holmes, *The Gentry in England and Wales, 1500–1700* (London, 1994).

2 For estimates of the population of England, see for example: Wrigley and Schofield, *The Population History of England*; Cornwall, 'English Population', pp. 32–44; I. S. W. Blanchard, 'Population Change, Enclosure, and the Early Tudor Economy', *EcHR*, 23 (1970), pp. 427–45; Campbell, 'The Population of Early Tudor England', pp. 145–54.

3 Hoskins, 'Harvest Fluctuations', p. 31; Harrison, 'Grain Price Analysis', pp. 147–51; E. H. Phelps Brown and S. V. Hopkins, 'Seven Centuries of Building Wages', *Economica*, 22 (1955), pp. 195–206; Phelps Brown and Hopkins, 'Seven Centuries of the Prices of Consumables', pp. 296–314; Braudel and Spooner, 'Prices in Europe from 1450 to 1750', pp. 378–486.

4 Tawney, *The Agrarian Problem in the Sixteenth Century*, pp. 177–260; Eric Kerridge, *Agrarian Problems in the Sixteenth Century and After* (London, 1969), pp. 32–93; Clay, *Economic Expansion and Social Change*, vol. 1, pp. 53–101; Wrightson, *Earthly Necessities*, pp. 132–41 and pp. 182–90. See also the essays in J. Thirsk (ed.), *The Agrarian History of England and Wales, Vol. 4: 1500–1640* (Cambridge, 1967); and these three recent volumes reassessing many of these themes: Whittle (ed.),

had undergone in the fifteenth century affected the ways in which these institutions could respond to the new challenges posed by inflation. After the dissolution, the newly formed dean and chapter of Durham Cathedral, for example, inherited an estate where most of the agricultural land had been steadily converted to leasehold tenure, whereas copyhold tenure had become entrenched on much of the bishops of Durham's lands. This chapter focuses upon how these two rentier landlords responded to the high levels of inflation of the sixteenth century and how far the divergent development of their estates influenced the options available to them.

The ability of rentier landlords to respond to the inflation of the sixteenth century has proven a controversial area of debate. Eric Kerridge, for instance, noted that 'the opinion is not yet dead that rents lagged behind prices in Tudor and early Stuart England, landlords as a class being either impoverished or in difficulties'.[5] He argued that rents across England may in reality have not only kept pace with prices in the sixteenth century but may have actually led them. With a slightly different focus, Tawney and Brenner argued that the rise in inflation caused landlords to increase rents and fines at the expense of customary tenures, to promote the growth of larger farm units, and to consolidate these farms through conversion to enclosed pasture.[6] Despite acknowledging that rents often stagnated behind prices, Peter Bowden argued that 'the basic premise of landlord embarrassment has been seriously overstated' and that 'if such theories carry great scholarship behind them, they also seem in the light of present evidence to be built on very uncertain foundations'.[7] He concluded that rent was not the landlord's only source of estate revenue, whilst 'in spite of rigidities due to the prevailing system of land tenure, there were probably few estates where rental revenues remained inflexible for any length of time'.[8] Alan Simpson similarly concluded that 'it is difficult to see how the mere landlord had suffered from the inflation', as he 'simply raised the rents, and found tenants – often the same tenants – who were able and willing enough to meet each rise'.[9]

This process was far from simple and, as this chapter explores, the dean and chapter of Durham Cathedral and the bishops of Durham faced a whole host of problems when trying to increase their rents, many of which were created by the previous development of their estates in the fifteenth century. Recent reassessments of Tawney's views have shown the importance of tenure and custom in affecting the ability of landlords and tenants to renegotiate rents in the sixteenth century, but it

Landlords and Tenants; Bowen and Brown (eds.), *Custom and Commercialisation*; and R. W. Hoyle (ed.), *Custom, Improvement and Landscape in Early Modern Britain* (Farnham, 2013).

5 Eric Kerridge, 'The Movement of Rent, 1540–1640', *EcHR*, 6 (1953), pp. 16–34.

6 Tawney, *The Agrarian Problem in the Sixteenth Century*, pp. 200–13; see the essays in Aston and Philpin (eds.), *The Brenner Debate*.

7 Peter Bowden, 'Agricultural Prices, Wages, Farm Profits and Rents', in Joan Thirsk (ed.), *AHEW, IV, 1500–1640* (Cambridge, 1967), pp. 694–5.

8 Ibid., pp. 694.

9 Alan Simpson, *The Wealth of the Gentry, 1540–1660* (Cambridge, 1961), pp. 201–2.

is vital to understand the development of these tenures from the medieval period.[10] There is now a much greater recognition of the strength of copyhold tenure and the role it could play in insulating some tenants from the high levels of inflation of the sixteenth century. In turn, it is increasingly thought that custom often 'served to limit a lord's income from his tenants', as 'the customary tenant's outgoings to his lord were relatively fixed', which 'brought substantial financial penalties to the landlord'.[11] However, custom and copyhold tenures had a period of germination after the decline of serfdom in the late fourteenth and fifteenth centuries and although they did not become sources of significant dispute until the population growth of the sixteenth century, it is important to study the previous development of these tenures because this often shaped the nature and outcome of those later disputes.

Some of the problems facing ecclesiastical landowners in particular in the sixteenth century arose from the religious divisions of the period, with both the dissolution of the monasteries and the long leases of Church lands by Tudor monarchs creating difficulties for the Church, the effect of which was 'to put most of the profits from lands so leased into the pockets of the lessees'.[12] This redistribution of wealth caused by low rents on Church lands was acknowledged by contemporaries like Hacket who argued that tenants 'enjoyed six parts out of seven in pure gain', whilst Laud at his trial noted that 'more than five parts in six' were kept by tenants.[13] It was not just the actions of the Crown or the leading gentry who acquired long leases of episcopal manors which hindered the ability of the higher clergy to respond to inflation, with tenurial developments on their estates greatly undermining any attempts to increase rents in the sixteenth century. Indeed, there has been a tendency among modern historians to downplay the role of the Crown in favour of seeing inflation as the greatest problem facing the bishops of England with, for example, Gina Alexander noting that 'the rigidities of leasehold and copyhold tenure on their manors made it difficult for the bishops [of London] to improve the long-term profitability of the see', concluding that 'the real income of the bishops of London was drastically reduced not by the direct action of the Crown but by inflation'.[14] Likewise, Rosemary O'Day concluded for the bishops of Coventry and Lichfield that 'if Elizabeth did nothing to worsen the see's economic position she did nothing to aid it positively. In an age

10 See the essays in Whittle (ed.), *Landlords and Tenants*; Bowen and Brown (eds.), *Custom and Commercialisation*.

11 R. W. Hoyle, 'Introduction: Custom, Improvement and Anti-Improvement', in Hoyle (ed.), *Custom, Improvement and the Landscape*, p. 4.

12 Christopher Hill, *Economic Problems of the Church: From Archbishop Whitgift to the Long Parliament* (Oxford, 1956), p. 6.

13 Ibid., p. 36.

14 Felicity Heal, 'The Tudors and Church Lands: Economic Problems of the Bishopric of Ely During the Sixteenth Century', *EcHR*, 26 (1973), p. 199. Gina Alexander, 'Victim or Spendthrift? The Bishop of London and his Income in the Sixteenth Century', in E. W. Ives (ed.), *Wealth and Power in Tudor England: Essays Presented to S. T. Bindoff* (London, 1978), pp. 144–5.

of inflation successive bishops were forced to seek a way out of a very real financial predicament.'[15] She went on to explain that the bishops chose short-term methods which were detrimental to the see's resources in the long term, with much episcopal property being leased out in reversion.[16] As we will see, the decisions taken during the depth of the mid-fifteenth-century recession, or indeed those not taken, continued to have an impact upon rural society for generations, long after those economic conditions were no longer prevalent.

Dean and Chapter of Durham Cathedral

On 31 December 1539, the monks of Durham Cathedral Priory surrendered the church to Henry VIII, but within seventeen months the dean and chapter of Durham Cathedral had been re-founded, with the former prior, Hugh Whitehead, as the dean of the new foundation.[17] Rather than housing fifty to a hundred monks divided into obediences and subordinate cells, the new cathedral was comprised of a dean, twelve prebendaries, twelve minor canons and numerous deputies, including choristers, deacons and the master of the school, but this transformation did not decrease the cathedral's expenses as much as might be expected, for each of these posts was paid a not inconsiderable stipend. For example, the dean was allocated £266 13s 4d per annum, clearly emphasising his prominence within the new foundation, whilst the twelve prebendaries shared £400 between them, and the minor canons were paid a further £120 divided between them.[18]

Much of the priory's land was restored to the new foundation, perhaps because of the potential for violence in the aftermath of the Pilgrimage of Grace in 1536, and such was the continuity that David Marcombe described 'the new cathedral as but old abbey writ large.'[19] There were many holdings which suffered little interruption in ownership across this turbulent period, but some of the priory's lands were not restored to it, whilst its subordinate cells lost much of their lands.[20] For example,

15 Rosemary O'Day, 'Cumulative Debt: the Bishops of Coventry and Lichfield and their Economic Problems', *MH*, 3 (1975), p. 91.

16 For a further discussion of the Crown's relationship with the bishops of England in this period see later in this chapter, pp. 101–4.

17 David Marcombe, 'The Dean and Chapter of Durham, 1558–1603' (Durham Doctoral Thesis), p. 6.

18 The other aspect of their pay, known as corpes land, and the gradual inroads many of these prebends were able to make into the landed society of the palatinate are discussed in greater detail in chapter 5, pp. 190–4.

19 Marcombe, 'Dean and Chapter of Durham', p. 6.

20 A. H. Thompson (ed.), *The Statutes of the Cathedral Church of Durham: With Other Documents Relating to its Foundation and Endowment by King Henry VIII and Queen Mary*, Surtees Society, 143 (1929), p. 15.

the manor of Ketton was not restored to the cathedral, which as late as the receiver's book of 1541/42 was accounted for as owing a rent of £27 6s 8d.[21] This manor was granted by the king to Sir Arthur Darcy, who alienated it to Sir William Bellasis of Newborough Abbey several years later.[22] Similarly, the manor of Haswell, a former possession of Finchale Priory, was granted out to the Andersons, a rich Newcastle merchant family, who eventually sold it in 1631 for £4,600, whilst the cell of Wearmouth was granted to Thomas Whitehead, presumably a relative of Hugh Whitehead who had surrendered the Priory of Durham to the Crown in 1539.[23]

Reconstructing the income of the dean and chapter for the first hundred years of its foundation is a singularly difficult proposition, partly because of the poor survival of some of the key accounting material, and partly because of the lack of information surrounding entry fines. The surviving receiver's rolls cover the period c.1550–1606, but the first nine rolls are now only small and virtually useless fragments. The transumpt books provide a useful summary of the annual accounts and so can cover some of this loss, but their survival is limited to the period c.1572–1614. Lastly, the receiver's books have survived in both the best condition and the best chronological coverage, but they are not without their limitations.[24] With these reservations in place, it is still possible to piece together much of the information concerning the dean and chapter's income – except, that is, for entry fines. Prior to 1660 there is scant information concerning this crucial piece of the puzzle, although several theoretical attempts will be made later in this chapter to suggest what could have been achieved from this source given the few indicators of the levels of entry fines which have survived.

The first glimpse of the reconstituted income of the dean and chapter comes from the receiver's book of 1541/42.[25] However, this is somewhat deceptive, for, as noted above, some of the possessions of the cathedral had not been seized by this date, whilst there is no information about the state of arrears, which thus provides a superficially buoyant picture of income. A much more detailed breakdown of this income can be found in the receiver's rolls, shown in Table 5 for 1569/70.[26]

21 DCM, Receiver's Book 1541/42.

22 R. Surtees, *The History and Antiquities of the County Palatine of Durham*, vol. 3 (1816), p. 330.

23 Ibid., vol. 1, pp. 119–20.

24 It is often unclear whether the rent recorded had been paid in full or whether this was simply the expected rent, whilst the sub-totalling is sometimes inaccurate, and there are often no annual totals even attempted.

25 DCM, Receiver's Books, 1541/42. The sum of all temporalities was £1554 16s 5d; the sum of all spiritualities was £599 8d; and the sum of decay was £32 13s 4d.

26 DCM, Receiver's Roll, 1569/70. Temporalities included rent and feudal dues from agricultural and urban tenants, and spiritualities generally consisted of tithes and offerings to the church.

Table 5. Revenue of the Dean and Chapter of Durham Cathedral, 1569/70

Sum of Temporalities in Durham	£1,388 2s 6d
Sum of decay and allowances	£49 4s 5d
Sum clear after decay and all deductions	£1,338 18s 1d
Sum of all receipts collected for year	£1,229 15s 5d
Sum of arrears	£109 2s 8d
Sum of Temporalities in Northumberland	£31 19s 7d
Sum of decay and allowances	3s 4d
Sum clear after decay and all deductions	£31 16s 3d
Sum of all receipts collected for year	£25 0s 12d
Sum of arrears	£6 15s 3d
Total of Temporalities (less decay and allowances)	£1,370 14s 4d
Sum of Spiritualties in Durham	£294 7s 8d
Sum of decay and allowances	55s 8d
Sum clear after decay and all deductions	£291 12s
Sum of all receipts collected for year	£260 5s 4d
Sum of arrears	£31 6s 8d
Sum of Spiritualties in Northumberland	£187 5s 6d
Sum of decay and allowances	76s 8d
Sum clear after decay and all deductions	£183 8s 10d
Sum of all receipts collected for year	£105 18s 8d
Sum of arrears	£77 10s 2d
Sum of Spiritualties in Yorkshire	£73
Sum of all receipts collected for year	£68 10s
Sum of arrears	£4 10s
Sum Total (less decay and allowances)	£1,918 15s 3d
Sum total receipts collected this account	£1,689 10s 6d
Sum of arrears	£229 8s 10d

Source: DCM Receiver's Rolls, 1569/70.

The total income of the dean and chapter was, therefore, £1,974, from which £56 was deducted for decay and allowances, so that the receiver was expected to account for £1,918, but only £1,689 was actually collected, with over £229 outstanding as arrears.[27] One of the reasons for these high levels of arrears must surely have been

27 DCM, Receiver's rolls: DCM/G/AA/5.

the Rising of the North, which took place earlier in the accounting year and in which many of the dean and chapter's tenants participated.[28] Another reason for these arrears, which are somewhat surprising given how well their early-sixteenth-century predecessors had managed to minimise their build-up, was the ongoing dispute with tenants concerning their tenure which came to a head in the 1570s.[29] Such high levels of decay are perhaps even more surprising given the rising agricultural prices in this period. However, when the rents and properties in decay are taken into consideration it becomes clear that decay had become an urban phenomenon in Durham.[30] Similarly, the cathedral's fishing rights in the River Tyne had become virtually worthless as a rent by the late sixteenth century, presumably as a result of the coal trade which meant that the river became much busier and more polluted from the mid-sixteenth century onwards.[31]

Although there are signs of high arrears and consistent allowances for decay in the dean and chapter's accounts, there are also occasional glimpses of improvements in their income, nowhere more so than at South Shields where the vast growth of the salt industry provided the dean and chapter with one of the most notable increases in annual rent. The history of the salt industry at South Shields goes back to before the dissolution, with, for example, a Lionel Bell surrendering his lease of a parcel of land and two salt pans there to the monks of Durham Priory in 1499.[32] It was not until the late sixteenth century, however, that the industry really took off, with revenue from South Shields more than tripling in the early seventeenth century. It was not that the rents of individual salt pans were increasing – the majority of salt pans were leased out at 10s per annum throughout this period – but that the overall scale of operations increased with the take-off of the coal trade.[33] An early seventeenth-century rental lists over 140 individual salt pans, many of which were leased out to rich Newcastle merchants like the Andersons and Selbys who made their fortunes in the coal trade.[34] This link with the Newcastle coal trade explains the success of the salt industry at South Shields, where the combination of 'pan coal' (which was rejected as unfit for the sea trade), sea water and water transport enabled

28 See chapter 6 for the pardons of dean and chapter tenants, p. 212.

29 See below for further details of the tenant-right dispute, pp. 81–7.

30 In 1614, for example, Saddlergate was recorded as in decay of £4 14s 4d out of a rent of £13 18s 2d; the burgh of Elvet was in decay of £5 6s 6d; the barony of Elvet was in decay of £4 9s 10d; Crossgate was in decay of £4 10s 8d; and the mills there were also in decay of £4 6s 8d. DCM, Transumpt of Accounts, 1571/72–1613/14.

31 Out of a rent of £11 1s 8d, the fishing rights were in decay of £9 8d: DCM, Transumpt of Accounts, 1613/14.

32 Surtees, *History and Antiquities*, vol. 2, pp. 94–5.

33 DCM, Receiver's Books: 1541/42–1639/40.

34 DCM/E/BA – list of tenants, with rents and valuations in the time of Dean Hunt [1620–38]. This had increased to some 200 salt pans in the hands of 47 proprietors in 1635. James, *Family, Lineage and Civil Society*, p. 88.

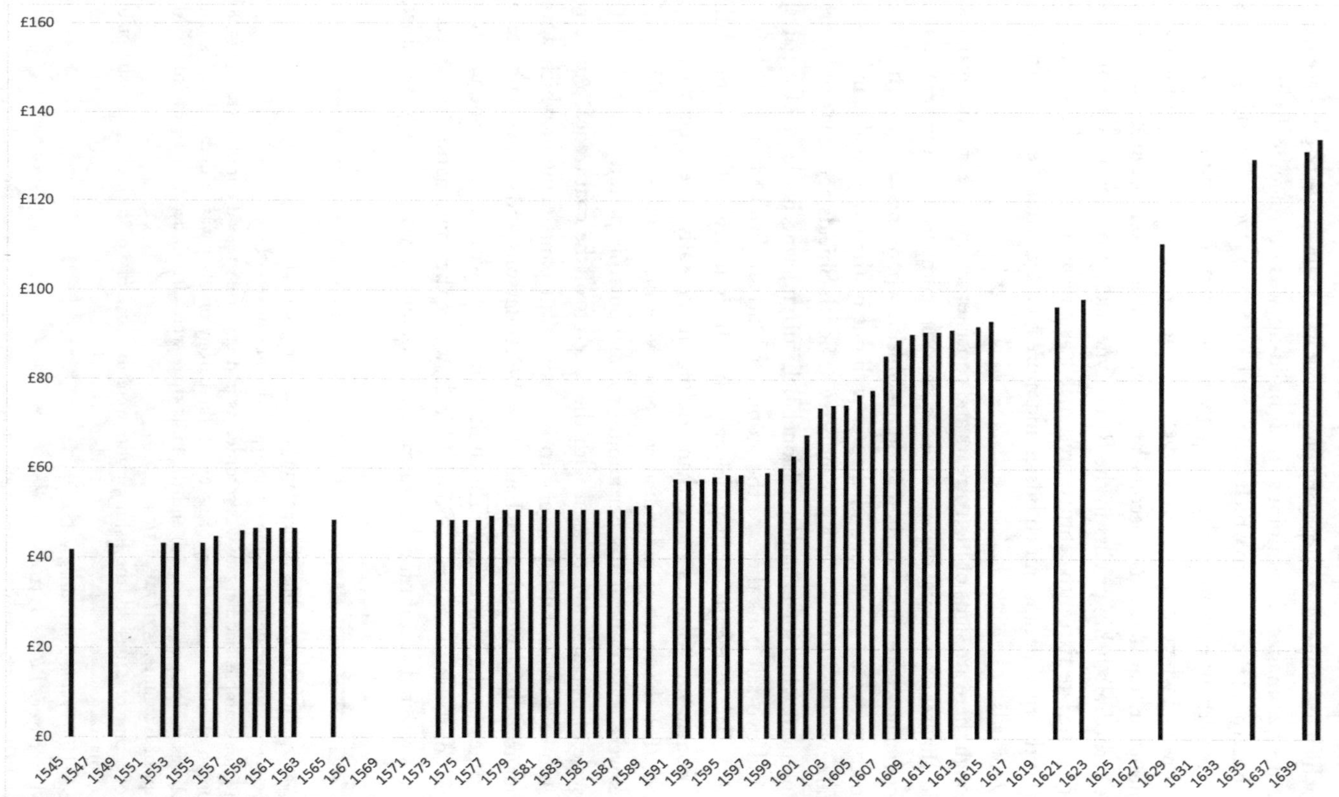

Figure 15. Dean and Chapter Receipts from South Shields, 1540–1640.
Source: DCM, Receiver's Books, 1541/42–1639/40.

the Tyne to become 'the most important sea salt manufacturer in the kingdom by the seventeenth century'.[35]

In order to understand the income of the dean and chapter in this period, especially the problems they encountered with arrears, we have to understand the controversy caused by the so-called 'lottery system' on their estate during the 1570s. David Reid has called this system 'legal chicanery' whereby the dean and chapter attempted to increase their revenues through granting reversionary leases, which in his words was 'leasing a holding to a man of substance able to pay a market rent during the lifetime of the customary tenant and by a legal chicanery denying the heir [of the customary tenant] the ancient right to inherit on the grounds of a lease already held'.[36] The core of the debate surrounding the lottery system is whether these tenants held by tenant-right, a customary tenure in northern England which guaranteed certain protections of inheritance and stable rents.[37] Did the process of syndication during the fifteenth century, which effectively converted their lands to leasehold tenure, undermine these claims to tenant-right? Naturally, the tenants argued that it did not, as they owed border service as part of their tenure and they considered their holdings to be inheritable, whilst the dean and chapter argued that syndication had clearly converted their tenants into leaseholders. It is a contentious point which not only divided contemporary opinions but has also provoked historical debate, with David Marcombe considering the tenants' claims of a 'vague and ill-defined local custom of "tenant-right"' as 'largely fictitious', whereas Jean Morrin has argued that the tenants genuinely believed in their tenant-right and their convictions were reinforced when their duty to perform border service was restated in their new leases.[38]

As has been shown in chapter 1, increasing numbers of Durham Priory's tenants held by leasehold tenure as the fifteenth century progressed.[39] This point must be emphasised because the dean and chapter had a strong claim that their tenants were in fact leaseholders, a point which has often been disregarded. For example, if we read the introduction to the Surtees Society edition of the 1580 Elizabethan survey, Longstaffe and Booth thought that there was 'no room for doubt' that in the fourteenth century the tenants 'had a recognised tenant-right in their holdings which was ripening into a customary freehold estate', but that soon after the foundation of the new dean and chapter they 'refused to recognise a customary estate in their tenants, who were induced to take leases of their lands under a system of renew-

35 Laura Tabili, *Global Migrants, Local Culture: Natives and Newcomers in Provincial England, 1841–1939* (Basingstoke, 2011), p. 17.

36 Reid, *Durham Crown Lordships*, p. 43.

37 For tenant-right see, Hoyle, 'Lords, Tenants, and Tenant-Right', pp. 38–63.

38 Marcombe, 'Dean and Chapter of Durham', p. 141; Morrin, 'The Transfer to Leasehold', pp. 117–32.

39 See chapter 1 above for some of these tenurial changes on Durham Priory's estate. See also chapter 6 for some of the consequences for their tenants.

able leases'.[40] However, the priory's lands had already undergone important tenurial changes in the fifteenth century, with Lomas concluding that 'whatever the conditions or arrangements prevailing in 1300, by 1500 leasehold tenure of customary holdings had become widespread if not universal'.[41] The changes which Durham Priory's lands had undergone during the fifteenth-century recession thus provided its successors with a headache which was not easily remedied. The fixed rents seemed to confirm their tenants' belief that they held by tenant-right, and a clause in their leases which required them to equip themselves with horse and armour for fifteen days' service a year only served to enhance this impression.[42] Under the administration of the monks in the fifteenth century, despite their holdings being leaseholds, tenants were still only charged with a fixed annual rent, and their lands were clearly considered inheritable with numerous families possessing the same holding from the fourteenth to the early seventeenth century.[43]

Although there were some examples of the dean and chapter granting reversionary leases of some holdings in the 1550s and 1560s, this practice came to a head in 1572 and 1575, when a large number of such leases were granted out. The dean and prebendaries granted out a reversion of the leases of over a hundred agricultural holdings to a friend or themselves in this period, thereby effectively disinheriting the sitting tenant and evicting them when the reversionary lease was due to come into operation. However, the much more common outcome was that the sitting tenant would pay a large entry fine and thus purchase the reversion of their lease, continuing to hold their lands uninterrupted. This was in itself a problem for many tenants because the fine was much higher than a regular entry fine, with fines made under the lottery system generally being between £20 to £30, representing around ten years' rent for most holdings, whereas a standard fine would usually be between three and four years' rent. Naturally this did not sit well with their tenants, over a hundred of whom signed a petition in 1575, describing how the prebendaries decided that 'all the tenements parcel of their possession being numbered should be put into several billes, which in the whole did amount to the number of eight tenements for every prebendary and sixteen for the dean' and that each of them should 'hold in severalty such tenement as by lot should fall unto them by the same lottery', denying 'your said poor orators' their land which they had held by 'the laudable custom of tenant right' for 'time out of mind'.[44]

40 W. H. D. Longstaffe and J. Booth (eds.), *Halmota Prioratus Dunelmensis: Containing Extracts from the Halmote Court or Manor Rolls of the Prior and Convent of Durham, 1296–1384*, Surtees Society, 82 (1886), pp. xxxv–xxxvi.

41 Lomas, 'Developments in Land Tenure', p. 43.

42 Thompson (ed.), *Statutes of the Cathedral Church of Durham*, pp. 95–7.

43 See chapter 6 below for more about the inheritability of these holdings.

44 Longstaffe and Booth (eds.), *Halmota Prioratus Dunelmensis*, p. xliii.

Table 6 shows a contemporary summary of the lottery system, which reveals that although the tenants were misinformed about the exact number of leases per stall, it is understandable why they felt aggrieved at the profits the dean and chapter so quickly raised. Unfortunately, there is insufficient evidence concerning the third, sixth and eighth stall, but even with these prebendaries missing, they were able to raise £3,687 13s 8d from the granting of 111 reversionary leases.[45] This meant that over half of the main agricultural holdings on the dean and chapter's estate were affected by the lottery system in the 1560s and 1570s, with nearly all of the tenants in certain townships, like Cowpen Bewley, having reversionary grants made of their lands in this period. When the dean and chapter's annual income from land only came to around £1,400, it is easy to see why they pursued this policy and why their tenants were so keen to resist it. The fact that all profits accrued in this fashion went directly into the hands of the Protestant prebendaries rather than the cathedral's coffers only served to increase the contentiousness of this lottery system amongst their tenants.[46]

Table 6. Income Generated by the Lottery System of the 1570s on the Dean and Chapter's Estates

Position	Dean and Canons	Number of Leases	Valuation of the Lotteries
Dean	William Whittingham	29 leases	£886 (and £40 for Jesus Miln)
First Stall	Robert Swift	11 leases	£411 13s 4d
Second Stall	John Pilkington	11 leases	£527
Third Stall			
Fourth Stall	William Bennet	12 leases	£356 6s 8d
Fifth Stall	Ralph Lever	5 leases	£126 13s 4d
Sixth Stall			
Seventh Stall	Leonard Pilkington	9 leases	£418
Eighth Stall			
Ninth Stall	William Stevenson	15 leases	£394
Tenth Stall	John Rudd	5 leases	£130
Eleventh Stall	Adam Halliday	7 leases	£322
Twelfth Stall	George Cliffe	7 leases	£136
Total		**111 leases**	**£3,687 13s 8d**

Source: W. H. D. Longstaffe and J. Booth (eds.), *Halmota Prioratus Dunelmensis: Containing Extracts from the Halmote Court or Manor Rolls of the Prior and Convent of Durham, 1296–1384*, Surtees Society, 82 (1886), pp. 249–50.

45 Ibid., pp. 249–50.

46 The dean and prebends normally shared the income received from regular entry fines between themselves as part of their annual dividend. During the lottery system, however, the fine went to the individual prebend who was assigned the reversionary lease. This is one of the reasons why there is so little evidence about fines as they were not included in the annual audit.

The whole dispute, which has been explored in greater detail by David Marcombe and Jean Morrin, resulted in over a hundred tenants, led by Roland Seamer, protesting, with many of them utterly refusing to take any lease.[47] Ultimately the case was referred to the Council of the North who in 1577 for the 'ending of which troubles, and for a quietness hereafter to be had', decided that whereas the tenants claimed that they held by tenant-right and the dean and chapter 'alleged them to be only their tenants at will, because some of them had taken no leases by a long time', it 'appeareth by an ancient book and register of the leases made by the predecessors of the said dean and chapter ... that the lands in contention belonging to that house, had many times been letten for years by lease', and that the tenements 'should not be holden by tenant right'.[48] It was in many ways a victory for the dean and chapter, as the council ordered that all tenants 'claiming by tenant right, shall relinquish and give over for them, their heirs and assigns forever, all their titles, rights and claims of tenant right in the premises and every part thereof'.[49] However, as we shall see in chapter 6, this did not lead to a wave of mass evictions, but rather to a more harmonious relationship with their tenants, many of whom went on to inherit the holdings which had been in the family name for over two centuries. The ruling of the Council of the North went on to confirm that tenants were bound to respond 'when they be commanded in warlike manner upon the frontiers, or elsewhere in Scotland, by the space of fifteen days without wages', as a result of which fines were to be two or three years' rent, whilst a son or his representative had the right to inherit his father's lands. Indeed, even those primary agitators around Merrington and Ferryhill seem not to have been disinherited, whilst the Crown pardoned many of the dean and chapter's tenants for their role in the Rising of the North.

This tenurial dispute which was brought to a head in the 1570s can be interpreted in two different ways: either as a genuine attempt by a landowner to convert any remaining customary holdings to leaseholds or at the least reintroduce leaseholds where they had lapsed; or as an attempt by a landowner to benefit from the increasing profits of the sixteenth century by burdening their tenants with increased fines through the granting of reversionary leases of their holdings. Certainly there is evidence of the former, with the dean and chapter seemingly trying to impose leases upon a reluctant tenantry. Morrin, for instance, found that only thirteen out of fifty of the sitting tenants in the Merrington area of the estate had accepted leases by the 1570s, the remaining tenants claiming that they had customary rights to the land.[50] Twelve tenants were listed at the end of the survey of 1580 as still refusing to

47 Jean Morrin, 'Merrington: Land, Landlord and Tenants, 1541–1840: A Study of the Estate of the Dean and Chapter of Durham' (Durham Doctoral Thesis, 1997); Marcombe, 'Dean and Chapter of Durham', pp. 140–50.

48 Longstaffe and Booth (eds.), *Halmota Prioratus Dunelmensis*, pp. xxxvii–xxxviii.

49 Ibid., p. xxxviii.

50 Morrin, 'Merrington: Land, Landlord and Tenants', p. 49.

take leases, including the whole of West Merrington, where the likes of John Laxe answered at the last court that he 'will pay three years' rent to fine at his own pleasure but neither will disclaim his tenant right neither take any lease at all'.[51] Even where tenants had taken up leases, there was a minority who had done so in the 1540s and 1550s but who then did not renew them until some years after the tenant-right dispute. At Westoe, for example, John Wilkinson took up a lease in 1551 but there is no evidence of him renewing it until 1587, whilst John Hodge did not renew his lease between taking it on in 1546 and renewing it in 1580; both leases would have been up for renewal in the 1570s and both were included in the lottery system.[52] However, there is a potential methodological problem here in creating an argument from the lack of a lease because although some tenants appear to have no lease prior to the 1570s from the evidence of the dean and chapter's leasehold registers, the 1580 survey suggests that they may have done so. For example, Thomas Kay and William Maltby were described in 1580 as having leases which 'are now expired and seek not to take new', and yet neither appear in the leasehold registers until 1587, despite both families holding land in Chilton from the late fifteenth to the early seventeenth centuries.[53]

It is also possible that tenants who had previously been content to hold by lease took up a claim to hold by tenant-right because of the actions of the dean and chapter in the 1560s and 1570s, and thus repudiated their leases. For example, Janet Brough of East Rainton had 'a lease hereof granted in her name four years since and unsealed, which she now refusith and standith to her widow right'.[54] If the lottery system was aimed at forcing such truculent tenants into compounding for new leases then it appears to have had the desired effect, with twenty-three tenants taking up leases between November and December 1575 after the successful eviction of Roland Seamer (one of the principal agitators against the dean and chapter and one of the handful of tenants actually evicted), with a further sixteen doing so between January and March the following year. Again, after the ruling of the Council of the North and Huntingdon's orders, thirty-seven tenants accepted leases in January and February 1578.[55] To return to Janet Brough, she took up a lease in 1575, 'being of late changed', paying £7 16s 10d for her holding which Robert Brough had held in 1539 and which George Brough would renew the lease of in 1588 and 1606.[56] Other than Seamer, who was deemed too quarrelsome by the dean and chapter and the Council of the North,

51 Longstaffe and Booth (eds.), *Halmota Prioratus Dunelmensis*, p. 238.

52 John Wilkinson (1551, 1587), DCM, Register 1, f. 174r and Register 5, f. 162v; John Hodge (1546, 1580), DCM, Register 1, f. 67v and Register 4, f. 4v.

53 Longstaffe and Booth (eds.), *Halmota Prioratus Dunelmensis*, p. 202; Thomas Kay (1587), DCM, Register 5, f. 168r.

54 Longstaffe and Booth (eds.), *Halmota Prioratus Dunelmensis*, p. 218.

55 Marcombe, 'Dean and Chapter of Durham', p. 154.

56 Longstaffe and Booth (eds.), *Halmota Prioratus Dunelmensis*, p. 218. George Brough (1588, 1606), DCM, Register 5, f. 177r and DCM, Register 6, f. 301r; Janet Brough (1575), DCM, Register 3, f. 177r.

there are few signs of sitting tenants being evicted. At first glance, therefore, the dean and prebends appear to have been intimidating their tenants in order to get them to buy out the reversionary lease, thereby admitting to being leaseholders in the process.

Although this may have been a motivating factor for the dean and chapter, it certainly does not explain the implementation of the lottery system over more than half of the estate, especially upon tenements which had a recent history of leases; here the motivation was surely financial. At Cowpen Bewley, for example, William Marshall and Janet Pickering were required to pay £20 fines under the lottery system, despite having seemingly valid 21-year leases still running, with the 1580 survey noting that both of these 'lotteries' were granted 'in reversion', to begin 'after the date of a former lease'.[57] Thomas Hixon, George Taylor, Giles Gowland and John Heighington were in a similar situation at East Merrington, where they were forced to pay fines of £26–£30 each, despite a recent history of leases on their holdings.[58] Indeed, at Merrington eleven of the properties included in the lottery system were the first lease on the property, but nine were reversionary leases to follow an existing lease to the sitting tenant.[59] There does not appear, therefore, to be any correlation between a tenant owning a recent lease and his or her inclusion in the lottery system, with tenants like Richard Punchon of Wallsend not being included whereas his neighbours Richard Stott and Christopher Preston were, despite the latter two having recent leases.[60] Although the dean and chapter may have been trying to coerce some of their more reluctant tenants to accept or renew their leases, the primary motive appears to have been financial rather than administrative. How else can we explain the inclusion of tenants in the lottery system who possessed seemingly valid 21-year leases? Indeed, it was the lottery system itself which brought about the widespread claims amongst the dean and chapter's tenants that they held by tenant-right; Janet Brough, for example, only seems to have repudiated her lease in the face of the financial pressure which the dean and chapter applied on her through the lottery system. As Marcombe noted, the difficulties which many prebends were experiencing in accessing their corpes lands undoubtedly contributed to the problem, whilst he argued that there is at least some evidence to suggest that individual prebends were

57 William Marshall (1564), DCM, Register 2, f. 202v; Janet Pickering (1566), DCM, Register 2, f. 217r; and yet both were included in the lottery system; Longstaffe and Booth (eds.), *Halmota Prioratus Dunelmensis*, pp. 242–3.

58 Thomas Hixon (1551, 1566), DCM, Register 1, f. 204v and Register 2, f. 220v; George Taylor (1551), DCM, Register 1, f. 165r; Giles Gowland (1568), DCM, Register 2, f. 242r; and Richard Heighington (1551, 1568), DCM, Register 1 f. 212v and Register 2, f. 238v.

59 Morrin, 'Merrington: Land, Landlord and Tenants', p. 54.

60 George Punchon (1562), DCM, Register 2, f. 177r; Richard Stott (1545, 1564), DCM, Register 1, f. 52r and Register 2, f. 192r; and Christopher Preston (1545, 1572), DCM, Register 1, f. 59v and Register 3, f. 52v.

trying to evict tenants close to their personal benefices and so accumulate land on the estate.[61]

The effects of this dispute with the tenants can be seen in the receiver's rolls which cover the period 1570–1605, and which record both the annual arrears and decay of rents on their estate.[62] Although it is difficult to know the state of arrears just prior to this dispute with tenants it seems unlikely that they were coming down from a high point given the ability of the dean and chapter's early sixteenth-century predecessors to control arrears. Indeed, it is much more likely that the 1570s brought these disagreements with their tenants to a head, with arrears spiralling upwards as tenants simply refused to take new leases, pay entry fines or, in some cases, even pay their rents. However, once the issue of tenant-right was resolved, arrears were once again brought under control as Figure 16 shows.

Taking all of this information into consideration, was the income of the dean and chapter keeping pace with inflation across the sixteenth century? Certainly, South Shields was one of the few townships which showed any real sign of improvement in this period, but this was because entry fines were increasingly becoming the dynamic element of a tenant's rental obligation. Thus, for a 21-year lease tenants would pay a lump sum entry fine to acquire the lease, or renew it, and then pay the annual ancient rent. It was therefore only newly created rents which noticeably increased the dean and chapter's overall income in this period, which fluctuated between £1,950 and £2,100 per annum, with the majority of this increase coming from their salt pans at South Shields.[63]

The relative stagnation of the dean and chapter's income throws the lack of information concerning entry fines into sharp relief: it seems unlikely that the dean and chapter's income was as stagnant as their rental income would suggest, with entry fines increasingly compensating for some of the shortfalls in the ancient rent. However, it is difficult to provide any definitive conclusion on this matter because evidence for entry fines is extremely limited. The Elizabethan survey of 1580 is one of the few documents which allows for a very speculative glance at the entry fines charged by the dean and chapter, as well as a closer investigation of the lottery system and its profitability.[64] Apart from the sums made by the prebends in selling reversionary 'lottery' leases, the dean and chapter seem to have asked for no more than a fine of three or four years' ancient rent as laid down by their own Chapter Act of 1574 and the order of the Council of the North in 1577. David Marcombe argued that the maintenance of fines at this level was not out of conservatism but self-interest, since many of the prebends themselves held land at 'ancient rents in just the same

61 For a full account of the legal proceedings, see Marcombe, 'Dean and Chapter of Durham', pp. 141–52. See chapter 5 for a description of the prebendal estates, known as corpes land, pp. 190–4.

62 DCM, Receiver's Rolls, 1570/71–1604/05.

63 Ibid.

64 Longstaffe and Booth (eds.), *Halmota Prioratus Dunelmensis*, pp. 189–250.

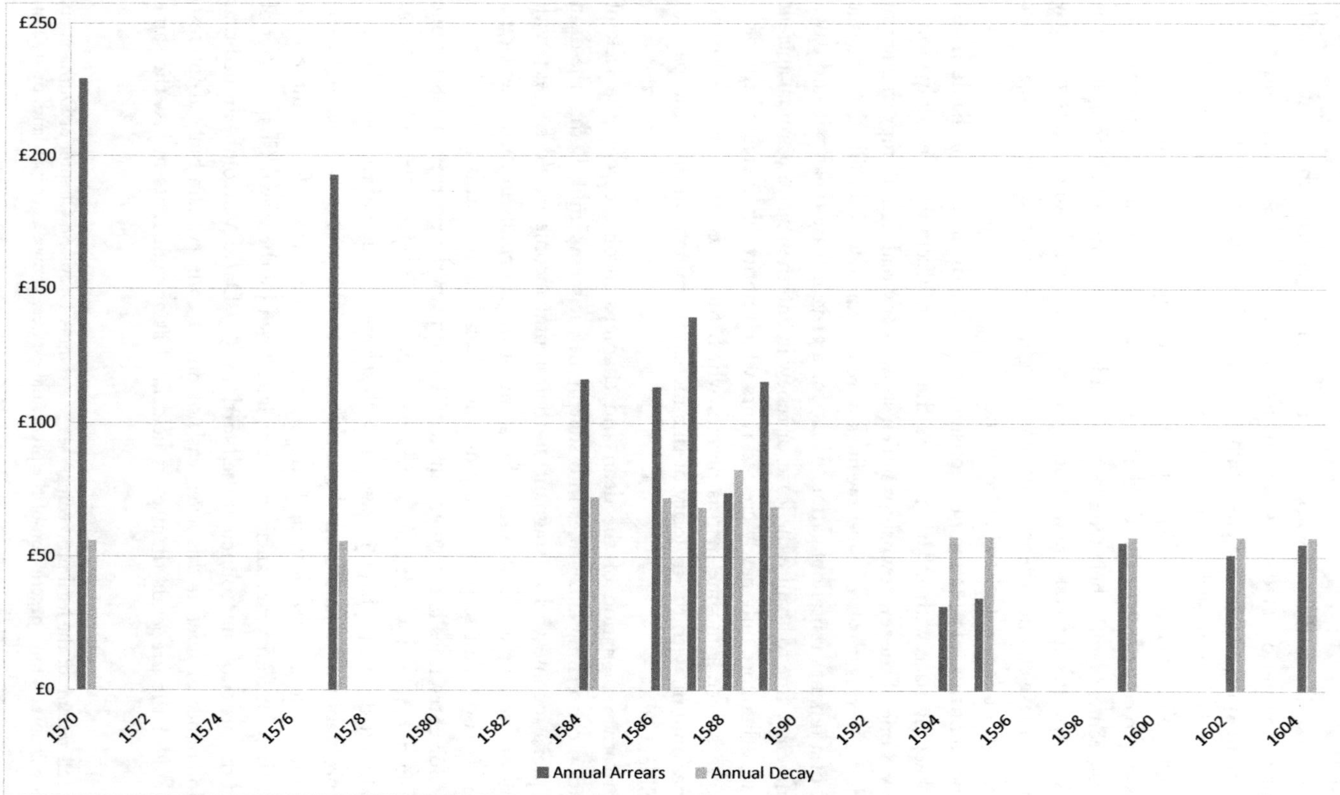

Figure 16. Arrears and Decay on the Dean and Chapter's Estate, 1570–1605.
Source: DCM, Receiver's Rolls, 1570/71–1604/05.

way as the bulk of their tenants did', and so any increase in rents 'would have been an attack on their own interests and on the interests of other prebendal families already established on the estates'. [65] He concluded that prebends such as Pilkington and Lever decided in favour of the 'status quo', preferring not 'to rock the boat too much'.[66]

Entry fines of between three and four years' annual value were not extortionate on a national level, where fines worth ten to thirty years' rent could be demanded, but, as will be seen below, this was higher than was achieved on the estate of the bishops of Durham who were often charging less than one year's rent for their copyholds even sixty years later.[67] Four townships (see Table 7) have been selected as a template for the estate, representing the best compromise between geographical diversity and sufficient evidence of entry fines, with as little interference from the lottery system as possible in the 1580 survey.[68]

Table 7. Approximate Annual Entry Fines on Four Manors of the Dean and Chapter in the 1580s

	Total Annual Rent	Total Entry Fines
Harton	£27 5s 10d	£132 10d
East Rainton	£24 8s 7.5d	£99 12s 1d
West Rainton	£20 4s 6d	£106 14s 8d
Dalton le Dale	£12 9s 2d	£53 9s 2d
Total	**£84 8s 1d**	**£391 16s 6d**

Source: W. H. D. Longstaffe and J. Booth (eds.), *Halmota Prioratus Dunelmensis: Containing Extracts from the Halmote Court or Manor Rolls of the Prior and Convent of Durham, 1296–1384*, Surtees Society, 82 (1886).

Entry fines thus appear as an important source of income, but it must be remembered that these fines were only collected once every 21 years as each lease fell in, and thus they were not in a position to replace the revenue derived from the annual rent. It must be emphasised that Table 7 represents an extremely provisional snapshot of the dean and chapter's income from fines in the 1580s, but it does suggest that additional income from these sources was significant, while there were still occasional

65 Marcombe, 'Dean and Chapter of Durham', p. 104.

66 Ibid., p. 106.

67 T. S. Willan and E. W. Crossley (eds.), *Three Seventeenth-Century Yorkshire Surveys*, The Yorkshire Archaeological Society Record Series, 104 (1941), p. viii; see below for the bishops of Durham, pp. 91–103.

68 Firstly, many of the entry fines were in fact amounts paid for reversions of leases granted out in the lottery system which were very often considerably more than any standard entry fine appearing in the survey: few lottery reversions were valued at less than £20, with most worth approximately £30, whereas almost all standard entry fines were below £20. Secondly, this survey can only provide a snapshot of entry fines, and so it is impossible to estimate annual fluctuations over the sixteenth century. Longstaffe and Booth (eds.), *Halmota Prioratus Dunelmensis*, pp. 189–250.

windfalls, such as the £200 fine taken on a lease of coal mines to Henry Anderson.[69] This was perhaps the best compromise between the dean and chapter and their tenants, with the cathedral able to access some of the unearned increment created by inflation whilst also enabling their tenants to retain some of their agricultural profits. Despite their foundation statutes prescribing that leases should contain no agreement to renew after the term was finished, their tenants were clearly inheriting these leases, often disposing of them in their wills, with some families inheriting holdings which stretched back to the bond tenants of the priory over two hundred years earlier. These tenants were able to make a modest profit in the late sixteenth century and were variously described as yeomen or husbandmen, many of whom possessed goods valued at between £100 and £200.[70] By the early seventeenth century, however, these fines do not appear to have greatly risen, with Marcombe describing them as 'a pitifully small sum', and there are signs that the prebendaries thought the same, especially Marmaduke Blakiston who replaced the dean and chapter's policy of taking three years' ancient rent as an entry fine with the idea of taking three years' *improved value* as a fine. 'For a while the chaos of the 1570s was recreated, with Blakiston on occasion demanding arbitrary fines' in the 1620s, whilst 'accusations of favouritism and bribery were rife'.[71] The Chapter Act of 1626 implemented this change to the improved value of the land and marked an 'important turning point in the leasing policy of the Dean and Chapter', because entry fines were now directly linked to the value of the land rather than the ancient rent and thus took inflation and land value into consideration.[72]

The way in which the monks of Durham Cathedral Priory and their tenants adapted to the fifteenth-century recession greatly influenced how the dean and chapter were able to respond to the challenges of the sixteenth century. The decision taken by the monks and their tenants to convert their holdings into leaseholds undoubtedly influenced the new statutes which ordered all leases to be 21 years in length. The history of leasing on their estate provided the prebends with the evidence taken before the Council of the North which proved that their tenants were in fact leaseholders; it was, after all, the 'ancient book and register of leases made by the predecessors of the said Dean and Chapter' which the Council of the North directly referred to in their decision. But the leniency of the monks in allowing the inheritability of these leases to become established, in keeping fixed rents and low entry fines, and in maintaining their tenants' duty of border service allowed the tenants to

69 Ibid., p. 197.

70 See chapter 6 below and A. T. Brown, 'The Rise of a Rural Elite? Leaseholders on Durham Cathedral's Estate, 1540–1640', in Adrian Green and Barbara Crosbie (eds.), *The Economy and Culture of North-East England, 1500–1800* (forthcoming)

71 David Marcombe, 'Church Leaseholders: The Decline and Fall of a Rural Elite', in Rosemary O'Day and Felicity Heal (eds.), *Princes and Paupers in the English Church* (Leicester, 1981), pp. 256–9.

72 Ibid., pp. 256–9.

assert their own claim to tenant-right, one which they likely believed in. After much wrangling, beneficial leaseholds became established on the dean and chapter's estate, allowing the prebends to improve their income and, if this did not enable them to keep pace with inflation entirely, then it at least provided them with a buffer against its worst effects. By the early seventeenth century, they had renegotiated these entry fines further and tied them to the real land value. This may not seem a significant achievement compared to the profits made by some lay landlords, but it was considerably more than their neighbour, the bishops of Durham, could accomplish in this same period.[73]

The Bishops of Durham, 1540–1640

In his seminal work on the *Economic Problems of the English Church* Christopher Hill highlighted many of the problems facing the clergy in the sixteenth century, but it was not until the 1970s and '80s that a flurry of historical activity produced coherent outlines of the economic position of the higher clergy.[74] The general conclusion of these works was that the Crown did not bear the lion's share of responsibility for the relative decline in their economic prosperity, but that inflation had eroded the value of these sees. For example, Claire Cross concluded that 'the myth that the archbishops of York in the sixteenth century endured grievous spoliation at the hands of the Crown which eighteenth-century historians had perpetuated should be recognised for what it is; a pious deception'.[75] It was often the inability of bishops to raise their incomes which caused their economic problems, and yet the long-term causes of these difficulties have not been analysed as extensively as has the political economy of Elizabethan England. Moreover, Durham has tended to feature as little more than a footnote in these broader studies because the experience of the bishopric was different to almost every other see in England and is traditionally described as an exceptional case. In her survey of the resources of the Elizabethan bishops, Felicity Heal concluded that Durham and Winchester were the only outstanding

73 For example, see the profits made by the Percys in this period. See chapter 3 and Gordon Batho, 'The Finances of an Elizabethan Nobleman: Henry Percy, Ninth Earl of Northumberland (1564–1632)', *EcHR*, 9 (1957), pp. 440–1.

74 Hill, *Economic Problems*, pp. 1–21. For later work on the higher clergy, see: Felicity Heal, *Of Prelates and Princes: A Study of the Economic and Social Positions of the Tudor Episcopate* (Cambridge, 1980); Rosemary O'Day and Felicity Heal (eds.), *Princes and Paupers in the English Church, 1500–1800* (Leicester, 1981); Felicity Heal, 'The Bishops and the Act of Exchange of 1559', *HJ*, 17 (1974), pp. 227–46; Heal, 'Economic Problems of Ely', pp. 198–217; Alexander, 'Victim or Spendthrift?', O'Day, 'Cumulative Debt'; Claire M. Cross, 'The Economic Problems of the See of York: Decline and Recovery in the Sixteenth Century', in Joan Thirsk (ed.), *Land, Church and People: Essays Presented to Professor H. P. R. Finberg*, *AgHR* Supplement (1970).

75 Cross, 'The Economic Problems', p. 81.

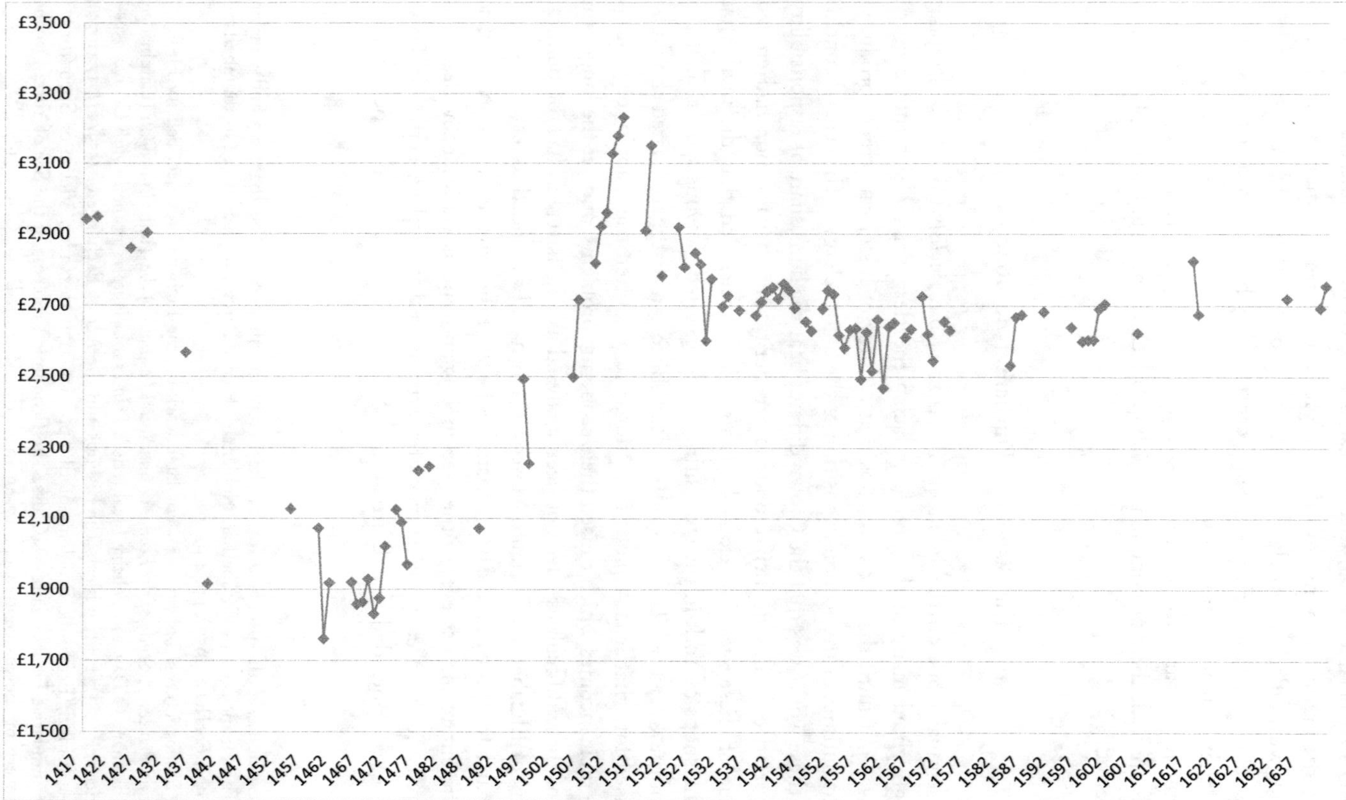

Figure 17. Total Receipts of the Receiver Generals of the Bishops of Durham, 1417–1640.
Source: DUL, ASC, Receiver General's Accounts, CCB B/1/1–CCB B/12/139.

cases of income loss during the Elizabethan era, whilst in most sees the erosion of money income, which had been so common in the mid-Tudor period, was halted under Elizabeth, and the bishops enjoyed a long period of comparative stability in the management of their property.[76] The intrusive intervention by the Crown only served to compound the problems facing the bishops of Durham during the late sixteenth century that were created by the evolution of customary and copyhold tenures upon their estate.

From the 1520s through until the 1640s, the receiver general's income shows a remarkable stability, with an average annual income of around £2,700 (Figure 17).[77] After the volatility of the bishops' income during the mid-fifteenth-century recession this appears at first glance to be a triumph for the receiver general, but given the increasing levels of inflation during the sixteenth century this inertia was in many ways more disastrous for the bishop than even the depths of the fifteenth-century recession had been. Given that grain prices, for example, had increased some six- or seven-fold across this period, it is clear that the remarkable continuity of the bishops' income represented stagnation rather than stability: in a period of rapid change and high inflation, the bishops found themselves in increasing financial straits.

There were two major problems that the bishops of Durham faced in this period with regard to their income: the first, arising from the long-term tenurial development of their estate, meant that they struggled to raise rents in line with inflation during the sixteenth century; the second, in the form of long leases taken by the Crown, compounded these problems by ensuring that the bishops could not use their other resources to supplement the declining value of their rental income. The Elizabethan survey of 1588 gives the tenure of all holdings upon the bishops' lands, grouped partly by ward and partly by the office responsible for each rent.[78] Table 8 shows the breakdown of tenures for the four wards of the bishopric, based upon the rents gathered by the collectors and coroners of the bishopric.[79] Why Easington ward should have a significantly larger proportion of leasehold land is unclear, although it could possibly be because of the commercialising effects of its close proximity to Newcastle and the emerging Sunderland.

76 Heal, *Of Prelates and Princes*, pp. 223–7.

77 DUL, ASC, Receiver General's Accounts, CCB B/5/47–CCB B/12/139.

78 DUL, ASC, Survey of Durham Bishopric Estates, CCB D/1981/185000B, ff. 1–66r.

79 There were approximately 6 collectors for Chester Ward, 21 for Darlington, 14 for Easington and 8 for Stockton. The coroner's duties consisted mainly of collecting the rents, free rents and dues from tenants of the bishops of Durham, who were in the main non-copyhold tenants. These were the more socially prominent and distinctive tenants with the larger and less common holdings: a whole vill or manor, a fishery, mill, aristocratic holdings or those of institutions. See the DUL, ASC Catalogue: Church Commission Deposit of Durham Bishopric Estate Records: Financial and Audit Records to 1649.

Table 8. Tenure of the Land in the Four Wards of the Bishopric of Durham in 1588

Ward	Copyhold		Leasehold		Total (£)
	Rent (£)	Percentage (%)	Rent (£)	Percentage (%)	
Easington	£93	24%	£290	76%	£383
Chester	£184	47%	£204	53%	£388
Stockton	£124	59%	£84	41%	£208
Darlington	£305	45%	£360	55%	£665
Total	**£706**	**43%**	**£938**	**57%**	**£1,644**

Source: Survey of Durham Bishopric Estates in County Durham, April 1588, Sede Vacante, P. M. Richard Barnes, DUL, ASC, CCB D/1981/185000B, ff. 1–66r.

The rents collected by the bailiffs of the bishops of Durham show a similar concentration of leasehold lands, primarily because they were responsible for the manors of Auckland, Coatham Mundeville, Darlington, Evenwood, Gateshead and Bishop Middleham, many of which were leased out.[80] Moreover, there was the high forester who was responsible for the bishopric's main forests and parks, which were primarily located in the west of the palatinate, in the Pennine foothills. There was an approximately equal ratio of customary to leasehold land here also, but again with a wide variation as a majority of tenants in Weardale Forest and Stanhope Park held by customary tenure, whilst the parks of Wolsingham, Evenwood and Bedburn were entirely leased out.[81]

Table 9. Total Rental Value of the Different Tenures on the Estate of the Bishops of Durham in 1588

	£	%
Copyhold Rents	£740.85	36.63%
Customary Rents	£83.38	4.12%
Leasehold Rents	£1,176.29	58.15%
(Of which was leased to the Queen)	(£420)	(20.77%)
Freehold Rents	£22.19	1.10%

Source: Survey of Durham Bishopric Estates in County Durham, April 1588, Sede Vacante, P. M. Richard Barnes, DUL, ASC, CCB D/1981/185000B, ff. 1–66r.

80 Leasehold land accounted for over £150 out of a rental income of £215 collected by the bailiffs of the bishops of Durham in 1588. Survey of Durham Bishopric Estates, DUL, ASC, CCB D/1981/185000B, ff. 1–66r.

81 The overall income of the High Forester in 1588 derived £83 7s from customary rents and £83 16s from leasehold land, but this was unevenly distributed: Weardale Forest and Stanhope Park accounted for all of the income from customary lands, whereas Wolsingham, Evenwood and Bedburn Parks were entirely leased out. DUL, ASC, Survey of Durham Bishopric Estates, CCB D/1981/185000B, ff. 1–66r. For the tenurial development of Weardale, see Drury, 'More Stout than Wise', pp. 71–100.

In total the survey of 1588 shows that approximately two-fifths of the bishops' income came from copyhold or customary rents (Table 9). On these copyhold lands, rents were fixed by custom at extremely low medieval values, as were entry fines which, from an analysis of the entire estate in the parliamentary surveys, were charged at an average of one year's old rental value.[82] These rents were difficult to improve because copyhold tenure gave much greater protection to tenants than was once thought.[83] A typical example is that of Newbottle, where approximately half of the land was held by copyhold tenure and the other half by leasehold. Unfortunately, there are few indicators of the level of entry fines on the bishops' leasehold land, but the parliamentary surveys of the 1640s show the trivial nature of entry fines for copyhold land, which did not even amount to a single year's rent here at Newbottle.[84] When the inflation of the sixteenth century is taken into consideration these copyhold rents had become nominal payments rather than reflecting the real economic value of the land.

The tenurial development of the bishops' estate made the long leasing of many of their manors all the more detrimental. There were long leases granted by the bishops of Durham during the sixteenth century which were completely unrelated to the mass leasing of manors to the Crown explored further below.[85] For example, Ricknell Grange was leased to Sir William Bellasis for 73 years in 1548 at a rent of £30, which was renewed by Sir Thomas Bellasis as a lease for lives in 1621. This lease was valued at £160 per annum in the parliamentary surveys of the 1640s.[86] Similarly, Tunstall township was leased at the low rent of £16, first to John Middleton for 70 years in 1550 and then to King James for 80 years in 1604: land which was valued at £120 per annum by the 1640s. It was impossible to renegotiate these rents or take new entry fines upon manors held by such long leases. This resulted in many agricultural tenants in the Durham region paying the same rents on the eve of the Civil War as their predecessors had done during the depths of the mid-fifteenth-century reces-

82 D. A. Kirby (ed.), *Parliamentary Surveys of the Bishopric of Durham*, vols. I and II, Surtees Society, 183 and 185 (1966 and 1968).

83 Tawney, *The Agrarian Problem in the Sixteenth Century*, pp. 19–54 and pp. 281–312; Kerridge, *Agrarian Problems*, pp. 65–93; R. W. Hoyle, 'Tenure on the Elizabethan Estates' and 'Customary Tenure on the Elizabethan Estates', in R. W. Hoyle (ed.), *The Estates of the English Crown, 1558–1640* (Cambridge, 1992), pp. 163–168 and pp. 191–203 respectively; and Hoyle, 'Tenure and the Land Market', pp. 1–20.

84 For example, William Ranson had a rent of £1 10s 8d but paid 15s entry fine; George Lilburne owed £2 6s 8d in rent but only paid 13s 4d in entry fine; Robert Chilton owed £3 6s 8d in rent with an entry fine of £1. Kirby (ed.), *Parliamentary Survey*, vol. 2, pp. 158–60. See chapter 7 for some of the consequences of this for their tenants.

85 DUL, ASC, CCB Registers of Leases and Patents, 1–5, c.1530–c.1640; see chapter 5 below for leases to the bishops' own families and friends, pp. 190–4.

86 Kirby (ed.), *Parliamentary Surveys*, vols. I and II; DUL, ASC, CCB Registers of Leases and Patents, 1–5, c.1530–c.1640.

sion and yet receiving six or seven times the income for their agricultural produce.[87] Members of the gentry in particular gained extremely advantageous leases of some of the bishopric's most valuable manors in this fashion, the consequences of which will be returned to in later chapters because of the considerable potential for profits that such arrangements offered to these fortunate lessees.

The financial problems of the bishops led them into making further estate changes that were not in the long-term interest of the see. The most important of these was the wholesale conversion of large numbers of leases from 21 years into leases for three lives in the early seventeenth century. Peter Clack argued that Bishops Howson (1628–32) and Morton (1632–59) especially converted these leases because they could charge a larger entry fine on a lease for three lives compared to a 21-year lease.[88] This was problematic because the entry fine was seen as the bishops' own income rather than as belonging to the bishopric, and so this move has been seen by many as an example of bishops sacrificing future profits for their own needs. Bishop Cosin, for example, was particularly critical of his predecessors, commenting that:

> most of the profitable and best leases were let out for three lives by my predecessors (and by Bishop Morton more than by any before him) ... which shall continue in being. They have one or two lives dead, refuse to renew their leases, unless they might have them for the fourth part of the value. I desire my successors to take special notice hereof, and to wait till all the lives of these tenants' leases become void; which will be a great advantage to him if he maketh use of his right to let their leases unto any others whom he shall be pleased to choose.[89]

Sherburn, in Easington ward, is perhaps one of the most explicit examples of this transition from 21-year leases to leases for three lives. In the 1580s, all leases were for 21 years; however, by the time of the parliamentary surveys of the 1640s this picture had radically changed so that all the larger holdings of the village were held by leases for three lives, with only the smaller cottages remaining on 21-year leases.[90]

These changes to their leasehold lands were problematic for future bishops because leases for three lives often ran for longer than 21 years and so restricted the future ability of bishops to take entry fines – a fact of which their tenants were clearly

87 As contemporaries like Hacket and Laud pointed out: tenants 'enjoyed six parts out of seven in pure gain', with 'more than five parts in six' being kept by tenants. Hill, *Economic Problems*, p. 36.

88 Peter Clack, 'Bishop Cosin's Survey of his Episcopal Estates', in Margot Johnson (ed.), *John Cosin: Papers Presented to a Conference to Celebrate the 400th Anniversary of his Birth* (Durham, 1997), pp. 228–36.

89 Ibid., pp. 230–2. This was perhaps unfair of Cosin, for he could rely on a much larger income than his predecessors because many of the long leases taken by the Crown fell in during his episcopate. See also his criticism of Bishop Neile for converting leases to three lives: G. Ornsby (ed.), *The Correspondence of John Cosin D.D., Lord Bishop of Durham: Together with Other Pages Illustrative of his Life and Times*, Surtees Society, 55 (1870), p. 240.

90 DUL, ASC, Survey of Durham Bishopric Estates, CCB D/1981/185000B, f. 7r; Kirby (ed.), *Parliamentary Surveys*, vol. 2, pp. 182–4.

aware. For example, at Heighington Martin Richmond put the lives of his lease as himself and two children who were aged one and three, whilst a John Tewart in the same township put down three children aged four, two and the final child just three months old.[91] If these children survived into adulthood there was a very real possibility that the bishops would not be able to charge an entry fine on these holdings for decades to come. Receipts from fines for leases for three lives also tended to be very unpredictable, something the bishops of Durham found even in the mid-eighteenth century when they received £2,902 19s 6d from fines in 1746 but only £1,149 18s in 1750.[92] Bill Sheils and Felicity Heal have both highlighted Laud's prohibition of the translation of years into lives upon renewal as a way of changing a system by which 'the present bishop puts a great fine into his own purse, to enrich himself … and leave his successors … destitute of that growing means which else would come in to help them'.[93] It is illustrative of the increasing financial straits that the bishops of Durham found themselves in by the early seventeenth century that they were resorting to this expedient to increase their personal revenues, highlighting the limited interest bishops might have in the long-term finances of their own bishopric.

The conversion of all leases from 21 years to three lives by successive bishops of Durham in the early seventeenth century is a clear example of how estate management directly shaped tenurial development, but why had copyhold tenure become entrenched in some villages and not others? Table 10 shows the long-term tenurial changes on a random selection of manors on the bishops' estate from the twelfth to the sixteenth centuries and clearly reveals a significant degree of continuity from the Boldon book of the 1180s to the Hatfield survey of the 1380s. At Norton, for example, the thirty villeins became twenty-nine bondmen (with one holding presumably unaccounted for), the leaseholders became malmen and the cottages continued throughout. However, there was a clear break in the tenurial development of holdings here during the fifteenth and early sixteenth centuries as this entire manor was converted to copyhold tenure. The situation at Newbottle is much more comprehensible if we think of the cottages becoming bondland, which in turn developed into copyhold land, whilst the demesne land was leased out after the late fourteenth century. There was no discernible geographical pattern to these variations, but it is clear that there was a real discontinuity in the tenurial development on the estate of the bishops of Durham between the 1380s and the 1580s, again highlighting that the consequences of the restructuring of rural society in the late fourteenth century did

91 Kirby (ed.), *Parliamentary Surveys*, vol. 1, pp. 65–70.

92 C. G. A. Clay, '"The Greed of Whig Bishops"? Church Landlords and their Lessees, 1660–1760', *P&P*, 87 (1980), p. 140.

93 Felicity Heal, 'Archbishop Laud Revisited: Leases and Estate Management at Canterbury and Winchester before the Civil War', in Rosemary O'Day and Felicity Heal (eds.), *Princes and Paupers in the English Church, 1500–1800* (Leicester, 1981), p. 130.

Table 10. Long-term Tenurial Changes on a Selection of the Bishop of Durham's Estate from the Twelfth to the Sixteenth Centuries

	1180s Boldon Book		
Village	**Tenure**	**Acres**	**Rent**
Norton	Villeins	30 villeins (900 acres)	3 days' work per week
	Leasehold	20 tenants, 40 bovates (600 acres)	½ mark and services
	Cottages	12 cottages	6s, 14 days' work p.a.
	Further	1 carucate and various holdings	For services rendered
Bishop Wearmouth	Demesne	At farm and renders with mill	£20
	Villeins	22 villeins (660 acres)	3 days' work per week
	Cottages	6 cottages (72 acres)	2 days' work per week
	Further	3 holdings of 12 acres (36 acres)	For services rendered
Cleadon	Demesne	At farm and renders in grain	50 chalders, 15 marks
	Villeins	28 villeins (840 acres)	3 days' work per week
	Cottages	12 cottages (144 acres)	2 days' work per week
	Further	4 holdings (196 acres)	For services rendered
Whitburn	Land here accounted for with Cleadon above		
Newbottle	Demesne	4 ploughs, sheep and pasture	In the lord's hand
	Cottages	19 cottages (210 acres)	2 days' work per week
	Further	4 holdings of 12 acres (48 acres)	For services rendered
Ryhope	Demesne	At farm and renders in grain	42 chalders, 6 marks
	Villeins	27 villeins (810 acres)	3 days' work per week
	Cottages	3 cottages (36 acres)	2 days' work per week
	Further	3 holdings (72 acres)	For services rendered
Burdon	Land here accounted for with Ryhope above		

Source: W. Greenwell (ed.), *Boldon Boke, A Survey of the Possessions of the See of Durham*, Surtees Society, 25 (1852); W. Greenwell (ed.), *Bishop Hatfield's Survey: A Record of the Possessions of the See of Durham*, Surtees Society, 32 (1857); Survey of Durham Bishopric Estates in County Durham, April 1588, Sede Vacante, P. M. Richard Barnes, DUL, ASC, CCB D/1981/185000B, ff. 1–66r.

1380s Hatfield Survey			1580s Elizabethan Survey		
Tenure	**Acres**	**Rent**	**Tenure**	**Description**	**Rent**
Bondland	29 bondlands (870 acres)	£20 10s			
Malmen	40 bovates (600 acres)	£8 2s 2d	Copyhold	50 messuages	£36
Cottages	12 cottages	Blank			
Demesne	150 acres in tenant hands	£14 2s 8d			
Bondland	20 bovates (300 acres)	£15	Copyhold	19 messuages	£39 9s
Cottages	10 cottages (90 acres)	£3 15s 6d			
Land at Tunstall was included here in 1180s			Leasehold	A windmill	55s 4d
Demesne	336 acres in tenant hands	£45 10s			
Bondland	56 bovates (840 acres)	Blank	Copyhold	11 messuages	£21 8s
Cottages	12 cottages (144 acres)	£9 12s			
Land here accounted for with Cleadon above			Copyhold	24 messuages	£51 1s
Demesne	315 acres in tenant hands	£22 12s	Leasehold	5 messuages	£18 9s
Bondland	26 bovates (312 acres)	£7 11s	Copyhold	5 messuages	£17 9s
			Copyhold	10 cottages	above
Demesne	292 acres in tenant hands	£29 15s			
Bondland	36 bovates (540 acres)	£28 6s	Leasehold	19 messuages	£41 7s
Bondland	20 bovates (300 acres)	£15 14s	Leasehold	7 messuages	£11 9s

not end with the middle ages but posed long-term consequences for landowners and their tenants into the early modern period.[94]

Although it is difficult to identify management decisions that could be described as a policy towards their landed estates, the end result of these changes is clear. It was the lack of widespread, centralised changes upon the estate of the bishops of Durham which set them apart from their neighbours, the monks of Durham Priory. While there may have been historic differences between the estates of Durham cathedral and the bishops of Durham which predate this period, it was changes wrought after the Black Death which really set these two estates apart in the sixteenth century. The political economy of Elizabethan England helps to explain why this divergence between the ecclesiastical estates of Durham became significant in the sixteenth century. There was no guarantee that the customary tenures which developed after the decline of serfdom would become a relatively secure form of tenure in the sixteenth century; the Crown could have refused to recognise such customary rights, much as they did with tenant-right in the early seventeenth century.[95]

The difficulties of employing a consistent estate management policy for bishops are most clearly seen in the tenant-right dispute between the bishops of Durham and their own tenants in Weardale. Tenants who held land in the High Forest of Weardale and Stanhope Park, in the far western reaches of the county at heights of up to 2,000 feet above sea level, did so by customary tenure rather than copyhold. These tenants fought a protracted battle with successive bishops over the nature of this tenure, the former claiming that they held by tenant-right and the latter sporadically trying to introduce leases into the region. Linda Drury concluded that the 'sixteenth century had seen the development of the tenants' position in Weardale from a well-established privilege to a legal right', primarily because the bishops' 'activity was intermittent, unsustained and often ill-prepared', especially from one episcopate to the next, which offered the 'tenants the chance they were too perspicacious to miss'.[96] Successive bishops found it particularly difficult to maintain a consistent policy towards their tenants and it was this inconsistency, especially in legal cases over tenure where precedence was so important, which could be the undoing of estate policies. As we have seen, the dean and chapter had a similar dispute with their tenants over the issue of tenant-right, but the continuity of personnel on their estate, with many of

94 By the fourteenth century there had been additions made to the agricultural land in these bishopric townships in the form of exchequer land. Table 10 does not include this and shows the continuity of the twelfth-century holdings by the time of Hatfield's Survey.

95 See for example: Hoyle, 'Tenure and the Land Market', pp. 1–20; Brenner, 'Agrarian Class Structure', pp. 10–64; and the essays in Whittle (ed.), *Landlords and Tenants*, especially Jennifer Holt, 'The Financial Rewards of Winning the Battle for Secure Customary Tenure', pp. 134–49, and J. Whittle, 'Introduction: Tawney's *Agrarian Problem* Revisited', pp. 1–18. See also Mark Bailey's recent book on serfdom, *The Decline of Serfdom*.

96 Drury, 'More Stout Than Wise', pp. 71–100.

the monks becoming prebendaries, ensured that they were able to respond in a more systematic and consistent fashion than the bishops were able to.[97]

Felicity Heal concluded for Ely that 'the cause of financial crisis lay in the failure actually to improve income in the face of the rise of prices, rather than in any direct action by the Crown or aristocracy'.[98] However, in many of the bishoprics and especially at Durham, it was often the Crown's direct intervention which contributed to the inability to improve their income. Under the Act of Exchange of 1559, the archbishop of Canterbury and the bishops of London, Ely, Hereford and Chichester were forced to surrender seventy-three manors with a total rental income of around £3,000 and received impropriated rectories, tithes and tenths of an equivalent value.[99] In the long term, this was to the bishops' disadvantage because they surrendered manors which could have provided an increased revenue for the next generation of incumbents in exchange for rigid incomes, but in the short term this meant that the annual income of these bishoprics was relatively little affected by Crown intervention.

By comparison, the bishopric of Durham was dealt with completely differently, having most of its Yorkshire estates, the ward of Easington and a variety of scattered properties confiscated. In a letter to Cecil, Bishop Pilkington protested against these seizures, explaining how the loss of so much land would greatly reduce his ability to aid in the defence of the realm. He went on to detail how:

> the danger is great; the shire is small. And yet if any of the wardens of the marches send for aid to the bishop on the sudden, he must give them help. The shire is divided into four wards. Of which is detained from me a ward and a half.[100]

The lands were later restored to the bishopric, but a rent charge to the Crown of £1,020, the approximate total value of the above lands, was imposed upon the see.[101] There was to be no exchange for the bishops of Durham and this represented nothing less than an overnight slashing of their total income by around a third of its previous levels. Given the stagnation of the bishops' income during this period of rapid inflation, the sudden and decisive loss of £1,020 per annum was a further blow to the financial health of the see.

Crown intervention did not stop there. With hindsight, historians have focused upon the Grand Lease of the coal mines of Whickham and Gateshead as being the

97 For example, the last prior, Hugh Whitehead, was made the first dean of the new foundation; the former sub-prior, Stephen Marley, was the prebend of the sixth stall; the former prior of Finchale Priory, William Benett, was the prebend of the fourth stall; and the former prior of Lindisfarne, Thomas Sparke, was the prebend of the third stall.

98 Heal, 'Economic Problems of Ely', p. 199.

99 Heal, 'The Bishops and the Act of Exchange', p. 239.

100 John Strype, *Annals of the Reformation and Establishment of Religion, and Other Various Occurrences in the Church* (London, 1701), p. 440.

101 Lapsley, *The County Palatine of Durham*, p. 294.

most detrimental to the bishops of Durham, primarily because of their future potential wealth under the Newcastle Hostmen. However, it was also crucially important because their medieval counterparts had relied on these other sources of income to supplement their ailing rent roll, thus enabling them to ride out the worst of the mid-fifteenth-century recession: the Grand Lease made it impossible to replicate this success and alleviate their difficulties with profits from the burgeoning coal industry.[102] The Grand Lease was assigned to Thomas Sutton, Master of the Ordinance in the North, in 1578 for 79 years, but was renewed several years later for 99 years. However, Sutton could not fully profit from this lease because the Newcastle merchants refused to make him a freeman of the city. In the end the mayor, Henry Anderson, and one of the aldermen, William Selby, were provided with funds from the city to supplement their own money to purchase the lease, and it was thus that the 'leaders of Newcastle's coal-owning oligarchy became prodigiously rich, above all those of them who retained personal shares in the Grand Lease'.[103] The bishops of Durham saw none of this increase in the overall value of the Newcastle coal trade because the rent of these mines was fixed at the low annual level of £117 15s 8d for 99 years.[104] By comparison, the jurors of the parliamentary surveys found fifteen coal pits on the manor of Whickham which they valued at £20 per annum 'for every several pit over and above the rent aforesaid in the Grand Lease', whilst on the manor of Gateshead the jurors valued the mines, tolls and salt meadows as being £2,555 10s per annum above the reserved rent.[105]

Furthermore, the Crown leased out many of the bishops' manors for extremely long periods. These manors represented some of the most prized assets of the bishopric, both in terms of agricultural land and as a source of financial wealth and patronage. For example, the previous lessees of these lands included the Lords Scrope and Eure, as well as the Bellasises, Ducketts, Cecils and Frevilles, whilst the bishops also used these manors to reward their own families with favourable leases.[106] Of course, patronage had been an integral part of the countryside for centuries, but it was particularly important to incoming bishops of Durham in this period who were expected to become one of the largest landowners in the predominantly Catholic north.[107] The local gentry may have owed loyalty to the bishopric as an institution,

102 See chapter 1 for the reliance of the bishops of Durham on their revenues from the coal industry.

103 For a fuller account of the history of the Grand Lease see: Levine and Wrightson, *The Making of an Industrial Society*, pp. 18–20; H. R. Trevor-Roper, 'The Bishopric of Durham and the Capitalist Reformation', *Durham University Journal*, 7 (1946), pp. 45–58; and Hatcher, *British Coal Industry*, pp. 70–96 and pp. 508–34. Also see chapter 5 for more on these Newcastle merchants.

104 DUL, ASC, Receiver General's Accounts, CCB B/5/47–CCB B/12/139.

105 Kirby (ed.), *Parliamentary Surveys*, pp. 105–41.

106 DCM, Dean and Chapter Registers, 1–15, 1541–1670; DUL, ASC, CCB Registers of Leases and Patents, 1–5, c.1530–c.1640.

107 See for example, Krista Kesselring, *The Northern Rebellion of 1569: Faith, Politics, and Protest in Elizabethan England* (Basingstoke, 2007), pp. 10–90; M. E. James, 'The Concept of Order and the

Table 11. Leases granted to Queen Elizabeth by Bishop Barnes

Property	Former Lease and Lessee	Crown's Lease	Rent	Estimated Value, 1640s
Middridge Manor	Thomas Tunstall, 40-year lease, 1558	80-year lease, 1583	£26 9s 8d	£250
Quarrington Grange	Henry and John Duckett, 21-year lease, 1546	80-year lease, 1584	£22 4s 8d	£138 18s
Rectory of Leake	Lord Scrope, 21-year lease, 1547	50-year lease, 1578	£18	
Crayke Manor	Henry Duckett, 21-year lease, 1549	80-year lease, 1586	£29	
	Thomas Cecil, 21-year lease, 1567			
Coundon Grange	William Drury, 21-year lease, 1572	70-year lease, 1585	£24	£106
Howden Manor, land in Howden	Sir Marmaduke Tunstall, 21-year lease, 1547	90-year lease, 1584	£34	
Weelhall Manor	Francis Tunstall, 21-year lease, 1550	80-year lease, 1586	£5 18s 5d	
Morton Grange	Richard Bellasis, 21-year lease, 1581	70-year lease, 1585	£6	£90
Sowerby Grange		80-year lease, 1584		
Wolsingham Park	Anthony Carleton, 21-year lease, 1558	80-year lease, 1584	£6 13s 4d	£30
	William Lord Eure, licence to hunt and hawk, 1561			
Norham Fisheries	Various tenants, 21-year lease, 1554	100-year lease, 1577	£82	
Byers Green	Sir George Freville, 21-year lease, 1576	80-year lease, 1585	£8	£38
Bishop Middleham Park		80-year lease, 1585	£18 1s	£88 15s 8d
Darlington and Blackwell Mills	Edward Atkinson and John Grene, 21-year lease, 1547	40-year lease, 1578	£22	£50
	George Kingesmill, 21-year lease, 1576			
Gateshead and Whickham	Anthony Thomlynson	99-year lease, 1578	£117 13s 6d	£2,555 10s

Source: DCM, Dean and Chapter Registers, 1–15, 1541–1670; DUL, ASC, CCB Registers of Leases and Patents, 1–5, c. 1530–c. 1640; D. A. Kirby (ed.), *Parliamentary Surveys of the Bishopric of Durham*, vols. I and II, Surtees Society, 183 and 185 (1971 and 1972).

but it was the judicious use of this patronage which bound men to the individual bishop. These long leases, therefore, greatly curtailed the ability of bishops to take entry fines, increase rents or even to garner support for themselves in the region as Table 11 shows.

As a large rentier landlord in this period, the bishops of Durham could not wrestle the unearned increment accrued by the divergence between prices and rents away from their tenants: the inflexibility of tenures and long leases rendered the bishops relatively helpless in the face of inflation. Bishops Matthew, James and Neile faced institutional constraints in the late sixteenth and early seventeenth centuries which their predecessors had allowed to develop and which hindered their ability to improve their stagnant income. High concentrations of copyhold and customary land with fixed medieval rents and low entry fines accounted for around two-fifths of their rental income, whilst Crown intervention only served to reinforce these difficulties. The Crown's long leases of many of the bishops' manors, alongside other long leases to the gentry, ensured that they could not use their leasehold land to supplement their stagnant copyhold rents, whilst the Grand Lease of their coal mines meant that they could not replicate the success of their fifteenth-century predecessors who had turned to their coal reserves as a means of bolstering their ailing rent roll.[108] The only estate management change available to the bishops in this period was one which ultimately proved detrimental: the wholesale conversion of many leases from 21 years to three lives, which has been roundly condemned by contemporary critics and modern historians alike as an attempt to sell the future for immediate profits.[109] This rental stagnation had much wider implications than the income of one man: the divergence between rents and prices enabled several generations of rural gentry and larger yeomen farmers to greatly benefit in the late sixteenth century, the results of which are explored further in chapters 4 and 7.

Conclusion

The two largest landowners between the Tyne and the Tees faced the same problem of how to increase their income in a period of rapidly rising inflation but did so from two distinctly different positions. The dean and chapter inherited an estate which had largely been converted to leasehold tenure and although this caused a considerable headache for the first few decades after their foundation, they were ultimately able

Northern Rising of 1569', *P&P*, 60 (1973), pp. 49–83; R. W. Hoyle, *The Pilgrimage of Grace and the Politics of the 1530s* (Oxford, 2001); R. W. Hoyle, 'Faction, Feud, and Reconciliation Amongst the Northern English Nobility, 1535–1659', *History*, 84 (1999), pp. 590–613.

108 Given the plans to create a bishopric of Newcastle out of the lands of the bishopric of Durham during Edward VI's reign, the extent of Crown intervention could have been more disastrous for the see, a fact which contemporary bishops were undoubtedly aware of.

109 Heal, 'Archbishop Laud Revisited', p. 130.

to take modest entry fines and experience a more harmonious relationship with their tenants. By comparison, the bishops of Durham, who possessed substantial amounts of copyhold land, found that they had little room to manoeuvre, and this was further curtailed by Elizabethan intervention through the forced long leasing of many of the bishopric's most valuable manors and coal mines. This chapter has shown how the tenurial development of these estates depended considerably upon changes made under the economic pressures of the fifteenth-century recession, directly affecting the ability of these landowners to respond to inflation in the sixteenth century. The final two chapters of this book explore the consequences of these developments for their tenants further because they provided them with a whole host of different challenges and opportunities.

Alan Simpson posed the question 'why should landlords suffer when agricultural prices were rising?'[110] One of the explanations for this view, he suggested, was the 'supposed inelasticity of tenures – such as the long lease or the inflexible copyhold – which prevented the landlord from getting his fair share of rising values'. At the heart of these differences in historical opinion lie debates surrounding tenure – a singularly dry but fundamental subject, which often determined the living standards and prosperity of landlords and tenants alike throughout this period. As Whittle has commented, 'forms of land tenure were the most significant legacy of the manorial system to the sixteenth century and beyond'.[111] Over a century ago, for instance, Frances Gardiner Davenport described the process whereby the rents on a Norfolk manor became fixed in the fifteenth century, and how this 'change to tenure at fee farm must ultimately have resulted in great profit to the tenants and loss to the lord' when prices began to rise from the middle of the sixteenth century onwards.[112] At Durham, the dean and chapter may well have inherited an estate which was entirely leasehold, but, as the tenant-right dispute showed, the reality of the situation was not so simple. The lottery system of the 1570s demonstrates both the profits which could be eked out of tenants by a landlord during the sixteenth century, but also the disputes such activities were likely to provoke. The duke of Lennox, for example, tried to raise entry fines on his Yorkshire manor of Wensleydale from 10 to 30 years' rent for 21-year leases, which caused considerable conflict with his tenants in the early seventeenth century.[113] The ruling of the Council of the North ultimately restricted the prebends from fully exploiting the leasehold nature of their estate in this manner, but they still succeeded in increasing entry fines to a level commensurate with rises in land value from the early seventeenth century. By comparison, the restrictive tenures on the estate of the bishops of Durham left them with little room for manoeuvre in

110 Simpson, *Wealth of the Gentry*, p. 179.

111 Whittle, *Agrarian Capitalism*, p. 64.

112 Frances Gardiner Davenport, *The Economic Development of a Norfolk Manor, 1086–1565* (Cambridge, 1906), pp. 77–8.

113 Willan and Crossley (eds.), *Three Seventeenth-Century Yorkshire Surveys*, p. viii.

the late sixteenth and early seventeenth century and it is hard to argue with Peter Horton's conclusion that 'the bishop can undoubtedly be numbered amongst the victims of the sixteenth-century price inflation'.[114]

The mechanisms for some of these changes and the consequences of them for Durham tenants are explored more fully in the final chapters, but the overwhelming difference between these often contiguous estates was the development of their tenurial structure from the late fourteenth to the early seventeenth centuries. Both responses to the fifteenth-century recession were rational and successful, made without the foresight of what was to come in the sixteenth century, but they created a path dependency which their successors found difficult to alter. It was these unintended and unforeseen consequences of decisions taken over a century before which became so important in affecting the incomes of landlords and tenants alike in the sixteenth century. The divergent development of these neighbouring ecclesiastical estates created wholly different tenurial structures upon their manors, which in turn greatly affected the rents and security of tenure of their tenants. It is all the more surprising, therefore, that as Hoyle has commented, there have been 'remarkably few recent studies of estates in the century following the dissolution of the monasteries (as opposed to studies of rural communities)'.[115] Management differences at the estate level produced tangible variations in rural society and could often act as an important driving force of change. Although demographic movements, commercialisation and class relations are often cited as the primary causes of change in pre-industrial society, estates were often the vehicle through which this change was carried out. The tenurial development of estates was important in creating a path dependency which sixteenth-century landowners found difficult, although by no means impossible, to overcome, whilst the structural imposition this created upon their tenants was considerable.[116]

114 P. Horton, 'The Administrative, Social and Economic Structure of the Durham Bishopric Estates, 1500–1640' (Durham Mlitt., 1975), p. 154.

115 R. W. Hoyle, 'Introduction: Aspects of the Crown's Estate, c.1558–1640', in Hoyle (ed.), *The Estates of the English Crown, 1558–1640*, p. 1.

116 See chapters 6 and 7 below for the impact of these developments on their tenants.

3

The Great Lay Landowners

Lay landlords differed from their ecclesiastical counterparts in two primary ways. Firstly, the laity were able to alienate their manors in the face of financial difficulties, whereas the likes of Durham Priory were forced to watch their total arrears outstrip their annual income twice over; and secondly, the laity had more than just a life interest in their landed estates when compared to the bishops of Durham. The broad differences between Church, lay and Crown estates are well documented, but the effects of these differences upon estate management and the broader countryside are still far from clear. For example, were ecclesiastical landowners more conservative than their lay counterparts? Miriam Muller has noted that 'larger ecclesiastical lords tended to have a reputation for conservatism, especially the regime of the abbey of Glastonbury and the bishopric of Ely, whereas smaller, and perhaps lay lords may have been more amenable' to peasant requests.[1] There are often good reasons for this reputation, with John Hare's study of Wiltshire showing that by 1400 there were only three out of twenty-five documented lay manors still involved in direct agriculture, whereas only six out of thirty-one ecclesiastical manors had been leased out by this date.[2] How did the transfer of land amongst the laity within the palatinate of Durham affect rural society in this period? The methodology used here is developed from that employed by Christian Liddy in his book on the Durham gentry between 1340 and 1430, in which he analysed changes in the balance of landed power and its subsequent implications for the political community.[3] However, because of the dates chosen for Liddy's study the long-term consequences of many of the trends he identified could not be fully explored, especially when related to the findings of Mervyn James and Diana Newton concerning the early modern gentry of Durham.[4] By combining the evidence of the fifteenth and sixteenth centuries it becomes clear that the late sixteenth-century emergence of the parish gentry which James commented upon was in fact a re-emergence of an important social group which had been hit particularly hard by the fifteenth-century recession.

1 Miriam Muller, 'A Divided Class? Peasants and Peasant Communities in Later Medieval England', in C. Dyer, P. Coss and C. Whickham (eds.), *Rodney Hilton's Middle Ages: An Exploration of Historical Themes*, *P&P* Supplement, 2 (2007), p. 120.

2 Hare, 'The Demesne Lessees', pp. 1–15.

3 Liddy, *The Bishopric of Durham*, pp. 1–75.

4 James, *Family, Lineage, and Civil Society*; Newton, *North-East England.*

The late fourteenth and early fifteenth centuries may well have been a time of hardship for many landowners, but were they also one of opportunity for larger and wealthier landlords? Simon Payling has observed that there was an accumulation of land in the hands of the aristocracy of Nottinghamshire across the late fourteenth and early fifteenth centuries, with Ralph, third Lord Cromwell, and Humphrey, earl of Stafford, making extensive acquisitions of land chiefly at the expense of non-resident gentry.[5] As will be seen below, this is very reminiscent of John, Lord Neville's purchases in Durham during the late fourteenth century which were 'based upon a willingness to exploit opportunities on the land market as they arose, notably from landholders whose principal interests lay outside the bishopric'.[6] Payling concluded that by the middle of the fifteenth century, the quantity of land in baronial hands had significantly increased, but unlike at Durham where the resident aristocracy came to dominate landed society for a further century, the large Nottinghamshire estate Ralph, Lord Cromwell, built up between 1429 and 1441 was gradually dismembered upon his death in January 1456, reminding us 'that the hegemony of a great magnate family within county politics was often a very short-lived phenomenon'.[7]

The experiences of the Nevilles and Lumleys in sixteenth-century Durham, by comparison, certainly seem to support Lawrence Stone's conclusions in his *Crisis of the Aristocracy*, with one family disappearing from landed society entirely and the other selling off whole tracts of land in the second half of the sixteenth century.[8] Stone used three snapshots of the manorial possessions of the aristocracy in 1558, 1602 and 1641 to show that although the total number of manors held by aristocratic families declined only slightly from some 3,390 to 3,080 by 1641, the average number of manors per family was nearly halved from fifty-four to twenty-five because the total number of aristocratic families had doubled in the intervening period.[9] He went on to describe that 'in terms of landownership, though not of course of gross

5 Simon Payling, *Political Society in Lancastrian England: the Greater Gentry of Nottinghamshire* (Oxford, 1991), pp. 8–9.

6 Liddy, *The Bishopric of Durham*, p. 67.

7 Payling, *Gentry of Nottinghamshire*, p. 10.

8 For the immediate response to Stone's *Crisis of the Aristocracy*, see for example: W. T. MacCaffrey, 'England: The Crown and the New Aristocracy, 1540–1600', *P&P*, 30 (1965), pp. 52–64; G. E. Aylmer, 'The Crisis of the Aristocracy, 1558–1641', *P&P*, 32 (1965), pp. 113–25; Edward Miller, 'The Elizabethan and Early Stuart Peerage', *HJ*, 9 (1966), pp. 133–6; Alan Everitt, 'The Peers and the Provinces', *AgHR*, 16 (1968), pp. 60–7; Stuart Woolf, 'The Aristocracy in Transition: A Continental Comparison', *EcHR*, 23 (1970), pp. 520–31.

9 Stone, *Crisis of the Aristocracy*, p. 764. For some of the controversy caused by this debate see Lawrence Stone, 'The Anatomy of the Elizabethan Aristocracy', *EcHR*, 18 (1948), pp. 1–54; Lawrence Stone, 'The Elizabethan Aristocracy – A Restatement', *EcHR*, 4 (1952), pp. 302–21; and Hugh Trevor-Roper, 'The Elizabethan Aristocracy: An Anatomy Anatomized', *EcHR*, 3 (1951), pp. 279–98. Stone estimated that in 1559 the total receipts from land for peers were about £135,000 and the mean receipts per peer £2,140. Dependent on various assumptions, the mean net income of a peer, as adjusted by the price index, was £2,200 a year in 1559 and £1,630 in 1602, a drop of 26 per cent.

landed income, much less total income from all sources, the top level of the English social pyramid had been substantially reduced between the accession of Elizabeth and the outbreak of the Civil War', with a severe period of sales from 1585 to 1606, 'during which time the net losses were so alarming that one may reasonably talk about a financial crisis of the aristocracy, which was arrested soon after the death of Queen Elizabeth.'[10] Tawney similarly pointed to the fact that a family 'inheriting great estates, often inherited trouble. Its standards of expenditure were those of one age, its income that of another.'[11] It was in the second half of the sixteenth century that the aging Lord Lumley was so prolific in selling manors, which saw the landed assets in the hands of Durham's resident aristocracy quickly disperse. This was done partly to cover the costs of his time at court and his political ambitions, but also to fund his retirement in all 'the pomp, pride and circumstance of ancient nobility'.[12]

This debate surrounding the structure of English society became inextricably linked with the causes of the English Civil War, but it has a broader conceptual utility for historians of rural society in this period, not least in the changing relationship between landlords and their tenants in the sixteenth century, especially with regard to tenure, custom and real incomes.[13] Tawney and Stone, for example, emphasised the conflict between the successful gentry and the aristocracy who found themselves in increasing financial difficulties. By comparison, Trevor-Roper argued that the key distinction was between the 'court' and 'country' gentry; the former achieved success through holding court office or by the practice of the law, and the latter retired to their estates, facing inevitable financial difficulties.[14] There were numerous problems with these interpretations, however, not least the fact that the gentry were a social group not an economic category and, as Hill pointed out, a more useful analysis might be made using the categories of rentier landlords and agricultural producers.[15] The Brenner debate renewed interest in many of these questions by revisiting Tawney's emphasis upon landlord and tenant relations in the sixteenth century, highlighting the importance of tenure, custom and commercialisation in

10 Stone, *Crisis of the Aristocracy*, pp. 72–3.

11 Tawney, 'Rise of the Gentry', p. 8.

12 For a brief history of the Lumleys in the palatinate of Durham, see Surtees, *History of Durham*, vol. 2, pp. 153–64.

13 See for example: Christopher Hill, *The English Revolution, 1640* (London, 1940); Lawrence Stone, *The Causes of the English Revolution, 1529–1642* (London, 1972); Lawrence Stone, 'The Bourgeois Revolution of Seventeenth-Century England Revisited', *P&P*, 109 (1985), pp. 44–54; J. C. D. Clark, *Revolution and Rebellion: State and Society in England in the Seventeenth and Eighteenth Centuries* (Cambridge, 1986); R. C. Richardson, *The Debate on the English Revolution Revisited* (London, 1988); and Stephen Taylor and Grant Tapsell (eds.), *The Nature of the English Revolution Revisited* (Woodbridge, 2013).

14 Trevor-Roper, *The Gentry*, pp. 24–31.

15 Hill, *Puritanism and Revolution*, p. 8.

this period.[16] Much of the research conducted since these publications, not least by Richard Hoyle, Jane Whittle, Keith Wrightson and Andy Wood, has focused upon the conflict between landlords and tenants in the sixteenth century, whilst there has been a renewed interest in Tawney's *Agrarian Problem* with the book's centenary.[17] It is argued here that the distinction between rentier landlords and agricultural producers helps to explain the economic history of rural society in Durham more so than the division between the aristocracy and the gentry, with several large landlords in the region selling off portions of their manors to the sitting tenants as agricultural profits descended the social ladder.

The following chapters explore these changes in the balance of lay landownership in county Durham and the reasons for the financial difficulties of landowners from the late fourteenth to the early seventeenth centuries. This is done primarily through the counting of manors, a technique which has many problems, not least the fact that one manor was not equal to another manor in terms of economic or landed wealth, nor was a manor always the same across time.[18] Some Durham manors were little more than moorland farms with a few dozen acres carved out of the waste, whilst others such as Raby and Brancepeth were the capita of entire baronies. In the absence of rental accounts of the gentry and with few sources for the aristocracy, however, this offers one of the few opportunities to trace changes in the composition of the rest of rural society in Durham.[19] Given Durham's exemption from national taxation, including the poll taxes of the 1370s and the income taxes of the early fifteenth century, there are precious few other sources available for exploring the landed assets of the laity in the palatinate of Durham, especially ones which are comparable across the fifteenth and sixteenth centuries.[20] In the following analysis, the overall number of manors is used to suggest general trends in the pattern of landownership amongst social groups, whereas more detailed case studies of selected families are undertaken to illustrate their changing living standards and economic activities. These chapters explore how the balance of landownership within county Durham was transformed under the pressure of the mid-fifteenth-century recession, and how this changed

16 See the essays in Aston and Philpin (eds.), *The Brenner Debate* and Whittle (ed.), *Landlords and Tenants*.

17 Hoyle, 'Lords, Tenants, and Tenant-Right', pp. 38–63; Hoyle, 'Tenure and the Land Market', pp. 1–20; Wood, *The Politics of Social Conflict*; Levine and Wrightson, *The Making of an Industrial Society*; Wrightson and Levine, *Poverty and Piety*; Whittle (ed.), *Landlords and Tenants*; Bowen and Brown (eds.), *Custom and Commercialisation*.

18 John P. Cooper, 'The Counting of Manors', *EcHR*, 8 (1956), pp. 377–89; Christopher Thompson, 'The Counting of Manors Reconsidered', *EcHR*, 25 (1972), pp. 124–31; Lawrence Stone, 'Counting Manors Again: A Reply to Mr Thompson', *EcHR*, 25 (1972), pp. 131–6.

19 Liddy, *The Bishopric of Durham*, p. 58; Pollard, *North-Eastern England*, pp. 81–3.

20 Even the feet of fines have not survived before 1535, although attempts have been made to analyse them based upon later indexes, see for example: M. L. Holford, 'Feet of Fines for the Palatinate of Durham, 1228–1457: Liberties, Law and the Local Community', *EHR*, 125 (2010), pp. 818–43.

when landlords were faced with a multitude of challenges in the sixteenth century: rebellion, religious dissidence and inflation.[21] This overview has potential flaws as the total number of manors under analysis fluctuates: it is not, therefore, a concrete statement of the ownership of all land in the county at a given time, but rather a general survey exploring the trends in the balance of that ownership.[22]

D. C. Coleman's deconstruction of the economic underpinning of Stone's *Crisis of the Aristocracy* revealed a number of problems with his approach, not least the use of the Phelps Brown-Hopkins index for deflating the incomes of the aristocratic elite of England. He went on to question the large scope for error within Stone's figures, which range from 20 to 40 per cent and then from 66 to 98 per cent, as well as the limited rental evidence produced. Finally, Coleman used Stone's own statistics to create a new table showing the considerable increase in mean landed income per manor held, from some £40 in 1558 to £77 in 1602 and finally to £208 in 1641, questioning 'how they had then contrived so remarkable an increase between 1602 and 1641'.[23] Although the potential inaccuracy of Stone's figures may account for some of this increase, it was in the early seventeenth century that the likes of the dean and chapter of Durham Cathedral, the ninth earl of Northumberland and the Crown were able to increase their revenues in north-eastern England through raising entry fines, renegotiating rents and leasing out former parks.[24] Nevertheless, Coleman's greatest criticism of Stone and the gentry debate rested not upon the economic analysis but upon the broader conclusions of the work: how to demonstrate a causal relationship between this supposed economic and social crisis and subsequent political events in an attempt to discover 'a new explanation of the central event of modern English history'.[25] These chapters make no claim to the latter, but seek to explore economic and social change in the Durham countryside across the late medieval and early modern divide.

The extensive use of probate inventories as a general indicator of wealth in the following chapters creates a further methodological concern. There are a whole host of warnings against this use of inventories as they 'can seriously underestimate a man's

21 It does so primarily through a combination of inquisitions post mortem, probate inventories, wills, charters and registers of ecclesiastical leases. Inquisitions post mortem (IPMs) were taken on the death of the king's tenants-in-chief, recording their landholdings and heirs. For more on IPMs, see the essays in Michael Hicks (ed.), *The Fifteenth-Century Inquisitions Post Mortem: A Companion* (Woodbridge, 2012).

22 Christian Liddy has argued that 'there are strong grounds for thinking that the figures given in Durham IPMs might be more accurate than those recorded in inquests taken in other parts of England', Liddy, *The Bishopric of Durham*, p. 29.

23 D. C. Coleman, 'The Gentry Controversy and the Aristocracy in Crisis, 1558–1641', *History*, 51 (1966), p. 174.

24 See chapter 2 for the dean and chapter of Durham Cathedral; for the earls of Northumberland, Batho, 'The Finances of an Elizabethan Nobleman', pp. 433–50; and for the Crown, Reid, *Durham Crown Lordships*, esp. chapters 1–3.

25 Coleman, 'The Gentry Controversy', p. 178.

total wealth' because they do not record a person's debts, nor his or her real estate.[26] However, there is little to be gained from dismissing such detailed sources of information which, if used in conjunction with other sources, can provide an indication of wealth, living standards and economic activities. The lack of information concerning real estate is obviously problematic since a person's landholding was almost certainly the most valuable asset he or she possessed.[27] It can be overcome in many ways: wills often give an indication of landed property which might otherwise be unknown; for the gentry, inquisitions post mortem obviously form a very informative counterpart to the probate inventory as they are essentially a survey of a person's landholding; and the estate records of the two largest landowners between the Tyne and the Tees enable a reconstruction of the leases and access to land of all sections of society.[28] It may never be truly possible to reconstruct the net total estate of various social groups because of the potentially ad hoc nature of these sources, but it is feasible to do so in smaller prosopographical studies of individual families and to explore these changes over time.

The second deficiency of probate inventories brings our ability to explore the financial position of families or individuals into question further: the lack of information about debts the deceased owed to other people at the time of his or her death. There is a consensus that probate inventories do not contain this vital piece of information as 'the great majority of surviving inventories were concerned only with a man's personal effects, not with his liabilities'.[29] John Moore put this in a national context, describing how 'unlike the Scottish "testaments", the English and Welsh inventories only give the gross values of moveable estates ... it is impossible to calculate the net values of estates'.[30] Naturally the lack of information about a

26 Michael Reed, *Buckinghamshire Probate Inventories, 1661–1714* (Aylesbury, 1988), p. ix. For similar warnings see: John S. Moore, 'Probate Inventories: Problems and Prospects', in P. Riden (ed.), *Probate Records and the Local Community* (Gloucester, 1985), p. 12; W. G. Hoskins, 'The Elizabethan Merchants of Exeter', in S. T. Bindoff, J. Hurstfield and C. H. Williams (eds.), *Elizabethan Government and Society: Essays Presented to Sir John Neale* (London, 1961), pp. 78–9; and Lorna Weatherill, *Consumer Behaviour and Material Culture in Britain, 1660–1760* (London, 1996), p. 2.

27 Margaret Spufford, 'The Limitations of the Probate Inventory', in J. Chartres and D. Hey (eds.), *English Rural Society, 1500–1800: Essays in Honour of Joan Thirsk* (Cambridge, 1990), p. 142.

28 DUL, ASC, CCB Registers of Leases and Patents, 1–5, c.1530–c.1640; DCM, Dean and Chapter Registers, 1–15, 1541–1670; Survey of Durham Bishopric, DUL, ASC, CCB D/1981/185000B, ff. 1–66r; W. Greenwell (ed.), *Bishop Hatfield's Survey: A Record of the Possessions of the See of Durham*, Surtees Society, 32 (1857); Kirby (ed.), *Parliamentary Surveys*.

29 B. A. Holderness, 'Credit in a Rural Community, 1660–1800: Some Neglected Aspects of Probate Inventories', *MH*, 3 (1975–76), p. 95. See also for example: Moore, 'Probate Inventories', p. 12; Rachel P. Garrard, 'English Probate Inventories and their use in Studying the Significance of the Domestic Interior, 1570–1700', in Ad van der Woude and Anton Schuurman (eds.), *Probate Inventories: A New Source for the Historical Study of Wealth, Material Culture, and Agricultural Development* (Wageningen, 1980), p. 62; and Mark Overton, 'English Probate Inventories and the Measurement of Agricultural Change', in the same volume, p. 206.

30 Moore, 'Probate Inventories', p. 12

person's debt would greatly distort any study of his or her overall wealth and financial position.[31] Contrary to the weight of this historical opinion, however, Durham probate inventories often contain the debts owed by the deceased, although whether these were the full extent of such debts is unclear. There are approximately 3,500 inventories surviving for county Durham between 1540 and 1650, of which around 2,250 provide some details of debts owed by the deceased.[32] The bishops of Durham required the executors and administrators to 'perform or administer the deceased's will or estate, *pay debts according to law* and exhibit a full and perfect inventory of all his goods and chattels'.[33] Whether including the debts owed by the deceased was a legal peculiarity of Durham is unclear, but it does provide us with the opportunity to work with the net moveable wealth of individuals on a much larger scale than probate accounts would allow. When exploring this aspect of probate inventories, Margaret Spufford concluded that they 'must be taken no longer with pinches of salt, but with whole salt-cellars of disbelief'.[34] Perhaps, through the use of supplementary sources such as inquisitions post mortem, wills, surveys and leasehold registers, we can reduce our salt intake slightly.[35]

Estate management and institutional constraints played a greater role in the medieval countryside than just affecting the economic opportunities of the Church, although because of the excellent survival of Church records it is often from its lands that most of our evidence derives. The tenurial development of lay estates was fundamentally important to their prosperity, and it is clear that the challenges and opportunities which lay landowners and their tenants faced in this period often originated from the composition of their landed estates. The withdrawal from direct-demesne production had a considerable impact upon lay landowners, with Dyer arguing that there 'was novelty in the leasing of some thousands of demesnes, varying in size between 100 and 500 acres, and amounting to a quarter or a fifth of the land

31 For example, Roger Widdrington, esquire, possessed an inventory naming goods worth £1,446, but he also had outstanding debts worth £4,468 in which he was the principal debtor, and a further £2,152 for which Widdrington stood as surety, his goods alone not remotely representing his financial position, DPRI/1/1641/W8/1–5.

32 DPRI/1, 2, 3; database of Durham Probate Records accessible online and viewable in Durham University's Archives and Special Collections: <http://familyrecords.dur.ac.uk/nei/data/intro.php>.

33 Linda Drury, 'Inventories in the Probate Records of the Diocese of Durham', *AA*, 5th series, 28 (2000), p. 178. My italics.

34 Spufford, 'Limitations', p. 174. There are other potential problems with using probate inventories, not least the fact that heirlooms and bequests were often excluded from the inventory and so they could provide a potentially distorted view of possessions.

35 As Cressy has argued, despite their problems 'inventories give an adequate indication of the distribution of wealth', whilst Zell concluded unreservedly that probate inventories 'were superior to taxation returns as a source for studying the changing distribution of wealth or relative wealth of the different trades in the Elizabethan Weald'. Cited in Tom Arkell, 'Interpreting Probate Inventories', in T. Arkell, N. Evans, and N. Goose (eds.), *When Death do us Part: Understanding and Interpreting the Probate Records of Early Modern England* (Oxford, 2000), pp. 95–100.

in lowland England' from the late fourteenth century.[36] Unfortunately, because of the lack of comparable evidence about the lay estates of county Durham we cannot follow these developments as clearly as on the ecclesiastical estates, but as will become apparent over the following chapters, whether a landowner was directly engaged in commercial agriculture or had become a rentier landlord was of extreme importance, especially from the mid-sixteenth century onwards. The withdrawal from the direct management of demesnes in the late fourteenth and early fifteenth centuries was thus of long-term importance to rural society because it influenced how landowners could respond to inflation during the sixteenth century.[37]

The Formation of Great Estates in the Fifteenth Century

The palatinate of Durham, like most English counties, possessed a group of resident aristocracy and larger gentry families, with the Nevilles of Raby, Lumleys of Lumley, Bowes of Streatlam, Hiltons of Hylton, Claxtons of Claxton and Old Park, Eures of Witton-le-Wear and Conyers of Sockburn amongst the major manor-holding families in the region.[38] These families held 40 of the 200 lay manors mentioned in the inquisitions post mortem (hereafter referred to as IPMs) at the time of the Black Death, resulting in 20 per cent of all lay manors resting in the hands of these eight families.[39] By 1500, however, these estates had been greatly consolidated so that the same families, less those who had died out in the male line, possessed some 113 of the 231 manors recorded. Thus over the course of the fifteenth century this handful of families had managed to nearly triple their holdings, coming to account for half of the lay manors in the palatinate of Durham (Table 12).

The consolidation was even greater than this suggests if we look at three of the principal lay families within the county: the Nevilles, Lumleys and Bowes. These three families possessed nineteen manors in 1350 but by 1500 they had accumulated no fewer than eighty-eight manors, coming to account for approximately 40 per cent

36 Dyer, *An Age of Transition*, p. 195.

37 Did landowners fully retreat from directly working their own lands? Did they lease out their demesnes in their entirety? Or did they do so piecemeal and allow customary tenures to develop on them? The process of disparking in the sixteenth century was to provide landowners with similar opportunities and potential problems.

38 Liddy, *The Bishopric of Durham*, pp. 58–75; James, *Family, Lineage, and Civil Society*, p. 30.

39 TNA, Inquisitions Post Mortem: DURH 3. General trends summarised here from the deputy keeper's reports: 'Durham Records: Cursitor's Records: Inquisitions Post Mortem', in *The Forty-Fourth Annual Report of the Deputy Keeper of the Public Records* (London, 1883), Appendix, pp. 310–542; 'Durham Records: Cursitor's Records: Inquisitions Post Mortem', in *The Forty-Fifth Annual Report of the Deputy Keeper of the Public Records* (London, 1885), Appendix, pp. 153–282. The original IPMs are held in The National Archives in DURH 3, but Durham Archives and Special Collections also possess microfilm copies of this collection, XM/film Palatinate 1.

Table 12. Number of Manors Held by the Aristocracy and Greater Knightly Families*

	1350	1400	1450	1500	1550	1600	1640
Nevilles of Raby	12	40	45	48	39	–	–
Lumleys of Lumley	5	6	8	18	20	8	8
Bowes of Streatlam	2	7	10	22	12	10	9
Hiltons of Hylton	6	8	8	7	8	8	8
Eures of Witton	5	8	10	10	9	9	8
Claxtons of Claxton	3	8	8	–	–	–	–
Claxtons of Old Park	3	5	5	5	5	3	2
Conyers of Sockburn	4	4	3	3	3	3	–
Total Number	**40**	**86**	**97**	**113**	**96**	**41**	**35**

* In the late-fourteenth century, there were also the Daldens (5), Grays, (7), Surtees (5), Bekes (8) and Cliffords (5), but these families quickly died out or sold off their lands. In the early-seventeenth century, the Vanes (c.15) entered the Durham scene, but certainly could not replace the Nevilles in terms of landholding in the region.

Source: TNA, Inquisitions Post Mortem, DURH 3. Abstracted on microfilm in DUL, ASC, XM/film Palatinate 1. Published lists in *The Forty-Fourth Report of the Deputy Keeper* (London, 1883), pp. 310–542 and the *Forty-Fifth Report of the Deputy Keeper* (London, 1885), pp. 153–282.

of the lay manors recorded in the Durham IPMs.[40] This represented a considerable consolidation of land across the fifteenth century, not only amongst the knightly group of families as a whole, but also in the hands of the resident aristocracy who came to dominate landed society across the century. Was there a specific strategy of estate-building which fuelled these mass acquisitions or were these purchases the result of opportunism at times when their neighbours experienced bad fortunes? Was the fifteenth century, as well as being a period of economic recession, paradoxically also a great period for estate-building for those with sufficient wealth and access to credit?

Unfortunately, it is 'difficult to study the value of the estates for the Neville family because no collection of accounts survives', unlike, for example, the sources used in Bean's study of the Percys.[41] The Nevilles appear in the Domesday Book of 1086 as a knightly family of no particular note, holding lands primarily in Lincolnshire. The family was able slowly to accumulate lands and influence across England through

40 In the early sixteenth century, the Nevilles held approximately 48 manors within the palatinate; after gaining the Thornton inheritance, the Lumleys held some 18 manors in the county; whilst the Bowes had accumulated around 22 manors through a succession of successful marriages and purchases. See below for more information about these families.

41 Much of the following twelfth- and thirteenth-century history of the Nevilles comes from Charles R. Young, *The Making of the Neville Family, 1166–1400* (Woodbridge, 1996), p. 2.

long-standing royal service. Alan de Neville served as chief justice of the forests under Henry II and, under King John and Henry III, various members of the family held the office of chief forester, chamberlain and chancellor. It was the marriage of Geoffrey de Neville of Burreth with Emma Bulmer prior to 1176 which brought the important manors of Brancepeth, Raby and Sheriff Hutton in Durham and Yorkshire into Neville ownership. The family, therefore, were relative late-comers to county Durham, only acquiring much of their land through marriage, which contemporaries remembered: 'when they were not such great lords that they had a marshal, butler and other household servants, since they then only held Raby with appurtenances, which then was not of such value as it is now, and they only acquired Brancepeth afterwards by marriage and Raskelf and other lands in the county of York and Richmond in the same way.'[42]

Ranulph Neville was summoned to Parliament in 1295 and was styled Lord Neville of Raby, whilst the family played an increasingly important role in the governance of the north of England, and especially in the prosecution of the war with Scotland. Military service became 'all important to the Neville family during the long reign of Edward III', with Ralph Neville becoming a warden of the marches in Northumberland, Cumberland and Westmorland, alongside Henry Percy, in 1334.[43] Ralph would go on to lead one of the armies in the battle of Neville's Cross just outside Durham in 1346, which saw the defeat of the Scottish attack and the capture of King David II of Scotland.[44] The consolidation of the family's power in the north of England was seemingly complete when Ralph's son, John Neville, was appointed as warden of both the eastern and western marches in the 1380s, seemingly supplanting the Percys as the military leaders of the north, whilst such was his financial success that he was able to loan the king £7,000 prior to January 1383.[45] John's son, Ralph Neville, went on to marry Joan Beaufort, the daughter of John of Gaunt, and finally, on 29 September 1397, he was created the earl of Westmorland. Thus the family rose from relative knightly obscurity in the eleventh century to the titular aristocracy in the fourteenth century through a combination of royal service, successful military campaigns and the occupation of a range of commissions and offices.

The rise of the Nevilles in the north, especially in the Durham countryside, saw them purchase manors hand over fist to increase the size of their estate from around a dozen manors in the mid-fourteenth century to over forty-five by the mid-fifteenth century.[46] In the middle of the fourteenth century the landed position of the Nevilles in Durham was 'basically limited to their patrimonial estates of Raby and Brancepeth'

42 Liddy, *The Bishopric of Durham*, p. 65.

43 Young, *Making of the Neville Family*, p. 112.

44 For the battle of Neville's Cross see the essays in D. Rollason and M. Prestwich (eds.), *The Battle of Neville's Cross, 1346* (Stamford, 1998).

45 Young, *Making of the Neville Family*, p. 122 and p. 129.

46 TNA, DURH 3/2, f. 110; DKR 45, pp. 243–4. TNA, DURH 3/3, f. 61; DKR 44, pp. 532–3.

to the west and south-west of Durham city.[47] By 1381 John, Lord Neville, had acquired a further fourteen manors, many of which were in the particularly fertile arable region of the south-east of the county rather than in the upland regions around Brancepeth and Raby. These acquisitions included, for example, the purchase of Stotfold in 1382, which in the sixteenth century was described as containing 1,500 acres of arable land, 800 of meadow, 1,000 of pasture, 10 of wood, and 2,000 of furze and briar, and the reacquisition of Winlaton after it had been granted to the Menvilles of Horden in the mid-fourteenth century.[48] Liddy has described this purchasing strategy as one 'based upon a willingness to exploit opportunities on the land market as they arose, notably from landholders whose principal interests lay outside the bishopric', including purchases from the Percys of Alnwick and Dacres of Cumberland.[49] In the economic context of the 1380s, when prices had recently declined and wages were climbing, these absentee landlords may well have found it preferable to sell off some of their outlying manors and in John Neville they found a ready purchaser.[50]

On the death of Ralph Neville, first earl of Westmorland, these lands had increased from around thirty at the time of Hatfield's survey in 1381 to forty-seven by 1425. In contrast to the opportunistic nature of his father's acquisitions, Ralph Neville 'seems to have concentrated his attention on properties close to the main patrimonial estates of Raby and Brancepeth'.[51] The Nevilles now held the manors of Crook, Billy Row, Brancepeth, East Brandon, Holywell, Tudhoe, Wooley Hill, Stanley, Stockley, West Brandon and Willington in Brancepeth parish, as well as the manors of Binchester, Byers Green, Cornsay, Hedley Hope, Helme Park, Langley forest, Rowley and Whitworth in the surrounding parishes.[52] Some of these manors, such as Tudhoe, were said to be worth £30 or more in the IPM of Ralph Neville in 1425, whereas others were little more than moorland farms, with the likes of the manor and vill of nearby Stanley and Billey Row only worth 40s per annum above reprises; the latter continued as a small settlement throughout this period with only eight households there in the mid-seventeenth century.[53] Much of this land, situated as it was in the Pennine spurs and over 400 feet above sea level, was primarily suited to pastoral farming, with the manor of Brancepeth having only 300 to 400 acres of arable land but some 2,000 acres of moor and pasture in the forest of Brancepeth in 1425. This

47 Liddy, *The Bishopric of Durham*, p. 64.

48 Surtees, *History of Durham*, vol. 3, p. 88.

49 Liddy, *The Bishopric of Durham*, p. 64.

50 For the economic context of the late fourteenth century, see for example, A. R. Bridbury, 'The Black Death', *EcHR*, 26 (1973), pp. 577–92; John Hatcher, 'England in the Aftermath of the Black Death', *P&P*, 144 (1994), pp. 3–35.

51 Liddy, *The Bishopric of Durham*, p. 68.

52 See Ralph Neville's IPM, a copy of which is in DCM, Registrum Parvum IV, f. 126r–127v.

53 For Brancepeth lordship in the seventeenth century, see D. E. Hamilton, 'Social Networks, Families and Neighbourhoods: Brancepeth Parish in the Seventeenth Century' (Durham Doctoral Thesis, 2000), pp. 76–7 and Reid, *Durham Crown Lordships*.

was as true in the seventeenth century as it was in the fifteenth century, with many of the tenants of the parish of Brancepeth possessing considerable numbers of sheep and cattle but relatively little grain, except on the east side of the parish where some tenants had arable agriculture similar to tenants in the Tees lowlands region.[54]

When taken together, however, this concentration of land meant that anyone riding west or south-west from Durham city after the early fifteenth century was travelling across Neville land, often for as far as the eye could see.[55] If our imaginary traveller continued on south-west, past the bishop's palace at Bishop Auckland which, along with the Eure's lands at Witton-le-Wear, divided the two Neville lordships, they would come to the other major accumulation of Neville landed power in the region centred on Raby castle. The castle and park there, along with the nearby manors of Bolam, Cockfield, Eldon, Gainford, Ingleton, Newsham, Snotterton, Staindrop, Summerhouse and the moiety of the vill of Cleatlam and Wackerfield, were said to be worth some £100 per annum in 1425.[56] Further to the east lay the solitary manor of Long Newton and, in the Tees lowlands around Hartlepool, lay the manors of Dalton Piercy, Elwick, Newton Hansard, Stotfold and Swainston. In total, the Nevilles' annual income from castles, manors, lands and tenements was valued at over £2,500 in 1434, half of which came from their Durham estate; there was no other lay landowner within the palatinate who had comparable landed resources and the Nevilles would form a major focal point of local politics right up until the forfeiture of this vast estate in the middle of the sixteenth century.[57]

By comparison, the Bowes family were relatively minor members of the gentry who made substantial gains of landed property within county Durham across the fourteenth century, primarily through marriage with two wealthy heiresses. The Bowes owed their initial acquisition of Streatlam manor, which was to become the family's home, to the marriage of Adam Bowes and Alice, the daughter and heiress of Sir John Trayne, and by the mid-fourteenth century, the family possessed six manors in the south-west of the palatinate.[58] Although this estate was relatively

54 Hamilton, 'Social Networks, Families and Neighbourhoods', p. 141.

55 The Homberston survey in 1570 noted that the area was 'nothing so well inhabited as the east part of the bishopric and few gentlemen of any land or living inhabited there', for the area was primarily owned by the bishop or the Nevilles. TNA, E164/37, p. 68 (using contents page references).

56 DCM, Registrum Parvum IV, f. 126r–127v.

57 Liddy, *The Bishopric of Durham*, p. 68. The division of the Neville family's estate on the death of Ralph, first earl of Westmorland, weakened the family's position, with his second wife, Joan Beaufort, succeeding to a third of the Brancepeth lordship in dower and the bulk of the estate outside of Durham, whilst Ralph, second earl of Westmorland, inherited the title and remainder of the Durham estate. See also, DCM, Registrum Parvum IV, ff. 126r–128r. Even after this division, the Westmorland Nevilles were still the paramount lay family within the palatinate until their forfeiture after the Rising of the North in 1569.

58 Christine M. Newman, 'The Bowes of Streatlam, County Durham: A Study of the Politics and Religion of a Sixteenth Century Northern Gentry Family' (York Doctoral Thesis, 1991), pp. 23–4.

modest, Alice brought with her the manor of Streatlam, which was no mere moorland farm, being valued at £40 per annum in 1399.[59] By the start of the sixteenth century, however, the Bowes had accumulated a much more considerable estate across county Durham, coming to own some twenty manors and various parcels of land throughout the region.[60] These lands were partly acquired by purchase, but again the marriage of a wealthy heiress was crucial to the family's fortunes, this time through the marriage of William Bowes, grandson of the above Adam, and Maud of Dalden in 1375. Maud was the cousin and heiress of Jordan de Dalden who brought with her substantial land in the Weardale region as well as the manors of Dalden, Seaham, Ryhope and Seaton, which together were valued at around £44 per annum.[61] Unfortunately, as Christine Newman has pointed out, the 'lack of coherent estate accounts and rentals has inhibited any major study of the family's land-holding practices and financial resources' and there is 'little evidence to show the full extent and actual economic management of the Bowes's patrimony during this period'.[62] By the end of the fifteenth century, the Bowes had made several other marriages to prominent north-eastern families, including the daughters of Henry, Lord Clifford, and Richard Conyers, accumulating a further five manors in this fashion and so securing the family's status as one of the most important landholding families in the palatinate of Durham by the sixteenth century.[63]

The Thorntons were the largest purchasers of manors from outside the traditional landed elite of the Durham countryside in the fifteenth century, and will be returned to again in chapter 5 in relation to the much broader phenomenon of mercantile purchases into rural society. However, Roger Thornton's acquisitions must be explored here first because they went on to secure the financial standing of an ancient Durham family by the end of the fifteenth century. This rich Newcastle merchant was perfectly positioned to take advantage of the troubles of many of his rural neighbours in the fifteenth century, which provided a unique opportunity for the widespread accumulation of manors for someone with ready cash and access to credit markets. Roger Thornton was a bailiff, alderman and mayor of Newcastle and one of its wealthiest inhabitants in the fifteenth century, accumulating numerous manors in the first half of the fifteenth century.[64] For example, in 1369 John Birtley died seized of High Friarside, which comprised of eight messuages and eight score

59 Liddy, *The Bishopric of Durham*, p. 42.

60 At the time of an inquisition in 1516, Ralph Bowes was said to hold the manors of Barnes, Berford, Bertfield, Bireside, Cleatlam, Clowcroft, Chilton Magna, Dalden, Eggleston, Elton, Hilton, Hamilden, Hepton, Medomsley, Middleton in Teesdale, Newton, Osmondcroft, Pavilion, Plawsworth, Stainton, Streatlam, Willington and various other moieties and parcels of land within the county. TNA, DURH 3/3, f. 36; DKR 44, pp. 330–1.

61 Surtees, *History of Durham*, vol. 1, p. 235; Newman, 'The Bowes of Streatlam', p. 28.

62 Newman, 'The Bowes of Streatlam', p. 13 and p. 29.

63 Ibid., pp. 31–2.

64 Liddy, *The Bishopric of Durham*, p. 56.

acres of land, valued at 20s.[65] The Thorntons purchased the manor sometime afterwards, along with Lyntz and Colfield which were parcels of the same manor.[66] The manor of Ludworth was held by Walter Ludworth in 1347, and was exchanged several times before it was eventually alienated by Thomas Holden to Roger Thornton in 1438, whilst the manor of Sheraton was acquired in an equally complex series of transactions.[67] The descent of the manor of Folansby was much simpler, it having been held by John Farnacres in 1339, his son Thomas who died in 1359, and his son William who alienated it to Roger Thornton sometime thereafter.[68]

Fugerhouse was acquired in a different fashion. In Hatfield's survey this land was included amongst the free tenancies of the manor of Whickham, held by the earls of Northumberland, and contained approximately 100 acres, but its real value was in a coal pit which the bishop leased to the earl for the rent of £26 13s 4d.[69] In 1405, Roger Thornton was granted the manor in the letters patent of Henry IV for his role 'in the defence of Newcastle' against Henry Percy, earl of Northumberland.[70] Another acquisition was made in the early fifteenth century when, in 1411, William Swalwell quitclaimed all of his father's lands to John Fenwick, chaplain, a trustee for Roger Thornton. Several more manors followed in similar fashion. The manors of Axwell, Redheugh and Bradley near Medomsley were held by the heirs of Hugh Redheugh in Hatfield's survey, and the IPM on the death of Hugh Redheugh in 1391 confirms this.[71] His brother, Thomas Redheugh alienated these manors to Roger Thornton, who received a pardon for purchasing without licence in 1411.[72] The manor of Stokerley Crook was described in Hatfield's survey as belonging to John Kirkby, whose heirs alienated the manor and vill to Roger Thornton.[73] The manors of Preston le Skerne, Little Chilton, Bradbury and Isle also passed from one of the most prominent former mercantile families, the de la Poles, into the rising house of the Thorntons.[74]

65 TNA, DURH 3/2, f. 82v; DKR 45, pp. 161–2.

66 By the death of Roger Thornton the elder the manor was said to contain three messuages, 100 acres of arable, ten of meadow, 100 of woodland, and twenty acres of pasture, Surtees, *History of Durham*, vol. 2, p. 233.

67 In 1347 the manor was said to contain four carucates of land, held of the bishop by the fourth part of a knight's fee and of a tenement and sixteen acres held of the prior of Durham by 12s, TNA, DURH 3/2, f. 30v; DKR 45, p. 228. Surtees, *History of Durham*, vol. 1, pp. 123–4.

68 TNA, DURH 3/2, f. 31v; DKR 45, p. 193; Surtees, *History of Durham*, vol. 1, pp. 123–4.

69 Greenwell (ed.), *Bishop Hatfield's Survey*, p. 93.

70 Liddy, *The Bishopric of Durham*, p. 56.

71 TNA, DURH 3/2 f. 114; DKR 45, p. 255.

72 TNA, DURH 3/2, f. 167; DKR 45, p. 269.

73 John Kirkby held the manor of Stokerley Crook, the vill of Crokheugh and 100 acres of arable and woodland, Greenwell (ed.), *Bishop Hatfield's Survey*, p. 124. The heirs of Kirkby alienated Crook to Roger Thornton, who died seized of the manor containing two messuages, 120 acres of arable, five of meadow, eight of pasture and twelve acres of woodland: Surtees, *History of Durham*, vol. 2, p. 352.

74 In 1381, Preston le Skerne was described as a messuage, three tofts, twenty oxgangs of land, five acres of meadow, and a watermill: Surtees, *History of Durham*, vol. 3, pp. 330–1.

The Thorntons were thus one of the most prolific purchasers of manors in the county during the early fifteenth century, second only to the newly created earls of Westmorland, because their wealth acquired in Newcastle meant they were one of the few families in the region who could afford such extensive purchases when others were no doubt struggling to make ends meet. Indeed, John Leland, the sixteenth-century antiquarian, described Roger Thornton as 'the richest merchant that ever was dwelling in Newcastle'.[75] Chapter 5 looks at this influx of mercantile wealth into rural society in further depth, exploring the social position of merchants and their motives for making such inroads into landed society, but Roger Thornton's purchases were to have a profound impact upon the Lumley family. In 1381, Sir Robert Lumley held the manors of Little Lumley, Murton, Cold Hesleden, Butterby, Stranton and Housefield in the palatinate of Durham, which made him one of the more important landowners in the region, but certainly not paramount.[76] It was the inheritance of the Thweng estate in Yorkshire, which descended to this Robert Lumley through his wife Lucy upon the death of her brother Thomas de Thweng, that gave the family a combined income of over £500 per annum, and 'it is little wonder' that Ralph Lumley was summoned to Parliament as Lord Lumley from 1384.[77] However, the involvement of Ralph, Lord Lumley, in the Epiphany rising of 1400 against Henry IV saw the family's title lapse until 1461, even though the Lumleys' lands had been restored in 1405, and so their position was not as secure as it at first seems.

Regardless, the Lumleys were the second most important lay family in Durham society, but the strength of this claim was really in their additional Yorkshire lands. Within the palatinate, there was relatively little to separate the Lumleys from other members of the upper gentry like the Hiltons of Hylton, the Claxtons of Claxton and the Conyers of Sockburn, that was, at least, until the death of Roger Thornton in 1471. George, Lord Lumley, inherited the vast Thornton estate through his wife Elizabeth who was the sole daughter and heiress of Roger Thornton. This included the manors of Bradley, Bolam, Friarside, Croke, Axwell, Swalwell, Folansby, Bradbury, Isle, Ludworth, Redheugh, Preston le Skerne and Little Chilton, as well as lands and tenements scattered across a dozen other townships. Lord Lumley made one of the smartest matches in this period, virtually doubling his family's inheritance with his marriage to this wealthy heiress, who brought with her the vast accumulations of her father and grandfather.[78] Thus overnight the name of Thornton disappeared from the Durham countryside and Lord Lumley gained a more than ample dowry, which assured the family's position as the second most important family in the county.

75 Edith Milner (ed.), *Records of the Lumleys of Lumley Castle* (London, 1904), p. 24.

76 TNA, DURH 3/2, f. 106; DKR, 45, p. 229.

77 Milner (ed.), *Records of the Lumleys*, p. 10; Liddy, *The Bishopric of Durham*, p. 66.

78 TNA, DURH 3/2, f. 31v; DKR 45, p. 193. Indeed, such were the stakes involved that a quarrel arose concerning this succession in which Lord Lumley slew Giles Thornton, his wife's bastard brother, in a duel in Windsor Castle ditch. Surtees, *History of Durham*, vol. 2, pp. 153–64.

How far the above purchases were sheer opportunism is unclear, for there were definite attempts at building consolidated areas of landed power within the palatinate of Durham. As would be expected, the Nevilles purchased manors and land around the lordships of Raby and Brancepeth, whilst the Bowes did similarly around Streatlam, and the Lumleys around Lumley castle. It is also clear, however, that there were concentrations of land away from these traditional power-bases, such as the Neville manors of Dalton Piercy, Elwick, Newton Hansard, Stotfold and Swainston in the south-east of the county.[79] The Bowes family, by comparison, had a consolidated estate in the south-west of the county centred on Streatlam, but the marriage of Sir William Bowes with Maud brought the family important lands in Easington ward around Seaham and Dalton, whilst the marriage of Lord Lumley with the sole daughter and heiress of Roger Thornton brought the family a whole host of coal-bearing manors just to the south of the River Tyne.[80]

The knightly and aristocratic families of the palatinate of Durham, therefore, slowly accumulated manors from their less fortunate and smaller neighbours as well as from absentee landlords across the late fourteenth and early fifteenth centuries.[81] The Nevilles, Lumleys and Bowes gained the most across this period and went on to rise out of this group in rural society – the two former families rising into the peerage and the latter just failing in their attempts to create a barony centred on Coldingham Abbey in the sixteenth century.[82] The Nevilles made extensive purchases in the late fourteenth and early fifteenth centuries, whilst the latter two families acquired substantial dowries through marriage: in the case of the Bowes this happened twice and thus they acquired the Streatlam and Dalden inheritances, whilst the Lumleys secured the substantial properties acquired by the Thorntons. These larger landowners were certainly facing the same recession and hardship as others in the late fourteenth and fifteenth centuries, but those financial struggles also gave rise to opportunities for expansion. It was the knightly and aristocratic families of Durham, whose commercial connections often extended outside of the county, who had superior access to credit and capital. The late fourteenth and early fifteenth centuries were not only a period of great hardship for landowners but also a great period for estate-building for those with sufficient resources and resourcefulness to take advantage of the opportunities provided.

Fragmentation and Forfeiture in the Sixteenth Century

The fifteenth century may well have been a period of opportunity for building large estates in Durham but, in complete contrast, the sixteenth century was a time of

79 Surtees, *History of Durham*, vol. 3, pp. 88.

80 Newman, 'The Bowes of Streatlam', p. 28; Surtees, *History of Durham*, vol. 1, p. 235.

81 See chapter 4 for the causes and consequences of this for the parish gentry of the county.

82 Newman, 'The Bowes of Streatlam', p. 167.

hardship for many of the larger landowners in the palatinate. During the sixteenth century there was a fragmentation of the larger estates created by Durham's aristocracy in the previous century, with an increasing number of families holding anything from a portion of a manor to several manors, but very few possessing more than five manors.[83] In 1500, the Nevilles, Lumleys, Bowes, Hiltons, Eures, Claxtons and Conyers held in total some 113 manors, or around a half of the lay manors of the county, but by 1640 this group only accounted for 35 manors (Table 12).[84] The Claxtons of Claxton died out in the male line in the late-fifteenth century; the Nevilles forfeited their vast estate and the Claxtons of Old Park suffered for their involvement in the Rising of the North in 1569; John, Lord Lumley, sold off whole tracts of land to fund his various political activities from the mid-sixteenth century onwards; the Bowes suffered a divided inheritance; and the Conyers of Sockburn died out in the male line in the early seventeenth century. Each family thus found their own way to disaster, but financial problems, especially from the mid-sixteenth century onwards, are a common theme in the history of each of these families.

The single most obvious event which affected the composition of rural society in Durham was the Rising of the North in 1569, which saw the forfeiture of the Neville estate and the redistribution of many other minor estates.[85] In many ways, the downfall of the Nevilles was an event exogenous to the palatinate, inspired by a heady mixture of religious convictions, uncertainty and fear of the Elizabethan court, but this interpretation would underestimate the local concerns of many of the rebels.[86] In 1569 around 6,000 people from Durham and North Yorkshire joined under the banners of the earls of Northumberland and Westmorland to secure the restoration of Catholicism and make Mary I of Scotland queen of England. After a short military campaign the rebellion was brought to a swift conclusion, leading to the forfeiture of the Percy and Neville estates, the latter permanently. In the aftermath, Sir George Bowes, who had remained loyal to the Crown, ordered the execution of around 600 rebels, whilst the Crown received land worth some £5,300 per annum from attainted rebels, although much of this was entailed to the earl of Northumberland's brother whose family were eventually restored to the earldom.[87]

By comparison, Charles Neville, the sixth and last earl of Westmorland, died a penniless pensioner of Spain and his extensive lands in Durham, which had formed the largest lay estate with approximately a fifth of all lay manors in the county, rested in the hands of the Crown. The political spectrum of the region became significantly

83 TNA, DURH 3; DKR, 44 and 45.

84 See Table 12 above, p. 115.

85 Kesselring, *The Northern Rebellion of 1569*, pp. 118–43.

86 David Marcombe, 'A Rude and Heady People: the Local Community and the Rebellion of the Northern Earls', in David Marcombe (ed.), *The Last Principality: Politics, Religion and Society in the Bishopric of Durham, 1494–1660* (Nottingham, 1987), pp. 117–51.

87 For more on the Rising of the North, see Kesselring, *The Northern Rebellion of 1569*, pp. 118–43.

narrower, at least in terms of the sources of local aristocratic patronage, and James has argued that this calamity was crucial in transforming Durham from a feudal to a civil society focused upon the Crown's representative in the region, the bishops of Durham.[88] In 1603, for example, the former Neville lordships of Raby and Brancepeth brought the Crown an income of £396 4s 8d and £480 2s 3d respectively, which, if added to the £265 9s 11d received from the lordship of Barnard Castle, the £429 9s 4d from former monastic lands and the £114 19s 4d from lands forfeited by gentry families attainted after 1569, made the Crown the largest landowner in the region after the two ecclesiastical estates.[89]

Although it is difficult to assess the prosperity and condition of the tenantry on the Neville estates, the Homberston survey of 1570 noted the general prosperity of the husbandmen tenants. The tenants at Brancepeth, for example, were said to be 'wealthy and substantial before this late rebellion' and 'have great waste ground to keep their cattle and plenty enclosed ground for the succour and maintenance of them in winter', with the surrounding country said to be 'plentiful of all things, the soil good and bountiful for corn.'[90] David Reid, who explored the Crown lordships in Durham from the late sixteenth century onwards, concluded that the tenants had 'never had it so good' and that 'they could hardly fail to have profited from low fixed rents and rising prices.'[91] This extended to the mineral resources of these lands, with a survey of the Crown's coal mines in 1621 noting that the leases of Sir Peter Riddell and others were a thirtieth of their real annual value, whilst an earlier survey in 1611 had shown that coal mines were being let at £137 6s 8d, while the clear profit to lessees was £1,053 7s 4d.[92] Once again, it was the Newcastle coal merchants who benefited from the take-off of the coal industry rather than the Crown or the Church.[93]

The Crown's policy towards its tenants shared many similarities with that of the Nevilles since they were motivated by the protection of the border and so did not wish to unduly burden their northern tenants. The Crown's tenants in the lordships

88 James, *Family, Lineage, and Civil Society*, p. 178. It is questionable how easy the bishops of Durham found this in reality as their real income was being eaten away by inflation, as were their sources of patronage by the Crown's long-leasing of bishopric manors. See chapter 2 above for more on the position of the bishops of Durham in the sixteenth century.

89 Barnard Castle had been forfeited to the Crown in 1471 after the defeat of Richard Neville, earl of Warwick. Gentry families whose lands were attainted include the Tempests, Swinburns, Trollopes, Claxtons, Blakistons and Conyers. Reid, *Durham Crown Lordships*, pp. 38–9. See, for example the accounts of land late in the possession of the earl of Westmorland and other attainted persons, TNA, Accounts of the land of the Earl of Westmorland and other attainted persons, SC 6/ELIZI/628.

90 TNA, Homberston Survey of the lands of the Earls of Northumberland and Westmorland, E164/37, p. 13.

91 Reid, *Durham Crown Lordships*, p. 20.

92 Ibid., pp. 18–19.

93 See chapter 2 for the difficulties the bishops of Durham experienced with their coal mines because of the Grand Lease, and chapter 5 for more on the Newcastle coal merchants.

of Barnard Castle and Middleham, for example, understood that they held by tenant-right, a customary tenure which guaranteed low rents, small fixed renewal fines and rights of inheritance, along with a provision to perform border service. Much like the dean and chapter's dispute with its tenants, the Crown refused to recognise this tenure, arguing that its Barnard Castle tenants 'pretend by colour of tenant right to have their farms to them and their heirs by prescription whereof no record appears' and that as a result they were mere tenants at will.[94] However, it was not in the Crown's interest to alienate the tenantry of the region and so the commissioners in 1564 were to 'treat with the tenants thereof' to take leases for 'life or lives or forty years', with lessees in the lordship of Barnard Castle to 'pay at first entry one year's rent only for fine in consideration of his accustomed service on the Borders and at the change of every Prince and Lord, death of the tenant or alienation one year's rent more by way of fine or gressum'.[95] Furthermore, after the decease of her husband a wife was entitled to 'her widow's estate in the same lands according to the custom of the manor', whilst the Crown was 'to covenant in every lease that the eldest son of a tenant or lessee for a term of life, lives or years shall after the lessee's decease have the preferment of the lands formerly in his father's tenure and under like terms'.[96] In the short term, therefore, former Neville tenants would find that many of their tenurial obligations were much as they had been under the earls of Westmorland, with no rent increase until the early seventeenth century. This must have come as a relief to the tenants in the lordships of Raby and Brancepeth because the Homberston survey noted that their lands were 'very good and finable' and that 'tenants hold all by indenture for terms of years', and so they undoubtedly viewed any change of landlord with wary apprehension.[97]

Fixed low rents and entry fines, guaranteed inheritance and border service should have meant that life continued much as before for many tenants in the lordships of Brancepeth and Raby. However, the replacement of the Nevilles as a local aristocratic landlord with the non-resident Crown had a considerable impact upon other areas of their lives. In 1614, for example, there was a commission into complaints from the tenants about the various abuses of power which Henry Sanderson, the constable, was accused of committing, which ranged from the felling of timber to the excessive hunting of deer in the parks of Brancepeth.[98] Undoubtedly part of the motivation for these numerous complaints was that Sanderson, as a Puritan, was busy persecuting Catholic recusants within Brancepeth parish with particular zeal, but the tenants

94 See chapter 2 for the tenant-right dispute between the dean and chapter and their tenants in the 1570s.

95 *Calendar of Patent Rolls Elizabeth, 1563–66*, pp. 182–4 and pp. 213–15.

96 Ibid., pp. 213–15.

97 TNA, E164/37, p. 13.

98 For the context of Brancepeth parish see Hamilton, 'Social Networks, Families and Neighbourhoods', chapter 2.

had underlying complaints about how other aspects of their lives had changed since the attainder of the last earl of Westmorland. Thomas Lonsdale of Helmington Row, aged eighty-four, for example, recalled how the county sheriffs could not serve warrants directly on tenants of Brancepeth lordship but had to give them to the earl's bailiffs to execute, a situation which led to the sheriff's bailiff being apprehended by the earl's officers and tenants when he circumvented this hierarchy. Lonsdale recalled how this bailiff was then made to eat the legal summons before being 'set upon his horse with his face backwards towards the horse's tail and so sent away out of the lordship.'[99] The tenants of Brancepeth had also lost some of their financial privileges, such as their freedom from tolls at Durham and Bishop Auckland, and their right to purchase coal from the bishop's mines at Hargill, near the Railey pits, at 4d per wain load since time out of mind.

These privileges were lost 'little by little' after the 'rebellion and attainder of Charles late earl of Westmorland', as was the right to buy cheap coal. The bishops' lessees of the Hargill pit tried to charge the Brancepeth tenants 8d per load whereupon the tenants offered to load coal at 6d per load and were 'forcibly resisted by the tenants of the said coal pits and many blows and some hurts were given on both sides', but an agreement of 6d per load was eventually made.[100] The tenants also blamed themselves for the loss of some of these privileges with John Rippon noting that they have 'been by degrees denied the said liberty and freedom and as he thinketh by their own weakness in this behalf are now altogether debarred thereof', whilst Thomas Mayor remembered how the tenants refused to pay the tolls at first but they had slowly agreed to the imposition.[101] Being a tenant of the Neville family in the sixteenth century was more than just an expectation of cheap rents, encompassing a whole range of financial and legal privileges; without the earls to defend them, these privileges were quickly eroded by the encroachment of the bishops' lessees and the indifference of the Crown. As Dorothy Hamilton concluded, 'these depositions give a clear sense of the dissatisfaction of the tenants with the loss of the customs and life-style associated with being tenants of the most powerful nobleman in the County Palatine of Durham.'[102]

With the defence of the border no longer a priority after 1603, the tenants of Brancepeth, Raby and Barnard Castle would soon find that even their traditional

99 TNA, Special Commission, Inquisition into the Privileges and Customs of Brancepeth Lordship, E178/3765, ff. 38–9.

100 The following all agreed with Thomas Lonsdale's deposition: Thomas Johnson of Crook and Billey Row, 79 years old; Percival Markendall of Willington, 76 years old; Roger Dowthwaite of Willington, 58 years old; Thomas Mayor of Helmeden Row, 58 years old; and Charles Watson and John White of Brancepeth, 69 and 68 years old respectively.

101 TNA, Special Commission, Inquisition into the Privileges and Customs of Brancepeth Lordship, E178/3765, f. 40.

102 Hamilton, 'Social Networks, Families and Neighbourhoods', p. 97.

Table 13. Rents and Valuations of the Lordships of Raby and Brancepeth, 1607

Place	Rent per annum	Value per annum
Raby	£35 3s 4d	£179 3s 10d
Staindrop	£51 17s 8d	£221 12s 8d
Ingleton	£12 18s	£76 7s 4d
Wackerfield	£18 18s 7d	£141 3s
Langton	£6 16s 8d	£34 10s
Houghton	£17 11s 10d	£109 13s 4d
Summerhouse	£23 12s 7d	£97 16s 4d
Eggleston	£42 15s 2d	£181 6s 11d
Langley	£53 6s 8d	£360 8s 4d
Shotton	£7 1s	£51 16s 6d
Woodland	£5 12s 8d	£44 13s 4d
Bolam	£1 16s 11d	£19 14s
Cockfield	£6 13s 1d	£43 6s 11d
Brancepeth	£36 11s 5d	£200 3s 1d
East Brandon	£33 8s 8d	£213 3s 4d
Crook and Billy Row	£20 0s 1d	£177 4s 1d
Thornley	£9 8s 8d	£63 16s 10d
Willington	£13 10s 1d	£92 17s 5d
Stockley	£18 8s 1d	£137 16s 2d
Eldon	£44 13s 8d	£256 8s 10d
Helmington Row	£12 7s 2d	£93 6s
Whitworth	£7 14s 1d	£54 1s
Byers Green	£28 11s	£198 10s
Helm Park	£8 10s	£75 0s 1d
Hedley	£2 1s	21 10s 6d
Cornsay	£21 13s 2d	£290 12s 4d
Elwick	£33 8s 4d	£163 16s 6d
Dalton Piercy	£25 6s 10d	£125 8s
Total	**£600 6s 4d**	**£3,725 11s**

Source: Survey of Crown Lands in Durham and Yorkshire, 1607, TNA, LR2/192.

rents were no longer protected from scrutiny. In 1607, the Crown commissioned a new survey to explore the potential for rent increases which noted that on average tenants were paying rents which were worth less than a sixth of the true value of the land (Table 13). The single most valuable lease was that of Waterhouse held by John Trollope who paid a rent of £8 per annum for 927 acres of land which was valued at £151 per annum.[103] More typical, however, were the tenants of Dalton Piercy who each held 30 acres of meadow and 24 acres of arable land spread across three fields and with pasturage for fifteen cattle; they each paid 53s 9d per annum, but these holdings were valued at £13 17s per annum.[104] No action to increase revenues was taken at this stage however.

Several years after the above surveys, the Crown sought to recreate the influence of the Neville family in the form of Robert Carr, soon to be earl of Somerset, who was granted the three Durham lordships in 1613 in an attempt to produce a loyal northern magnate, but this experiment failed shortly afterwards when Somerset fell out of favour.[105] Somerset's own man, Thomas Emerson, became steward of Raby and Brancepeth during this time and would survive the downfall of his master before going on to suggest a method for a sixfold increase in rents, roughly in line with the above survey and the inflationary trends of the sixteenth and early seventeenth centuries, which the former Neville tenants had largely been protected from until now. In many cases this would take the form of a doubling of the old rent, with a fine of as much as 80 years' rent for a lease of 40 years: a significant demand given the relative stagnation of rents on the two ecclesiastical estates in the region. The resulting rent increase brought the predicted revenues from the three lordships up from £892 to £2,155 15s 8d per annum by 1623. The example of Stockley in Table 14 shows the large entry fines now demanded of tenants who had previously been expected to pay a more symbolic gressum of one or two years' rent; a tenant holding land with a rent of around 20s per annum was now expected to find £100 in three annual instalments of £33 6s 8d.[106]

As Reid has noted, 'it soon became apparent however that it was one thing suddenly to impose greatly "improved" rents and quite another to collect them', with arrears accumulating to £4,957 9s 8d in 1622 and reaching £6,769 13s by 1628.[107] Sir Henry Vane, who had replaced Emerson as steward, agreed a new deal with the tenants whereby much of their indebtedness would be written off and they would take out new leases for three lives or thirty-one years, with a doubling of the old rent and a fine of 25–30 years' rent, which the tenants appear to have found more agreeable. The final compositions made at Stockley in Table 14, for example, show the smaller entry fines which were now being demanded of tenants.[108] It was at about this time – in 1626 – that the dean and chapter replaced their policy of taking three years' ancient rent as an entry fine with three years' improved value as a fine, as

103 TNA, Survey of Crown Lands in Durham and Yorkshire, 1607, LR2/192, f. 66a.

104 TNA, LR2/192, f. 67b.

105 Reid, *Durham Crown Lordships*, pp. 44–5.

106 TNA, A Book of Fines Compounded for by Sir Henry Vane and other Commissioners, 1617–27, LR2/214, ff. 137–8.

107 Reid, *Durham Crown Lordships*, p. 47.

108 TNA, LR2/214, ff. 137–8.

Table 14. Rents and Entry Fines on the Manor of Stockley, 1617–27

Tenant	Rent	Fine	Payments of fines over three years	
Cawen Forrest	3s 4d	£20	£6 13s 4d	1618, 1619, 1620
Robert Fawden	17s 8d	£80	£26 13s 4d	1618, 1619, 1620
William Fawden	20s 11d	£100	£33 6s 8d	1618, 1619, 1620
Raphe Wilson	16s 4d	£70	£23 6s 8d	1618, 1619, 1620
Oswald Mason	20s	£90	£30	1618, 1619, 1620
George Tripps	20s 11d	£100	£33 6s 8d	Blank
Martin Nicholson	16s 2d	£60	£20	1618, 1618, 1619
Robert Johnson	26s 10d	£100	£33 6s 8d	1618, 1619, 1620
William Sley	16s 2d	£80	£26 13s 4d	1618, 1619, 1620
William Bulsey	16s 2d	£80	£26 13s 4d	1618, 1619, 1620
Humphrey Wall	27s 7d	£100	£33 6s 8d	1618, 1619, 1620
Perceval Markendall	27s 1d	£100	£33 6s 8d	1618, 1619, 1620
Robert Lydall	8d	£8	53s 4d	1619, 1620, 1620
George Bell	3s	£10	66s 8d	1619, 1620, 1620
George Colson	8d	£8	53s 4d	1619, 1620, 1620
Nicholas Tyndall	8s 3d	£37	£12 6s 8d	1619, 1620, 1620
Robert Marley	26s 8d	£70	£23 6s 8d	1620, 1620, 1621
George Comyn	8d	30s	10s	1622, 1623, 1623
George Tripps	20s 11d	£60	£20	1623, 1624, 1625
Nicholas Fawden	6s 9d	£5	£1 13s 4d	1625, 1626, 1627
George Brabant	5s 5d	£5	£1 13s 4d	1625, 1626, 1627
John Brack	3s 4d	£3	20s	1625, 1626, 1627
John Hull	4s 1d	£4	£1 6s 8d	1625, 1626, 1627
Nicholas Fewster*	26s 8d	£30	£10	1625, 1626, 1627
George Wilkinson	17s 2d	£20	£6 13s 4d	1625, 1626, 1627
Total	**£17 13s 7d**	**£1,241 10s**		

* Nicholas Fewster agreed to pay double the ancient rent from this composition onwards.

Source: A Book of Fines Compounded for by Sir Henry Vane and other Commissioners, 1617–27, TNA, LR2/214, ff. 137–8.

landlords were slowly able to redress the balance of rental payments in their favour in the early seventeenth century.[109]

The Crown's financial needs would ultimately dictate the destiny of these three lordships which were sold, except for the castles, parks and demesne, for a total

109 It was also in the first decades of the seventeenth century that the ninth earl of Northumberland was able to increase his rent rolls. Batho, 'The Finances of an Elizabethan Nobleman', pp. 433–50.

of £25,000 to the City of London, who in turn sold the lands to local gentry and Newcastle merchants. However, given the recent agreement between the Crown and its tenants to take new leases in the 1620s, much of this land was not improvable, at least in the short term. Indeed, Reid estimated that the Crown had managed to raise over £20,000 from the fines for these new compositions, whilst the new owners of these lands would only receive a rent twice the ancient customary value, at least whilst these leases still ran, and they still had to pay an annual fee-farm to the Crown of one year's old rent.[110] In 1636, Ralph Cole, a wealthy Newcastle coal merchant, set about purchasing the manors of Brancepeth and Stockley, along with Brancepeth castle and the extensive parks there, from the original purchasers. The Coles do not seem to have challenged their tenants' rents, acting 'like traditional lords of the manor, continuing the customs of the manor, including the manor courts, and even the medieval-style views of frankpledge, up until the end of the seventeenth century', even 'trying to claim the right to stray animals because the right had belonged to his predecessor, the earl of Westmorland'.[111] This is in stark contrast to Sir Henry Vane who had purchased Barnard Castle, Raby castle and many of the other manors of these lordships. Already by 1641, he had increased numerous rents, such as at Staindrop Carres where the ancient rent of £27 2s 8d had been increased by £82 7s 4d, and the colliery at Cockfield where he had increased the rent by £90, although the potential for profitable increases was still hindered by the previous compositions of the 1620s.[112]

It was the parks of Raby and Brancepeth and the demesne of Barnard Castle which offered the best opportunities for commercial exploitation, primarily because of these recently agreed Crown leases on much of the remaining lands in the lordships. In the Homberston survey of 1570, the two parks at Brancepeth had been described as 'well paled and a very park like ground', containing fallow deer and 'many wild cattle which are for the most part all white and black spotted'.[113] The three parks at Raby were described in similar terms, seemingly well stocked with fallow deer, but the primary difference was that these parks were described as 'very barren of wood' compared to those at Brancepeth which were 'well planted with timber and wood'.[114] An inventory of Henry Neville, the late earl of Westmorland, noted a total of 1,313 sheep, 112 cattle and 15 horses spread across land at Langley Chase and Staindrop Carres, and the parks at Raby and Brancepeth in 1564, although somewhat surprisingly these latter only accounted for 29 cattle in the West Park and 150 sheep in the

110 Reid, *Durham Crown Lordships*, p. 50.

111 Hamilton, 'Social Networks, Families and Neighbourhoods', p. 358. See chapter 5 for more on the Coles and the Newcastle coal merchants.

112 DUL, ASC, Mickleton and Spearman MS 7, A Rental of the Lordship of Barnard Castle and Raby, 1641, ff. 1–14.

113 TNA, E164/37, p. 13.

114 Ibid., p. 68.

East Park of Raby, and 7 cows and 13 horses in the two parks at Brancepeth.[115] By the 1640s, however, the parks had been disparked and were producing a respectable income for their new owners. In 1646, for example, Nicholas Cole received £508 9s for Brancepeth park against the king's fee-farm rent of £44 6s 8d, whilst Raby park had a fee-farm rent of £51 10s but was producing an income of £324 17s 2d for Sir Henry Vane in 1641.[116] The former Neville tenants were, therefore, paying rents and fines much closer to the commercial value of the land by the middle of the seventeenth century, but the difficulty the Crown faced in increasing these rents shows the problems rentier landlords were confronted by in this period, even when their tenants held land by 21-year leases and were considered to be 'very good and finable'.[117]

The Lumleys suffered not from outright forfeiture like the Nevilles but from the long list of imprudent sales made by John, Lord Lumley, who, in trying to fund the extravagant expenditure of his father-in-law, the earl of Arundel, and his own substantial art and book collections, slowly sold off the family's patrimonial estate in Durham.[118] John, Lord Lumley, married Jane, the daughter of the earl of Arundel, and it was through these connections that Lumley was introduced into the court, being made a Knight of the Bath two days before the coronation of Queen Mary. Although many of the financial difficulties John, Lord Lumley, experienced were caused by events outside of Durham, they were exacerbated by his stagnant income, whilst their consequences reverberated throughout rural society in the region. The nineteenth-century antiquarian Surtees recounted how the earl of Arundel thought that his son-in-law Lord Lumley had sold and mortgaged 'most part of his own lands, tenements, hereditaments and patrimony for the discharge and payment of his (the earl's) debts and causes'.[119] Contemporary letters from the likes of Guerau de Spes, the Spanish ambassador, make it clear that the political machinations of the earl of Arundel and the duke of Norfolk were buoyed by their association with Lord Lumley. In 1569, for example, Guerau de Spes noted that the former were:

> begging me to let them have a sum of money, as the Duke and the Earl are deeply in debt. As Lord Lumley, son-in-law of the one and brother-in-law of the other, is also concerned in it, I do not see any great objection to take their pledge.[120]

115 Given that the Homberston survey just a few years later makes reference to the fact that both parks were well stocked with fallow deer and wild cattle, it seems likely that the Nevilles possessed more livestock than is included in this inventory. TNA, Inventory of the property of Henry Neville, late Earl of Westmorland , DL 44/96.

116 Reid, *Durham Crown Lordships*, p. 55. DUL, ASC, Mickleton and Spearman MS 7, ff. 1–14.

117 TNA, E164/37, p. 13.

118 In 1525, Lord Lumley lost the office of master forester and the coroner of Chester ward, which the family had been linked with for over a century, see James, *Family, Lineage and Civil Society*, pp. 43–4.

119 Surtees, *History of Durham*, vol. 2, pp. 153–64.

120 Milner (ed.), *Records of the Lumleys*, p. 55.

Lord Lumley also bore considerable expenses because of his jointly taking on the 'Florentine's debt' with the earl of Arundel, which was described in 1570 as a 'debt of £11,245 16s 8d owing to King Henry VIII by the Florentines to be paid by £500 a year.'[121] This debt was a source of long-standing financial difficulty for John Lumley, who spent the next forty years of his life in negotiations with the Crown in attempts to lessen his financial obligation. As will be seen, it is far from clear that the 'new Lord Lumley would be enormously enriched through his marriage to one of the co-heiresses of the earl of Arundel', as Mervyn James thought.[122]

John, Lord Lumley, was involved in both the Rising of the North and the Ridolfi plot and shared in the displeasure his father-in-law incurred during the late 1560s and early 1570s, especially with his involvement in the plans to place Mary Queen of Scots on the English throne, and he was repeatedly imprisoned in the Tower of London.[123] He was later released and spent the rest of his life in 'the pomp, pride and circumstance of ancient nobility', much of which was spent in the south of England, especially at Nonsuch Palace, Surrey, before returning to Lumley castle and undertaking considerable rebuilding there.[124] If there was anywhere in England to retire to in pomp, then Nonsuch was an appropriate place to do so, having cost Henry VIII some £24,536 7s 7d by 1545. The earl of Arundel and John Lumley finished its construction and furnishing, so that by 1598, the German Paul Hentzner described the palace as being built 'with an excess of magnificence and elegance, even to ostentation.'[125]

In order to meet the increasing costs of his life at court, the extravagant expenses of his father-in-law and the rising costs of his own aristocratic lifestyle in this period of high inflation, John Lumley was forced to sell the majority of his inheritance: not just the vast estate accumulated by the Thorntons during the fifteenth century and many of the lands inherited from Arundel but also much of the ancestral lands of his family. Murton, for example, was alienated to his husbandmen tenants of the manor in eight portions in 1566 for £341 6s 8d, reserving a free rent of £21 6s 8d.[126] It is of particular significance that it was Lumley's own husbandmen tenants who purchased portions of this manor, as agricultural profits slowly trickled down the social scale.[127] The manor of Bainbridge Holme was similarly alienated by John Lumley, with a fishery in the Wear, to Thomas Whitehead, gentleman, for £276 12s 4d in 1560.[128] The

121 Ibid., p. 64.

122 James, *Family, Lineage and Civil Society*, p. 50.

123 John Guy, *Tudor England* (Oxford, 1988), pp. 273–77.

124 Surtees, *History of Durham*, vol. 2, pp. 153–164.

125 Leo Gooch, *A Complete Pattern of Nobility: John, Lord Lumley, c.1534–1609* (Sunderland, 2009), p. 20.

126 The purchasers were: Richard Rede, Thomas Yonge, Thomas Shadforth, Anthony Dune, John Gregson, William Unthank, John Shaklock, and John Robinson; Surtees, *History of Durham*, vol. 1, pp. 8–9.

127 See chapter 7 below for more on these yeoman families, especially the Shadforths.

128 Surtees, *History of Durham*, vol. 1, p. 234.

manor of Ludworth, valued at £22 per annum on the death of George, Lord Lumley, in 1511, was alienated to Richard Bellasis of Morton.[129] The manor of Twizel was sold to Humphrey Cole, goldsmith, who in turn sold the manor on to the Tempests.[130] A whole host of other manors were disposed of during this flurry of sales by John, Lord Lumley. The manor of High Friarside was alienated to James Rawe, merchant of Newcastle, for £243 in 1562, whilst the manor of Butterby was similarly sold to another Newcastle merchant, Christopher Chaytor, who died seized of the manor in 1591. Waldridge manor was alienated in 1607, shortly before Lumley's death, to George Smith, whose descendant Thomas Smith appeared amongst the disclaimers at St George's Visitation in 1615.[131] The list of these sizeable sales goes on: the manors of Swalwell and Axwell were alienated to Matthew Ogle, gentleman; the manor of Bradley near Medomsley was sold to the Newtons; the manors of Bradbury and Isle were alienated to the Nevilles in the sixteenth century for they appear in the forfeiture of Charles, earl of Westmorland, in 1569; the manor of Folansby was alienated to the Hiltons, with Sir Thomas Hilton holding the manor and vill there in 1561; the manor of Bolam was alienated in parcels to a whole host of small freeholders; and the manors of Stranton and Seaton Carew were alienated to Sir Thomas Gresham, who settled his estates on his wife Anne Gresham in 1577.[132]

There was a definite trend in the overall balance of these transactions which not only saw the slow and steady alienation of John, Lord Lumley's inheritance to those of a lower social status, but also the fragmentation of landownership within county Durham.[133] These manors which in the early sixteenth century had been in the hands of a single aristocratic family had, by the death of John Lumley in 1609, come to rest in the hands of nearly a dozen different families. Several of these families belonged to the knightly group of the palatinate who were following the trends laid down by their ancestors in the fifteenth century, but a number of newer groups were emerging as purchasers across the sixteenth century. Gentlemen were now purchasing their way back into the countryside on a scale matched only by the alienations of this social group in the late fourteenth and early fifteenth century, whilst a wide variety of Newcastle merchants and even husbandmen were amongst the purchasers. The increasing ability of these sections of society to make such extensive purchases is

129 TNA, DURH 3/3, f. 5; DKR 44, pp. 453–4. The Bellasis family are returned to in chapter 4, for they were one of the wealthier and more prominent families of the Durham gentry who increasingly profited from the financial struggles of the Lumleys and the bishops of Durham.

130 Surtees, *History of Durham*, vol. 2, p. 199.

131 Ibid., p. 196.

132 Ibid., pp. 153–64.

133 Murton was sold to his husbandmen tenants; Bolam was alienated to various small freeholders; Twizel, Butterby and High Friarside were sold to merchants; Hamilden, Swalwell, Axwell, Waldridge, Bainbridge Holme and Bradley near Medomsley were alienated to gentlemen; Ludworth, Folansby, Stranton and Seaton Carew were sold to knights; and only Bradbury and Isle were alienated to an earl, who very quickly forfeited them.

Table 15. Land Sold by John, Lord Lumley, in the Bishopric of Durham

Land Sold	Rent	Land Remaining Unsold	Rent
Hawthorn	£3 6s	Newcastle	£5 9s 5d
Cleadon	11s 9d	Lumley	£48
Rykendell	£3 15s	Murton*	£21 6s 8d
Housefield and Wearmouth	£5	Hesleden	£19
Harverton	26s 8d	Coal pits about Swalwell	£30
Ludworth	£24	Waldridge	2s
Butterby	£18 13s	Woodstonhouse	£4 10s 8d
Swalwell and Axwell	£16	Chester	£6
Bradley	£4 0s 12d	**Total of Land Unsold**	£134 9s 9d
Colehouse	17s 8d		
Spenne	20s 4d		
Bishopton	£3 6s 8d		
Whessoe and Ringfield	8s		
Windlestone	£4 0s		
Durham	33s 4d		
Darlington	£3 6s 8d		
Pichard	£4		
Shelmore	26s 8d		
Rykendell	£3 15s 1d		
Crook	27s 8d		
Friarside	£5 9s		
Haughton	24s 4d		
Sheraton	£7 13s 8d		
Foxden	7s 0d		
Bradbury	£28 3s 2d		
The Isle	£20		
(Preston le) Skerne	£4 5s 4d		
Little Chilton	£4 9s 8d		
Bolam	£12 4s 9d		
Fishburn	40s		
Gateshead	35s 10d		
Newcastle	£18		
Stranton	£112		
Total of Land Sold	£323		

* Murton was sold to the sitting tenants with a reserve rent of £21 6s 8d.

Source: Rentals and Accounts of John, Lord Lumley, 1532–1608, Surrey History Centre 836/2.

explored in greater depth in the following chapters, but it is noteworthy that even Lumley's own husbandmen tenants were amongst these purchasers as fixed rents and high inflation greatly benefited those directly working the land. A note written by John, Lord Lumley, late in his life lists the rental income of land sold during this period, estimating that £30 worth of land was sold in Northumberland; £323 worth of land in the bishopric of Durham; and £116 worth of land in Yorkshire.[134]

In total, therefore, the land sold by John, Lord Lumley, and listed in Table 15 represented over half his rental income from the north of England, the bulk of which came from within the palatinate of Durham.[135] The rents, moreover, are comparable to the rent rolls of his medieval ancestors, showing little signs of the inflation which was rapidly eroding their real value. Nor are there many signs within much of the surviving accounting material of direct agriculture being practised. For example, a list of livestock at Lumley Park in 1542 includes a pitifully small inventory of forty-five cows, twenty-seven calves, fifteen sheep and ten horses – numbers not even sufficient to meet his household requirements let alone to suggest commercial production on any large scale.[136] The consequences of this meant that in 1588/89, for example, John Lumley spent £1,338 on food alone, a staggering sum given that by this stage in his life he had largely withdrawn from court and its attendant expenses.[137] Undoubtedly, many of these sales were prompted by his financial needs arising from his political machinations, but it is no coincidence that they also took place during the 1560s and '70s when inflation was increasingly hurting rentier landlords.[138]

On the earl of Arundel's death in 1580, John, Lord Lumley, as his sole executor and residuary legatee, inherited not only Nonsuch Palace and considerable lands in the south of England, but also his father-in-law's debts. Out of the lands valued at £1,900 per annum on the earl's death, the earl of Surrey acquired lands to the value of £700 per annum, whilst the residue 'being of the value of £1,200' was conveyed to John, Lord Lumley; but along with these lands the latter also inherited the Florentines' debt, still valued at £11,000, as well as the 'reckoning of my Lord of Arundel's debts

134 This was 'a note of my Lordes owne Hand towchinge his Landes in the North', which listed these extensive sales. Surrey History Centre (SHC) 836/2.

135 The same note describes the remaining land in northern England as worth: Witton Castle and land in Northumberland, £101; in the bishopric, £134 9s 9d; in Hart and Hartlepool (land purchased in 1586), £174 17s 4d; and in Yorkshire, £78. SHC 836/2.

136 A more extensive but undated list of livestock on Lumley's estate includes: 50 animals at Kilton Park; 19 animals at Stanho Hagg; 65 animals (mostly cattle) at Moresam More; 113 animals at Lumley Park; 105 ewes and lambs at Laverokes Close; and a further 168 sheep. SHC 836/1, f. 61r–62r.

137 Stone, *Crisis of the Aristocracy*, p. 783.

138 See figure 18 in chapter 4 for a graph showing the divergence in agricultural wages and prices. This could be very problematic for rentier landlords if they could not take land back in hand or increase rents, p. 160.

due to other persons' said to amount to some £13,000.[139] John Lumley had further reason to feel aggrieved as 'it is well known that the £1,200 worth of land which the Lord Lumley is to have is not further to be improved other than by disparking of parks', showing the contemporary concern that rentier landlords had when faced with unimprovable rents and little direct access to the land they nominally owned.[140] The only improvement in Lumley's fortunes was in his ability to purchase Hart and Hartlepool from George Clifford, the third earl of Cumberland, for £5,350 in 1586, a purchase which led Tom Beastall to claim that 'Lord Lumley's affairs in the North seem to have been less strained'.[141] Given the sale of the vast majority of the family's patrimonial estate within the bishopric of Durham, Lumley's finances were certainly strained and this purchase was perhaps only really afforded by his recent second marriage to Elizabeth Darcy in 1582. Although Lord Lumley's finances showed some signs of improvement with his involvement in the coal industry in the last decades of the century, he was still forced to surrender Nonsuch Palace to Elizabeth in 1592 in lieu of his remaining debts to the Crown, though he remained as keeper there with an annual allowance of £300.[142]

In the last decade of his life, John Lumley still possessed a considerable income, but one which was derived more from his inherited lands in Sussex and Hampshire than from the family's ancient holdings in Durham. Indeed, the majority of income deriving from the palatinate of Durham, beside the later additions of Hart and Hartlepool, came from the park and fishery of Lumley, as well as several coal mines which he had retained. Despite this, the income and influence of the Lumleys in the north of England had deteriorated in both absolute and real terms as inflation ate into his stagnant income and the alienation of such vast tracts of land left the family with few sources of patronage. Table 16 gives an impression of his income at the turn of the century. Even this is somewhat deceptive since these totals include arrears, which Martin Hallyman, the receiver for Durham, Northumberland and Yorkshire, noted amounted to some £302 0s 16d in 1608, with the income from the lordship of Lumley actually only producing £184 8s 4d after arrears and allowances.[143]

How far Lord Lumley spent the rest of his life in 'the pomp, pride and circumstance of ancient nobility' can be seen from the inventory taken on his death in 1609. The total value of his moveable goods came to £1,404, but there is no mention of agricultural goods, and the vast majority of this valuation came from his famous collection of hangings, paintings and books for which he is now particularly remem-

139 Arundel's funeral expenses were said to add at least a further £1,000 to these debts. Milner (ed.), *Records of the Lumleys*, p. 71.

140 Ibid., p. 71.

141 T. W. Beastall, *A North Country Estate: The Lumleys and Saundersons as Landowners, 1600–1900* (London, 1974), p. 7.

142 Milner (ed.), *Records of the Lumleys*, p. 82.

143 SHC 836/4.

Table 16. Annual Income of John, Lord Lumley, in the Early Seventeenth Century

Sum Totals with Arrears	1598	1608
Land in Sussex and Hampshire	£1,441 13s 1d	£1,355 17s 2d
Tower Hill, London	£108 15s 10d	£132 2s 8d
Liberties in Sussex and Hampshire	£87 16s 7d	£19 10s 2d
Land in Surrey	£192 16s 9d	£181 14s 2d
Greenwich, Kent		£31 19s 1d
Kilton in Yorkshire	£199 11s 11d	£216 7s 7d
Hart and Hartlepool	£242 7s 8d	£344 15s
Lordship of Lumley	£205 13s 4d	£276 19s 8d
Witton and Northumberland	£108 0s 12d	£86 19s 8d
Totals	**£2,586 18s**	**£2,646 4s**

Source: Rentals and Accounts of John, Lord Lumley, 1532–1608, Surrey History Centre 836/3–4.

bered by historians.[144] He possessed hangings retelling the stories of Troy, Hector, Scipio and Hannibal, Jason and Medea, and King Pluto which were valued at £80 each, with yet more hangings of the story of the Amazons worth £60, those retelling the story of Paris and the story of St George worth £40 each, and a 21-piece hanging of the story of King Saul and David worth £120. His collections of paintings and statues were valued at considerably less than the hangings, but included pictures of Henry VIII, Edward VI, Queen Mary, Queen Elizabeth and 'my Lord Arundel'. In the great chamber he possessed fifteen pictures of 'my Lord Lumley's ancestors with a pillar of his pedigree' worth £8, as well as a picture of Lord Lumley in armour with his two wives and the old castle of Arundel valued at £13. Such was his love of ancestry and lineage that this preoccupation has been described as bordering on 'genealogical megalomania'.[145] When James I was visiting Lumley castle on his way south in 1603, he was heard to remark: 'Oh mon, gang na further. I maun digest the knowledge I have this day gained, for I didna ken Adam's ither nam was Lumley.'[146] There was also the library at Nonsuch, which comprised some four hundred manuscripts and over three thousand printed works, and was one of the largest libraries in

144 M. Evans, *Art Collecting and Lineage in the Elizabethan Age: The Lumley Inventory and Pedigree* (London); for the following, see his probate inventory: DPRI/1/1609/L5/2–4.

145 R. Strong, *The English Icon: Elizabethan and Jacobean Portraiture* (London, 1969), p. 45. In the hall he also possessed seventy-six little pictures worth £12, and fifteen great pictures worth £5, as well a further nineteen pictures in the drawing chamber worth £6 6s 8d, and ninety-one other pictures in the gallery and four others in the wardrobe, valued altogether at £40.

146 Milner (ed.), *Records of the Lumleys*, p. 92.

Elizabethan England.[147] An even fuller inventory made around 1590 values 'certayne stuffe', mostly musical instruments, carpets, cushions and luxurious furnishings, in Lumley's houses as worth some £5,380, but this luxurious interior seems to have come at the cost of whole tracts of the family's lands.[148]

Perhaps one of the motivating factors in his extravagant expenditure was the fact that John, Lord Lumley, had no son and the family was facing extinction in the direct line: his three children by his first wife, Jane Fitzalan, had died in infancy, and his second wife, Elizabeth Darcy, was childless.[149] Given the commemoration of his ancestors, it is clear that Lord Lumley was very conscious of this fact and 'throughout the 1590s and into the early seventeenth century John Lumley worked tirelessly to identify and to secure the patrimony for his next heir'.[150] In this context, the widespread alienation of his ancestral lands would have remained a last resort for a man who was so clearly concerned with his family's pedigree and position, and who made such careful provisions for the future inheritance of his estate.[151] Before his death he chose to settle his lands on Richard Lumley who was a second cousin; he inherited the estate, which had been greatly reduced by his predecessor's sales and mortgages, received a knighthood in 1616 and was created an Irish peer in 1628 as the viscount Lumley of Waterford.[152] Thus the entire estate founded by the Thorntons and much of the ancient inheritance of the Lumleys was sold piecemeal in the second half of the sixteenth century.

In this regard, John Lumley represents the archetypal aristocrat of Lawrence Stone's *Crisis of the Aristocracy*: living beyond his means at court, he faced the irreconcilable problems of balancing high inflation with a lifestyle of conspicuous consumption. What compounded these problems still further, however, was his inability to increase rents to match the high levels of inflation of the period, and it was precisely this situation which enabled his own tenants to purchase portions of his estate as they profited from the increasing agricultural prices of the sixteenth century. After all, the income described for these lands by John, Lord Lumley, himself at the start of the seventeenth century had not improved since the start of the sixteenth century despite high levels of inflation undermining their real value. The financial difficulties which rentier landlords experienced were clearly acknowledged by contemporaries, as was the short-term expediency of sales: 'it is well known that the Lord Lumley

147 Stone, *Crisis of the Aristocracy*, pp. 705–6; Gooch, *A Complete Pattern of Nobility*, pp. 59–63.

148 Milner (ed.), *Records of the Lumleys*, pp. 335–6.

149 Surtees, *History of Durham*, vol. 2, pp. 153–64.

150 C. D. Liddy and C. Steer, 'John Lord Lumley and the Creation and Commemoration of Lineage in Early Modern England', *The Archaeological Journal*, 167 (2010), p. 215.

151 Although John, Lord Lumley, now held substantial lands in Sussex, Hampshire and Surrey which were inherited from the earl of Arundel, it is highly unlikely that a landowner as conscious of his ancestry as Lord Lumley would have sold his ancestral estate without dire financial reasons. SHC 836/3–4.

152 Liddy and Steer, 'John Lord Lumley', p. 216.

hath departed with £600 land of old rent for other causes of his lordship, the which land at this day is worth £1,200 of yearly rent improved'.[153] Undoubtedly many of the financial problems John Lumley experienced had their origins in the high level of expenses and debts incurred in his political manoeuvrings. However, his inability to improve his landed income clearly compounded these problems and meant that he spent much of his life living on credit extended by merchants.[154] It was in his role as a rentier landlord – as much as in his role as a member of the aristocracy – that he struggled in this period, with few signs of direct agriculture to cushion the effects of inflation. Whatever the cause of his financial problems, however, the consequences are clear: a further lessening of the amount of land held by the resident aristocracy of the palatinate of Durham.

The Bowes family similarly suffered significant losses over the course of the sixteenth century, partially as the result of a divided inheritance after the death of George Bowes in 1545 and partially because of mounting debts incurred in service to the Crown. Already by 1568 Sir George Bowes could be seen raising £1,000 by mortgaging his principal manors of Streatlam, Cleatlam and Barforth.[155] But it was in the following year, with Sir George Bowes' decision to defend Barnard Castle against the rebel forces during the Rising of the North in 1569, that financial struggles became particularly pronounced, as he set himself against many influential northern families, including the Nevilles and Percys.[156] Although William, Robert and George Bowes acquired leases of property in Stockton and in Evenwood Park from the bishops of Durham in 1569, perhaps for their involvement in the defence against the rebels, the family did not gain as much from their loyalty as they might have hoped for.[157] Sir George estimated that the damage inflicted by the rebels to his goods and property was in excess of £4,000, whilst a letter from the earl of Sussex to William Cecil in 1570 noted that he had granted certain goods seized from the rebel earl of Northumberland to Bowes after the 'spoil of all he had'.[158] The Bowes had already received the office of moor men for a term of lives, which put them in charge of all the

153 Milner (ed.), *Records of the Lumleys*, p. 71.

154 See, for example, his repeated borrowing of £1,300 and £600 from Alderman Jackman and Alderman Lambert in the 1560s, upon forfeiture of a group of manors 'being late parcel of the possessions of the right honourable, the Earl of Arundel'. Milner (ed.), *The Records of the Lumleys*, pp. 66–7.

155 Newman, 'The Bowes of Streatlam', p. 271.

156 It was this Sir George Bowes who ordered the execution of 600 rebels in the aftermath of the rising; see Kesselring, *The Northern Rebellion of 1569*, pp. 118–43. He also served in the Ecclesiastical Northern High Commission and the Council of the North until his death in 1580.

157 DCM, Dean and Chapter Registers, vol. 3, ff. 8, 12v. He petitioned the Crown for the land of several attainted families, but received only the following: the Tempests' manor of Bradley in the bishopric, the former Markenfield manors of Scruton and Markington in North Yorkshire, along with various other adjacent properties, to the annual value of only £66 11s 4.5d, Newman, 'The Bowes of Streatlam', p. 267.

158 Newman, 'The Bowes of Streatlam', p. 267.

bishops' lead workings in Stanhope and Wolsingham in 1565, an occupation which they increasingly became synonymous with as the seventeenth century progressed.[159] However, this combination of faith, loyalty and capitalism was a sword which could cut both ways, with Sir George Bowes, as well as his son, incurring many financial debts in service to the Crown and in trading deals. In 1577 he took out a further mortgage, of slightly more than £1,600, by assignment of the leases of Gainford rectory and manor.[160] Sir George's son, Sir William, suggested in 1598 that his father's debts had cost him more than £30,000, though Christine Newman has estimated this sum as more likely to be 'in the region of several thousand pounds'.[161]

Perhaps the most financial damage to the Bowes family was done, however 'by the division of the estates in 1545 when, upon the death of the first Sir George, that part of the inheritance not entailed in tail male descended to the heirs-general, his three daughters and co-heirs'.[162] Newman has estimated that the Bowes' estate at the start of the sixteenth century was worth in the region of £600–£800 per annum, but after this division of land it was only worth around £400 per annum. This divided inheritance on the death of Sir George Bowes in 1545 saw his three daughters inherit much of the family's estates in the east of the county and furthered the trends of fragmentation already explored in this chapter. Dorothy married Sir Cuthbert Collingwood of Eslington in Northumberland; Elizabeth married John Blakiston; and Anne married Robert, the younger son of Richard Bowes of Aske.[163] Although Sir George Bowes' purchasing activities in the 1560s likely saw his rental income increase to around £600 per annum as suggested by Mervyn James, it was still less than his ancestors had enjoyed, with inflation rendering it still lower in real terms.[164]

The Claxtons were another family whose large estates disappeared across this period, with the Claxtons of Claxton dying out in the male line towards the end of the fifteenth century and the Claxtons of Old Park suffering for recusancy and yet another divided inheritance in the second half of the sixteenth century. William Claxton of Claxton possessed the manors of Claxton, Fishburn and Holom in 1380, but it was the marriage to Isabel, the only daughter of William Laton, which brought the manors of Horden, Haswell, Pespol, Boisfield and Hawthorn into the Claxton family, and so greatly improved their financial and social standing.[165] However, Sir

159 DCM, Dean and Chapter Registers, vol. 2, f. 211v; see also John Brown, 'Lead Production on the North-East Periphery: A Study of the Bowes Family Estate, c.1550–1771' (Durham Doctoral Thesis, 2010).

160 Gainford rectory and manor had been held since 1546 by the Bowes on a 95-year lease from Trinity College, Cambridge.

161 Newman, 'The Bowes of Streatlam', p. 272.

162 Ibid., p. 308.

163 Surtees, *History of Durham*, vol. 4, pp. 101–26.

164 James, *Family, Lineage and Civil Society*, p. 30; Newman, 'The Bowes of Streatlam', p. 314.

165 It was thus that on the death of Sir Robert Claxton in 1483, the family possessed the manors of Bruntoft, Claxton, Fishburn, Haswell, Holom, Horden, Pespol and Boisfield, and Ponthop in

Robert Claxton died in 1483 leaving four daughters as co-heiresses, and so this substantial estate was partitioned approximately as follows: Margaret, wife of Sir William Bulmer, acquired the manors of Claxton, Bruntoft and Ponthop and a third of Fishburn; Joan, wife of John Cartington, Northumberland, acquired the ancient possessions of the Tyndales at Dilston and Whitchester in that county; Elizabeth, wife of Richard Conyers, acquired the manor of Horden and lands in Easington and a third of Fishburn; Felice, wife of Sir Ralph Widdrington, acquired the manors of Haswell, Pespol and Boisfield and the remaining third of Fishburn.[166] Purchases and alienations fragmented this estate still further in the sixteenth century, with Richard Bellasis acquiring the manor of Haswell, whilst the manor of Pespol and Boisfield was acquired by the wealthy Newcastle merchant Henry Anderson. The manor of Ponthop descended with the Bulmers until 1600 when it was sold to Anthony Meaburne, whilst Bruntoft was sold to John Featherstonhaugh, esquire, of Stanhope in 1608.[167] This estate, which had been held by a single knightly family of the palatinate in the middle of the fifteenth century, had been divided amongst a whole host of families by the early seventeenth century, continuing the trend of fragmentation.

One of the more important landowning families besides the Nevilles, Lumleys and Bowes were the Conyers, who possessed a unique role in welcoming the new bishop of Durham into the palatinate. The Conyers held the manor of Sockburn for over five centuries, having been granted the manor along with other lands both north and south of the Tees during the episcopate of Ranulf Flambard (1099–1128), and were amongst 'a small group of families who formed the baronial elite of the palatinate in the twelfth century known as the *barones et fideles Sancti Cuthberti*'.[168] The Conyers were amongst the first to greet the bishop, meeting him in the middle of the River Tees and presenting the falchion with which their ancestor supposedly slew the fabled Worm of Sockburn. This ceremony was clearly a memorable event, for on 22 August 1661 Bishop John Cosin wrote to William Sancroft relating the welcome he received as he crossed the Tees from the south:

> The confluence and alacrity both of the gentry, clergy and other people was very great; and at my entrance through the river Tees there was scarce any water to be seen for the multitude of horse and men that filled it, when the sword that killed the dragon was delivered to me with all the formality of trumpets and gunshots and acclamations that might be made.[169]

the palatinate, making them one of the most substantial families outside of the Nevilles, Lumleys and Bowes: DKR 44, p. 352.

166 Surtees, *History of Durham*, vol. 3, p. 142.

167 Ibid., p. 89.

168 Aird, *St Cuthbert and the Normans*, pp. 211–12; Christian Liddy, 'Land, Legend and Gentility in the Palatinate of Durham: The Pollards of Pollard Hall', in Christian Liddy and Richard Britnell (eds.), *North-East England in the Later Middle Ages* (Woodbridge, 2005), p. 70.

169 Ornsby (ed.), *The Correspondence of John Cosin*, p. 21.

As Christian Liddy has argued, the medieval ancestors of the Conyers must have enjoyed a 'semi-mythical status' because of these legends.[170]

The Conyers were described as barons of the bishopric from as early as the twelfth century, owning the manors of Sockburn, Bishopton, Harperley, and Clowcroft and further lands in the palatinate of Durham and Yorkshire for much of this period.[171] In total the family's landed revenue was in the region of £50–£100, which was sufficient to enable them to weather the harsh economic conditions of the fifteenth century, but the Conyers appear to have suffered a similar fate to many of the larger families of the county in the sixteenth century. Sir George Conyers died in 1567 with £281 worth of moveable goods, although it is unclear whether this was the whole inventory or just a valuation of goods at Harperley.[172] Regardless, it is the composition of this wealth which is revealing, for although he possessed corn, hay and wool worth approximately £20 and livestock worth £133, his household goods only came to £31, primarily composed of a large quantity of low-value items. He also died with jewellery valued at £72 6s, which included a gold chain presumably for official ceremonies that alone was valued at £40 and which was worth more than the entire sum of his household goods. Clearly, the social expectations of the age could not be spurned, especially for a family such as the Conyers who played such a prominent role in the ceremonies of the diocese. His will also provides an annual valuation of his lands from which Sir George Conyers empowered Robert Aske of Aughton, John Dawney of Seassey and John Saier of Worsall, esquires, to 'have the said lands till they receive from them 500 marks to the use of Elinor Conyers, my daughter, for her preferment in marriage, or when she reaches twenty-one; and the same sum to Mary Conyers, my daughter'.[173] Sir George Conyers thus possessed an estate worth around £100 per annum, but this rent had hardly improved since the fifteenth century and was quickly being eroded by high levels of inflation. As agricultural prices increased sixfold across the sixteenth and early seventeenth centuries, these stagnant rents became increasingly problematic for the family and there are signs that the Conyers were financially struggling to maintain their position in society, especially when they were burdening their estates with such large marriage portions.

Sir John Conyers, who died in 1609, possessed a considerably larger moveable wealth than his predecessors, with goods and chattels valued at £647 18s.[174] He had over £18 worth of gold and £15 17s in ready cash, with around £85 worth of plate and

170 Liddy, 'Land, Legend and Gentility', p. 77.

171 For the earlier history of the Conyers, see J. P. Boniface, 'The Durham Gentry: Social Stability and Change in the Palatinate of Durham, c.1286–1346' (Durham Doctoral Thesis, 2006), pp. 157–9.

172 J. Raine and W. Greenwell (eds.), *Wills and Inventories from the Registry at Durham, Part I*, Surtees Society, 2 (1835), pp. 266–8.

173 Land in: Girsby, Dinsdale, Hornby and Worsall worth £19 11s 4d; Bishopton worth £26 4s 5d; Wintringham, Yorkshire, worth £21 22d; Newbiggin and Little Stainton worth £18 19s 6d; Harperley worth £4 4s 5d; and the home manor of Sockburn worth £8 17s 10d. Ibid., pp. 34–5.

174 DPRI/1/1609/C14/1.

jewellery, and also apparel worth £50: a respectable wardrobe for the period. The scale of his agricultural activities appears to have been quite limited for he is only recorded as possessing eight draught oxen, which was the average for many of the tenants on the lands of the two ecclesiastical estates in Durham.[175] He also possessed twenty-two cows with ten suckling calves and a further thirteen calves and eleven two-year-old beasts and around £13 6s 8d worth of corn on the ground, suggesting that the majority of his income was primarily derived from rents, although it is unclear if this was the full extent of the family's agricultural pursuits. Despite the considerable total valuation of his moveable goods, it is unclear whether the family were enjoying any financial success in this period, for Sir John Conyers also died with debts worth £520: notably £120 to the aldermen of York, and a further £400 to Anthony Applebie.[176]

On Sir John's death in 1609, his son and heir Sir George Conyers inherited the estate, but by 1613 Sir George had alienated the family manor of Bishopton and other lands in Stainton and Newbiggin to his own tenants.[177] This was not the sale of surplus lands, but the alienation of important family manors which had been held by the Conyers for centuries. It is also revealing that once again it was his own tenants who were purchasing these manors as stagnant rents passed the profits of agriculture down the social scale, much akin to the sales by the Lumleys. A list of 115 non-armorial gentlemen dating from the first half of the seventeenth century includes six individuals from Bishopton, more than any other place in the county, with the likes of Francis and Ralph Welfoot, whose family purchased portions of land in Bishopton and Stainton from the Conyers, described as non-armorial freeholders.[178] This need not necessarily have been the end of the Conyers at Sockburn, but a series of early deaths in the family sealed their fate. When Sir George Conyers died in 1625, he left William Conyers as his 13-year-old heir to the ancestral homes of Sockburn and Harperley; William died just ten years later, leaving three daughters as co-heiresses.[179]

As Trevor-Roper would have highlighted, those looking for failure amongst the aristocracy and success amongst the gentry are bound to find it, and so a particularly pertinent example of aristocratic success for the current study is that of the Percy family, the earls of Northumberland, whose gross income increased fourfold during the life of the ninth earl, from some £4,595 in 1582 to £13,847 in 1636.[180] Batho argued

175 See for example the probate inventory of a Durham husbandman tenant: DPRI/1/1594/L1/1–4, discussed further in chapters 6 and 7.

176 DPRI/1/1609/C14/1.

177 DKR 44, p. 362.

178 Charles Henry Hunter Blair, 'Durham Armorials of the Seventeenth Century', *AA*, 4th series, 15 (1938), pp. 156–203. Once again showing the opportunities available to the tenants of these struggling landlords in the second half of the sixteenth century.

179 DKR 44, p. 365.

180 From 1582 to 1636 their income changed as follows: Yorkshire, £1,530 to £5,485; Northumberland, £796 to £4,150; Tynemouth, £786 to £698; and Cumberland, £371 to £650. See M. E. James

that the earl achieved this through the creation of large leaseholds out of demesnes: 'in this way the receipts at Alnwick were nearly trebled between 1581 and 1612'. He went on to conclude that 'more important still were the replacements of customary tenancies by leaseholds for twenty-one years, and as copyhold tenancies fell in, new tenants were being pressed to take out leases at increased rents'.[181] This is the archetypal example of an improving, rack-renting landlord, converting customary tenures into large leaseholds and substantially increasing rents. Much of the Percys' success did indeed come from increasing the rents owed by customary tenants or tenants at will. For example, at Wressel in Yorkshire, income from their tenants at will increased from £17 to £88, whilst at Newsholme rents increased from £9 to £73.[182] What is also particularly interesting is that there was a relatively high continuity of families at Wressel, with 60 of the 116 families in 1536 surviving in 1577, and 40 surviving in 1620.[183] This is a perfect example of what Alan Simpson described as landlords simply raising their rents and finding tenants, 'often the same tenants, who were able and willing enough to meet each rise'.[184]

If the entire Percy estate is looked at, however, the increases in income made in Yorkshire came much more from the leasing out of demesnes and parks rather than from rent increases. For example, the breaking up of the parks at Leconfield increased rents from £56 to £580; at Spofforth from £2 to £428; and at Topcliffe from £29 to £1,048.[185] At the start of the sixteenth century, the rental income from these demesnes and parks stood at £87 out of a total of £185 for the three lordships, just under 50 per cent; by the start of the seventeenth century they came to form £2,056 out of £2,504, or just over 80 per cent. Of course, part of the reason the ninth earl was so intent on leasing out his parks and demesnes was because he never visited his northern manors. After the debacle of the Rising of the North it was politically expedient for the earls of Northumberland to reside in the south of England at Syon House. Thus their northern lands became a source of profit not patronage or pleasure, and so their parks were slowly converted to leasehold pastureland. This process was continued after the Gunpowder Plot in 1605, after which the earl was imprisoned in the Tower of London for his role in the conspiracy.

(ed.), *Estate Accounts of the Earls of Northumberland, 1562–1637*, Surtees Society, 163 (1948). 'The history of Elizabethan and Jacobean gentry is strewn with their casualties, although Tawney's searchlight, seeking to illuminate only prosperity among the gentry and aristocratic decline, has seldom lit upon them', Trevor-Roper, *The Gentry*, p. 7.

181 Batho, 'The Finances of an Elizabethan Nobleman', pp. 440–1.

182 Eric J. Fisher, 'Some Yorkshire Estates of the Percys, 1450–1650', vol. 2 (Leeds Doctoral Thesis, 1954), p. 121.

183 This is considering the Pilgrimage of Grace in 1536 and the Rising of the North in 1569, both of which affected the inheritance of holdings in northern England.

184 Simpson, *Wealth of the Gentry*, pp. 201–2.

185 For the lordship of Leconfield see Fisher, 'Some Yorkshire Estates', vol. 1, pp. 1–129; for the lordship of Spofforth, see idem, pp. 1–185; and for the lordship of Topcliffe, see idem, vol. 2, pp. 1–165.

One of the reasons the Percys stand out is because their parks and forests acted as extra demesne land in the sixteenth century and unlike much of their other lands had no restrictive tenures entrenched upon them. This enabled the ninth earl to lease out these lands when they were in peak demand in the early seventeenth century, and thus the Percys were able to augment their rental incomes whereas other landlords, such as the bishops of Durham who had exploited these resources in the fifteenth century, were not able to respond in the same way.[186] It was, after all, one of Lord Lumley's complaints that the only way to improve the land he inherited from the earl of Arundel was by the 'disparking of parks', whilst it was the parks of Raby and Brancepeth that offered the Coles and Vanes the most commercial opportunities after their sale by the Crown. There were, of course, other ways for landowners to increase their revenues, but the leasing out of former parks for pasture was clearly a financial opportunity which several northern landowners decided to exploit in the early seventeenth century.

Although Batho focused upon the large rent increases achieved by the Percys from the late sixteenth century, the stagnant rents they were collecting from Tynemouth are also particularly interesting as the road not taken can often be as revealing about society as the way events played out. Why did this improving landlord not increase his rents from these Tynemouth lands when he was busy rack-renting and throwing up large enclosures elsewhere on his estate? All of the possessions of Tynemouth Priory were seized by the Crown in 1538/39 and were leased out to several people before falling to the eighth earl of Northumberland, descending with the earldom until the family eventually acquired the full freehold rights to the estate.[187] Were these lands treated differently to the ancestral estate of the family and how far did the previous monastic ownership of these lands provide a puzzle for the Percys which not even the ninth earl could unravel? Arable demesne lands no longer existed at the dissolution except in Tynemouth and Preston townships, the original demesnes having been turned into pasture and appropriated by the customary tenants so that each husbandry holding had extensive rights of common appurtenant to it. It does not appear that the lordship was treated any differently than the other lands, but that the previous tenurial development of the estate hindered the earl's ability to make the desired changes. The earl endeavoured to induce his copyhold tenants, not only in Tynemouth but on all his copyhold lands, to exchange their copies for 21-year

186 This process of disparking in early modern England was important because it essentially freed up land which could be used for pastoral farming or leased out at highly commercial rents in the late sixteenth century. But it could also prove controversial with the sale of forests, for example: *Calendar of State Papers: Elizabeth*, vol. 3, p. 289. See chapter 1 for the use of the bishops' forests in the fifteenth century.

187 This included the townships of Tynemouth, Preston, East Chirton, Whitley, Monkseaton, Murton, Earsdon and Backworth.

leases.[188] However, the previous history of the lordship of Tynemouth frustrated the earl's attempts to improve his income, with much of the land being held by copyhold of inheritance. In contrast to the success the earl achieved on his other lands which were part of the traditional patrimony of the Percys, the tenants took a petition to the king arguing that they were copyholders of inheritance according to the custom of the manor. In 1610, it was decreed 'that the said copyholders are and always have been copyholders of inheritance, and so from henceforth shall be'; that the continuance of their ancient rights and custom was just; and that the forms of surrenders and admittances should be such as were commonly used before the twentieth year of Queen Elizabeth.[189] In other words, it was the long-term tenurial development of these estates which provided the laity of rural England with many of the same headaches that the ecclesiastical landlords faced in chapter 2.

Conclusion

These two centuries were of completely contrasting fortunes for the larger lay landowners of county Durham; the late fourteenth and fifteenth centuries proved to be a great period for estate building, whilst the late sixteenth and early seventeenth centuries were quite the reverse and saw the fragmentation of many of these estates. Natural contingency played its part in these processes. The marriages of the Bowes and Lumleys in the fourteenth and fifteenth centuries, for example, saw them acquire significant estates which led to a greater accumulation of land amongst a smaller territorial elite, whereas some of these larger landowners died out in the male line leading to a fragmentation of their lands in the sixteenth and early-seventeenth centuries. However, there was a balance to these trends that mere individual misfortune does not account for, with a whole host of purchases being made in the earlier period which were only matched in scale by alienations in the latter. In the mid-fourteenth century, the balance of landed power in the palatinate was, if not uniform, then certainly less stratified than it was to become by the end of the fifteenth century when the Nevilles, Lumleys and Bowes held over two-fifths of lay manors in the region and a group of knightly landowners just below them held perhaps another fifth. This concentration of territorial power was not to last into the sixteenth century, however. Each family found its own way to disaster: the Nevilles led the Rising of the North in 1569; the Bowes faced a divided inheritance and increasing financial difficulties in the service of the Crown; the Lumleys sold over half their ancestral lands in the north; the Claxtons died out in the male line; and the Conyers shared a mixture of the fates of these last two families.

188 H. H. E. Craster, *A History of Northumberland*, vol. 8, *The Parish of Tynemouth* (London, 1907), p. 238.

189 Ibid., p. 239.

In many ways, therefore, this chapter supports the idea of a 'crisis of the aristocracy', and yet in a number of important ways it does not.[190] After all, the Bowes, Conyers and Claxtons were never members of the titular aristocracy, however important they were as landowners in the palatinate. It was in their roles as larger landowners, and more specifically as rentier landlords, in which they suffered the same vicissitudes as the Lumleys and the bishops of Durham. The dual pincers of high inflation and stagnant rents gave rise to a crisis, not of a social group, but of a type of landowner who struggled to benefit from the unearned increment which their tenants slowly accumulated. It was no coincidence that it was the tenants of these landowners who were increasingly able to purchase portions of their lord's manors. Rather than thinking of this problem as a crisis of the aristocracy it is more useful to conceptualise it as a crisis of rentier landlords: the problem of stagnant and unimprovable incomes had its origins in the tenurial development of their estates rather than in their social status and it is here where the answer to many of the problems rural society faced in the sixteenth century lies. The withdrawal from the direct-demesne management of land in the fourteenth and early fifteenth centuries had long-term consequences for rural society because it divorced the ownership of land from its use, and so the successors of these rentier landlords struggled to access the profits of their lands in the sixteenth century. That is not to say that all landlords failed in this struggle, but they did all face significant difficulties from the mid-sixteenth century onwards, just as their predecessors had done during the fifteenth-century recession. Some, such as the ninth earl of Northumberland, the Crown and the dean and chapter of Durham Cathedral, were able to mitigate these problems or even overcome them entirely, but others like the bishops of Durham and John, Lord Lumley, faced increasing difficulties as inflation slowly eroded their real incomes. By comparison, the smaller landowners who tended to keep some land under direct management throughout this period were in a position to take advantage of the rising agricultural prices in the sixteenth century, often benefiting directly from the stagnant rents on the estates of their larger neighbours.

190 See the conclusion to chapter 4 for a further discussion of the crisis of the aristocracy in relation to the rise of the gentry debate.

4

The Fortunes of the Gentry

Alan Everitt's concept of the county community has proven fertile ground for research into county studies of the gentry, not only in seventeenth-century studies exploring the Civil War, but also in works exploring the emergence of the gentry in the fourteenth and fifteenth centuries. The point Everitt was investigating was 'the recurring problem that faced so many provincial people in this period, the conflict between loyalty to the local community and loyalty to the state'.[1] The idea of a county community, fundamentally interested in local not national affairs, and whose social and political lives were lived 'almost wholly within the confines of their county', has been explored in a range of different contexts and chronologies.[2] For example, Bennett found that 'the county community of late medieval Cheshire represented a social unit of considerable convenience, both at a personal and an institutional level', whereas Carpenter has expressed doubt at the utility of the concept and its reality in the political lives of the late medieval gentry of Warwickshire.[3]

The social and political lives of the Durham gentry have been explored extensively within this framework in recent studies. This has involved the broadening of the concept from the county to the region, with Mark Arvanigian emphasising the importance of military service in the wars against Scotland in the late fourteenth century and Diana Newton showing the broad range of social connections between families in the north-east of England in the sixteenth and early seventeenth centuries.[4] Within the county itself, Christian Liddy has explored whether the Neville family's affinity dominated society and how far the palatinate status of the county gave rise to a specific community, the *haliwerfolc*, whereas Mervyn James argued that the disappearance of the Neville influence after 1569 gave rise to a civil society focused

1 A. M. Everitt, *The Local Community and the Great Rebellion* (London, 1969), p. 5. See also Clive Holmes, 'The County Community in Stuart Historiography', *Journal of British Studies*, 19 (1980), pp. 54–73, and the essays in Jacqueline Eales and Andrew Hopper (eds.), *The County Community in Seventeenth-Century England and Wales* (Hatfield, 2012).

2 A. M. Everitt, *The Community of Kent and the Great Rebellion, 1640–1660* (Leicester, 1966), p. 13.

3 M. J. Bennett, 'A County Community: Social Cohesion among the Cheshire Gentry, 1400–25', *NH*, 8 (1973), p. 42; C. Carpenter, 'Gentry and Community in Medieval England', *Journal of British Studies*, 33 (1994), pp. 340–80.

4 Mark Arvanigian, 'A County Community or the Politics of the Nation? Border Service and Baronial Influence in the Palatinate of Durham, 1377–1413', *Historical Research*, 82 (2009), pp. 41–61; Newton, *North-East England*.

upon the bishops of Durham.[5] Rather than enlarging this literature on the political lives of the gentry, the current chapter explores the economic foundations of this social group and how they fared under the pressures of the fifteenth-century recession and the sixteenth-century inflation.

The debate surrounding the economic fortunes of the laity in this period has an even longer history than the county community debate, with the storm over the gentry having taken place well over half a century ago, and many other studies of individual counties arising since.[6] Tawney's argument for the rise of the gentry and Lawrence Stone's thesis of a crisis of the aristocracy combined to create a narrative of economic, social and political upheaval in rural society in the century leading up to the English Civil War. Although there have been many criticisms of this older historiography, not least its tendency to portray the Civil War as inevitably rising out of these conflicts, there have been numerous studies which have shown that there were significant changes in the composition of rural society across the fifteenth and sixteenth centuries.[7] Simon Payling and Christine Carpenter, for example, found a contraction in the number of smaller gentry families holding manors from the late fourteenth century, which in turn facilitated the accumulation of larger estates by members of the aristocracy and knightly families.[8] By comparison, the work of Cliffe on the Yorkshire gentry and that of James on Durham have both shown that there was a great proliferation of gentry families from the late sixteenth century onwards as yeomen increasingly took advantage of the rise in agricultural profits and the eclipse of the aristocratic families of northern England.[9] Stone and Tawney believed it was during this period that many noble families faced a financial crisis in contrast to the rise in the prosperity of gentry families.[10]

5 Liddy, *The Bishopric of Durham*, esp. pp. 174–235; James, *Family, Lineage and Civil Society*, pp. 147–98.

6 For the debate surrounding the rise of the gentry, see: Tawney, 'The Rise of the Gentry', pp. 1–38; Tawney, 'The Rise of the Gentry: A Postscript', *EcHR*, 7 (1954), pp. 91–7; Trevor-Roper, *The Gentry*; J. H. Hexter, 'Storm over the Gentry', *Encounter*, 10 (1958), pp. 22–34; Clay, *Economic Expansion and Social Change*, pp. 142–64.

7 For surveys of the gentry see: Simpson, *Wealth of the Gentry*; and Heal and Holmes, *The Gentry in England and Wales*; for county studies of the gentry see: Susan Wright, *The Derbyshire Gentry in the Fifteenth Century* (Derby, 1983); Christine Carpenter, *Locality and Polity: A Study of Warwickshire Landed Gentry, 1401–99* (Cambridge, 1992); Payling, *Gentry of Nottinghamshire*; Liddy, *The Bishopric of Durham*; Newton, *North-East England*; Everitt, *The Community of Kent*; and J. T. Cliffe, *The Yorkshire Gentry from the Reformation to the Civil War* (London, 1969).

8 Carpenter, *Locality and Polity*, pp. 83–4; Payling, *Gentry of Nottinghamshire*, pp. 8–10.

9 James, *Family, Lineage, and Civil Society*, p. 31; Cliffe, *The Yorkshire Gentry*, p. 19.

10 Lawrence Stone argued that there was an inflation of honours in the early seventeenth century which saw a 'remarkable increase in the number of upper classes, which trebled at a period when the total population barely doubled. The number of peers rose from 60 to 160; of baronets and knights from 500–1,400; of squires from perhaps 800–3,000; and of armigerous gentry from perhaps 5,000–15,000'; Lawrence Stone, 'Social Mobility in England, 1500–1700', *P&P*, 33 (1966), pp. 23–4; Stone, *Crisis of the Aristocracy*, pp. 72–3; Tawney, 'Rise of the Gentry', p. 10.

James went on to describe the 'smaller parish gentry, a group which, practically non-existent as such at the beginning of the [sixteenth] century, was in the process of emerging from the ranks of the rich farmers, yeomen, and merchant-shopkeepers.'[11] This is one of the most interesting groups in rural Durham because the parish gentry were not emerging but were in fact re-emerging as the economic conditions changed in their favour during the sixteenth century. There were undoubtedly differences between these two groups, not least the fact that many single-manor families of the fourteenth century possessed local jurisdiction whereas their counterparts of the seventeenth century tended to be freeholding yeomen, but they shared many characteristics, especially in their economic role as employers and direct producers. As prices and rents declined and real wages increased during the late fourteenth and early fifteenth centuries, the parish gentry were perhaps the section of society most vulnerable to this pincer movement: families who possessed considerable martial responsibilities and social pretensions, and yet whose landed estates were often precariously balanced between profit and loss. As will be seen, the lesser gentry struggled during these socio-economic conditions and were gradually forced to sell their lands as the recession continued to bite. By the start of the sixteenth century, however, the majority of gentry and yeomen farmers found themselves in a favourable position to benefit from rising agricultural prices. As was explored in the previous chapter, the misfortunes of the lesser gentry in the early fifteenth century provided their larger neighbours with a perfect opportunity for estate building.[12] As the sixteenth century progressed, however, these larger families struggled because of political follies, financial difficulties and divided inheritances, providing the gentry with opportunities for economic, social and political advancement. Many of these problems were caused by the restrictive tenures which had developed on the lands of the aristocracy who struggled to improve their incomes in line with inflation, especially from the second half of the sixteenth century onwards.[13]

The north-east of England thus forms an important case study where the debates surrounding the crisis of the aristocracy and rise of the gentry have traditionally come together to form a coherent outline of events in the sixteenth century.[14] As Diana Newton concluded, 'with the counties of Northumberland and Durham no

11 James, *Family, Lineage, and Civil Society*, p. 31.

12 The Nevilles and Thorntons purchased between them around a fifth of all lay manors in the palatinate during the late fourteenth and early fifteenth centuries, whilst many other knightly families can be seen making opportunistic acquisitions on a smaller scale, see chapter 3 above for more details.

13 These tenures also made it difficult for larger landowners to return to direct cultivation as they would have needed to buy out any remaining customary interest in the land. However, even where landowners could have engaged in direct agriculture (such as using their parks for livestock), many of the aristocracy seem to have preferred leasing these assets out, with the Percys, Lumleys and later the Vanes choosing this method of increasing their rent rolls.

14 Stone, *Crisis of the Aristocracy*; Tawney, 'Rise of the Gentry', pp. 1–38; Trevor-Roper, *The Gentry*.

longer dominated by the Nevilles and the Percys, the lesser peers and gentry filled the political (and social) vacuum'.[15] This goes far beyond the Rising of the North and subsequent forfeitures, however, and was part of a much broader shift in rural society which saw rentier landlords struggle in the face of inflation, whilst agricultural producers were able to accrue a higher return for their goods than had been possible for generations. It was not simply the overnight disappearance of the Nevilles which brought about this shift in power in the palatinate, but also the financial struggles of the Lumleys, the Bowes and the bishops of Durham which enabled this shift in landed society. By comparison, the gentry, many of whom were directly managing their own manors on a commercial scale during the sixteenth century, were enjoying the fruits of their labour. It was this economic shift, as much as the political downfall of the Nevilles and the take-off of the coal industry, which brought about the overall redistribution of landed power within the palatinate.

Financial Crisis in the Late Fourteenth Century

There is another side to the story outlined in chapter 3 as the greater consolidation of manors in the hands of fewer families during the late fourteenth and fifteenth centuries led to a reduction in the number of families holding a single manor in the palatinate. There was remarkable stability in the overall number of families who held more than one manor but less than five across this period: in 1350, there were thirty such families holding a combined total of eighty-four manors, and there were thirty-one families in this category who held eighty-three manors by 1500.[16] Although the actual families within this category changed, the overall composition of this section of rural society was relatively stable, with some families accumulating manors to join the upper gentry and others dropping downwards into the parochial gentry. By comparison, there was a dramatic decrease in the number of single-manor families. In the late fourteenth century there were fifty-five such families, each holding a single manor and so accounting for approximately 30 per cent of lay manors in total.

By 1500, there were only thirty-two such single-manor families, an approximate halving of this group across the fifteenth century and, as Table 17 shows, much of this decline came in the late fourteenth and early fifteenth centuries. Liddy has noted that the 'most marked feature of the tenurial landscape was the numerical dominance of a group of parish gentry' who often had little economic power, but possessed political status through their involvement in the community.[17] Why did this seem-

15 Newton, *North-East England*, p. 45.

16 TNA, Inquisitions Post Mortem: DURH 3; DKR 44 and 45; and DUL, ASC, XM/film Palatinate 1.

17 Liddy, *The Bishopric of Durham*, p. 65.

Table 17. Distribution of Manors among Durham Lay Landowners, 1350–1640*

	1350		1400		1450		1500		1550		1600		1640	
Categories	**Families**	**Manors**	**Families**	**Manors**	**Families**	**Manors**	**Families**	**Manors**	**Families**	**Manors**	**Families**	**Manors**	**Families**	**Manors**
> 5 manors	8	53½	8	88	9	108	6	110	7	99	5	41	6	54
1–5 manors	30	84	31	85	30	82	31	83	30	82	32	89	37	90
1 manor†	55	55	43	43	31	31	32	32	34	34	42	42	56	56
< 1 manor	15	7½	14	7	11	6	12	6⅓	14	7¼	18	9	30	12½
Totals	**108**	**200**	**96**	**223**	**81**	**227**	**81**	**231⅓**	**85**	**222¼**	**97**	**181‡**	**129**	**212½**

* These figures are estimates of the overall number of families and manors in each category at fifty-year intervals, derived from the inquisitions post mortem and, where these are lacking, from contextual information of the descent of the family's manors. This is why the overall number of manors fluctuates slightly as certain parcels of land disappear from the records, often to reappear later under a different name.

† The majority of families in this category were very small landowners on the cusp of gentility, such as the Alansheles of Alansheles, the Henknolls of Henknoll, the Edmondsleys of Edmondsley, the Grooms of Burseblades, the Guildfords of Collierley, the Gourlays of Ponthop, the Hagthorpes of Nettlesworth, the Milots of White Hill, the Blackheads of Woodcroft, the Eppletons of Eppleton and the Chancellors of Woodfield.

‡ The Crown held much of the Neville estate and some other forfeited estates, reflecting the shortfall in the overall number of manors here.

Source: TNA, Inquisitions Post Mortem, DURH 3. Abstracted on microfilm in DUL, ASC, XM/film Palatinate 1. Published lists in *The Forty-Fourth Report of the Deputy Keeper* (London, 1883), pp. 310–542 and *The Forty-Fifth Report of the Deputy Keeper* (London, 1885), pp. 153–282.

ingly dynamic group in rural society slowly diminish across the late fourteenth and early fifteenth centuries? How far is this representative of national trends and, importantly, how far was this disappearance caused by the financial difficulties following the decline in prices after the 1370s?

These are harder questions to answer than they might at first appear, primarily because it was 'these people's farming practices about which we know least', but this difficulty has been further exacerbated by the time-frame on which most gentry studies have focused.[18] Liddy's study of the gentry and lesser landowners of Durham is one of the few which specifically aims to explore the late fourteenth century in conjunction with the fifteenth century.[19] It is also difficult to make direct comparisons because other studies have used social status as their springboard into the wealth of these lesser landowners, whereas the current book uses IPMs to explore the distribution of landownership first and foremost, and thus this chapter captures families who were often on the cusp of gentility and whose claims to such status were often fleeting. Susan Wright's description of Derbyshire landed society in the early fifteenth century, for example, is not unlike that of Durham, with:

> two peers constituting our upper dividing line. Below this, only eight Derbyshire families are known to have provided one or more knights throughout the period and a further twenty-four families were distrained … Below the knightly group a second tier can be identified of families with at least £20 p.a. from land. In theory JPs also had a minimum income of £20 p.a. making the total membership of this second strata twenty and with the knightly families a grand total of fifty-two.[20]

Although the absolute numbers in each category were different in Durham, the overall social structure is broadly comparable, with a 'much more complex' group of 'parochial gentry' existing below these knightly families, who were 'accorded the distinction of gentility, however ephemeral and open to ambiguity the status was in the fifteenth century'. Wright concluded that a comprehensive list of landowners with over £5 per annum's worth of landed income totals over 200 families, forming a broad group of landowners not unlike at Durham, but unfortunately this is as far as any comparisons can be taken because she decided to exclude 'this rather ill-defined group of gentlemen-yeomen in the £5–£20 income range' from any further analysis.[21] Even so, she touched on the financial difficulties of these smaller landowners in Derbyshire during the fifteenth century when discussing the potential accumulations

18 Carpenter, *Locality and Polity*, p. 194.

19 Liddy, *The Bishopric of Durham*. Christine Carpenter's study of the Warwickshire gentry focused upon 1401–99; Susan Wright's study of the Derbyshire gentry was of the fifteenth century but focused primarily on c.1430–1509; Simon Payling's work on the gentry of Nottinghamshire used the 1412 tax returns as its start point; and Eric Acheson's study of the Leicestershire gentry began around 1422.

20 Wright, *Derbyshire Gentry*, p. 6.

21 Ibid., p. 6.

of the larger gentry, as the need to settle debts may occasionally have forced the gentry into realising their landed assets and so sometimes it was possible to acquire single manors in their entirety from small local landowners.[22]

Christine Carpenter's study of Warwickshire provides much better comparative data. Broadly speaking, her findings show an erosion of the property of the lesser gentry similar to that found at Durham, with seventeen gentlemen holding two to four manors in 1410, but only five holding the same by 1500, the redistribution in this instance greatly favouring the earls of Warwick, akin to their counterparts in Durham, the earls of Westmorland. The main difference between Warwickshire and Durham is in the stability of the single-manor families, who show relatively little change across the fifteenth century, but part of this may be because of the start date chosen by Carpenter. She was, however, willing to make some provisional judgements on the financial difficulties faced by landowners during the fifteenth century, concluding that 'it is probably safe to assume that the greater lords were in a better position to cope with these difficulties than the gentry' and that 'it is probable that it was the gentry who suffered most, squeezed between the demands of the Crown and the resistance of the peasantry'.[23]

> What we can do is decide how well, on the evidence before us, lesser landowners were likely to have surmounted arguably one of the worst periods for them in the agrarian history of England. The indisputable conclusion is that although most of them must have been under some strain, if they responded effectively, as most apparently did, they had nothing to fear. It is probable that the smaller landowners, nearer the base of the gentle hierarchy, struggling to provide for their families while sustaining a level of consumption superior to that of the richer peasants, lived closer to the margin of their income. Unfortunately, it is these people's farming practices about which we know least.[24]

It was these smaller landowners, whose claims to gentility were often most tenuous, who struggled the most in the half-century following the decline in prices from the 1370s. Many of the parish gentry owned little more than moorland farms but possessed all the pretentions of their larger neighbours, and so were gradually forced out of the land market as poor economic conditions continued to erode their incomes.

Some members of the lesser gentry fell upon hard times but were still determined to carry out their roles in society, such as Walter Hawick, who settled his manor of Little Eden on the trustees John Trollope, gentleman, and John White, chaplain, as he proposed to journey to France in the service of the king. This manor was returned in the IPM of Johanna Hawick in 1371, held by homage, fealty and service,

22 Ibid., p. 27.

23 Carpenter, *Locality and Polity*, p. 58 and p. 155.

24 Ibid., p. 194.

and was given an annual value of 10 marks.[25] The trustees were to pay his wife 40s a year out of the profits of the manor, and any remainder was to 'pay his debts', although the nature of these debts is unclear.[26] If his line should fail the manor would pass to the heirs of John Trollope, and so when his daughter Joan died without issue, the manor duly passed to John Trollope of Thornley's son. Was this nothing more than a series of unfortunate events? Perhaps, but clearly Walter Hawick was in debt, although whether as a result of his determination to serve abroad or from the problems of recession is unclear. There are a whole host of similar examples of these single-manor families who sold their lands, often to the more substantial knightly families who could afford to purchase manors during the harsh economic conditions that troubled landowners after the Black Death, or more specifically after the 1370s.[27] Eppleton gave name to its family occupiers from a very early period and the family had resided there for nearly three centuries prior to its alienation by Robert Epplinden to Sir John Heron in the late fourteenth century.[28] Similarly, the manor of Ponthop belonged to the Gourlay family in the mid-fourteenth century with John Gourlay dying seized of the manor in 1361.[29] The description of the manor in Hatfield's survey in the 1380s shows the minor nature of these lands, which were little more than a large farmstead.[30] William Gourlay died seized of the manor in 1395, but his son and heir, Richard Gourlay, alienated the manor to Sir William Claxton in 1409.[31]

The Gildfords were another lesser gentry family who alienated their manor to members of the knightly community of the palatinate, in this case to Sir William Tempest, Sir William Lumley and others in 1428. Thomas Gildford died seized of Collierley in 1349, presumably as a result of the pestilence of that year, with the manor valued at £4–5 per annum.[32] In Hatfield's survey, John Gildford is described as holding the manor of Collierley, containing 200 acres of pasture, arable and woodland by foreign service and suit at the county court and the same John died seized of the manor in 1385.[33] The manor continued in the hands of the Gildfords until

25 TNA, DURH 3/2, f. 87; DKR 45, p. 212.

26 Surtees, *History of Durham*, vol. 1, pp. 36–7.

27 Despite population decline after the Black Death, prices remained buoyant until the 1370s when they declined significantly, leading to the well-known 'price-scissors' as high wages continued unabated. See, for example, John Munro, 'The Late Medieval Decline of English Demesne Agriculture: Demographic, Monetary and Political-Fiscal Factors', in Mark Bailey and Stephen Rigby (eds.), *Town and Countryside in the Age of the Black Death* (Turnhout, 2012), pp. 299–350.

28 TNA, DURH 3/2, f. 59; DKR 45, p. 154; Surtees, *History of Durham*, vol. 1, pp. 217–19.

29 TNA, DURH 3/2, f. 63; DKR 45, p. 201.

30 In Hatfield's Survey, William Gourlay held the manor containing sixty acres of land with a rent of 2s; a messuage and forty-eight acres with an ancient rent of 16s, now only 8s; and a messuage and thirty acres called Shippinstele, with a rent of 2s; Greenwell (ed.), *Bishop Hatfield's Survey*, p. 115.

31 Surtees, *History of Durham*, vol. 2, p. 350.

32 TNA, DURH 3/2, f. 37; DKR 45, p. 200.

33 Greenwell (ed.), *Bishop Hatfield's Survey*, p. 124; on John's death, the manor was described as

John Gildford sold the manor and all his land to the aforementioned Sir William Tempest, Sir William Lumley and others in 1428.[34] Another example of a gentry family who took the name of their manor were the Alansheles who held a messuage and 100 acres of arable and meadow ground there by homage, fealty, suit of court three times a year and 6s 8d rent; the manor was valued at 60s.[35] William Alansheles died seized of the manor in 1364; his daughter and heir, Alice, married Richard Laton.[36] The manor was purchased by the Nevilles, and appears in the inquisition on the death of Ralph Neville, earl of Westmorland, as a messuage and 100 acres of land.[37] The manor of Farnacres followed a similar pattern to that laid out above: held by the Farnacres family until it was sold to Sir Robert Umfraville who in turn founded the chantry of Farnacres with much of this land.[38] Whether all of these families were under financial pressure because of the economic trends of the period remains unclear, but there was a definite pattern which involved the smaller parish gentry alienating their ancestral manors to the established knightly families of the palatinate. This was not the occasional sale of unimportant land, but was often the last desperate act of ancient landowning families whose names never reappear in the Durham countryside.

Given the high attrition rate of the lesser gentry noted above, it seems all the more remarkable that there were many gentry families who survived and even prospered on their single manors throughout this period. Many of these will be discussed below with regard to their sixteenth-century descendants who found themselves in a favourable position because their ancestors had managed to retain the family manor. This included the Bellasises of Henknoll who were to feature so prominently in the leases of the bishops in the sixteenth century and, for example, the Blackheads of Woodcroft, the Egglestons of Bradwood, the Hagthorpes of Nettlesworth, the Sayers of Preston-on-Tees and the Wards of Consett – all instances of single-manor families who survived the fifteenth century and went on holding their manor for generations. It is the high attrition rate amongst the lesser gentry, however, that reveals just how troubling the late fourteenth and fifteenth centuries were for lesser landowners as many ancient families had their names stricken from the rolls, either through failure of the male line because of increased outbreaks of disease and war, or through forced alienation as the recession continued to bite into their inheritances. There can be little doubt that there was an overall balance to these alienations which saw the number of these single-manor families slowly diminish as their lands were

containing a messuage and 180 acres, and a further thirty acres called Smethystrother, in 1385; TNA, DURH 3/2, f. 155; DKR 45, p. 203.

34 Surtees, *History of Durham*, vol. 2, p. 359.

35 Ibid., p. 367.

36 TNA, DURH 3/2, f. 71; DKR 45, p. 154.

37 TNA, DURH 3/2, f. 230; DKR 45, pp. 279–82.

38 Surtees, *History of Durham*, vol. 2, pp. 243–4.

accumulated, either piecemeal by knightly families or else in the wholesale purchases of the Nevilles and Thorntons.

The relatively large number of families who held on to their family manor and modest inheritances speaks to the resilience of many during the fifteenth-century recession, whilst there are signs that this situation stabilised in the second half of the century. In the latter part of the fifteenth century, there was a halt to the accumulation of larger estates, and the number of single-manor families stabilised. In 1350, there were 55 such families, but by 1400 this number had been reduced to 43 families, and by 1450 had fallen to just 31 families. However, there were still 32 single-manor families in 1500 and 34 such families in 1550, suggesting that their numbers had steadied from the middle of the fifteenth century onwards.[39] Was this perhaps a sign that the smaller members of the gentry, at least those who had survived this long, had adapted to the socio-economic conditions of the fifteenth century? Or perhaps rather than the supply of manors drying up, did this in fact reflect the increasing difficulties that larger families were finding themselves in as the recession continued to take its toll on them, especially during the 1450s and '60s?[40] Without the estate records of these smaller landholders it is difficult to tell why some families were able to survive whilst so many of their neighbours were forced to alienate their lands. There are signs of a geographical trend to these alienations with many of the smaller landowners in the western half of the palatinate particularly struggling, but equally small landowners like the Milots of White Hill were able to go from strength to strength across the fifteenth and sixteenth centuries, using their coal reserves to great effect.

The other main trend of these fifteenth-century transactions was that the knightly group of county society tended to be among the main recipients of these manors, but how far were they the beneficiaries of the struggles of their smaller neighbours nationally? In his study of the greater gentry families of Nottinghamshire, Simon Payling concluded that there was a 'significant tendency' for failure in the male line and profits available from office-holding to 'bring about a concentration of wealth in the hands of fewer families' and as 'this wealth became increasingly concentrated, county administration and representation became more exclusively the preserve of the greater shire gentry, and it was they, distinguished from the bulk of their gentry neighbours by their wealth, who were the natural recipients of royal and baronial patronage'.[41] Thus for Payling there was a definite accumulation of wealth by the knightly families of Nottinghamshire which was very reminiscent of that found here for Durham, but there were significant differences in the social, political and

39 See Table 17 above for the overall numbers and distribution of landholding in the county, p. 152.

40 This is, of course, not taking into consideration the potential impact that the Wars of the Roses had upon the land market in Durham from the 1450s onwards.

41 Payling, *Gentry of Nottinghamshire*, p. vii.

economic consequences of this stratification of rural society between these two counties during the fifteenth century. This was primarily because Lancastrian Nottinghamshire was a county with a much lower concentration of both ecclesiastical and aristocratic wealth, which helped the knightly families of Nottinghamshire rise to much greater prominence than their counterparts achieved in the palatinate of Durham. It was this small group of leading county families who 'had a much more continuous corporate existence' that made them 'as a body, less susceptible to such misfortunes', which broke apart the estate built up by Ralph, Lord Cromwell, on his death in 1456, tipping the balance of landholding 'further in favour of the greater gentry'.[42] The knightly families of Durham may well have benefited from the financial struggles of their smaller neighbours but it was not to the same degree as managed by those in Nottinghamshire, for the Nevilles and Lumleys still dominated local society, whilst the large estates of the bishops of Durham and Durham Priory curtailed the opportunities for further expansion. It was not until the sixteenth century that such opportunities would come for the Durham gentry, with the political downfall of the Nevilles, and the financial struggles of the Lumleys and the bishops of Durham.

'The Rise of the Gentry' in the Sixteenth Century

The 'storm over the gentry' is an historiographical debate which raged between Tawney and Trevor-Roper concerning the fortunes of the gentry, and which has become inextricably linked with discourses surrounding the causes of the English Civil War, the origins of that conflict being sought in the upheavals of rural society in the century prior to its outbreak.[43] It is argued here that the rise of the gentry is a misnomer more adequately phrased as a rise of the agricultural producer who increasingly profited from the rising prices of the sixteenth century.[44] The sixteenth century was a period of rapid inflation, with landowners facing the problem of how to increase rents when their estates had been focused upon retaining tenants not exploiting them for the past century. In Tawney's words: 'such difficulties confronted all conservative landowners, both peers and commoners, in proportion to the magnitude of their commitments and the rigidity of their incomes. The most that can be said is that the former usually carried more sail than the latter, and found it, when the wind changed, more difficult to tack.'[45] When the landowners explored in the

42 Ibid., p. 10.

43 For the original debate surrounding the rise of the gentry, see: Tawney, 'The Rise of the Gentry', pp. 1–38; Tawney, 'A Postscript', pp. 91–7; Trevor-Roper, *The Gentry*. For a summary of this debate, see for example: Hexter, 'Storm over the Gentry', pp. 22–34.

44 The rise of the yeomen is in many ways as important as the rise of the gentry. Although there is significant overlap between these groups, their success depended on their exploitation of agricultural land in the sixteenth century.

45 Tawney, 'Rise of the Gentry', p. 37.

first three chapters of this book retreated from direct-demesne agriculture across the course of the late fourteenth and fifteenth centuries, they left a gap in rural society. As Eric Acheson has argued for Leicestershire during the fifteenth century, the gentry rarely leased their demesnes entirely because their households still needed supplies, and so they found it easier to profit from the rising prices of the sixteenth century.[46] If landlords like the Lumleys and the bishops of Durham wished to increase their income from land they faced the difficult tasks of trying to recover demesne land leased out over a century before or of attempting to increase their rents; neither was an easy proposition and both could lead to considerable dispute with their tenants over the course of the sixteenth century.[47]

By comparison, those agricultural producers of the sixteenth century who could create a large marketable surplus, namely the parish gentry and to a lesser extent the yeomanry, were in a much stronger position. It was often this section of society who stood to gain the most from the rise in agricultural prices, taking beneficial leases of the bishops' manors, directly managing their own lands and taking advantage of the increased economic opportunities associated with the burgeoning coal industry. Figure 18 shows the overall movements of agricultural wages and prices across this period, revealing the relative equilibrium which had been established during the fifteenth century, but also the challenges and opportunities which population growth and inflation provided in the sixteenth century. From the start of the sixteenth century, the rise in agricultural prices began to outstrip increases in wages, a process which rapidly increased from the second half of the century onwards. This provided a generation or two of agricultural producers with increasing opportunities for profits, provided, of course, that they held land by either freehold tenure, copyhold of inheritance or particularly long leases.

In Durham, the case for the 'rise of the gentry' is compelling but equally shows many of the problems of the thesis; should families which rose into the gentry be classified as evidence of this success or of the 'rise of the yeomanry'? For example, James noted that there was a striking increase in the number of families claiming gentry status, which doubled between the visitations of 1575 and 1615, as 'rich farmers, previously content with the traditional title of "yeoman", were eager to be called gentry'.[48] The successful freeholding yeoman will be discussed more in chapter 7, but they have a significant impact in Table 17 above, not least in the burgeoning numbers of single-manor families and those holding a portion of a manor, the former totalling at least fifty-six by 1640. These were families like the Shepherdsons and Shadforths

46 Eric Acheson, *A Gentry Community: Leicestershire in the Fifteenth Century, c.1422–c.1485* (Cambridge, 1992), p. 57.

47 See chapter 2 above for the disputes which arose on the dean and chapter's lands, as well as the financial problems facing the bishops of Durham. See chapter 3 above for the financial difficulties facing John, Lord Lumley, whose rental income from the palatinate of Durham had not increased by the early seventeenth century.

48 James, *Family, Lineage and Civil Society*, p. 71.

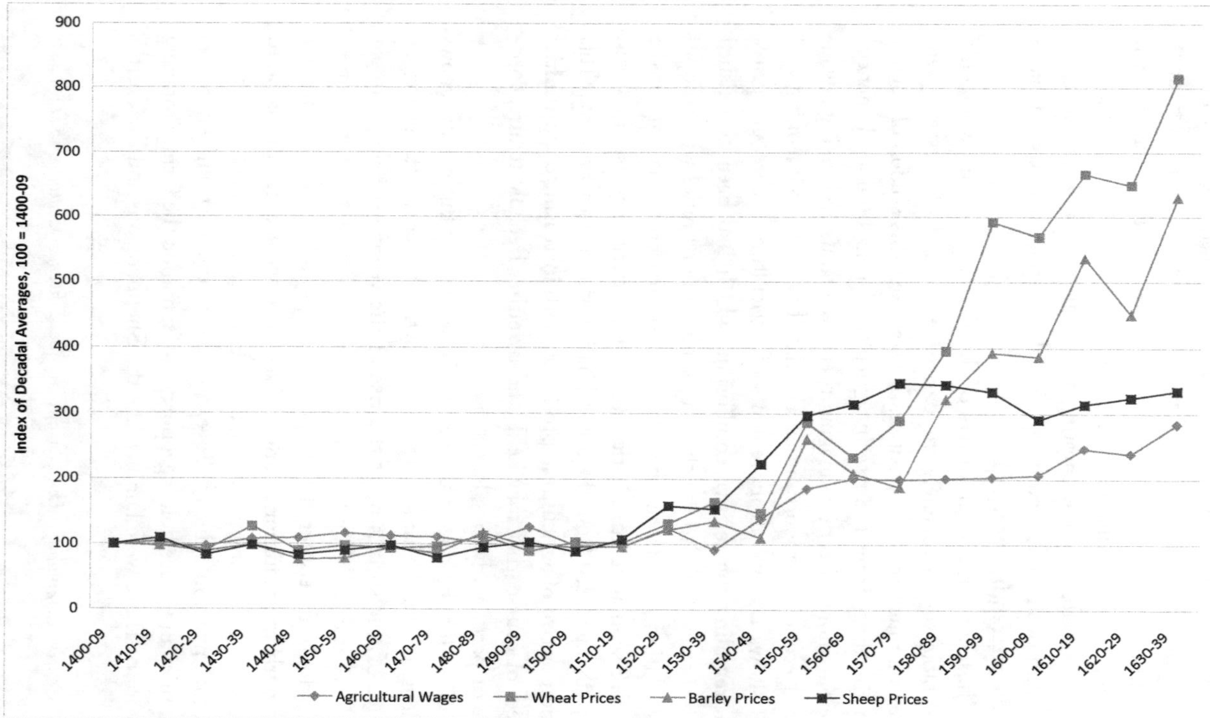

Figure 18. Index of Agricultural Wages and Prices, 1400–1640

This graph was created by making an index of the decadal averages of prices for wheat, barley and sheep and agricultural wages. As such, and given that much of the data is from the south of England, it is only intended to give a broad outline of the chronology of inflation.

Source: Gregory Clark, 'The Long March of History: Farm Wages, Population, and Economic Growth, England 1209–1869', *EcHR*, 60 (2007), table 1; and 'The Phelps Brown and Hopkins Basket of Consumables Commodity Price Series and Craftsmen's Wage Series, 1264–1700; Revised by John H. Munro', <http://www.economics.utoronto.ca/wwwfiles/archives/munro5/ResearchData.html> (accessed 1 February 2015).

who benefited from the financial problems of their landlords, the bishops of Durham and the Lumleys respectively, and were able to purchase the freehold rights to their lands.[49] Similarly, there was a greater proportion of families who held a portion of a manor like John, Lord Lumley's tenants of Murton who each gained an eighth of the manor, or the Conyers' tenants of Bishopton. There were, however, many families who had survived the fifteenth-century recession and who were able to prosper in the economic conditions of the sixteenth century.

The Lambtons are a particularly important example of this continuation of one of the ancient families of the palatinate, being another family whose name and identity were bound up with their manor. This was especially so for the Lambtons because of their association with the Worm of Lambton, a tale which involved one of their ancestors killing a great worm, warning against the dangers of procrastination and sloth.[50] Lambton was the ancestral home of the family, being returned in the IPM on the death of Robert Lambton in 1350, and remained in the hands of the family throughout this period. They were granted their other manor of Tribley in 1427 from John Arrowsmith, William Hutton and Thomas Brancepeth, clerk.[51] They also acquired several other parcels of land, the most important being their estate in Penshaw, which was purchased piecemeal. In 1370, Robert Lambton died seized of a messuage, a carucate of land and fourteen acres there, but by 1431, William Lambton had died with a messuage, three cottages, 100 acres of land, forty-eight acres of meadow, and ten acres of wood there.[52] Within another two generations the Lambtons had purchased a further messuage, sixty acres of land and two acres of wood in Penshaw and a messuage and forty acres in Bishop Houghton. Thus the Lambtons had two principal manors, Lambton and Tribley, as well as land at Penshaw, but how far were they engaged in commercial agriculture on this estate and thus reaping the profits of rising agricultural prices in the sixteenth century?

The evidence from their probate inventories suggests that the Lambtons not only retained much of this land in hand but were involved in commercial agricultural on a considerable scale. For example, the inventory taken on the death of Robert Lambton, esquire, in 1583 valued his total goods at £744 5s and shows the agricultural activity on his lands immediately after his death, with a total of over £76 worth of corn and hay and over £300 worth of livestock.[53] This included a team of ten oxen, eight horses, over 150 sheep, seventy-six lambs and over sixty cows at Lambton; eight oxen, eighteen cows and over 220 sheep at Tribley; and fifteen double acres of corn

49 See chapter 7 for more on the Shepherdsons and Shadforths, as well as the freeholding yeomen of the county.

50 A. L. Hind, *The Story of the Lambton Worm* (Durham, 1978), pp. 1–16.

51 Tribley consisted of sixty acres of arable land worth 30s per annum, twenty-four acres of meadow worth 33s 4d, and 100 acres of pasture worth 6s 8d per annum; Surtees, *History of Durham*, vol. 2, pp. 200–1.

52 TNA, DURH 3/2, f. 84–5; DKR 45, p. 229; TNA, DURH 3/2, f. 255; DKR 45, p. 232.

53 DPRI/1/1583/L1/2.

worth £20 at Penshaw. This agricultural activity, which was distributed across all of Robert's lands, was far beyond the family's own consumption requirements and was clearly intended for the market, especially the substantial numbers of cattle and sheep. Robert Lambton also had a considerable wealth of household goods valued at £51 18s, with, for example, linen worth £12 and pewter vessels valued at £5. There were also four featherbeds, five other beds and five servants' beds, suggesting substantial amounts of hired labour was employed by the family throughout the year. Furthermore, he possessed plate and jewellery worth £20, and around £110 in ready money, whilst his funeral expenses were equal to his social status, coming to a total of £80. In his will Robert made bequests of £32 a year to his four younger sons, Roger, John, William and James, as well as £100 for each of his daughters' marriage portions: Margery, who married John Tempest, esquire, and Jane, who married Sir William Blakiston of Gibside.[54] His will also makes mention of a coal mine at Lambton, which was being leased out to Mr Heath for £20 annually.

The inventory taken on the death of Ralph Lambton, esquire, the eldest son and heir of Robert, also survives, for he died just over a decade later in 1594 with a total moveable wealth estimated at £996 7s.[55] Ralph appears to have purchased further land at Beddick, and with this was able to increase the size of the family's agricultural activities. At Lambton there were now sixty-four cows, twenty-two calves, two bulls, 240 sheep, eight horses and fifteen swine; at Tribley there were seventeen cows and 150 sheep; at Penshaw there were thirty-two acres of corn in the ground, twenty draught oxen, fifteen cows, 130 sheep and four work horses; and at Beddick, there was corn on the ground and in the yard worth nearly £60, twenty-one draught oxen, eight cows and a handful of horses. In total, Ralph possessed £184 worth of corn and hay and over £500 worth of livestock. He was not just expanding the agricultural pursuits of the family, for he was very aware of the profitability of the coal industry and, along with the coal mine at Lambton, possessed coal and gear at Penshaw worth £34, his own keel worth £30 and three salt pans at Sunderland valued at £100.[56] The value of his household goods was considerable at £80, with, for example, £18 worth of napery and a selection of claret and white wine worth £7, although much of his plate and jewellery had been bequeathed as heirlooms before the inventory was taken. The Lambtons were thus an archetype of the successful gentry family in this period, taking advantage of all the economic activities in the region, not just passively reaping the benefits of increasing agricultural prices, but also engaging in the burgeoning coal industry and its ancillary operations whilst they ploughed these profits back into the countryside.

The Bellasises were a similarly long-standing family in the Durham countryside who found themselves able to fill the void created by the problems of the larger

54 DPRI/1/1583/L1/1.

55 DPRI/1/1594/L1/1–4.

56 Ibid.

landowners of the palatinate during the sixteenth century. They were not only able to command the leases of some of the bishops' best manors because of their loyal service, but were in such an economically advantageous position that they purchased several manors, one of which was from Lord Lumley himself. Peculiarly the Bellasises were no longer of Bellasis, having exchanged their ancestral manor with Durham Priory for the manor of Henknoll near Auckland, and thus the primary land of the family throughout these two centuries was at Henknoll, which was valued at £5 in the IPM of John Bellasis in 1409.[57] It was in the sixteenth century, however, that the fortunes of the family significantly improved, especially with the leasing of the bishops' manors. The manor and grange of Morton were leased to Richard Errington, gentleman, for forty years by Bishop Fox but the lease soon found its way into the hands of Richard Bellasis who had married the daughter and heir of Errington, and in 1525 Cardinal Wolsey confirmed the lease with a fixed rent of £6.[58] It was in these years that Richard Bellasis leased the Railey coal mines as part of a consortium, whilst he also acted as a bailiff of Stockton and constable of Durham Castle.[59] Morton grange appears to have remained in the hands of the Bellasis family for generations, with a lease for twenty-one years granted to Richard Bellasis in 1580 and, even after the manor was leased to the Crown for seventy years in 1585, it was Richard Bellasis who retained the manor.[60] In the 1640s it was still in the hands of the Bellasis family with a rent of £6, but was valued at £90 per annum by the parliamentary surveyors.[61] Bishop Cosin was particularly troubled by these preferential leases, especially when William Bellasis tried to persuade him to convert the lease of Morton to three lives, complaining that:

> He maketh great instance (having deserved well for his service done to the King and his country in the late rebellious times) that ... his lease for years may be changed into a lease for 3 lives ... because it was let for 70 years before. But I am not willing to do it. If his importunity chance hereafter to prevail with me or my successors, let the rent at least be advanced to £10 from £6.[62]

Through these advantageous leases of the assets of the bishopric, the Bellasis family were able to purchase further land in the sixteenth century. It has already been seen how John, Lord Lumley, was approaching financial disaster and sold the manor of Ludworth to Richard Bellasis of Morton.[63] This manor was then inherited

57 TNA, DURH 3/2, f. 165; DKR 45, p. 166.

58 Surtees, *History of Durham*, vol. 1, pp. 202–4.

59 Britnell, 'The Coal Industry', p. 463.

60 DUL, ASC, CCB Registers of Leases and Patents, 1–5, c.1530–c.1640.

61 Kirby (ed.), *Parliamentary Surveys*, vol. 2, p. 157.

62 Clack, 'Bishop Cosin's Survey', pp. 228–36.

63 See chapter 3 above for the financial problems that John, Lord Lumley, was experiencing in the second half of the sixteenth century, pp. 131–9.

by Brian Bellasis, esquire, who succeeded his uncle, and then by William Bellasis, esquire, son and heir of Brian, who had livery in 1614 and became high sheriff of the county of Durham from 1628 until his death in 1641, receiving King Charles on his Scottish progress in 1633 at the head of the gentry.[64] Similarly, Richard Bellasis gained the manor of Great Haswell from the Widdrington family, which he settled in trustees on himself for life and the remainder, failing his own issue, to his nephews, Brian, Charles and James Bellasis. The manor of Owton also came into the possession of the family. In 1574, the queen granted the manor of Owton, a parcel of the lands of Robert Lambert who was attainted for high treason, to Edmund Gresham and Percival Gunston. After a series of transfers it came into Richard Bellasis' hands and he settled the manor on his nephews.[65]

The revealing will of Richard Bellasis shows that he had hardly over-extended his wealth with these acquisitions. Indeed, his purchases pale in comparison to the stores of ready cash he possessed at Morton. He made various bequests of goods to his family, the most notable cash bequests being the £64 to his sister Jane Hedworth; £30 each to his nieces Katherine Bainbridge, Elizabeth Fenwick, Margery Constable and Anne Conyers; £200 to his nieces Isabell and Margaret Hedworth for their marriage portions; £100 to his servant Margaret Lambert; £100 each to his nephews Richard Pullen and Richard Hedworth; £10 to each of his servants, Michael Myers, William Thursby, William Rudd and Robert Rutter; £100 to the mending of highways in county Durham; and lastly, £100 each to his nephews Brian, Charles and James Bellasis.[66] Unlike many testators, he was not anticipating that these large bequests would be financed by the sale of his personal goods or from mortgaging his property but instead expected them to be made from the ready coin he possessed at Morton, which is shown in a schedule of gold and silver attached to his will in 1597.[67] At his house in Morton he possessed £500 which had been walled away in his staircase; a further £300 which was also walled away there; £200 which was hidden under the highest step of the staircase; £200 which had been put into a wooden box and walled away in the great chamber; £100 which was within the bottom of the table chair in his bedchamber; £400 which was hidden in a presser in the study; £200 which was in his chamber in Jarrow; and a further £64 which had been hidden within a shoe in his study.[68] This ready cash accrued partly because Richard never married, nor had

64 Surtees, *History of Durham*, vol. 1, pp. 202–4.

65 Ibid., pp. 123–4.

66 DPRI/1/1599/B6/1–2. He also made bequests of around £6 to each of the following parishes for the relief of the poor: Jarrow, Houghton, Easington, Pittington, Kirkletham (co. York), Cockwold (co. York), and Blacterne (co. Westmorland), St Andrew in Auckland, and to the prisoners of Durham gaol, as well as £5 to the School of Kepier.

67 DPRI/1/1599/B6/3–4.

68 For example, this list starts: 'Firstly in current coin of gold, of several sorts all of which is now wrapped up in one several thin piece of lead, as follows: viz: in old angells 760, containing £380. Item in old rials at 15s a piece 100, containing £75. Item in new rials or sovereigns 90, containing

children, but even if this is taken into consideration, it was an extraordinary list of ready money to have sequestered away at his home, especially if his previous land purchases are taken into consideration. Through the sound management of his lands and the advantageous leases acquired from the bishops of Durham, Richard Bellasis had thus been able to purchase a further three manors and accumulate quite literally thousands of pounds' worth of ready gold and silver by the time of his death.

There were a whole host of gentry families in the sixteenth century whose experiences were similar to that of the Bellasis family and none more so than the Blakistons, who, in the words of the nineteenth-century antiquarian Surtees, 'reached the zenith of [their] wealth and honours under John Blakiston the *paterfamilias*, of 1575'.[69] The Blakistons held the manors of Blakiston and Coxhoe throughout this period, which in 1418 were valued at £40 per annum, as well as further parcels of land throughout the palatinate, and prospered during much of the sixteenth century.[70] By comparison to the ancient lineage of the Lambtons, the Milots of White Hill had very humble beginnings in the late fourteenth century, being one of those families who used the opportunities of the post-Black Death period to accumulate a manorial holding. John Milot was originally a free tenant at Pelaw, a village a mile to the north-east of White Hill, who was active in the local land market and acquired the estate of White Hill from its previous owners in the 1380s. It was families like the Milots who, Christian Liddy concluded, 'remained, in financial terms, gentry landholders of very modest rank'.[71] Indeed, White Hill was little more than a freehold farm, which on the death of William Milot in 1437 was comprised of a hall, a chamber, a kitchen, a granary, a stable and a kilnhouse, with sixty-seven acres of arable land and three closes containing forty-four acres of arable and six of meadow.[72]

The Milots are more representative of those families who were established in the west of the bishopric, whose landed estates were small, but who had other sources of income upon which to rely, one of the most important being coal. Using the natural resources of their holdings, these smaller members of the gentry were able

£45. This said some is £500; And all these parcells, aforesaid, being thus laid up, and put, in three several sorts, are now together walled upon the left hand, and west side, of the little dark stair, that goes down out of my bedchamber at Morton, into my study there, about three quarters of a yard above the upper step or stair, and Margaret Lambert is only privy thereto, who helped me to lay it there', and continues in this vein until the 'further £64 of gold which was put within a bag, thrust into an old leather shoe, and lies upon the upper floor of the said presser, in my study, where the glasses stand, on the west end, behind two books'.

69 Surtees, *History of Durham*, vol. 3, pp. 159–64.

70 In an inquest on the death of Thomas Blakiston, esquire, in 1483 Blakiston was described as containing a hall, pantry and buttery, 6 chambers, a kitchen, a stable and other buildings, an orchard, 44 oxgangs of land, each of 15 acres, 60 acres of meadow and 100 acres of pasture: TNA, DURH 3/4, f. 81; DKR 44, p. 324. In 1418, the manor house and mill of Coxhoe were described as ruinous, along with 10 messuages, 10 cottages, 300 acres of arable land, 30 acres of meadow and 1,000 acres of moorland, Surtees, *History of Durham*, vol. 3, pp. 159–64.

71 Liddy, *The Bishopric of Durham*, p. 74.

72 TNA, DURH 3/2, f. 286; DKR 45, p. 241.

to fund further purchases of land. By the end of the fifteenth century the manor of Mayland and the vill of Newton had been acquired by the Milots, as had a moiety of the manor of Beddick Waterville. During the sixteenth century the Bowes family purchased this moiety of the manor from Thomas Milot, esquire, and so united the manor in the Bowes family (the other half having descended to the Bowes through inheritance). An interesting document, written by George Bowes in 1595, describes the manor as containing 464 acres of meadow and pasture, of which no part had been arable for the past sixteen years, being rented for two years together at £114 per annum. He then described the ample salmon fishing there and a seam of coal which he estimated would yield £200 per annum clear benefit when fully exploited, and attested that he had purchased the land for £1,640 and would take no less than £2,200 for the sale of the property.[73]

By the start of the seventeenth century, the Milots were relatively prosperous and could no longer be dismissed as amongst the poorest of the squirearchy, with the inventory of Robert Milot, esquire, of Chester-le-Street worth £379 16s 2d in 1622.[74] The agricultural pursuits of Robert were not significantly dissimilar to those of the yeomanry, with at White Hill corn in the ground worth £17, eight oxen, nine cows, six mares, fifty sheep and a handful of swine, geese, hens and ducks; and at Mayland six oxen, seven cows, seventy-eight sheep and five horses. It was his household goods, however, that confirmed his gentry status and high living standards: valued at a total of £90, they included linen worth £18, pewter worth £5, plate and jewellery worth £16 and a clock described as an heirloom. In total he possessed £31 worth of corn and hay and £107 in livestock, but the family had clearly diversified into the coal industry, for he also owned a keel worth £20 and 'coals wrought at the pit and staithes' worth £96 13s 4d. Thus over the course of this period the Milots went from being free tenants in the middle of the fourteenth century to important members of the squirearchy by the sixteenth century with the financial base to support such claims, primarily it appears through the exploitation of the subterranean wealth of their lands.

Conclusion

Discussing the economic fortunes of the gentry in this period is ultimately impossible, but equally irresistible. It is not only because the term 'gentry' is a social construct that so much debate has ensued, but also because they formed the middle section of rural society, sharing characteristics of both the aristocracy and the yeomanry at either extremity. As Holt observed, the 'gentry are always rising; it is their habit': a habit they share with the middle-class.[75] Indeed, Saul went so far as to argue that

73 Surtees, *History of Durham*, vol. 1, pp. 198–201.

74 DPRI/1/1622/M6/1–3.

75 J. C. Holt, *The Northerners: A Study in the Reign of King John* (Oxford, 1961), p. 60.

'were we to seek "the rise of the gentry", we would do well to look to the fourteenth century as much as to the sixteenth'.[76] In many ways he is right, for it was in the fourteenth century, especially after the increasing stratification of society following the Black Death, that the newer social ranks of esquire and gentleman arose. But if so, it was a relatively short-lived rise, at least for the poorer members of the gentry whose numbers were savagely halved by the middle of the fifteenth century in the palatinate of Durham: showing that the gentry as a social group were not always rising. It was members of this section of society who were so vulnerable to the joint pincers of low prices and high wages as they tried to maintain a social status and military function that their declining real incomes simply could not sustain. These parish gentry had all of the social ambitions of their larger neighbours but without the economic base to justify them, thus experiencing a much higher level of expenditure than their yeomen counterparts. Indeed, some of these parish gentry may have even emulated larger landlords by renting out their lands, which would likely have proven disastrous in the late fourteenth century since they would have faced mounting arrears and declining incomes without the assets to ride out any cash-flow problems. Although this is impossible to prove given the lack of evidence, many of these families may well have been facing the same problems evident in the account rolls of much larger rentier landlords but with very little room to manoeuvre. Family after family, some of whom had held their ancestral manors since the Norman Conquest, were forced to sell their lands to their larger neighbours in the palatinate of Durham from the late fourteenth century onwards.

By comparison, if the sixteenth century was a period of crisis for many rentier landowners, it was a century of opportunity for the gentry, who, because of their very nature, often possessed characteristics of both the yeomanry and aristocracy. These gentry figures in the sixteenth century were able to capitalise on the rising profits of agriculture in a fashion often more reminiscent of the yeomanry than the aristocracy. It was the likes of the Lambtons, Bellasises and Blakistons who, having survived the crucible of the fifteenth-century recession, were able to take advantage of the problems of their rentier neighbours. Richard Bellasis, notably, exploited both the long leases of the bishops' lands and the financial difficulties of John, Lord Lumley, accumulating a considerable fortune in the process. Stone argued that the great rebuilding between 1575 and 1625 saw more 'country-house building than any other fifty-year period in our history, which is itself significant proof of a "rise of the gentry"'.[77] Again, the Durham gentry were often at the forefront of this improvement in living standards and comfort, with the likes of Lady Bellasis recorded in the Hearth Tax of 1666 as occupying a twelve-room house in the borough of Elvet and Robert Lambton,

76 Nigel Saul, *Knights and Esquires: The Gloucestershire Gentry in the Fourteenth Century* (Oxford, 1981), p. 262.

77 W. G. Hoskins, 'The Rebuilding of Rural England, 1570–1640', *P&P*, 4 (1953), pp. 44–59; Stone, 'Social Mobility', p. 26.

gentleman, living in considerable comfort in a fifteen-room house at Penshaw.[78] This is not to say that all the gentry rose, for many continued as befitting their station, but there was a new opportunity for this group in society which had not been there a generation before. It was an opportunity arising not only from the problems of larger landowners but also from increasing prices, especially in the north-east of England, where the take-off of the coal industry not only stimulated high demand for agricultural goods but also offered investment opportunities for enterprising families from the mid-sixteenth century. If, in 1600, 'it could be said that the richer gentry had the incomes of an earl and, in 1628, that the House of Commons could buy the House of Lords three times over', then Durham, with the forfeiture and fragmentation of two aristocratic estates, the financial problems of the Church and the opportunities for advancement amongst the gentry, was at the forefront of this redistribution of economic power.[79] The sixteenth century was a period of rapid inflation, with landowners facing the problem of how to increase rents when their estates had been focused upon retaining tenants rather than commercially exploiting them for the past century.[80] It was this long-term tenurial development of their estates which provided landowners and tenants in the sixteenth century with so many problems as they tried to renegotiate leases, custom or legal practice in their favour.[81]

Was there a crisis of the aristocracy in the sixteenth century, with a corresponding rise of the gentry? Certainly in Durham this is the overwhelming impression of the period: the Nevilles disappeared from the Durham countryside because of their political misadventures; the landed estates of the Lumleys, the Bowes and the Conyers were greatly diminished through a long period of sales or divided inheritances; whilst the Claxtons died out in the male line in the late fifteenth century. Coupled with the seizure of land from various monasteries at the dissolution, this led to a significant redistribution in the landed assets of the palatinate, which saw an influx of mercantile wealth from Newcastle, alongside an increase in the number of yeomanry and minor gentry purchasing portions of manors. As David Reid concluded, 'local power then in [the sixteenth and seventeenth centuries] had come to lie in the hands of a gentry whose strength was based on a fusion of mercantile and mining wealth with the land of Durham'.[82] He went further, arguing that:

> The older gentry, if they were to maintain their political influence, it became increasingly necessary for them to pursue wealth through marriage alliances and

78 A. Green, E. Parkinson, and M. Spufford (eds), *County Durham Hearth Tax Assessment Lady Day 1666*, introduced by Adrian Green (London, 2006), p. 58.

79 Tawney, 'Rise of the Gentry', p. 37.

80 Ibid., p. 10.

81 Acheson, *A Gentry Community*, p. 57.

82 Reid, *Durham Crown Lordships*, p. 7.

> business connections in Newcastle, by a more commercial exploitation of their lands, or by the fostering of industry or mining where such possibilities existed.[83]

Many members of the gentry could be seen commercially exploiting their lands on a scale three or four times that of their yeomen neighbours, whilst they were increasingly turning to the mineral deposits on their property as a source of wealth. Of course, this was nothing novel – many members of the laity were engaged in the coal industry in the fourteenth and fifteenth centuries as the grants of wayleave by the bishops of Durham confirm – but it was the sheer scale of operations which increased during the sixteenth century.[84] One of the most consistent trends in the historiography of the sixteenth and early seventeenth centuries is the agreement that it was a prosperous period for certain groups of producers in the English countryside.[85] This is explored further in the following chapters in relation to the decline of the peasantry and rise of the yeomanry, but this idea has a much wider significance in these transitional debates.

Instead of suggesting the rise or fall of an entire social group such as the gentry, one which was open at both ends of the spectrum and incorporated a whole host of different families, it is perhaps more useful to think of the problem in terms of land usage: between rentier landlords and agricultural producers. That is not to say that all landlords declined, but it is probably safe to say that all faced problems: some such as the dean and chapter of Durham and the Percys were able to overcome them; others such as the Lumleys and bishops of Durham were not. Even the Crown faced difficulties when trying to increase the rents of the former Nevilles' leasehold tenants. Social status was less important in this respect than the management of landed resources. As agricultural prices rose, farmers were able to create larger surpluses and thus members of the gentry and yeomanry were able to prosper. The reason why members of the gentry tended to prosper more in this relationship was simply one of scale: upon Ralph Lambton's death, for example, he possessed corn and hay worth £184 and livestock worth over £500 – commercial agriculture on a scale that relatively few yeomen could accomplish, primarily because of his greater access to land. Social station, however, was very important in terms of expenditure, with families like the Conyers burdening their estates with large marriage portions; the Lumleys maintaining all the pomp of ancient aristocracy; and the Bowes incurring considerable expenses in their service to the Crown. For these families, managing the clash of income as an economic group and the expenditure expected of a social group proved an insurmountable challenge, which often resulted in the sale or mortgage of land

83 Ibid., p. 8.

84 For the grant of wayleaves to lay landowners for permission to take coal across the bishops' lands, see Britnell, 'The Coal Industry', pp. 445–6; and DUL, ASC, Receiver General's Accounts, CCB B/1/1–CCB B/6/69.

85 Stone, 'Social Mobility', p. 26; Trevor-Roper, *The Gentry*, p. 9.

and the fragmentation of their estates. Rents alone were rarely enough to improve the position of most families, with successful gentlemen needing the profits of either farming or coal in order to thrive; the combination of increasing agricultural prices and the take-off of the coal industry provided amble reward for men such as Richard Bellasis who were able to exploit the stagnant rents on the estates of both the bishops of Durham and the Lumleys.

Rather than think of the sixteenth century as a period of conflict between Tawney's gentry and Stone's aristocracy, or between Trevor-Roper's 'court' and 'country' gentry, it is more useful to analyse rural society in economic categories; so many of the disputes of the sixteenth century arose between 'those who were becoming mere rentiers, and those who were actively engaged in productive activities, whether in agriculture, industry, or trade'.[86] If we are to think of the problems of this period in terms of the rise of agricultural producers and the crisis of rentier landlords we must do so cautiously. It was not an inevitable decline for all rentier landlords, but it was perhaps a crisis for all rentiers, and this period is littered with legal disputes between tenants and landlords over access to the profits provided by inflation.[87] Likewise, agricultural profits were no shortcut to wealth; that was still the preserve of coal in the north-east, which quickly became monopolised by Newcastle merchants, intent upon not only controlling the ecclesiastical collieries but also acquiring as much coal-bearing land as possible.[88] However, agricultural profits did allow for the slow accumulation of wealth across several generations, which, if combined with other industrial ventures, could ensure the prosperity of an ancient gentry family or a member of the burgeoning yeomanry.[89]

The reason many of the aristocracy seem to have struggled was because they tended to be large rentier landlords with priorities elsewhere in the realm, whereas the local gentry tended to maintain some form of direct-demesne production, or at least found it easier to revert to this kind of land-usage in the sixteenth century. The inability of the ninth earl of Northumberland to increase his rental income from Tynemouth is illustrative of this problem, as are the financial difficulties John, Lord Lumley, encountered compared to the prosperity of Richard Bellasis. It was this slow and steady redistribution of wealth down the social scale, especially helped by the long leases of the bishops' manors, which saw a gradual fragmentation of large estates

86 Hill, *Puritanism and Revolution*, p. 8.

87 See the essays in Whittle (ed.), *Landlords and Tenants*, especially Holt, 'The Financial Rewards of Winning the Battle for Secure Customary Tenure', pp. 134–49; Harold Garrett-Goodyear, 'Common Law and Manor Courts: Lords, Copyholders and Doing Justice in Early Tudor England', pp. 35–51; and Jean Morrin, 'The Transfer to Leasehold', pp. 117–32; and also Chris Brooks, *Law Politics and Society in Early Modern England* (Cambridge, 2008), pp. 307–51.

88 See chapter 5 for a discussion of the inroads made into Durham landed society by Newcastle merchants across the fifteenth, sixteenth and early seventeenth centuries.

89 See chapter 7 for more on the opportunities available to yeomen in this period, especially in the Wearside coal industry which was not monopolised by a handful of Newcastle merchants.

across the sixteenth century. Alongside the influx of new wealth from the prebendaries of the cathedral and Newcastle merchants explored in the following chapter, this represented a wholesale redistribution of the landed resources of the palatinate of Durham by the seventeenth century, with remarkably few large landowners where just a century before there had been many.[90] The upheavals of the sixteenth century have a much longer history than is often recognised, however, dating back to at least the withdrawal from the direct management of demesnes by landowners in the late fourteenth and early fifteenth centuries. The tenurial development of estates across this period influenced the shape that many agricultural disputes took in the sixteenth century, often affecting the real incomes and economic opportunities available to landlords and tenants alike.[91] It is no coincidence that many of the tenants of John, Lord Lumley, and Sir George Conyers were purchasing their lords' lands as agricultural profits came into the hands of those who worked the land rather than owned it in the second half of the sixteenth century.[92]

90 Of course, this was a deliberate Elizabethan policy, with the downfall of the Nevilles; the Percys and Lumleys becoming largely southern landowners at Syon House and Nonsuch Palace respectively; and no new creations in the north, much to the chagrin of Sir George Bowes. See for example: Stone, *Crisis of the Aristocracy*, pp. 252–4. However, this redistribution of landed resources goes beyond Crown intervention, representing many of the problems and opportunities that inflation created in the region during the sixteenth century.

91 See chapter 2 for the financial struggles of the bishops of Durham and the dean and chapter during the sixteenth century. See chapter 3 for the example of John, Lord Lumley, who was forced to sell over half of his ancestral lands in the north of England because of mounting financial problems.

92 This was probably the case for much of England in the mid-sixteenth century as a generation or two of successful yeomen and gentry were able to benefit before landlords could increasingly make inroads into the unearned increment created by inflation by the end of the century. Even so, the Lumleys and bishops of Durham never managed to increase rents in this period, whilst it was only in the early seventeenth century that the Percys, the Crown and the dean and chapter succeeded in increasing rents and entry fines on their lands.

5

The Influx of 'New' Wealth

John Hatcher's work on the British coal industry highlighted the rapid take-off of coal exports in the late sixteenth and early seventeenth centuries from Newcastle, as 'we are driven unerringly to the 1570s and 1580s as the turning-point' in the history of the coal trade.[1] Between the late 1560s and the 1590s shipments of coal rose fourfold for the sea trade alone. In the ensuing twenty-five years shipments virtually doubled again to reach an average of over 400,000 tons a year in the early 1620s.[2] It was at this time that power over the coal industry was passing into the hands of a 'few rich men of Newcastle', who had obtained a 'plain monopoly or staple of coal' and, through the Grand Lease, had 'dealt a final blow to the aspirations of the bishops of Durham to share in the coal trade'.[3] The Newcastle Hostmen, or Lords of Coal as they were christened by the local inhabitants, were a small group of Newcastle merchants, led initially by Henry Anderson and William Selby, who formed an oligarchy at the pinnacle of Newcastle society in terms of both office-holding and wealth.[4] How far did the increasing mercantile wealth derived from this precocious development of the coal industry find its way into the Durham countryside and so disrupt the balance of lay landownership outlined in the preceding chapters?

Nef described these merchants as frequently acquiring 'great estates and set[ting] up as country gentlemen, allying themselves by marriage with the local gentry, and eventually retiring from direct participation in the trade of Newcastle'. He then reeled off a whole host of such examples:

> Thomas Liddell's purchase of Ravensworth and Ralph Cole's purchase of Brancepeth are only two examples of a general movement among the coal merchants to buy up local manors. The Selbys set up at Winlaton, the Tempests at Stella. The Andersons formed connections by marriage with the Collingwoods and the Gascoignes; the Selbys formed connections with the Bellasis, the Curwen, the Delaval, and the Darcy families.[5]

1 Hatcher, *British Coal Industry*, p. 78.

2 Ibid., p. 78; Nef, *Rise of the British Coal Industry*, vol. 1, p. 25.

3 Nef, *Rise of the British Coal Industry*, vol. 2, p. 120. See chapters 1 and 2 for the use of coal by the bishops of Durham in the fifteenth century and the effects of the Grand Lease upon them in the sixteenth century.

4 Ibid., p. 121. Newton, *North-East England*, pp. 35–6.

5 Nef, *Rise of the British Coal Industry*, vol. 2, p. 121.

Mervyn James used particularly militaristic language to describe this process and thought that it was only natural that these Newcastle coal merchants should '*invade* the Durham countryside' and were 'present *in force* by 1615', when ten coal-owning families recorded their arms at the heraldic visitation.[6] This view represents a much broader historiographical tradition which has seen these acquisitions as being a general sign of merchants' desires to integrate into landed society, seeking validation and status through such purchases. Thus far, much of this book has focused upon people already established in rural society, but this chapter explores the influx of other groups into the Durham countryside and how far they upset the traditional balance of landed power in this period.

The debate surrounding the position of merchants in English society has proven controversial not only because of the ambiguities of the social structure of medieval and early modern England, but also because of a tendency amongst historians to discuss merchants as a group with one aim, one ambition, and as a result to judge their achievements by one yardstick. As F. M. L. Thompson commented, 'merchants and manufacturers did not form a monolithic class, but were socially differentiated, entertaining different social ambitions just as they held different political opinions'.[7] This is particularly important for any study of landed society in the north-east of England because the acquisitions made by Roger Thornton in the fifteenth century, seen in chapter 3, were but a precursor for a series of much broader purchases made by merchant families throughout the sixteenth and seventeenth centuries. But what were the economic, social and political motivations for such acquisitions and was the ultimate ambition of these merchants to withdraw from the city and assimilate into landed society?

It has often been thought that the aspiration of merchants was to gain enough money to leave their trade and acquire gentility through landed possessions, to retire and, in Nef's words, set up as country gentlemen.[8] This belief is founded upon assumptions about English society in this period which often sit ill at ease with much of the surviving evidence. In this historical interpretation it is assumed not only that gentry status could only be acquired through landed possessions, but also that it was the ambition of all merchants to assimilate into rural society. In his general survey of medieval England, for example, Pollard noted that the 'ultimate goal was the acquisition of land, title and lordship and entry into the ranks of the gentry'.[9] Despite acknowledging that there was a close affinity in culture and outlook between urban oligarchs and the country gentry of early modern England, J. A. Sharpe still commented that, 'above all, successful merchants often left the counting house for the

6 James, *Family, Lineage, and Civil Society*, p. 70. My italics.

7 F. M. L. Thompson, *Gentrification and the Enterprise Culture: Britain, 1780–1980* (Oxford, 2001), p. 15.

8 Nef, *Rise of the British Coal Industry*, vol. 2, p. 121.

9 A. J. Pollard, *Late Medieval England, 1399–1509* (Harlow, 2000), p. 185.

pleasures of country life and the desirable status of country gentleman'.[10] Such a view has dominated the thinking of many historians of late medieval and early modern England and has been compounded by the contemporary problem of placing wealthy merchants into the traditional categories of those who worked, those who prayed and those who fought.[11]

It is a debate which has followed mercantile and industrial wealth well into the eighteenth and nineteenth centuries, with Michael Flinn arguing that 'the first goal of many a merchant was the acquisition of a landed estate with a stately home, and an unknown proportion of all mercantile profits in the eighteenth century was poured into this form of conspicuous consumption'.[12] Richard Wilson built on this to claim that 'the peak of *any* merchant's ultimate ambition was not to build up the largest firm in his trade, but ultimately to found a prominent and stable landed dynasty'.[13] Although he conceded that the merchant was not 'ashamed of his activities or felt compelled to hide his profits beneath the garb of broad acres', Wilson went on to note that 'because the way of life of the landowner was the ideal of commercial society, because land conferred political and social privileges and because it was often the best means of holding wealth, landownership was *always* the goal of the wealthiest merchants'.[14] Certainly some merchants fit this traditional narrative very well and made the transition from urban oligarch to landed gentleman within a generation or two, but many did not and instead formed urban dynasties for generations. When discussing the merchants of the seventeenth century, Keith Wrightson has argued that they belonged to an 'independent ladder of status' from the land-related scale of the gentry, but still noted that 'there was no doubt' that 'their urban status was inferior to that of established landowning families'.[15] The rise of the legal profession has been relatively well documented and it is now commonplace to allow for their place amongst the gentry, showing that the term itself was not synonymous with landowning in England, with particular emphasis upon service, office-holding and wealth as indicators of status.[16]

10 J. A. Sharpe, *Early Modern England: A Social History, 1550–1760* (London, 1987), p. 182.

11 S. H. Rigby, 'Introduction: Social Structure and Economic Change in Late Medieval England', in R. Horrox and W. M. Ormrod (eds.), *A Social History of England, 1200–1500* (Cambridge, 2006), p. 5.

12 M. W. Flinn, *Origins of the Industrial Revolution* (London, 1966), pp. 44–5.

13 R. G. Wilson, *Gentlemen Merchants: the Merchant Community in Leeds, 1700–1830* (Manchester, 1971), p. 220. My italics.

14 Ibid., p. 220 and p. 230. My italics.

15 Keith Wrightson, *English Society, 1580–1680* (London, 1982), p. 27.

16 Maurice Keen, *The Origins of the English Gentleman: Heraldry, Chivalry, and Gentility in Medieval England, c.1300–1500* (Stroud, 2003), p. 131; for a review of early modern urban culture, see Philip Withington, 'Two Renaissances: Urban Political Culture in Post-Reformation England Reconsidered', *HJ*, 44 (2001), pp. 239–67 and his book, *The Politics of Commonwealth: Citizens and Freemen in Early Modern England* (Cambridge, 2005). See also, Heal and Holmes, *The Gentry in England and Wales*, pp. 8–9.

Merchants, by comparison, have often been seen as ostentatiously aping characteristics of gentry behaviour, with their elite mentality and evident wealth interpreted as pretensions above their social status rather than as reflections of it.[17] Maurice Keen has partially challenged this assumption by arguing that mercantile activity in itself was not contrary to gentility in medieval England, with no laws of *derogeance* comparable to those on the Continent, but he maintained that mercantile activities were not sufficient to guarantee gentry status.[18] Caroline Barron has shown the distinctly mercantile and civic view which medieval London merchants had of themselves, pointing to the fact that they were not necessarily covetous of the lifestyles of the landed elite.[19] But the most important contribution to this debate was Rosemary Horrox's essay on the urban gentry in which she presented the idea of an urban gentry who bore many of the same attributes that historians have noted for the landed gentry, but who lived, worked and died in towns.[20] Even though some medieval merchants undoubtedly desired to become landed gentlemen, many seem to have had comparatively little interest in the chivalric pursuits of their landed counterparts, neither reading their literature nor participating in their tournaments and, although merchants adopted some traditional forms of authority, it was often to suit their own, specifically civic, ideals.[21] For example, they used armorial bearings in memorial works, but often combined them with their own merchants' marks, not only making a distinctly urban statement, but also revealing pride in their mercantile identity.[22] In their use of pageantry and heraldry merchants created an urban answer to the chivalry of the landed hierarchy, adopting the elements that suited their purposes but choosing to ignore others.

Merchant brasses, for example, show a pride in their trade that seems quite at odds with the image of gentrification that has since become the received idea amongst historians studying this period.[23] The brass of the London vintner Simon Seman

17 W. M. Ormrod, *The Reign of Edward III* (Stroud, 2000), p. 166. See for example: Chris King, 'The Interpretation of Urban Buildings: Power, Memory and Appropriation in Norwich Merchants' Houses, c. 1400–1660', *World Archaeology*, 41 (2009), pp. 471–88.

18 Keen, *Origins of the English Gentleman*, p. 126.

19 C. Barron, 'Chivalry, Pageantry and Merchant Culture in Medieval London', in Peter Coss and Maurice Keen (eds.), *Heraldry, Pageantry and Social Display in Medieval England* (Woodbridge, 2002), p. 225.

20 R. Horrox, 'The Urban Gentry in the Fifteenth Century', in J. Thompson (ed.), *Towns and Townspeople in the Fifteenth Century* (Gloucester, 1988), p. 22.

21 Out of the sixty-one wills that may be broadly characterised as those of London citizens studied by Susan Cavanaugh only three of these testators mention chivalric or romantic books, cited in Barron, 'Chivalry, Pageantry and Merchant Culture', p. 220.

22 Merchant marks were often seen as interchangeable with merchants' armorial bearings. See for example, C. M. Barnett, 'Memorials and Commemoration in the Parish Churches of Late Medieval York' (York Doctoral Thesis, 1997), p. 207.

23 See for example: Barron, 'Chivalry, Pageantry and Merchant Culture', p. 238; Nigel Saul, 'Bold as Brass: Secular Display in English Medieval Brasses', in Peter Coss and Maurice Keen (eds.), *Heraldry, Pageantry and Social Display in Medieval England* (Woodbridge, 2002), pp. 169–194.

at St Mary's Church, Barton-on-Humber, Lincolnshire, is a very good example of this pride that merchants took in their occupations as he is depicted standing on wine casks surrounded by an inscription and his merchant's mark.[24] Similarly, the inscription on William Greville's memorial brass at Chipping Campden in Gloucestershire proudly proclaims him to be 'late citizen of London and the flower of the wool merchants of all of England'.[25] This style is so reminiscent of the language used to proclaim a knight the flower of English chivalry that it is likely this was an intentional comparison between mercantile activities and those of knights. Moreover, contemporary literature on precedent, like John Russell's *Boke of Nurture*, directly compared urban and landed elites, where 'worshipful merchants' were to be seated before gentlemen, whilst the mayor of London was seen as the equivalent of a viscount.[26] As will be seen below, it was this social status and identity which the likes of the Thorntons, Andersons and Selbys of Newcastle demonstrably possessed, with Jenny Kermode concluding that 'to be a successful merchant and civic dignitary was to be at the apex of society'.[27]

Merchants, in their capacity as municipal office-holders, acted as justices of the peace with full powers of enquiry, trial and punishment.[28] These urban merchant elites provided the Crown with the same qualities as men of local standing that the traditional landed gentry did and it is clear from the perspective of royal government that merchants were in many ways comparable to the landed gentry. This is made explicit in the direct comparisons drawn between the two groups in the legislation of the fourteenth century where merchants were often seen as comparable in status to the titular nobility in their role as office-holders, whilst in their occupation as merchants they were considered the equals of the landed gentry. The sumptuary legislation of 1363 is a clear example of this, having been brought in to combat the situation whereby 'people of various conditions wear various apparel not appropriate to their estate'.[29] The legislation goes on to suggest that merchants, citizens and burgesses:

24 Barron, 'Chivalry, Pageantry and Merchant Culture', p. 237.

25 C. D. Liddy, *War, Politics, and Finance in Late Medieval English Towns: Bristol, York, and the Crown, 1350–1400* (London, 2005), pp. 153–4.

26 J. Russell, 'The Boke of Nurture', in F. J. Furnival (ed.), *Manners and Meals in Olden Time* (London, 1868), pp. 186–7. See also, for example, Wynkyn de Worde, 'The Boke of Kerunge', in Furnival (ed.), *Manners and Meals*, pp. 284–5. The author of this work also considered worshipful merchants as ranking above gentlemen in order of precedence, noting that they could sit at an esquire's table. Also, see Edmund Dudley, *The Tree of Commonwealth* (ed.) D. M. Brodie (Cambridge, 1948), p. 58.

27 Jennifer Kermode, *Medieval Merchants: York, Beverley and Hull in the Later Middle Ages* (Cambridge, 1998), p. 17.

28 E. G. Kimball, 'Commissions of the Peace for Urban Jurisdictions in England, 1327–1485', *Proceedings of the American Philosophical Society*, 121 (1977), p. 453.

29 Chris Given-Wilson (ed.), *The Parliament Rolls of Medieval England, 1274–1504*, vol. 5 (Woodbridge, 2005), p. 165.

> who clearly have goods and chattels to the value of £500, and their wives and children, may take and wear in the same manner as the esquire and gentlemen who have land and rent to the value of £100 a year. And that the merchants, citizens and burgesses who clearly have goods and chattels above the value of £1,000, and their wives and children, may take and wear in the same manner as the esquires and gentlemen who have land and rent to the value of £200 a year.[30]

The schedule of charges for the poll tax of 1379 reflects very similar views of society. The mayor of London was expected to pay the equivalent of an earl, whilst the aldermen of London and the mayors of other great towns were to pay as a baron.[31] From the perspective of royal authority, merchants were seen as social, economic and political equals to the landed gentry, with the wealthiest Newcastle merchants serving as members of Parliament and as sheriffs of Durham and Newcastle.[32] As Wrightson has noted, 'with distinction in a man's trade or profession came not only wealth, but also status and power', whilst the successful merchant could wield 'authority comparable to, and sometimes far in excess of, that of a country justice'.[33] Of course, this is not to deny that there were dissenters from this view such as John Blount, translator of Nicholas Upton's *De Studio Militari*, who noted that gentlemen 'ought not to meddle with tilling or ploughing of lands nor keeping of beasts nor occupying of merchandise'; but there is at least as much contemporary evidence to the contrary, whilst there is also considerable evidence to suggest that many merchants were not as covetous of landed society as has often been assumed.[34]

Mercantile Inroads into the Palatinate

Many of the reinterpretations of the position of merchants in medieval society have focused upon London and the immense wealth of its citizens, but similar claims

30 Ibid., p. 167.

31 C. C. Fenwick (ed.), *The Poll Taxes of 1377, 1379 and 1381* (Records of Social and Economic History, New Series 27, 1998), p. xv. All other municipal office-holders and great merchants of the realm were to pay 20s, which was the same as a strenuous knight, whilst 'sufficient merchants' were to pay 13s 4d, the same as a brother knight of the Hospital of St John.

32 C. M. Fraser (ed.), *Durham Quarter Sessions Rolls, 1471–1625*, Surtees Society, 199 (1987–88), pp. 200–35. C. H. Hunter Blair, 'The Mayors and Lord Mayors of Newcastle upon Tyne, 1216–1940, and the Sheriffs of the County of Newcastle upon Tyne, 1399–1940', *AA*, 4th series, 18 (1940), pp. 1–64; C. H. Hunter Blair, 'The Members of Parliament for Newcastle upon Tyne, 1559–1831', *AA*, 4th series, 23 (1945), pp. 102–55; C. H. Hunter Blair, 'Members of Parliament for Newcastle upon Tyne (1377–1558), for Berwick upon Tweed (1529–1558), and Morpeth (1553–1558)', *AA*, 4th series, 14 (1937), pp. 22–66.

33 Wrightson, *English Society*, p. 29.

34 John Blount's translation of Nicholas Upton's *De Studio Militari*, quoted in Keen, *Origins of the English Gentleman*, p. 103.

can be made for the merchants of Newcastle in the north-east of England.[35] It becomes apparent that Roger Thornton was a member of this urban gentry and, rather than seeking validation from his purchases, he was in fact investing further in his trade. The sixteenth-century antiquarian John Leland referred to Thornton as 'first a merchant and then a landed man', but as Liddy has emphasised, 'there is no evidence at all that Thornton sought to become a landed gentleman'.[36] This might at first seem contrary given that Roger Thornton was the second largest purchaser of manors in the Durham countryside in the fifteenth century, but his will makes it clear where his social identity lay. He was buried next to his wife in the church of St Nicholas in Newcastle, where his brass still remains, whilst he gave bequests for the repair and maintenance of several Newcastle churches and a donation of 100 marks to the upkeep of Tyne Bridge.[37] Liddy has described Thornton's numerous purchases as a 'commercial investment' because he looked upon land 'not as a source of social status, but as an economic asset, as the foundation of future wealth'.[38] For example, five of his acquisitions were just south of the Tyne, in Chester ward parishes known for their rich coal deposits: Swalwell and Axwell in Whickham, Redheugh in Gateshead, Crookhall in Lanchester and Friarside in Chester-le-Street. It is clear that these manors did indeed yield coal in this period because the bishop of Durham was paid wayleave to carry coal across his land by the lessees of the Lumley's coal mines here.[39] There are few signs that Roger Thornton was seeking legitimation through his purchases: he was rather securing the assets upon which his wealth was predicated, whilst his social identity was always centred on Newcastle and his mercantile background rather than in the Durham countryside. Although he is depicted in his great Flemish brass as wearing a partially concealed sword, the inscription reads 'here lies Roger Thornton, merchant of Newcastle upon Tyne', despite 'the fact that he possessed a coat of arms and that his family intermarried with the greatest families

35 Barron, 'Chivalry, Pageantry and Merchant Culture'; C. Barron, *London in the Later Middle Ages: Government and People, 1200–1500* (Oxford, 2004); S. Thrupp, *The Merchant Class of Medieval London, 1300–1500* (Chicago, 1948); S. O'Connor, 'Adam Fraunceys and John Pyel: Perceptions of Status Among Merchants in Fourteenth Century London', in D. Clayton, R. Davies and P. McNiven (eds.), *Trade, Devotion and Governance: Papers in Later Medieval History* (Stroud, 1994), pp. 17–35; for other provincial examples, see: Kermode, *Medieval Merchants*; Liddy, *War, Politics, and Finance in Late Medieval English Towns*; M. Kowaleski, 'The Commercial Dominance of a Medieval Provincial Oligarchy: Exeter in the Late Fourteenth Century', in R. Holt and G. Rosser (eds.), *The Medieval Town, 1200–1540* (London, 1990), pp. 184–216.

36 Liddy, *The Bishopric of Durham*, pp. 56–7.

37 The churches of Newcastle included: St Nicholas, All Saints, St John's, St Andrew's and St Thomas.

38 Liddy, *The Bishopric of Durham*, pp. 56–7.

39 This was after the Lumleys had inherited the Thorntons' manors, see chapter 3 for more information regarding this: DUL, ASC, Receiver General's Accounts, CCB B/1/1–CCB B/12/139. Similarly, Fugarfield and Swalwell were described as possessing coal mines in the IPMs of the Lumleys, the later inheritors of Thornton's purchases.

in the county'.[40] He was first and foremost a merchant of Newcastle and it was as such that he wished to be remembered.

How far did the Newcastle merchants of the sixteenth century follow the pattern laid down by the Thorntons, and were they trying to establish landed dynasties or to secure the resources upon which their wealth was largely founded? A list of the gentry of the palatinate of Durham dating to the first half of the seventeenth century includes two baronets, seventeen knights, thirty-seven esquires, eighty-one gentlemen bearing arms, and 115 non-armorial gentlemen. Out of this list of 252 people, some twenty individuals are readily identifiable as being recently descended from Newcastle merchant stock: a significant number, but ultimately less than 10 per cent of the total number of gentry in the county.[41] The settlement of these merchant families was not uniform across the county, however, with a disproportionate number settling on Tyneside and parishes just south of the river; fourteen of the individuals were to found in Chester ward, four in Easington, two in Darlington and none in Stockton, the most south-eastern ward, which contained very fertile land but relatively little coal. This suggests not only a preference amongst these families to maintain their close links with Newcastle, but also their desire for land in the rich coalfields of county Durham, especially those situated in Chester ward, which included the parishes of Jarrow, Whickham, Gateshead, Ryton and Chester-le-Street. Even those families who, like the Selbys, acquired land in the south-east of the county described lands in Chester ward as their primary residences, in this case at Winlaton. It was here, then, that the influx of mercantile wealth was most heavily felt, with at least one baronet, three knights, five esquires and five gentlemen settled in Chester ward tracing their lineage back to a Newcastle merchant within several generations.[42] However, it is far from obvious that these families had abandoned their urban roots in preference for a landed lifestyle and, as will become clear, they often retained their links to the city for many generations. The impact of these Newcastle merchants was, therefore, much more geographically constrained than the invasion envisaged by James and Nef.

The Andersons, for example, were one of the wealthiest merchant families of Newcastle who made increasing inroads into the Durham countryside across the

40 P. Coss, 'An Age of Deference', in Rosemary Horrox and W. M. Ormrod (eds.), *A Social History of England, 1200–1500* (Cambridge, 2006), p. 72.

41 This is closer to 15 per cent of purely armigerous families. See Blair, 'Durham Armorials of the Seventeenth Century', pp. 156–203. This list includes the Andersons of Haswell Grange; the Brandlings of Felling; the Carrs of St Helen Auckland; the Chambers of Cleadon; the Chaytors of Butterby; the Claverings of Axwell House; the Coles of Gateshead; the Dudleys of Chopwell; the Halls of Ellimore Hall; the Hodgsons of Hebburn; the Jenisons of Walworth; the Lawsons of Usworth; the Liddells of Ravensworth; the Maddisons of Unthank; the Mitfords of Pespol; the Riddells of Gateshead; the Sandersons of Brancepeth; the Selbys of Winlaton; and the Tempests of Stella.

42 In total Chester ward was described as having: one baronet, eight knights, twelve esquires, twenty gentlemen and twenty-seven non-armigerous gentlemen.

course of the sixteenth century, and they were especially prominent in the leases of the dean and chapter of Durham Cathedral. An early Stuart apologist for the merchant, Thomas Mun, claimed that:

> the memory of our richest merchants is suddenly extinguished; the son being left rich, scorneth the profession of his father, conceiving more honour to be a gentleman (although but in name), to consume his estate in dark ignorance and excess, than to follow the steps of his father as an industrious merchant.[43]

The Andersons, by contrast, formed a dynasty of urban office-holding in Newcastle for at least four generations: Henry Anderson's son, grandson and great-grandson all followed in his footsteps as sheriff, alderman, mayor and MP of Newcastle between 1520 and 1640.[44] Although we should be cautious of equating this with the gentry's emphasis 'upon ancestry, upon pedigree, [and] upon all that was invested in the continuance of a specific family name', it is clear that 'dynasties of elite families were to be found in all the major provincial towns' of early modern England.[45] The inventory taken on Henry Anderson's death in 1559 estimated his moveable goods to be worth £3,133: far beyond the wealth of most of his rural counterparts in the middle of the sixteenth century.[46] He possessed nearly £1,500 worth of mercantile and industrial goods, including sixty-eight fothers of lead worth £493 and coals wrought at Elswick worth £594. His personal and very visible wealth included £130 in ready money and £176 worth of plate and jewellery, including a nest of bowls weighing eighty-eight ounces worth £22, and he owned various shares in what can only be described as a veritable fleet of ships.[47]

The family made steady inroads into the Durham countryside, but given their immense wealth, this was not on a scale that would suggest they were trying to establish themselves as landed gentry. For example, the manor of Haswell had belonged to Finchale Priory since the twelfth century, but the foundation of the new cathedral only included the grain tithes of Haswell Grange; the manor had been granted by the Crown to Henry Anderson and it descended in the family for several generations.[48]

43 Sharpe, *Early Modern England*, p. 183.

44 Henry Anderson was sheriff of Newcastle in 1520, mayor of Newcastle in 1532, 1539, 1542 and 1546, and MP for Newcastle in 1529; his son, Bertram Anderson, was sheriff in 1543, mayor in 1551, 1557 and 1563, and MP in 1553, 1554 and 1563; his grandson, Henry Anderson, was sheriff in 1571, mayor in 1575, 1583 and 1594, and MP in 1584, 1586, 1589 and 1593; whilst his great grandson, also Henry Anderson, was mayor in 1613 and MP in 1614, 1621, 1624, 1625, 1626 and 1640.

45 P. Coss, *The Foundations of Gentry Life: the Multons of Frampton and their World, 1270–1370* (Oxford, 2010), p. 2; R. Grassby, *Kinship and Capitalism: Marriage, Family, and Business in the English-Speaking World, 1580–1720* (Cambridge, 2000), p. 358.

46 DPRI/1/1558/A1/2–3.

47 This included three-quarters of a ship called *Michael* worth £100, another three-quarters in *Anthony* worth £100, half of *John* worth £100, part of *Andrew* worth £80, three-quarters of *Barbara* worth £40 and a half of *Christopher* worth £15.

48 TNA, DURH 3/4, f. 84; DKR 44, p. 314.

The Andersons similarly gained the manor of Ouston which had belonged to St Edmund's Hospital in Gateshead before the dissolution, the manor being conveyed to Bertram Anderson by the original grantees and his son, Henry Anderson, sold half of the grange to Nicholas Tempest of Stella in 1584.[49] There were many other manors and portions of land which passed through the hands of these wealthy merchants but they showed no sign of trying to hold on to them for their status value, nor made any attempts to build up a landed estate. Their interest could take the form of investment during urban commercial recessions, opportunism when land appeared on the market, or even the gains of mortgages and money-lending.[50] The moiety of Consett was one such acquisition: purchased from Richard Ruthall in 1572 by Henry Anderson, it was then sold on to Robert Blenkinsop of Newcastle in 1579. Similarly, the messuage of Swainston and the manor of Newton Hansard, former lands of the earls of Westmorland, were granted to Thomas Calverley and Henry Anderson in 1575, the former becoming sole owner, presumably upon purchase of Anderson's interest in them.[51] But alongside this rural landownership must be placed the Andersons' extensive network of urban property in Newcastle itself.[52] The site of the nunnery of St Bartholomew, for example, was conveyed to Bertram Anderson in the 1540s and was added to the grounds of the Grey Friars to form the extensive Newcastle property known as Anderson Place.[53] Property was a worthwhile investment, whether it was rural or urban.

Much akin to the interest that the Thorntons took in coal-bearing land, Henry and his son Bertram appear to have had few intentions of settling in the Durham countryside, often treating manors and land as commodities to be bought and sold rather than inherited towards building a consolidated estate. The family's interest in land was not primarily for the social status it bestowed nor its financial security but for the subterranean wealth which was so vital to their positions as Newcastle merchants. This becomes widely apparent when their leases of bishopric and dean and chapter lands are taken into consideration. Between 1523 and 1533 Henry Anderson, along with Richard Hedworth and several partners, leased the bishop's coal mines at Whickham.[54] His son, Bertram Anderson, similarly took on the lease

49 Surtees, *History of Durham*, vol. 2, p. 192.

50 See for example Edward Miller, 'Medieval York', in P. M. Tillott (ed.), *The Victoria County History of Yorkshire: City of York* (London, 1961), pp. 25–116.

51 Surtees, *History of Durham*, vol. 3, p. 54.

52 Henry Anderson's will, for example, makes mention to 'my house at the Bridge-end', 'the tenement before my door which I had of the king', 'the house that I dwell in', 'the house that Henry Gray dwelt in at the White Cross', 'my house in Sandgate that Robert Tomson dwelt in', 'my house at the White Cross that Alexander Robson dwelt in', 'my house that Thomas Swanne dwelt in'; while his inventory details shop goods and goods at the cellar 'on the hyll under the chapell', at the new house, at Elswick and in the houses of Christopher Cook, Mr Davell and Swan. DPRI/1/1558/A1/1–3.

53 R. Welford (ed.), *History of Newcastle and Gateshead*, vol. 2 (London, 1884–87), p. 221.

54 DUL, ASC, Receiver General's Accounts, CCB B/5/50–CCB B/6/66.

of bishopric mines in the Whickham coalfield at Crosse Moor, whilst his grandson, Henry Anderson, was a prodigious lessee of coal mines and salt pans from the dean and chapter of Durham Cathedral and was one of the principal lessees in the Grand Lease.[55] Henry Anderson was also involved in less successful exploits as he sought profits wherever he felt there were opportunities, such as the leasing of the dean and chapter's coal mines and salt pans at Hayning for £20 per annum in the 1570s. The Elizabethan survey of 1580 described this as 'a lease hereof made about six years since to the men aforesaid, and now do not work coal there and therefore pay no rent, occupying also the salt pans without rent'.[56] Perhaps he deliberately acquired the lease to take the mine out of production, but if so it was an expensive proposition, for he is recorded as having paid £200 for the privilege of taking on the lease.

Henry Anderson and William Selby are best known for the very prominent roles they played in securing the Grand Lease in the late sixteenth century.[57] Queen Elizabeth acquired the long leases of Whickham and Gateshead from the bishops of Durham before transferring her interest in these lands to Thomas Sutton in 1578. Unfortunately for Sutton, the merchants of Newcastle viewed him as an interloping outsider and simply refused to make him a freeman of the city, which excluded him from direct participation in the coal trade. Not able to exploit the lease fully, he soon decided to sell it to the mayor and burgesses of Newcastle. However, since the city had never been formally incorporated they were unable to acquire the lease and so the mayor, Henry Anderson, and one of the aldermen, William Selby, were provided with £5,500 from the city's treasury towards the £12,000 purchase price on the understanding that they would transfer their rights once a new charter for the city had been acquired. For over a decade Anderson, Selby and a handful of merchants who had funded the rest of the purchase became 'the Lords of Coal' and refused to hand over the Grand Lease, only doing so in 1599 upon the creation of a separate trading company for the Hostmen who thereafter had exclusive rights to trade in coal in Newcastle.[58]

55 These leases include: to Bertram Anderson, a 21-year lease of the bishop's coal mines at Crosse Moor in Whickham in 1570 which stipulated that only three pits were to be opened at once, with a rent of £30 per annum; to his son, Henry Anderson, a 21-year lease of the dean and chapter's coal mines in Jarrow and salt pans in South Shields for £20 per annum in 1575 and which was renewed in 1595, 1599, 1601, 1606 and 1613; also to Henry Anderson, a 21-year lease of further salt pans in South Shields, who paid 10s per annum for each in 1589 and which was renewed in 1606; and also to Henry Anderson, a 21-year lease of the manor of Pittington for £27 13s 4d per annum in 1606, which he renewed in 1613. See the DCM, Dean and Chapter Registers, 1–15, 1541–1670.

56 Longstaffe and Booth (eds.), *Halmota Prioratus Dunelmensis*, p. 197.

57 For a fuller account of the history of the Grand Lease see: Levine and Wrightson, *The Making of an Industrial Society*, pp. 18–20; Trevor-Roper, 'The Bishopric of Durham', pp. 45–58; and Hatcher, *British Coal Industry*, pp. 70–96 and pp. 508–34.

58 For the records of the Newcastle Hostmen see F. W. Dendy, (ed.), *Extracts from the Records of the Company of Hostmen of Newcastle-upon-Tyne*, Surtees Society, 105 (1901). For some of the

The wealth that coal provided these merchants hardly needs to be laboured, but it can be illustrated with a passing glance at Bertram Anderson's inventory of 1570, which was valued at £2,766.[59] He possessed over £1,400 in mercantile and industrial goods, including twenty-four score tons of coal lying by the waterside worth £640, a further 126 tons of coal at the Crosse Moor pits worth £139, and more coal at the south-west pit worth £295. Even though the wealth of the family was based in coal and trade, they were not ignorant of the financial rewards of agriculture in this period, although it is equally clear that they were not abandoning trade in favour of more rural pursuits with a total of corn and hay valued at £117 and livestock worth some £264. The wealth and high living standards Bertram enjoyed, however, can be more adequately seen in the list of household goods which totalled over £250, clothes which were worth £43, and plate and jewellery worth over £370. Indeed, his plate and jewellery together were worth more than the total inventory of many Durham and Northumberland knights at this period of the sixteenth century.[60] He also possessed shares in ships worth £266, including two keels, whilst his will lists bequests of 400 marks to each of his children.[61] Another of his bequests also reveals his keen financial acumen: 'eighty coals to be given to the poor people of Hambrough taken from my staithes on the Tyne, and they to pay for the fetching of them from the staithes and for the customs with all other charges'. All of this was achieved by Bertram Anderson before 1570, long before the family had acquired either the Grand Lease or the monopoly of coal in Newcastle which followed.

The Selbys, the partners of the Andersons in the Grand Lease, similarly acquired land in the bishopric, some of it quite extensive. The manor of Stotfold was alienated by Charles, the last earl of Westmorland, to William Selby just prior to the earl's rebellion and subsequent forfeiture; it was comprised of 1,500 acres of arable land, 800 of meadow, 1,000 of pasture, 10 of wood and 2,000 of furze and briar.[62] The manor of Winlaton was similarly purchased from the last earl of Westmorland by Richard Hodgeson, Humphrey Scrivener, William Selby and Robert Anderson, merchants of Newcastle, for £2,000, for the use of Selby and Hodgeson in equal

controversy this caused, such as the accusation that Anderson and Selby were working 'the town's mines to the value of £2,000 without paying any rent to the town', see R. Welford, *Men of Mark 'twixt Tyne and Tweed*, vol. 1 (London, 1895), pp. 72–3.

59 DPRI/1/1570/A1/2–6.

60 Although probate inventories are notoriously difficult to use for determining wealth, the vast difference in moveable goods is noticeable. Between 1540 and 1640 the average probate inventory total of Newcastle merchants/aldermen was £2,509 and Newcastle merchant adventurers was £1,388. By comparison, the average Durham esquire had £483 worth of goods and the average gentleman only had £250. Even if we take the inventories of some of the most successful gentry in this period they still fall short: Robert Lambton, esquire, £744 in 1583, DPRI/1/1583/L1/1; Ralph Lambton, £996 in 1594, DPRI/1/1594/L1/1–4; Richard Bellasis, esquire, £2,493 in 1599, DPRI/1/1599/B6/3–4; and John, Lord Lumley, £1,404 17s 8d, DPRI/1/1609/L5/2–4.

61 DPRI/1/1570/A1/1.

62 Surtees, *History of Durham*, vol. 3, pp. 88.

moieties.[63] A plan of the lordship of Winlaton in 1632 states that Sir William Hodgeson held 1,601 acres of land, whilst Sir William Selby held 2,121 acres and Robert Anderson also held a further 519 acres, the Andersons retaining an eighth of the manor after the initial purchase.[64] It is perhaps illustrative of William Selby's intentions that he chose to settle in Winlaton, where he only held half of the manor, rather than Stotfold in the south-east of the county; the former had the dual benefits of ample coal and close proximity to Newcastle. A glimpse of the high status, living standards and wealth that could be achieved by these Newcastle merchants in this period is visible in the probate inventory taken on the death of George Selby, son of the above William, in 1625. This estimated his moveable goods to be worth the sum of £9,765 15s 10d, a figure comparable to that of the titular aristocracy like the ninth earl of Northumberland.[65] The items are far too numerous to detail in full, but just a brief summary reveals the wealth of this mercantile family. At White House, he possessed nearly £400 worth of household goods, which included items like the linen appraised at £46 15s. His house in Newcastle was only slightly less opulently furnished with around £340 worth of goods, whilst his apparel came to £100 and he had over £1,200 in ready money. He also possessed a chain of gold worth £120 and plate weighing a total of 1,024 ounces, estimated to be worth £330.

George Selby's inventory also shows why the family had expended so much money on the purchase of Winlaton, with coals wrought at the staithes and pits at Winlaton and Elswick valued at £1,508 3s and seven keels with their riggings worth £280. John Hatcher drew attention to the rare glimpse into the capacity of this Winlaton colliery when a dispute amongst its partners revealed that between Martinmas 1581 and Martinmas 1582 around 25,000 tons were produced.[66] It is little wonder that these Newcastle merchants were willing to part with £2,000 to acquire such a productive coal mine. George Selby's largest asset was the debts that were owed to him, which had been divided into those upon bonds (£4,267 15s) and those without formality (£1,977 12s 2d), leading Nef to call these Newcastle Hostmen a 'nucleus of money-lending' in the region.[67] Selby's expenses were no less extravagant than his goods, with funeral expenses totalling £574 13s 4d, an amount that would have bankrupted many

63 It is likely that this sale of land by the Nevilles was an attempt to fund the Rising of the North and who better to turn to for ready cash than the merchants of Newcastle. See W. Gibson, 'The Manor of Winlaton', *AA*, 4th Series, 23 (1945), pp. 8–26.

64 Surtees, *History of Durham*, vol. 2, pp. 272–3.

65 George Selby's inventory: DPRI/1/1625/S4/12–22. For a comparison, the ninth earl of Northumberland died with goods worth £6,432 12s 8d at Petworth House, including £700 in his lordship's coffers, £80 in wearing apparel and 6,254 ounces of plate worth £1,563 10s; and with goods valued at Syon House worth £2,281 4d. See G. R. Batho (ed.), *The Household Papers of Henry Percy Ninth Earl of Northumberland, 1564–1632*, Camden 3rd Series, 93 (1962), pp. 112–33.

66 Hatcher, *British Coal Industry*, p. 80.

67 Nef, *Rise of the British Coal Industry*, vol. 2, p. 120. Henry Anderson above also had debts owed to him on his death worth £886, of which £346 were desperate debts and £540 were good debts.

landed esquires in the Durham countryside, whilst he left £2,000 for each of his two daughters.[68] Once again, though, the emphasis upon Newcastle is present in his last will and testament, with bequests to each of the four almshouses of Newcastle and a further £6 13s 4d to the poor of Winlaton. Although he was now described as 'of Winlaton', in his probate material he clearly envisaged and prepared for his final return to Newcastle: 'I will that my body be buried within the church of St Nicholas at Newcastle Upon Tyne or near where my tomb is already erected there', giving to the churchwarden one mark per annum out of his rent from a house in Newcastle so that the said tomb 'be well kept and clean in a comely manner'. It was a common wish for these merchants to be buried in St Nicholas church in Newcastle, often long after the family possessed land in the surrounding countryside, revealing where their social identity was strongest.[69]

The Liddells were a further prominent Newcastle family whose members served as mayors and sheriffs of the city and who were also commented upon by Nef because they purchased various manors in the Durham countryside from the late sixteenth century onwards.[70] Thomas Liddell received a pardon from Bishop James in 1607 for acquiring the manors of Ravensworth and Lamesley and other lands in the palatinate without licence from Sir Henry Gascoigne.[71] As would be expected, the manor of Ravensworth included a very extensive and valuable coalfield, with grants of wayleave occurring in the bishops' accounts.[72] By 1700 Ravensworth 'was one of the very largest collieries in Britain, with an output of 65,000 tons'.[73] The Liddells, like many other Newcastle merchants, can be seen in transactions involving manors, often acting as intermediaries and quickly reselling them. For example, in 1619 Giles Burton of Pespol and Boisfield granted these manors to Thomas Liddell, alderman of Newcastle, who conveyed them to Robert White, gentleman, who in turn sold them to Thomas Mitford, merchant of Newcastle, in 1623. Similarly, Thomas Liddell purchased Darncrook from John and Thomas Heath, esquires, and devised the estate to his youngest son Roger Liddell in 1615, once again showing no intention to establish a landed dynasty, but using these properties to endow his younger son in an interesting role-reversal. It is often thought that younger sons of the gentry became

68 DPRI/1/1625/S4/1–10.

69 The following were, for example, buried in St Nicholas' church, Newcastle: Henry Anderson (d. 1559), Bertram Anderson (d. 1570), Roger Anderson (d. 1622), Robert Anderson (d. 1640), William Carr (d. 1572), Peter Riddell (d. 1641), Henry Brandling (d. 1578), William Selby (d. 1613), George Selby (d. 1625), Thomas Liddell (d. 1577), Thomas Liddell (d. 1619), William Jenison (d. 1587), Lionel Maddison (d. 1624), Henry Maddison (d. 1634), James Clavering (d. 1630), and Alexander Davison (d. 1644).

70 Thomas Liddell was sheriff of Newcastle in 1563 and mayor in 1572; his son, Thomas Liddell, was sheriff in 1592 and mayor in 1609; his grandson, also Thomas Liddell, was sheriff in 1609 and mayor in 1625 and 1636.

71 Surtees, *History of Durham*, vol. 2, pp. pp. 208–11.

72 DUL, ASC, Receiver General's Accounts, CCB B/1/1–CCB B/12/139.

73 Hatcher, *British Coal Industry*, p. 92.

merchants because their older brothers inherited the estate, but how often did the younger sons of prominent merchants become gentlemen because the oldest brother had inherited the family business? This also reveals an important difference between the inheritance patterns of merchants and their landed counterparts, with Grassby noting that 'even merchants who had turned landowners retained their preference for partible inheritance and were generous to their younger sons'; this suggests, yet again, that the establishment of landed estates was not the primary aim of many merchants.[74] The Liddells were also busy leasing coal mines from the bishops of Durham, with Thomas Liddell leasing certain coal mines in Whickham in 1601 for twenty-one years at a rent of £10 per annum and pits at Chester-le-Street in 1609 for three lives at a rent of £20 per annum.[75] Thomas Liddell's inventory reveals a glimpse of the high living standards and opulence of these Newcastle merchants; it included six featherbeds, eighteen pairs of linen sheets and thirty-six banqueting dishes, whilst his son, Thomas Liddell, was said to be worth some £2,000 per annum.[76]

Historians have tended to emphasise the social and political motivations driving the acquisition of land in the surrounding countryside by merchants.[77] There were few political gains to be had from a transition into the Durham countryside for Newcastle merchants, however, especially if they were to sever their ties with the city at the same time. For example, there were fifty potential MPs of Newcastle for the twenty-five parliaments between 4 November 1547 and 13 April 1640, but only sixteen different family surnames represented the city.[78] The Andersons represented Newcastle the most often and, with the Riddells and the Jenisons, accounted for over half of the MPs that represented the city.[79] As a landed comparison, Northumberland was represented by a larger and more diverse group of twenty-four different families in the same period, whilst the three most common families, the Widdringtons, the Greys and the Fenwicks, only accounted for a third of MPs; Durham, of course, returned no members of Parliament in this period because of its palatinate status.[80] Any move into the Durham countryside, therefore, was unlikely to have been motivated by political ambition. It was, after all, the two Newcastle members of Parliament, Henry Anderson and William Jenison, who were at the forefront

74 Grassby, *Kinship and Capitalism*, p. 353.

75 DCM, Dean and Chapter Register 6, f. 108r; Register 7, f. 138r.

76 Thomas Liddell's probate inventory (1577) in Raine and Greenwell (eds.), *Wills and Inventories*, Part I, pp. 413–16; Levine and Wrightson, *The Making of an Industrial Society*, p. 23. If this was the clear profit of his annual business transactions then he was worth more per year than John, Lord Lumley, at the time of his death.

77 Wilson, *Gentlemen Merchants*, p. 223.

78 Blair, 'Members of Parliament for Newcastle, 1377–1558', pp. 22–66; Hunter Blair, 'The Members of Parliament for Newcastle, 1559–1831', pp. 102–55.

79 The two branches of the Andersons were MPs of Newcastle fifteen times; the Riddells seven times; and the Jenisons five times.

80 The Widdringtons were MPs of Northumberland seven times; the Greys six times; and the Fenwicks four times.

of the campaign for parliamentary representation for the Durham gentry in 1614.[81] The coal-owning merchants exercised a similar control over the office of mayor of Newcastle, with 121 individuals possible between 1520 and 1640 but only 44 surnames represented and the most common ten families accounting for over half of the mayors of Newcastle in this period.[82] Merchants like the Andersons and Riddells could, moreover, straddle the urban–rural divide and act as mayors and MPs for Newcastle as well as JPs for Durham; there were few, if any, offices in the north-east of England closed to them.[83]

If the descendants of these Newcastle merchants felt any shame in their ancestry, we would expect to see a dissociation with the city and their mercantile past in the pedigrees they provided in the sixteenth and seventeenth centuries. The heraldic visitations of this period were, after all, attempts to register and ultimately restrict the usage of armorial bearings, a traditional symbol of the landed gentry, and so connections with a mercantile background might be moderated or even omitted if they were seen to damage a family's position. However, quite the reverse is the case, with many descendants not only acknowledging this descent, but actually placing their merchant ancestors prominently at the head of the family's pedigree, suggesting that there was a certain social cachet in being a merchant of Newcastle in this period.[84] Christopher Chaytor of Butterby, for example, placed his father, John Chaytor 'of Newcastle, merchant', at the head of the family's pedigree in 1575, whilst the Davisons' pedigree similarly begins with Sir Alexander Davison 'of Newcastle-upon-Tyne and of Blakeston in the County Palatine of Durham'. The Liddells of Ravensworth and the Sandersons of Brancepeth were descended from the Newcastle merchants Thomas Liddell and John Sanderson respectively, both of whom were prominently placed at the head of their pedigrees in the visitation of 1615, just as Christopher Mitford of Newcastle was for the Mitfords of Pespol in the 1666 visitation. Even when these merchants were described as residing in the Durham countryside, many retained their links with Newcastle to create a dual identity: Henry Anderson was described as from Haswell and Newcastle; Thomas Chamber was styled 'of Cleadon in the Bishopric, and merchant of Newcastle' in 1615; Alexander Davison was described as

81 Andrew W. Foster, 'The Struggle for Parliamentary Representation for Durham, 1600–41', in David Marcombe (ed.), *The Last Principality: Politics, Religion and Society in the Bishopric of Durham, 1494–1660* (Nottingham, 1987), pp. 176–201.

82 The two branches of the Andersons were mayor of Newcastle fifteen times; the Brandlings eight times; the Riddells eight times; the Jenisons six times; the Selbys six times; the Chapmans five times; the Liddells five times; the Maddisons five times; the Ellisons four times; and the Mitfords three times.

83 Newcastle merchants like the Andersons, Chaytors, Lawsons, Riddells and Selbys served alongside the Durham gentry as justices of the peace at the Durham Quarter Sessions. Fraser (ed.), *Durham Quarter Sessions*, pp. 337–49.

84 For the following, see Joseph Foster (ed.), *Pedigrees Recorded at the Visitations of the County Palatine of Durham Made by William Flower, Norroy King-of-Arms, in 1575, by Richard St George, Norroy King-of-Arms, in 1615, and by William Dugdale, Norroy King-of-Arms, in 1666* (London, 1887).

'of Newcastle and of Blakeston'; whilst a figure as prominent as Sir Thomas Tempest, who died a baronet, was styled as 'of Stella and Newcastle'.[85]

Undoubtedly there were merchants of Newcastle involved in the coal trade who desired to integrate into landed society and did so at the first available opportunity. The Coles, eventually of Brancepeth, were perhaps one such family, who made the 'meteoric rise' from 'butcher' to the owners of the manor and castle of Brancepeth in a single generation.[86] Ralph Cole was admitted to the Hostmen's company in 1605, where he was described as 'butcher', before becoming sheriff of Newcastle in 1625 and mayor of the city in 1633, and eventually purchasing Brancepeth, formerly owned by the earls of Westmorland.[87] Neither his father Nicholas nor his uncle Thomas were able to prove their right to arms at the visitation of 1615 and so were included in a list of those disclaimed who were found 'presumptuously and without any good ground or authority to have usurped the names and titles of gentlemen, contrary to all right', which the family no doubt found particularly galling, but as mayor, Ralph Cole acquired an official grant of arms for the family.[88] It was during his tenure as mayor that he was rather unflatteringly described by contemporaries as 'fat and rich, vested in a sack of satin'.[89] Ralph Cole went on to purchase the lordship of Brancepeth from Lady Ann Middleton who had acquired the estate after the Crown's sale to London merchants in the 1630s.[90] Ralph's son, Nicholas, was to be the main beneficiary; he married Mary, daughter of Thomas Liddell, and became a baronet in 1641. In her study of Brancepeth lordship in the seventeenth century, Dorothy Hamilton concluded that 'this clearly non-aristocratic lord of the manor took up residence in the castle, and shortly after reinstated the manorial court, even trying to claim the right to stray animals because the right had belonged to his predecessor, the earl of Westmorland'.[91] In many ways, then, the Coles represent the traditional story of gentrification: urban financial success providing the foundations for a landed lifestyle within a generation or two, with social status being a prime motivating factor for the image-conscious merchant. But this example also reveals the problems with this narrative, not least the fact that the Coles were not from amongst the traditional ruling elite of the city and could be considered as much upstarts in Newcastle as in the surrounding countryside. The more established merchant families of Newcastle,

85 These links to Newcastle were more than just a commercial necessity and show that many of these merchants had no desire to abandon their urban roots upon the acquisition of land in Durham and Northumberland.

86 Newton, *North-East England*, pp. 35–6.

87 Blair, 'The Mayors of Newcastle', pp. 1–64.

88 Nicholas and Thomas were disclaimed at the 1615 visitation, Foster (ed.), *Pedigrees Recorded at the Visitations*, p. 344.

89 Welford (ed.), *History of Newcastle and Gateshead*, vol. 3, p. 325.

90 Ibid., p. 340.

91 Hamilton, 'Social Networks, Families and Neighbourhoods', p. 89.

by comparison, show far fewer signs of preferring the formation of a landed dynasty over enjoying the place they had secured for themselves within this urban oligarchy.

The influx of 'new wealth' from mercantile sources in the sixteenth century certainly had an impact upon the Durham countryside, but caution is needed when discussing its novelty, its extent or the intentions of the individuals behind these purchases. Many of these merchants were quite content to buy and sell manors, often treating them as a commodity rather than as potential building blocks for a landed estate. They married into Durham landed society, but did so more often as equals rather than as inferiors seeking legitimation through such contacts.[92] The sons and grandsons of these merchants followed in their fathers' footsteps in becoming merchants, sheriffs, aldermen and mayors of Newcastle rather than retreating from the city.[93] The impact of these men on the Durham countryside was felt more often through their roles as coal merchants and citizens of Newcastle rather than as landed gentlemen. Levine and Wrightson concluded that the Grand Lessees were 'not remotely interested in agricultural estate management' in their ownership of Whickham manor, not challenging the 'security of their tenures', whilst 'rents and fines remained small and stable': it was coal first and foremost which interested these Newcastle merchants.[94] Given the wealth, living standards and social status of these coal merchants of Newcastle, there was little to be gained from a move into the countryside and much to be lost. Daniel Defoe described the villages of Essex where stood 'handsome large houses ... chiefly for the habitations of the richest citizens, such as either are able to keep two houses, one in the country and one in the city; or for such citizens as being rich, and having left off trade, live altogether in these neighbouring villages, for the pleasure and health of the latter part of their days'.[95] It is hardly surprising that many of the rich Newcastle coal merchants sought to acquire a country retreat, especially given the urban nature of many outbreaks of disease in this period, but there is much less evidence of their desire to assimilate into landed society; just as Bishop Matthew fled to his manor of Stockton from Durham in 1597, many Newcastle merchants also fled to their country houses during pestilence years. Of course, this is not to deny that the likes of George Selby purchased country retreats, being described as 'of Winlaton', but he also maintained a house in Newcastle

92 It could even be argued that the Durham gentry were eager to marry into Newcastle merchant families by the early seventeenth century. For example, Thompson suggested that the 'critical cultural shift in the eighteenth century might have been in the readiness of the aristocracy and gentry to behave commercially, not in the intensity or prevalence of the desire among businessmen to become gentry'. Thompson, *Gentrification and the Enterprise Culture*, p. 20. The same might be said of the Durham gentry in the coalfields of the north-east.

93 Grassby, for example, found that 56–60 per cent of all sons became businessmen, with more first sons becoming businessmen than gentlemen. Grassby, *Kinship and Capitalism*, pp. 356–7.

94 Ibid., p. 96.

95 Daniel Defoe, *A Tour Through the Whole Island of Great Britain* (London, 1971), p. 48 quoted in Thompson, *Gentrification and the Enterprise Culture*, p. 10.

almost as well furnished, whilst it was to Newcastle that he looked on his deathbed: just as Roger Thornton had done before him, he envisaged his last journey being a home-coming to Newcastle.

The Emergence of Ecclesiastical Dynasties

Mervyn James suggested that 'perhaps the most significant group of new recruits to the middle and lesser gentry [by 1615] were the now married upper clergy'.[96] He went on to list a whole host of prebendaries, deans and indeed bishops who established dynasties in the Durham countryside, slowly intermarrying with established members of the gentry. They included Henry Ewbank, prebendary of the twelfth stall, who established his son and heir at Snotterton; Dean Whittingham, whose heir became the squire of Holmside; Marmaduke Blakiston and John Hutton, prebendaries who founded landed families at Newton Hall and Houghton-le-Spring respectively; and the relatives of Bishop Barnes and Bishop James who also acquired estates in the countryside.[97] Diana Newton argued that the new composition of the Elizabethan chapter:

> impacted adversely on the county gentry, for the prebendaries were recruited from a much wider area than the monks they replaced and they were drawn from higher up the social scale. Thus these were outsiders who regarded themselves as the social equals of the resident gentry, presenting a double challenge to them as a discrete and coherent gentry.[98]

James went on to argue that this Church faction came to dominate political control of the county in the early seventeenth century, especially under Bishop Neile, when they asserted themselves 'with a consistency and comprehensiveness previously lacking'.[99] Under Neile, for example, the archdeacons of Durham and Northumberland and a selection of prebendaries were appointed as justices of the peace in the 1620s, whilst Church families became the captains to command the levies of the four Durham wards. But what were the economic foundations of this political power? As was explored in chapter 2, the dean was allocated an annual stipend of £266 13s 4d, a not inconsiderable income by any means, but the prebendaries shared a much more modest £400 between the twelve of them. Although they were also paid a dividend derived from the income of entry fines, this could hardly account for their many purchases of Durham manors. How were these churchmen able to establish

96 James, *Family, Lineage, and Civil Society*, p. 72.

97 Ibid., p. 72.

98 Newton, *North-East England*, p. 48.

99 James, *Family, Lineage, and Civil Society*, pp. 163–4.

ecclesiastical dynasties in the Durham countryside from the middle of the sixteenth century onwards?

The answer can be found in the beneficial leases which bishops of Durham granted out to their relatives and in the land which was attached to each prebendal stall of the cathedral. The bishops were hindered by long leases granted to the gentry, but they were also often hampered by grants their predecessors had made to members of their own extended families. This brings the problems facing bishops and prebendaries in the late sixteenth century into sharp relief; they only had a life interest in their office and yet many had families to provide for.[100] One of the most extensive examples of this in the sixteenth century is Cuthbert Tunstall, who was bishop of Durham for some of the most turbulent years of the diocese, from 1530 to 1559.[101] Table 18 lists leases made by Bishop Tunstall to his relatives and friends. Some of these leases were very favourable indeed, such as those to Thomas Tunstall which included the manor of Middridge for forty years and the manor of Windlestone which had been forfeited to the bishop. Although it is unclear how all of these Tunstalls relate to Cuthbert Tunstall, a Francis Tunstall was given £40 in Bishop Tunstall's will and appears to have been his great-nephew, whilst Sir Marmaduke Tunstall was Francis's father. Bishop Cuthbert's will also made provision for the care of 'little Thomas Tunstall, son to Thomas Tunstall, late my servant', who was to receive ten marks, as was 'Roger Tunstall his brother'.[102] Similarly, the Thornell connection is not entirely clear but Nicholas Thornell was one of the prebendaries of the Collegiate Church of Norton, and was favoured by Bishop Tunstall who made him an executor and witness to his will, as well as providing £5 for 'John Thornell waiting on me in my chamber'. It is likely that this is the same John Thornell who received the extremely favourable lease of property in Stockton for a rent of £23 14s 10d, but which would have been greatly devalued by inflation over the 60-year period of the lease. Many of these leases were made in the final years of Bishop Tunstall's life and undoubtedly represented an attempt to reward loyal service – an attempt that presumably added to his successors' headaches in the second half of the sixteenth century.[103]

100 For example, before the Grand Lease of the manors of Gateshead and Whickham was due to end in Bishop Cosin's episcopate, he granted it in advance to provide for his daughter Mary and her husband, Sir Gilbert Gerard. For more on post-Restoration bishops see Clay, '"The Greed of Whig Bishops"', pp. 128–57.

101 For the life of Cuthbert Tunstall, see Charles Sturges, *Cuthbert Tunstall: Churchman, Scholar, Administrator* (London, 1938); for bishopric leases, see: DUL, ASC, CCB Registers of Leases and Patents, 1–5, c.1530–c.1640.

102 For Bishop Tunstall's will see Sturges, *Cuthbert Tunstall*, pp. 378–82.

103 For the problems facing the bishops of Durham in the sixteenth and early seventeenth centuries, see chapter 2.

Table 18. Leases Made by Bishop Tunstall to Relatives and Friends

Property	Lease	Rent of Property
Property in Howden	Sir Marmaduke Tunstall, 21-year lease, 1547	£13 6s 8d
Manor of Weelhall	Francis Tunstall, 21-year lease, 1550	£5 18s 5d
Property in Thorpe	Roger Tunstall, 40-year lease, 1551	£5
Property in Weardale	Anthony Tunstall, 30-year lease, 1551	£10
Water Mill in Norton	Anthony Tunstall, 30-year lease, 1554	£16 13s 4d
Property in Norton	Roger Tunstall, 31-year lease, 1554	Blank
Property in Stockton	Roger Tunstall, 31-year lease, 1554	£5
Manor of Middridge	Thomas Tunstall, 40-year lease, 1558	£26 9s 8d
Manor of Windlestone	Thomas Tunstall, grant after treason, 1558	Blank
Property in Wolsingham	Ralph Tunstall, 21-year lease, 1559	£1
Property near Wiske	Nicholas Thornell, 21-year lease, 1543	£5 18s 5d
Property in Lumley	John Thornell, 30-year lease, 1548	£1
Water Mills, Bakehouse, etc.	Laurence Thornell, 50-year lease, 1550	£11
Property in Darlington	Laurence Thornell, 21-year lease, 1551	£7
Various Properties	John Thornell, 21-year lease, 1556	£1 4s
Property in Stockton	John Thornell, 60-year lease, 1559	£23 14s 10d

Source: DUL, ASC, CCB Registers of Leases and Patents, 1–5, c.1530–c.1640.

James Pilkington, the first of these successors, did not flood the lease books of the bishopric in the same way. This was because Queen Mary had granted the bishop of Durham the right of presentation to the cathedral stalls in 1556, which had been a right preserved by the Crown in the Henrician foundation statutes. David Marcombe emphasised the importance of this new source of patronage as:

> These were amongst the most valuable livings in the Bishop's gift and were therefore frequently used as rewards for his relatives, friends, and administrators: this process, still often uncharitably referred to as nepotism, represented no more than the bishop's attempt to build up his own sphere of influence in the diocese which was necessary if he was to free himself from over-dependence on the local gentry and a consequent involvement in their squabbles.[104]

He went on to describe how Bishop Pilkington, 'by far the most prolific distributor of prebends, promoted his two brothers and seven known kinsmen and friends, whilst his successors Barnes and Hutton presented a son and a nephew respectively'.[105]

104 Marcombe, 'Dean and Chapter of Durham', p. 72.
105 Ibid., p. 72.

Emanuel Barnes, for example, was installed in the fifth stall in 1585 where he remained until 1603 when he moved to the fourth stall until 1614, whilst Robert Hutton held the third stall between 1589 and 1623. Pat Mussett explained the financial importance attached to these stalls:

> The Durham stalls, unlike those in other Cathedrals of the New Foundation, were genuine prebends; each stall (including the deanery) had assigned to it from the Cathedral's estates its own endowment in land or in tithes or both, and any dean or canon of Durham received each year not only the sums of money authorised by the Cathedral statutes and his share of any surplus on the Cathedral's central accounts, but also the income from his own decanal or prebendal estate.[106]

It was these prebendal estates which were so valuable in this period, and it was out of the profits arising from these lands that many prebendaries and deans were able to branch out into the countryside.

John Pilkington, brother of Bishop Pilkington, was installed in the second stall of the cathedral from 1561–1602, whilst his other brother, Leonard Pilkington, was installed in the seventh stall between 1567 and 1599.[107] It was the land that they leased from the dean and chapter as part of their prebendal estate, known as corpes land, which was so valuable to them, with the Pilkington name flooding into the dean and chapter's lease-books.[108] The sheer scale of this leasing is all the more impressive when two factors are taken into consideration. Firstly, the surname Pilkington did not appear in any of the priory's rent books of the early sixteenth century before Bishop Pilkington's brothers became prebendaries. Secondly, the prebendal estate was only supposed to belong to the prebend whilst he was an incumbent of the cathedral: once he left his stall, all of the land assigned to that stall was supposed to pass to his successor. For example, the second and seventh stalls of the cathedral, occupied by the Pilkingtons in the late sixteenth century, held half of the manor of Elvet Hall and the manor of Finchale respectively; the rest of their extensive leasing came from their ability to give preferential leases to their relatives and friends as leases fell in.

As will be seen in chapter 6, many of the smaller leases which the Pilkingtons acquired were sufficient to provide a comfortable existence, but these additional

106 Patrick Mussett, *Lists of Deans and Major Canons of Durham, 1541–1900* (Durham, 1974), introduction.

107 Marcombe, 'Dean and Chapter of Durham', p. 72.

108 Anne Pilkington leased two holdings in Merrington in the 1620s; Barnaby Pilkington leased land at Cowpen Bewley and Burdon for £7 4s 10d in 1572; Jacob and Joseph Pilkington leased land in Monkwearmouth, Hedworth and Merrington throughout the 1580s and '90s; Francis Pilkington leased land in Harton, Cowpen Bewley, Cleatham and Coatsay Moor in the 1560s and '70s; Hugh Pilkington leased the parsonage of Norham for £13 in 1566; Isaac Pilkington leased half the manor of Elvet for £8 6s 8d in 1599; John Pilkington leased half the manor of Elvet in 1569; Nehemiah Pilkington leased land in Monkwearmouth, Heworth and Merrington in the 1590s, as well as the manor of Finchale for £9 19s 8d in 1598. See the Dean and Chapter leases: DCM, Dean and Chapter Registers, 1–15, 1541–1670.

corpes lands could prove extremely profitable. For example, the half of Elvet Hall attached to the second stall with its rent of £8 6s 8d was in fact valued at around £150 per annum, whilst Finchale, for which a rent of £9 19s 8d was paid, was valued at £200 per annum.[109] David Marcombe concluded that 'a man like Leonard Pilkington, for example, in possession of the wealthy manor of Finchale and the greater part of his bye-corpes (tithes), could perhaps expect an income from them somewhere in the region of £300 per annum in the 1590s'.[110] By 1617/18, the dean had an estimated personal revenue of £1,130 per annum from his corpes lands, bye-corpes, and his stipend and dividend, which was more than half the reserved rent of the property of the entire cathedral combined.[111] This income would have placed these incoming church families on a level with many members of the established gentry in the sixteenth century: an income, moreover, which could keep pace with inflation since this was not a stagnant rent and these lands could either be sublet at a commercial rent or directly managed by the prebends and their families.[112]

Conclusion

As we have seen in chapters 3, 4 and 5, the period from the late fourteenth to the early seventeenth century saw a radical change in the balance of landed possessions in the palatinate of Durham. This shift was initially in favour of the larger knightly families who were able to benefit from the financial straits which many members of the parish gentry found themselves in after the fall in prices during the 1370s. By the end of the fifteenth century, almost half of the lay manors of the palatinate had been accumulated within the hands of a few families, representing the highest concentration of land amongst a territorial elite in the region in this period. From this point, however, there was a gradual fragmentation of these large estates. By the early seventeenth century, there were very few families in the palatinate who owned over ten manors, something which had been much more common in the fifteenth century, whilst there was an influx of relative newcomers into the market, including wealthy merchants from Newcastle and the prebendaries of Durham cathedral. The advantageous leases of Church lands formed the platform from which new prebendaries could purchase their way into the Durham countryside and make permanent

109 Marcombe, 'Dean and Chapter of Durham', p. 136.

110 Ibid., p. 136.

111 This income was comprised of the following: £157 8s from Bearpark, £30 from Ravenflatt, £192 from Holme, £320 from the tithes of the rectories of Billingham and Merrington, £266 13s 4d from his stipend, and a further £114 10s 6d for his dividend, as well as £50 14s 4d from arrears. In total: £1,130. See the deanery accounts, DCM/H/DRA/10.

112 Depending on whether or not the prebendal stall had access to the land – several prebends faced struggles removing the families of previous incumbents who had tried to grant the land in perpetuity upon their families even though the land was attached to the office.

acquisitions of property. These leases enabled prebendaries to enter the region and quickly gain a foothold of important agricultural lands, especially of the larger leases which amounted to whole manors. The likes of Dean Newton, with an income over £1,000 per annum from his Durham office in the 1610s, were able to accumulate enough capital to purchase whole manors at a time when some members of landed society were facing increasing financial difficulties. The monks who had preceded these canons had left little impact on the ownership of land outside of their monastic community, but with the reformation of the cathedral, these new prebendaries created an increasingly important flow of wealth into the Durham countryside.

But just how far did these new prebendaries, together with the merchants of Newcastle, upset the traditional balance of landed power within the palatinate? Certainly, they increasingly made their presence felt, especially in their growing control of local politics, but it is easy to overemphasise their importance. James argued that a 'particularly striking' feature of the Durham countryside in the century preceding the Civil War was the influx of this new wealth into landed society: 'nowhere else in England, Northumberland included, were there so many landed fortunes founded on this kind of industrial basis'.[113] However, the acquisition of manors by Newcastle merchants was neither novel nor as extensive as it perhaps could have been, suggesting their intention was never to relocate to the countryside *en masse*. It is likely that some of these coal merchants sought entry into the ranks of landed society, but their acquisitions were more often aimed at securing the mineral resources upon which their wealth was founded rather than out of a desire to 'set up as a country gentleman'.[114] The Andersons, for example, formed a dynasty of urban office-holding in Newcastle and acquired considerable wealth long before they had secured the Grand Lease and the monopoly of coal which followed. Similarly, the large-scale purchases of Roger Thornton in the fifteenth century were primarily aimed at acquiring coal-bearing lands rather than establishing a landed dynasty. Even when they did move into the Durham countryside, this was overwhelmingly in Chester ward which was effectively in the process of becoming Newcastle's hinterland in this period. Likewise, the prebendaries of Durham cathedral were increasingly putting down permanent roots in the countryside, but this was still restricted to a relatively small group of families. There was a general shift in the overall balance of landed power in the palatinate across the sixteenth and early seventeenth centuries which saw the gradual fragmentation of larger estates into the hands of an ever-increasing number of families: this influx of 'new' wealth into the Durham countryside was but one facet of the overall redistribution of land in this period.

It must also be remembered that we are discussing a relative minority of Newcastle merchants and ecclesiastical families in this period: an elite within an elite. The majority of smaller merchants undoubtedly benefited from the take-off

113 James, *Family, Lineage and Civil Society*, p. 69.

114 Nef, *Rise of the British Coal Industry*, vol. 2, p. 121.

of the coal industry through provisioning the burgeoning city but not on the same scale as the Newcastle Hostmen. It was this group of merchants who formed an urban oligarchy and who shared many of the same concerns of the landed gentry surrounding hierarchy, wealth and social status.[115] Although it has been emphasised here that these merchants formed their own civic ideals, this is not to suggest that they were either in competition or conflict with the landed elite of Durham, as they can be seen intermarrying with many of the greatest families in the region. Some of these merchants may well have 'retreated' into the countryside, but they often maintained equally as well-furnished houses in Newcastle, with the city retaining its importance to both their future financial endeavours and their social identities. As Rigby has noted, wealthy merchants made 'relatively little overall impression on the character of the landed gentry in particular counties' in medieval England, whilst 'for many townsmen the use of the title of "merchant" may have been, in effect, a proclamation of their own gentility'.[116] The influx of this new wealth into the Durham countryside certainly never approached flood levels, but represented a gradual trickle of wealth which permeated society across the sixteenth and seventeenth centuries, with Newcastle increasingly forming a regional focal point. Against an economic, social and political backdrop which included the downfall of the Nevilles, the withdrawal from the north-east by the Percys and Lumleys, and the financial difficulties of the bishops of Durham, the success of Newcastle coal merchants like Henry Anderson and William Selby placed them amongst the most powerful men remaining in the north-east of England, landed or not.

115 See for example, Susan Reynolds, *An Introduction to the History of English Medieval Towns* (Oxford, 1977) and S. H. Rigby, 'Urban 'Oligarchy' in Late Medieval England', in John A. F. Thomson (ed.), *Towns and Townspeople in the Fifteenth Century* (Gloucester, 1988), pp. 62–86.

116 S. H. Rigby, 'English Society in the Later Middle Ages: Deference, Ambition and Conflict', in Peter Brown (ed.), *A Companion to Medieval English Literature and Culture, c.1350–c.1500* (Oxford, 2007), p. 30.

6

The Rise of the Church Leaseholder

One of the main issues in the transition from feudalism to capitalism debate has been the role of the peasantry who have been seen by many as a hindrance to the progress of agricultural development: their decline, and the transition from a rural society dominated by feudal lords and peasants to a tripartite society of land-owners, capitalist farmers and wage labourers, has been seen as crucial in setting England apart from much of early modern Europe.[1] It is illustrative of the changes which many historians of this period think rural society underwent between the fifteenth and sixteenth centuries that medievalists generally refer to the majority of small-scale agricultural producers as peasants whilst their early modern counterparts refer to this group in society by the more neutral terms of their form of tenure.[2] The decline of the peasantry is a narrative, moreover, which has been fraught with disagreements, ranging from Alan MacFarlane's view that England has never possessed a true peasantry to the debate surrounding peasants and class conflict in the eighteenth and nineteenth centuries between Michael Reed, Dennis Mills and Roger Wells.[3] These disputes have often arisen at a terminological level rather than an historical one, primarily because of problems with defining the peasantry: how important were property rights, market-orientation and cultural inheritance in peasant societies?[4]

1 For the transition debate, see for example: Dobb, *Studies in the Development of Capitalism*; Paul Sweezy et al., *The Transition from Feudalism to Capitalism* (London, 1954); R. H. Hilton (ed.), *The Transition from Feudalism to Capitalism* (London, 1976). For more recent studies on this period of rural history, see French and Hoyle, *Earls Colne*; Whittle, *Agrarian Capitalism*; L. R. Poos, *A Rural Society After the Black Death: Essex, 1350–1525* (Cambridge, 1991); Marjorie McIntosh, *Autonomy and Community: The Royal Manor of Havering, 1200–1500* (Cambridge, 1986); Marjorie McIntosh, *A Community Transformed: The Manor and Liberty of Havering, 1500–1620* (Cambridge, 1991); Dodds, *Peasants and Production*; Yates, *Town and Countryside*; Dyer, *An Age of Transition?*

2 See, for example, the indexes of Dyer's *An Age of Transition?* and Wrightson's *Earthly Necessities* for a comparison of the use of the term 'peasants'.

3 Alan MacFarlane, *The Origins of English Individualism: The Family, Property and Social Transition* (Oxford, 1978), pp. 32–3; see the articles in *The Journal of Peasant Studies*, reprinted in Michael Reed and Roger Wells (eds.), *Class, Conflict and Protest in the English Countryside, 1700–1880* (London, 1990).

4 The term 'peasant' is one which many have sought to avoid. For example, Sreenivasan refused to engage with the problem because 'to date the essence of that controversy has been the definition of a peasant. It seems to me that the question has to be settled at a terminological level before it can be dealt with at a historical one', G. Sreenivasan, 'The Land-Family Bond at Earls Colne (Essex), 1550–1650', *P&P*, 131 (1991), p. 4; Leigh Shaw-Taylor refused to engage directly with the term but

Peasants have traditionally been presented as a hindrance to agricultural progress, with Postan, Hilton and Brenner emphasising their inability to reinvest in agriculture because of the high levels of feudal rent they endured.[5] They placed the blame for this squarely on the shoulders of feudal lords, many of whom 'tended to spend up to the hilt on personal display, on extravagant living, on the maintenance of numerous retinue, and on war'.[6] Mark Bailey has criticised these interpretations as 'a tendency to stereotype medieval lords as rapacious extractors of peasant surpluses', but he went on to concede that 'landlords did not develop sophisticated notions of profit or returns to capital invested ... they certainly expected good returns ... but did not look to maximise profits. Their landed estates continued to be regarded more as a mark of status and privilege than as business enterprises.'[7] Hilton calculated that average reinvestment levels on the estates of Canterbury Cathedral Priory were less than 5 per cent, which, although enough to ensure the land and infrastructure were maintained in relatively good condition, were hardly entrepreneurial.[8] Even with the broadest definition of reinvestment, Postan argued that 'we cannot escape the conclusion that lords as a rule invested very small proportions of their incomes'.[9] He went on to estimate that the direct impact of these seigniorial exactions on peasants meant that something like 50 per cent of an unfree peasant's total product was taken by the lord, and that 'this was entirely unproductive profit, for hardly any of it was ploughed back into production; most was squandered in military expenditure and conspicuous consumption'.[10] Martin Stephenson has more recently challenged these low estimates of investment levels, arguing that capital investment by medieval landlords was more in the region of 17 per cent, which was not only over three times higher than Postan and Hilton calculated but also nearly double that of improving eighteenth-century landlords.[11] Even with this caveat in place, it is clear that investment and profits were

acknowledged that 'the terms are far too deeply embedded in numerous discourses to be excised from public discussion and they are not without value', Shaw-Taylor, 'Rise of Agrarian Capitalism', pp. 4–5. See especially J. V. Beckett, 'The Peasant in England: A Case of Terminological Confusion', *AgHR*, 32 (1984), pp. 113–23.

5 R. H. Hilton, 'Rent and Capital Formation in Feudal Society', in R. H. Hilton (ed.), *The English Peasantry in the Later Middle Ages: The Ford Lectures for 1973* (Oxford, 1975), p. 177; M. M. Postan, 'Investment in Medieval Agriculture', *EcHR*, 27 (1967), p. 578; Brenner, 'Agrarian Class Structure', p. 31.

6 Hilton, 'Rent and Capital Formation', p. 177.

7 Bailey, 'Commercialisation of the English Economy', p. 309.

8 Hilton, 'Rent and Capital Formation', p. 186.

9 Postan, 'Investment in Medieval Agriculture', p. 578.

10 Brenner, 'Agrarian Class Structure', p. 31.

11 M. Stephenson, 'Risk and Capital Formation: Seigneurial Investment in an Age of Adversity', in M. Bailey and S. Rigby (eds.), *Town and Countryside in the Age of the Black Death: Essays in Honour of John Hatcher* (Turnhout, 2012), p. 188. One of the reasons for this favourable comparison with eighteenth-century landlords may well be because medieval landowners invested heavily in livestock whereas these later landlords were rentiers and so their only capital investments tended to be in the maintenance of the land.

not the sole, nor indeed primary, aim motivating the actions of many medieval landowners. The widespread building of mills was one of the few areas where manorial lords did provide structural investment in the medieval economy, but this was often undertaken as an extension of their seigniorial rights as much as in an attempt to improve agricultural productivity.[12]

This medieval society is traditionally thought to have undergone a feudal or Malthusian crisis at the start of the fourteenth century as the soil was slowly exhausted by over-exploitation, with diminishing rates of return meaning that an increasing proportion of the population was living at subsistence levels.[13] This was because capital formation amongst the peasantry was restricted by the lack of any available surplus from production above basic subsistence needs and so 'they could not, so to speak, put back what they took out' of the soil.[14] The extent to which fourteenth-century society was facing a Malthusian crisis has been questioned more recently, especially by Campbell and Overton who have shown that yields may not have declined in the face of increasing population pressure. [15] Similarly, Hatcher and Bailey have suggested that serfdom may have been less exploitative than has often been argued because custom constrained the ability of lords to act arbitrarily or even increase rents in line with market values in the thirteenth century.[16] This situation bears many similarities with some of the advantages of copyhold tenure in the sixteenth century, but it is easy to over-emphasise the benefits for peasants in the earlier period, especially as many of them were facing increasing problems created by the fragmentation of traditional holdings. Kosminsky, for example, found that up to 57 per cent of unfree holdings and up to 80 per cent of free holdings had less than eight acres of land in four East Midlands counties in 1279–80, whilst in Bedfordshire in 1297, 85 per cent of taxpayers had either one draught animal or none at all.[17] Postan and Hilton both estimated that there were 'next to nil' opportunities to accumulate

12 John Langdon, 'Was England a Technological Backwater in the Middle Ages?', in Grenville Astill and John Langdon (eds.), *Medieval Farming and Technology: The Impact of Agricultural Change in Northwest Europe* (New York, 1997), pp. 275–92.

13 There has been considerable controversy over yields in thirteenth-century England, with Postan, Farmer and Titow believing that yields declined because of, amongst other things, under-manuring: Postan, 'Medieval Agrarian Society in its Prime: England', pp. 548–59; Farmer, 'Grain Yields', pp. 555–66; Titow, *Winchester Yields*.

14 Brenner, 'Agrarian Class Structure', p. 33.

15 Bruce M. S. Campbell and Mark Overton have shown that yields did not decrease because of population growth in Norfolk, Campbell and Overton, 'A New Perspective', pp. 38–105; see also, Campbell, 'Arable Productivity', pp. 379–404. For a re-evaluation of the early fourteenth century crisis, see Campbell, 'Arable Productivity in Medieval England: Some Evidence from Norfolk', *JEcH*, 43 (1983), pp. 3–70.

16 John Hatcher, 'English Serfdom and Villeinage: Towards a Reassessment', *P&P*, 90 (1981), pp. 3–39; Mark Bailey, 'Villeinage in England: a Regional Case Study c.1250–1349', *EcHR*, 62 (2009), pp. 430–57; Bailey, *The Decline of Serfdom in Late Medieval England*, p. 6.

17 Kosminsky, *Studies in the Agrarian History of England*, pp. 216–22; Hilton 'Rent and Capital Formation', p. 197.

any surplus for peasants holding a half-virgate or less, which is a particularly significant threshold given that as many as half of all peasants in pre-plague England may have held this amount of land.[18] The peasant, alongside his manorial lord, has thus been seen as hindering the formation of agrarian capitalism because the former could not create a large enough surplus to reinvest in agriculture, whilst the latter had little interest in doing so.

This vicious cycle is thought to have been broken with the Black Death because peasants had increasing opportunities to accumulate holdings afterwards, enabling the creation of larger surpluses and the gradual formation of capital which their ancestors had been deprived of by a combination of feudal exactions and fragmented holdings.[19] However, this was not a straightforward and linear process because there were many difficulties for agricultural producers during the fifteenth century in the form of low prices and high wages, which reduced the potential profit margins for peasants seeking to work their engrossed holdings intensively. It was in the sixteenth century that the widespread enlargement of peasant holdings took on a new social and economic significance. The high inflation of the sixteenth century provided these tenants with increasing potential for profits, not least because many of their rents stagnated behind the rise in agricultural prices, whilst smallholders were generally disadvantaged because wages did not increase in line with grain prices.[20] This process increasingly gave rise to two new groups in society: the yeomanry who thus rose out of the peasantry, reinvested in commercial agriculture and sometimes even purchased the freehold rights to their lands and entered the ranks of the gentry; and a growing group of landless agricultural labourers who worked on the farms of their yeomen neighbours and who suffered from this decline in real wages. This was not to be the end of the peasantry in the English countryside because they were able to survive on smallholdings on various estates where restrictive tenure, stagnant rents and common grazing rights ensured their viability, but the economic conditions did help to create these increasingly important social groups within rural society.[21]

Alan MacFarlane developed a particularly controversial definition of a peasant society which sought to undermine this traditional narrative. He drew upon anthropological literature describing Polish and Russian peasantries of the late nineteenth century to establish the characteristics of a peasant society in which there were no institutional property rights but land was vested in the family group. There could, therefore, neither be sale nor inheritance of goods, for no individual 'owned' them, and

18 Postan, 'Investment in Medieval Agriculture', p. 585; Hilton, 'Rent and Capital Formation', pp. 199–200.

19 See for example, Poos, *A Rural Society* and Dyer, *An Age of Transition?*, p. 175.

20 Kerridge, 'Movement of Rent', pp. 16–34; Tawney, *The Agrarian Problem in the Sixteenth Century*, pp. 200–13; Bowden, 'Agricultural Prices, Wages, Farm Profits and Rents', pp. 694–5. Hoskins, 'Harvest Fluctuations', p. 31; Harrison, 'Grain Price Analysis', pp. 147–51; Phelps Brown and Hopkins, 'Seven Centuries of Building Wages', pp. 195–206.

21 Dyer, *An Age of Transition?*, pp. 242–6; Wrightson and Levine, *Poverty and Piety*, p. 2.

so English society displayed a remarkable degree of individualism which precluded the existence of a peasantry.[22] His hypothesis was 'that the majority of ordinary people in England from at least the thirteenth century were rampant individualists, highly mobile both geographically and socially, economically 'rational', market-oriented and acquisitive, ego-centred in kinship and social life'.[23] Elements of MacFarlane's ideas of English peasants have survived revisionism surprisingly well, not least the increasing acknowledgement that medieval society was far more commercialised than was once thought.[24] In emphasising the continuity of the individualism of English society from the thirteenth century through until the eighteenth century, however, MacFarlane minimised the significance of the numerous transformations which rural society underwent in the intervening period.[25] Jane Whittle has more recently provided a concise and useful definition of peasants as 'smallscale agricultural producers who are in possession of land which is farmed primarily with family labour and with the main aim of providing the family directly with a means of subsistence'.[26]

The accumulation of land by a minority of richer peasants has been seen as a necessary precursor to the development of agrarian capitalism in works ranging from Lenin's *Development of Capitalism in Russia* to Hoskins' *Midland Peasant*. The latter, for example, noted that 'during the fifteenth and sixteenth centuries there emerged at Wigston what may be called a peasant aristocracy, or if this is too strong a phrase as yet, a class of capitalist peasants who owned substantially larger farms and capital resources than the general run of village farmers'.[27] In his study of agrarian capitalism, Glennie argued that there was an intensification of the polarisation of tenant landholdings under the pressure of inflation in the sixteenth century but that this was already a marked feature of the countryside in the fifteenth century, being well advanced prior to the increases in prices or leasehold rents.[28] Did the long-term

22 MacFarlane, *Origins of English Individualism*, pp. 32–3.

23 Ibid., p. 163.

24 Ben Dodds and Christian Liddy, 'Richard Britnell: An Appreciation', in Ben Dodds and Christian Liddy (eds.), *Commercial Activity, Markets and Entrepreneurs in the Middle Ages: Essays in Honour of Richard Britnell* (Woodbridge, 2011), pp. xi–xv. See Britnell, *The Commercialisation of English Society, 1000–1500* (Manchester, 1997); and the essays in Britnell and Campbell (eds.), *A Commercialising Economy*.

25 Jane Whittle has disputed MacFarlane's usage of the term peasant as an 'unusually constrictive definition of peasant society and economy, stressing an almost total lack of market relations in peasant societies', whilst Henry French and Richard Hoyle similarly criticised it for there 'seemed to be no good reason why one historically specific form of peasantry should be the standard against which all others should be judged'. Whittle, *Agrarian Capitalism*, p. 13; Henry French and Richard Hoyle, 'English Individualism Refuted: And Reasserted: The Land Market of Earls Colne (Essex), 1550–1750', *EcHR*, 56 (2003), p. 596. Steve Rigby has also questioned the force of MacFarlane's argument because medievalists had not based their studies of the period on his model, see Rigby, *English Society*, pp. 23–5.

26 Whittle, *Agrarian Capitalism*, p. 11.

27 Hoskins, *The Midland Peasant*, p. 141.

28 Paul Glennie, 'In Search of Agrarian Capitalism: Manorial Land Markets and the Acquisition

survival of families in a village aid this process? Dyer, for example, has noted the tendency for well-established families to occupy offices in the village, and they would ensure that traditions and memories were carried forward through time.[29] It was often these core families who had survived throughout the fifteenth century that became defenders of custom from the mid-sixteenth century onwards as landlords increasingly sought to combat inflation by increasing entry fines or rents, much akin to the tenant-right dispute on the dean and chapter's estate.[30] But were they also the same tenants who came to form a rural elite characterised by social ambition and economic entrepreneurship? As will be seen, although the long-term survival of families was a factor in the formation of agrarian capitalism, the tenurial and institutional context was also vital because it affected the ability of tenants to retain and reinvest capital.[31]

Durham Cathedral's Estate

The Durham region was characterised not only by a precocious development of industry, but also by a high concentration of ecclesiastical landownership: Durham Cathedral Priory was one of the most substantial landowners in the palatinate of Durham, second only to the bishop himself, and so the fortunes of the priory's tenants was of crucial importance to rural society in the region.[32] David Marcombe introduced his article on the decline of these Church leaseholders in the nineteenth century thus:

> In most English shires the Church was a very substantial landowner, and the tenants who leased its lands came to form an *elite group* in county society characterised by an *economic independence and a degree of social aspiration* not common to the English tenantry at large; the fact that this important social and economic group has been almost wholly neglected by historians is all the more difficult to understand when we remember that in the third and fourth decades of the nineteenth century the position of the Church leaseholder provoked heated debate in and out of Parliament.[33]

of Land in the Lea Valley', *Continuity and Change*, 3 (1988), p. 18. See also A. B. Appleby, 'Agrarian Capitalism or Seigneurial Reaction? The Northwest of England, 1500–1700, *American Historical Review*, 80 (1975), pp. 574–94.

29 C. Dyer, 'Were Late Medieval English Villages "Self-Contained"?', in C. Dyer (ed.), *The Self-Contained Village? The Social History of Rural Communities, 1250–1900* (Hatfield, 2006), p. 6.

30 For the idea of core dynastic families, see A. Mitson, 'The Significance of Kinship Networks in the Seventeenth Century: South-West Nottinghamshire', in C. Phythian-Adams (ed.), *Societies, Cultures and Kinship, 1580–1850: Cultural Provinces in English Local History* (Leicester, 1993), pp. 24–76.

31 Compare, for example, the Newtons and Taillours at Harton on the dean and chapter's estate in this chapter with the Shepherdsons or Shadforths on the bishop of Durham's estate in the following chapter.

32 See chapters 1 and 2 for more information about the estates of Durham Cathedral and the bishops of Durham in this period.

33 Marcombe, 'Church Leaseholders', p. 255. My italics.

The leaseholders on the estate of the dean and chapter of Durham Cathedral were, however, unlike those studied by Clay in the seventeenth and eighteenth centuries. He noted that most Church lands were 'leased out to laymen at very low rents, generally in large blocks to gentlemen and substantial freeholders, who in turn let to cultivating sub-tenants'.[34] Clay concluded that: 'everywhere (or almost everywhere), from the properties of the dean and chapter of Carlisle in the far north-west to those of the archbishop of Canterbury ... in the south-east, the immediate tenants of the church on its rural estates were mostly gentlemen and esquires'.[35] This was not the case on the estate of the dean and chapter of Durham Cathedral, where the majority of their tenants were husbandmen farmers, directly working and living on the land they leased from the cathedral throughout the period under study here.

The following chapters explore the longevity of families in certain villages on the two largest ecclesiastical estates in Durham and the effect that this institutional context had upon their opportunities for wealth accumulation and social mobility. Did certain families persist on the estate of Durham cathedral across the fifteenth and sixteenth centuries despite the numerous obstacles to such long-term inheritance and did this represent the survival of a 'peasant mindset'? Bailey has recently argued that 'there is no doubt the dissolution of villein tenure was a significant and beneficial contributor to economic development, because conditions in late sixteenth-century England were much better suited to the accumulation of wealth among the peasantry than they had been in the late thirteenth century'.[36] In essence, therefore, was capital formation possible in the sixteenth century in a manner not achievable before and did this situation emerge because of a cultural change away from a peasant mentality or as a result of the combination of demographic changes, removal of institutional constraints and increasing market opportunities?

In his study of the structure of Durham Priory's estate, Richard Lomas estimated that before the Black Death the estate of the priory contained some 825 holdings, which were in the hands of approximately 740 tenants.[37] He estimated that of these tenements over 100 were freeholds, of originally between thirty and sixty acres, with a further 148 bondlands whose tenants owed no money rent but rendered labour services only and which could range in size between eighteen and forty-eight acres although they were predominantly thirty acres, whilst there were also sixty-one husbandlands who owed money rent rather than labour services. Below this was a group of smallholders of perhaps half a virgate, with twelve acres being 'by far the

34 C. G. A. Clay, 'Landlords and Estate Management in England', in J. Thirsk (ed.), *The Agrarian History of England and Wales, Vol. 5: 1640–1750, part 2* (Cambridge, 1985), p. 156.

35 Clay, '"The Greed of Whig Bishops"', p. 137. For the survival of the yeoman on ecclesiastical and collegiate estates, see Michael Turner, 'The Demise of the Yeoman, c.1750–1940', in John Broad (ed.), *A Common Agricultural Heritage? Revising the French and British Rural Divergence*, AgHR supplement series, 5 (2009), pp. 83–106.

36 Bailey, *The Decline of Serfdom in Late Medieval England*, p. 8.

37 Lomas, 'Developments in Land Tenure', p. 28.

most common', whilst most townships also contained a group of cottages with a small amount of land attached to them, some of which survived as cottage-holdings throughout this period, although they often became a place of retirement for elderly family members or widows.[38] During the population growth of the late thirteenth and early fourteenth centuries many of these holdings fragmented so that the structure of landholding in some townships was radically altered. For example, at West Rainton there had been seven bondlands and six husbandlands in the early thirteenth century, all consisting of thirty-two acres, but after a century of population growth and inheritance they had fragmented into thirty-three holdings ranging from half an acre to forty-eight acres with, in Lomas' words, 'very few of like size and with almost all including fractions of an acre'.[39]

The monks of Durham Priory, in concert with their tenants, reorganised their estate across the fifteenth century so that 'the structure of the estate was completely altered ... although new arrangements were not everywhere complete in detail until the sixteenth century'. The most obvious change was that wrought by the Black Death and subsequent outbreaks of disease which reduced the number of tenants from 740 to 330 by 1495, with a similarly drastic decline in the number of holdings from 825 to no more than 375. Naturally this led to the engrossment of the surviving holdings, which will be explored in more detail with reference to case studies at Harton and Cowpen Bewley below, but there was another equally significant change which was wrought in this period: the conversion of these holdings to leasehold tenure. Around 1360, 'with very few exceptions, tenants were granted their holdings for life', but by the mid-fifteenth century this form of tenancy had 'given way completely to the short lease'.[40] It was this conversion to leasehold tenure which provided the dean and chapter with such headaches in the mid-sixteenth century. However, as will be seen below, it caused surprisingly little discontinuity in landholding. The conversion to leasehold was more significant because it made the engrossed holdings achieved after the Black Death the standard holding on their estates, and thus when population grew in the sixteenth century their holdings did not fragment in the same way they had during the thirteenth century. Although both Timothy Lomas and Peter Larson have shown how the priory's land market and this restructuring of holdings enabled certain families to prosper in the fifteenth century, the process of syndication ultimately led to a more even distribution of land in the following generations.[41]

38 Ibid., p. 32; See chapter 1 above for some of these tenurial changes in the fifteenth century on Durham Priory's estate.

39 Lomas, 'Developments in Land Tenure', p. 33.

40 Ibid., p. 37. All agricultural land was essentially brought together in syndications; all land was divided equally amongst the remaining tenants of the township who each had an equal responsibility for the total rent. Case studies below show this process at work.

41 Lomas, 'Land and People in South-East Durham', pp. 107–33; and Larson, *Conflict and Compromise*, pp. 225–40.

Table 19. Rental Value and Standard Deviation of Holdings on the Dean and Chapter's Estate, 1580

Manor	Number and Rent of Holdings	Standard Deviation
Wallsend	7 leaseholds, 34s 7d*	0
Over Heworth	4 leaseholds, 43s 10d–£10	63.85
Nether Heworth	4 leaseholds, 51s 10d	0
Monkton	5 leaseholds, 36s 10d	0
Hedworth	3 leaseholds, 44s 5.5d	0
Harton	10 leaseholds, 54s 7d	0
Westoe	9 leaseholds, 55s 4d*	0
Southwick	4 leaseholds, 88s 11d*	0
Fulwell	4 leaseholds, 108s 6d	0
Monkwearmouth	4 leaseholds, 60s 13d	0
Dalton le Dale	5 leaseholds, 49s 10d*	0
East Rainton	8 leaseholds, 52s 3.5d	0
West Rainton	8 leaseholds, 50s 7d	0
Moorsley	3 leaseholds, 45s 6d	0
North Pittington	5 leaseholds , 23s 10d–95s 4d; 2 cottages	29.1
Cowpen Bewley	10 leaseholds, 60s 2d; 13 cottages	27.47
Newton Bewley	9 leaseholds, 80s 1d; 3 cottages	22.7
Wolviston	13 leaseholds, 60s 4d; 21 cottages	27.39
Billingham	16 leaseholds, 75s 7d; 17 cottages	35.86
Burdon	4 leaseholds, 64s 4d; 4 smaller holdings	26.38
Newton Ketton	2 leaseholds, 106s 8d	0
Aycliffe	10 leaseholds, 48s 8d; 36 cottages	18.4
Chilton	2 leaseholds, 40s and 46s 8d	3.33
Ferryhill	13 leaseholds, 49s 2d	0
East Merrington	14 leaseholds, 49s	0
Mid Merrington	7 leaseholds, 48s 4d	0
West Merrington	4 leaseholds, 60s 5d	0

* Each of these townships had a solitary cottage, often attached to the village mill or held by a widow.

Source: DCM, Dean and Chapter Registers, 1–15, 1541–1640; W. H. D. Longstaffe and J. Booth (eds.), *Halmota Prioratus Dunelmensis: Containing Extracts from the Halmote Court or Manor Rolls of the Prior and Convent of Durham, 1296–1384*, Surtees Society, 82 (1886), appendix.

By the mid-sixteenth century, this reorganisation of land and tenure had produced a very distinctive pattern of landholding on the dean and chapter's estate, whereby the bulk of agricultural land in each township was held in roughly equal shares by tenants who owed the same rent as their neighbours. This uniformity can be seen in Table 19. Although there were obvious differences in the size of holdings and rental obligations of tenants in different townships across the estate, there was no variation within the same village in eighteen cases by 1580. There are few examples of these holdings breaking apart under inheritance in the sixteenth and early seventeenth centuries and the structure of landholding laid down in the syndication of holdings across the fifteenth and early sixteenth centuries remained largely intact for generations.[42] There were, however, several townships which did not conform to this pattern of uniformity, with Over Heworth and North Pittington showing genuine signs of stratification in the landholdings there. These townships were anomalies on the estate and represent the influence of Thomas Whitehead, a relative of Dean Whitehead, who gained half of the village of Over Heworth, and the wealthy Newcastle merchant Henry Anderson, who acquired several leases at North Pittington. These engrossed holdings were clearly a rarity on the dean and chapter's estate in the sixteenth century and were only held by prominent members of the gentry or Newcastle merchants throughout this period.[43]

The south-eastern townships of the dean and chapter's estate also show signs of variance, but this is because of the survival of a large number of cottage holdings rather than a stratification of the primary agricultural holdings of the villages. Billingham, Cowpen Bewley, Newton Bewley and Wolviston were in Billingham parish in the south-east of the county and contained some of the most fertile land in the region, while Aycliffe was further to the west of this group of townships. This pattern of landholding was partly related to the denser population settlement in this area of the county. Lomas, for example, estimated that the average population of these villages varied between 300 and 600 people in the fifteenth century, and so the survival of a considerable number of cottages is perhaps unsurprising.[44] The history of Durham Priory's demesne management is also significant here because Bewley was 'by far the priory's most important centre' and was its largest demesne with close to 700 sown acres, twenty-two ploughmen and 104 oxen in 1304/05, nearly twice that of any other priory demesne.[45] The survival of the cottagers in this group of south-eastern villages, therefore, reflected the long-term agricultural history of the region. Despite this, the bulk of the land here shows the same uniformity as elsewhere once these villages were syndicated and leased out. Case studies of the villages of Harton and Cowpen Bewley are explored in greater depth below to show the similarity between this group of southern villages and the rest of the cathedral's estate. The

42 Jean Morrin, for example, found only one example in the Merrington area of the estate where a farm was divided between two sons, leading to the granting of separate leases. Morrin, 'Merrington: Land, Landlord and Tenants', p. 41.

43 The lease for half the village of Over Heworth was owned first by Thomas Whitehead (1543, 1577), then George Bowes (1597), then Thomas Blakiston (1612) and then Ralph Cole (1616, 1625). Two-fifths of North Pittington was owned by Henry Anderson from the mid-sixteenth century onwards.

44 Lomas, 'Land and People in South-East Durham', p. 183.

45 Britnell (ed.), *Durham Priory Manorial Accounts*, pp. xlii– xlvi.

restructuring of tenure and landholdings in the fifteenth and early sixteenth centuries was of utmost importance, therefore, even when individual villages had significant differences in their long-term agricultural histories.

There is, of course, the potential problem posed by subletting: how far did the enlarged leasehold farms actually break up in the sixteenth century without the dean and chapter's recognition? In so far as it is possible to answer this question, there is little surviving evidence to suggest that this was commonplace and many signs that it was not. The surviving probate inventories of dean and chapter tenants, for example, include references to thirty to forty acres of sown corn on the ground, which, when land under fallow and pasture is taken into consideration, suggests little land was available for sub-tenancy to develop. Furthermore, the amount of livestock owned by these tenants, which is explored in greater depth below, reinforces this view: most tenants owned on average around eight oxen, eight cows, thirty sheep and a handful of horses, swine and poultry. Morrin, moreover, has noted that only two farms were completely sublet in the Merrington area of the estate before the Civil War, both by tenants who lived in Durham city; she argued that it was only really after 1660 that sub-tenancy increased apace on the estate.[46] It thus appears that the holdings discussed in Table 19 represented both the structure of landholding and the size of farming units, neither of which seem to have been significantly fragmented in the sixteenth and early seventeenth centuries.[47]

Peter Larson has recently suggested that the 'priory's conversion to leasehold would cost tenants in the long run by eliminating heritable right'.[48] It is far from clear, however, that the tenurial changes of the fifteenth and early sixteenth centuries did in fact destroy the ability to inherit holdings upon the priory's estate. The survival of surnames on the dean and chapter's estate suggests that in the 1620s around forty families remained in the village where their ancestors had resided in 1495/96.[49] The townships which experienced the highest levels of turnover often did so because outsiders purchased substantial portions of the village, such as at North Pittington and Over Heworth. However, this was rare and most townships contained a core group of families in the early seventeenth century who had been there since at

46 Morrin, 'Merrington: Land, Landlord and Tenants', p. 43 and p. 207.

47 This was, of course, a situation which was likely preferred by the dean and chapter since resident lessees were thought of as more likely to maintain the farm buildings and land in good condition.

48 Larson, 'Peasant Opportunities in Rural Durham: Land, Vills and Mills, 1400–1500', in B. Dodds and C. Liddy (eds.), *Commercial Activity, Markets and Entrepreneurs in the Middle Ages: Essays in Honour of Richard Britnell* (Woodbridge, 2011), p. 148.

49 Lomas and Piper (eds.), *Durham Priory Rentals*; Longstaffe and Booth (eds.), *Halmota Prioratus Dunelmensis*, appendix; DCM/E/BA: List of Tenants, With Rents and Valuations, Temp ~ Dean Hunt (1620–38). This represents the number of family names present on the main agricultural holdings of the dean and chapter's estate rather than either the number of tenants in total or the number of holdings. For instance, at Harton multiple holdings were leased by the Newtons, and likewise the Laws and Cliftons held multiple leases at Cowpen Bewley which would only be counted once.

least the fifteenth century, and some from the late fourteenth century. For example, Chilton was held in two halves by the Maltby and Kay families from the end of the fifteenth century until the early seventeenth century, as Newton Ketton was by the Cotesforths and Stellings. The Cliftons, Lawes and Marshalls remained in the village of Cowpen Bewley throughout this period, as did the Willeys, Whites and Heighingtons at East Merrington and the Robinsons and Laxes at West Merrington. This is surprising not because it represents the survival of a latent peasant mentality, but because these tenants were leaseholders during some of the largest upheavals in rural society in this period: the Pilgrimage of Grace in 1536; the dissolution of the cathedral which was their landlord just a few years later; the Rising of the North in 1569 in which many of these tenants participated; and the tenant-right dispute between the dean and chapter and their tenants in the 1570s. It is this last event which may go some way towards explaining why there was such a strong inheritance of holdings because although the Council of the North rejected the tenants' claims of tenant-right, beneficial leaseholds developed on the dean and chapter's estate which offered numerous rights to their owners.[50]

Harton and Cowpen Bewley

The following case studies of Harton and Cowpen Bewley explore the experiences of these core families and whether or not their survival for multiple generations enabled the rise of a rural elite. These two townships were chosen because of their geographical diversity, with Harton on the south banks of the Tyne and Cowpen Bewley amidst the more densely populated townships in the fertile south-east of Durham, and because the latter contained a group of cottages which survived into the sixteenth century.[51] Harton and Cowpen Bewley were both returned to the newly formed dean and chapter of Durham Cathedral, and both saw the survival of a core group of families from at least the late fifteenth century to the early seventeenth. Harton township was an appendage of Jarrow and had been one of the priory's original possessions, containing no demesne land or freeholdings, but comprising of twenty-one bondlands of forty-eight acres each.[52] The bursar's rent books provide

50 See chapter 2 above for more discussion of the dean and chapter of Durham Cathedral in the sixteenth century. See also Morrin, 'The Transfer to Leasehold', pp. 117–32, and J. Whittle, 'Leasehold Tenure in England, c.1300–c.1600: its Form and Incidence', in B. van Bavel and P. R. Schofield (eds.), *The Development of Leasehold in North-Western Europe, c.1200–1600* (Turnhout, 2008), pp. 147–50.

51 The townships in the south-east of the palatinate were generally much more densely settled than elsewhere on the priory's estate. T. Lomas, 'South-East Durham: Late Fourteenth and Fifteenth Centuries', in P. D. A. Harvey (ed.), *The Peasant Land Market in Medieval England* (Oxford, 1984), pp. 252–327.

52 Lomas and Piper (eds.), *Durham Priory Rentals*, p. 203.

snapshots of the tenants of Harton from the late fourteenth century onwards as shown in Table 20.

By the late fourteenth century the pre-Black Death holdings were still largely intact at Harton but the remaining tenants had accumulated them so that each person held at least two bondlands. Henry Smith, the village blacksmith, held a cottage with a forge and several other cottagers still existed, with the remaining tenants each holding between 96 and 144 acres of land and showing few signs of stratification. This was before the monks had implemented any kind of uniform process of syndication or centralised reorganisation of land, perhaps suggesting that this was the tenants' preferred distribution of land. By the rent book of 1495, these engrossed holdings had become officially recognised by the monks, and thus the entire township was leased out to the remaining tenants as a syndicate with each tenant holding a tenth portion of Harton. If there were initially twenty-one bondlands of forty-eight acres each, this represents a total acreage of approximately 1,000 acres, and so each new holding was just over 100 acres, for which tenants owed 54s 4d rent per annum.[53] Although it is unclear how far this was at the behest of their tenants, it was this official recognition of these enlarged holdings by the monks which was significant: if the holdings had remained as they were in the 1396/97 rent book, then tenants would have retained the option of fragmenting their holdings as had happened across the fourteenth century, but this was less likely to happen after the syndication of their lands.[54]

The Newton and Taillour families both survived the fifteenth-century recession, but the Kitchins, Pages and numerous other families had disappeared by 1495. However, the Kitchins reappear in the 1539 rent book and again in the Elizabethan survey of 1580, suggesting that this disappearance was only temporary, perhaps because of a minority at the time of the 1495 rent book.[55] The tenants at Harton had also acquired pasture rights in the nearby township of Simonside, which similarly belonged to Durham Priory.[56] Simonside had become depopulated across the course of the fifteenth century and from 1489 onwards was leased as enclosed pasture to the priory's tenants from the surrounding townships of Harton, Southwick, Fulwell,

53 Ibid., pp. 142–3 and p. 203. This was comparable to the size of holdings on much of the estate. In Kirk Merrington, Hett and Great Chilton each farm was about 100 acres. In Middlestone and Ferryhill it was about 120 acres and in Westerton 160 acres. Morrin, 'Merrington: Land, Landlord and Tenants', p. 32.

54 There are only a handful of examples of holdings being sub-divided across the sixteenth century. For example, a lease of a tenth part of Aycliffe was divided into two parts, as was a fifth part of North Pittington. However, these were anomalies on the dean and chapter's estate.

55 DCM, Bursar's Book M; Longstaffe and Booth (eds.), *Halmota Prioratus Dunelmensis*, pp. 225–6.

56 At Simonside there were originally nine husbandlands of thirty acres, nine cottages of six acres and nine cotterels, three of which were three acres and six of half that size. Lomas and Piper (eds.), *Durham Priory Rentals*, p. 203.

Table 20. Durham Cathedral Tenants of Harton from the Late Fourteenth Century to the Mid-Seventeenth Century

Bursar's Rent Book, 1396/97			Bursar's Rent Book, 1495/96		Elizabethan Survey, 1580			Survey ~ Dean Hunt, c. 1620–38	
Tenants	Holdings	Rent	Tenants	Rent	Tenants	Rent	Fine	Tenants	Rent
Thomas Neuton	2 bondlands	56s 8d	William Newton	54s 4d	Thomas Newton	54s 7d	£20	Thomas Newton	54s 7d
John Neuton	2 bondlands	56s 8d	Richard Newton	54s 4d	Richard Newton	54s 7d	£20*	Widow Newton	54s 7d
William Taillour	2 bondlands	53s 8d	Robert Taillyour	54s 4d	Robert Taylor	54s 7d	Unknown	Edward Taylor	54s 7d
William Page junior	3 bondlands	77s	John Person	54s 4d	Thomas Pearson	54s 7d	£14 10s	Thomas Pearson	54s 7d
William Page senior	2 bondlands	56s 8d	Jacob Atkinson	54s 4d	Andrew Atkinson	54s 7d	£11 3s 4d	William Atkinson	54s 7d
Ralph Kitchin	2 bondlands	50s	Thomas Grayden	54s 4d	Thomas Kitchin	54s 7d	£8 3s 9d	Rowland Sotheron	54s 7d
Robert son of William	2 bondlands	48s	Richard Betson	54s 4d	Thomas Hutchinson	54s 7d	£10	George Sheffield	54s 7d
John son of William	3 bondlands	72s 6d	William Bertram	54s 4d	Vidua Brompton	54s 7d	£8 3s 9d	Thomas Brompton	54s 7d
John son of Robert	3 bondlands	75s	Robert Alanson	54s 4d	Robert Chamber	54s 7d	£20*	John Smart	54s 7d
William Taillour	1 toft and 16 acres	9s 8d	John Newton	54s 4d	Vidua Wilkinson	54s 7d	£20*	John Smart	54s 7d
John son of William	1 cottage with garden	10d							
Henry Smith	1 cottage with forge	3d							
John Smith	1 cottage	6d							
Total	**21 bondlands**	**£27 12s 11d**		**£27 3s 4d**		**£27 5s 10d**	**£132 10d**		**£27 5s 10d**

* Land included in the lottery system; the entry fine represents the amount to be paid for the reversionary lease of their holdings (see chapter 2).

Sources: R. A. Lomas and A. J. Piper (eds.), *Durham Cathedral Priory Rentals, Vol. 1: Bursar's Rentals*, Surtees Society, 198 (1989); W. H. D. Longstaffe and J. Booth (eds.), *Halmota Prioratus Dunelmensis: Containing Extracts from the Halmote Court or Manor Rolls of the Prior and Convent of Durham, 1296–1384*, Surtees Society, 82 (1886), appendix. DCM/E/BA: List of Tenants, With Rents and Valuations, Temp ~ Dean Hunt (1620–38).

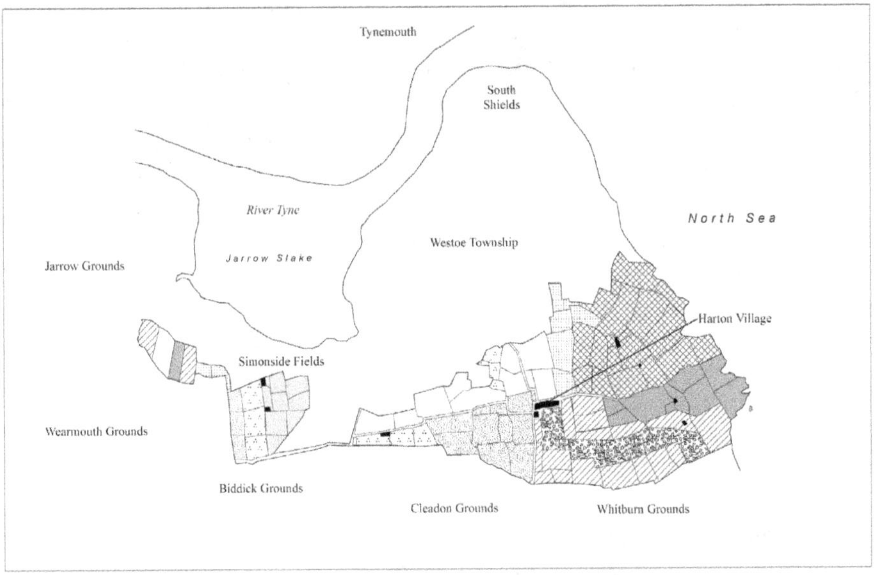

Map 3. Harton Township Survey Map, 1768.
Source: DCM/E/AA/1–2: Dean and Chapter Survey of Westoe and Harton, 1768.

Wearmouth, Westoe, Monkton and Hedworth.[57] This is an example of depopulation and enclosure which was undertaken by negotiation between landlord and tenants during the relative abundance of land in the fifteenth century.[58] Map 3 shows these holdings at Harton in the eighteenth century, with the enclosed fields at Simonside to the west of the village belonging to each of the main Harton holdings. Although two holdings had been accumulated and two others had been fragmented, there had been surprisingly little change in the overall distribution of land in the township since the fifteenth century.

Despite the Henrician Statutes of the cathedral explicitly stating that these 21-year leases were not to be inherited, and many of the disputes between the dean and chapter and their tenants arising because of this issue, it is clear that there was nothing hindering sons from inheriting the family holding.[59] The leases of the dean and chapter show that most holdings were renewed at least once, and the majority were inherited across several generations. Similarly, the wills of these lessees show that one of their main preoccupations was with the inheritance of their leases, whilst the few times these leases appear in their inventories they are valued at between £40 and £100.[60] This is surprising given that many of these tenants, or their close

57 DCM, Dean and Chapter Registers, 1–15.

58 Blanchard, 'Population Change', pp. 427–45.

59 Thompson (ed.), *Statutes of the Cathedral Church of Durham*, pp. 95–7.

60 DPRI/1/1605/A6/2–3; DPRI/1/1617/N1/2.

relatives, were involved in the Rising of the North in 1569.[61] Given the difficulties the dean and chapter were experiencing with their tenantry in these decades this might have provided an ideal reason for eviction, but would undoubtedly have caused further discontent in a region which had proven so volatile in the previous thirty years. The status quo was, therefore, to be maintained. The inheritability of these leases continued into the seventeenth century with the holdings in Table 21 being renewed by their families.[62] Despite the upheavals of this period, therefore, there was a surprising degree of continuity in village life, but what were the consequences of this?

Table 21. A Reconstruction of the Lease Renewals of the Primary Holdings at Harton, c.1540–c.1640

Lease Renewals, 1540–1640
Thomas Newton (1566, 1585, 1594, 1610, 1628)
Richard Newton (1585, 1595, 1627)
Thomas and William Pearson (1560), Thomas Pearson (1578), William Pearson (1595, 1611)
Richard Pearson (1573, 1593), Thomas Pearson (1611, 1627)
Robert Taylor (1560, 1575), Robert and Edward Taylor (1593), Edward Taylor (1610), Robert Taylor (1627)
William Atkinson (1591), James Atkinson (1601)
John Chamber (1588), Robert Chamber (1597, 1615)
Thomas Hutchinson (1587, 1607)

Source: DCM, Dean and Chapter Registers, 1–15, 1541–1640.

One of the greatest problems facing the English peasantry in the thirteenth century was their inability to acquire sufficient capital to either reinvest in agriculture or to significantly improve their standard of living.[63] This was because a combination of seigniorial exactions, fragmented holdings and the inherent unpredictability of medieval agriculture often meant that they could not produce a large enough marketable surplus to achieve anything more than meeting their basic subsistence needs. Were the sixteenth-century descendants of these medieval peasants able to use their enlarged holdings to engage in commercial agriculture and so profit from the

61 *Calendar of Patent Rolls Elizabeth, v, 1569–72*, pp. 81–114. Tenants at Harton receiving pardons include: Christopher Newton, Thomas and Richard Pereson, Thomas Hutcheson, Andrew Atkinson, John Chamber and John Carr the younger, reflecting the involvement of a large part of the village in the Rising.

62 The two leases held by the widows of Brompton and Wilkinson are difficult to trace. One was certainly lost to the Pilkingtons and then to the Tunstalls, whilst Thomas Brompton reappears in the village in a lease of 1617. DCM, Dean and Chapter Registers, 1–15.

63 For this traditional view of capital formation amongst the peasantry see: Kosminsky, *Agrarian History* and Hilton, 'Rent and Capital Formation', pp. 174–214.

rise in agricultural prices across this century? Was capital formation now possible in rural society in a manner not achievable before and did this emerge because of a cultural change from a peasant mentality or as a result of impersonal factors like demographic growth, the removal of institutional constraints and increasing market opportunities?[64] In their probate inventories, William Pearson (d. 1616) and Thomas Hutcheson (d. 1609) were both described as yeomen, whilst James Atkinson (d. 1605) was described as a husbandman, with the moveable goods of each of them being valued at over £100.[65]

Although much of the value of their inventories came, as would be expected, from livestock and agricultural goods, they also possessed modest household goods, with two of the oldest families, the Newtons and Pearsons, owning the highest valued household goods, livestock and clothes (Table 22). The longevity of these families in the township may have enabled wealth accumulation amongst these older families, allowing them a slightly higher standard of living than their neighbours, but it must also be noted that these amounts were not so far removed as to suggest the emergence of a rural elite nor were the items of significantly different quantity or, as far as can be determined, quality to those of their neighbours. John Chamber, for example, possessed eight candlesticks and James Atkinson had fourteen pieces of pewter, whereas the likes of William Pearson still possessed wooden vessels, despite the higher valuation of his total household goods. Although the possessions here suggest a reasonably comfortable standard of living, it is far from clear that they were either quantitatively or qualitatively different from those that the families' medieval ancestors would have possessed. Despite being problematic sources, medieval court roll inventories show that medieval peasants could possess significant numbers of agricultural and household goods. For example, Robert Osebern of Thornborough (Buckinghamshire) had a feather mattress, sheets and brass cooking implements on his death in 1297, despite only holding half a virgate.[66] With improving living standards and increased opportunities for landholding after the Black Death, peasants could accumulate more luxury items, such as the eight cushions and maple wood drinking cup bound in silver which the Yorkshire peasant Thomas Kirkeby possessed on his death in 1482.[67] The material culture of the dean and chapter's tenants does not, therefore, appear to be significantly different from wealthier tenants in the fifteenth century, nor do they appear to constitute a rural elite by the early seventeenth century.

64 For a methodological comment on the use of probate inventories for discussing wealth see the introduction to chapter 3 above.

65 DPRI/1/1596/C2/2; DPRI/1/1605/A6/2–3; DPRI/1/1609/H12/2; DPRI/1/1616/P5/3; DPRI/1/1617/N1/2.

66 Chris Briggs, 'Manorial Court Roll Inventories as Evidence for English Peasant Consumption and Living Standards, c.1270–c.1420', in A. Furio and F. Garcia-Oliver (eds.), *Pautes de Consum i Nivells de Vida al Món Rural Medieval* (Valencia, forthcoming).

67 P. M. Stell (ed.), *Probate Inventories of the York Diocese, 1350–1500* (York, 2006), pp. 647–8.

Table 22. A Breakdown of the Types of Wealth in the Surviving Probate Inventories of Harton Tenants, 1540–1640

Testator	Date	Arable	Livestock	Household	Clothes	Owed	Total	Owing
John Chamber	d. 1596	£42	£50	£7 11s	£2	6s 7d	£103 1s	-£9 13s
James Atkinson	d. 1605	£40 10s	£14	£6 10s	£2	£1 19s	£164 3s*	-£56 5s
Thomas Hutcheson	d. 1609	£54 6s	£56	£7 3s	£6	£5 1s	£129 13s	-£29 15s
William Pearson	d. 1616	£44	£70	£33 13s	£6	–	£153 13s	–
Thomas Newton	d. 1617	£49 13s	£70 8s	£22 15s	£7	–	£189 15s*	-£12 16s

* In their inventories, James Atkinson's lease was valued at £90, Thomas Newton's at £40.

Source: DPRI/1/1596/C2/2; DPRI/1/1605/A6/2–3; DPRI/1/1609/H12/2; DPRI/1/1616/P5/3; DPRI/1/1617/N1/2.

The sizes of the farms owned by these tenants would suggest that they were commercially producing for the market, whilst their probate inventories reveal a large degree of mixed agriculture on their primary holdings, supplemented by the additional pasture in the nearby fields at Simonside. In their work on Whickham, Levine and Wrightson have argued that the 'agriculture practised on these lands was predominantly pastoral' especially in the highland areas but 'even in the intermediate foothills and the eastern lowland zone, where crops of oats, rye, barley, wheat and peas were grown, animal husbandry remained the mainstay of the rural economy'.[68] They concluded that livestock generally accounted for 70–80 per cent of the total valuation of farm goods of copyholders on Whickham; this proportion is true for William Pearson and Thomas Newton, but there was a greater degree of parity between livestock and grain on the other farms. These tenants generally possessed around eight oxen, between six and ten cows, around thirty sheep and a handful of horses, swine and poultry, whilst James Atkinson's inventory shows the composition of grain they tended to grow: six-score thraves of wheat and ten of barley, oats and peas worth in total £36 13s 4d.[69]

The numbers of livestock were not enough to suggest commercial pastoral agriculture on any large scale, with oxen often accounting for half the value of their livestock, clearly emphasising the importance of arable farming to these tenants. This is somewhat surprising given the township's close proximity to South Shields, a fishing community with little agricultural land that had prospered due to the take-off of the salt industry in the early seventeenth century. Moreover, because the Tyne was difficult to navigate all the way upriver to Newcastle, the majority of ships which traded

68 Levine and Wrightson, *The Making of an Industrial Society*, p. 87.

69 James Atkinson's inventory: DPRI/1/1605/A6/2–3. For example, Thomas Newton (d. 1617) possessed eight oxen worth £36, five kyne and four stirkes worth £12 10s, thirty-six sheep worth £9 10s, one cow worth £2 10s, one nag worth £1 10s, a horse and mare worth £7, three hens and two pigs worth £1 8s, and hay worth £2, as well as corn in the garth and sown worth £41: DPRI/1/1617/N1/2.

with the city were anchored near Tynemouth, providing potential informal markets which tenants at Harton would have been ideally positioned to exploit. Harton tenants, therefore, were well situated to benefit from supplying the burgeoning coal and salt industries in Newcastle and South Shields, with vast throngs of keelmen and watermen rowing up and down the river, and yet, despite these potential commercial opportunities, they do not appear to have specialised for these markets.

The other notable difference between these Harton tenants and those of Whickham is in the grain grown, with Levine and Wrightson finding that 'oats and rye occur in the largest quantities, with wheat coming a poor third', whereas the inventories show much greater quantities of wheat being grown at Harton.[70] The overall impression created is not one in which animal husbandry was the mainstay of agriculture and is a far cry from other regions in England, such as the midlands where Hoskins found that the average farmer's livestock was worth almost twice the value of his crops.[71] Tenants in the lowland regions of Durham tended to have enough livestock to keep their lands well fertilised but possessed insufficient numbers for large-scale commercial farming: the six or seven cows which many of these tenants possessed being in Hoskins' mind 'enough for the milk, butter and cheese that were made and mostly consumed on the farm'.[72] It is only in the probate inventories of much more substantial yeomen tenants or the gentry that we tend to find pastoral farming on a significant scale, with livestock worth twice the value of arable farming.[73]

One of the other main concentrations of land owned by Durham Cathedral was focused on the heavily populated townships in the fertile south-east of the county. Cowpen Bewley is broadly representative of these townships and shows that the processes at work at Harton were not unique to the north-east of the county, with a similar gradual engrossment of holdings and the survival of certain families throughout (Table 23). It does, however, reveal the continuation of smaller cottage-holdings, something seemingly absent at Harton. At Cowpen Bewley there were originally sixteen bondlands of thirty acres. By the end of the fourteenth century, there was still a core group of bondlands but with a diverse range of cottagers holding fragments of land.[74]

The major tenants in 1396/97, holding two bondlands each, were William Pulter junior, William Arsom, William Schephird, John Pulter, Richard Golding, Gilbert Johnson, Thomas Schorueton and William Thorp. However, there were many

70 Levine and Wrightson, *The Making of an Industrial Society*, p. 88.

71 Hoskins, *The Midland Peasant*, p. 159.

72 Ibid., p. 159.

73 George Shadforth, who is explored further in chapter 7, possessed £150 worth of grain and livestock valued at £300, whilst Ralph Lambton possessed £184 worth of corn and over £500 worth of livestock. See chapter 4 for the Lambtons and chapter 7 for the Shadforths, pp. 161–2 and 245–6.

74 Lomas and Piper (eds.), *Durham Priory Rentals*, pp. 93–6.

Table 23. Durham Cathedral Tenants of Cowpen Bewley from the Late Fourteenth Century to the Mid-Seventeenth Century

Bursar's Rent Book, 1396/97			Bursar's Rent Book, 1495/96	
Tenants	**Holdings**	**Rent**	**Tenant**	**Rent**
Bond tenants			Robert Clifton	62s 2d
W. Pulter junior	2 bondlands	(10s) 20s	William Clifton	59s 9d
William Arsom	2 bondlands	20s	William Lawe	26s 10d
William Thorp	2 bondlands	20s	William Lawe junior	28s 2d
William Schephird	2 bondlands	20s	Robert Lawe	10s 1d
John Pulter	2 bondlands	20s	Robert Shoroton	£4 17s
Richard Golding	2 bondlands	20s	Thomas Shoroton	58s 5d
Gilbert Johnson	2 bondlands	20s	John Stevenson	59s 5d
Thomas Schorueton	2 bondlands	(7s) 20s	Thomas Cuke	21s 6d
William Thorp	1 bondland	7s	Edward Dawson	53s 8d
Cottagers			William White	£4 15s
John Wodroffe	1 cottage and 6 acres	(3s) 5s 10d	Thomas Marshall	29s 7d
Richard Pulter	1 cottage and 6 acres	5s 10d	John Robinson	6s 8d
William Monc	1 cottage and 6 acres	5s 10d	William Cleveland	6s 10d
John Steuenson	1 cottage and 6 acres	6s 8d	John Lawe	4s
William Roger	1 cottage and 6 acres	5s 10d	Thomas Marshall	9s
Thomas Murt	1 cottage and 6 acres	5s 10d	Robert Shoroton	3s 4d
Agnete Postell	1 cottage and 1 acre	(2s) 3s	Thomas Shoroton sen.	5s 10d
William Monc	1 cottage with garden	18d	John Shoroton sen.	18d
The same	1 cottage with garden	12d	Rel. William Calvert	3s
William Pulter j.	1 toft 6 acres	4s 3d	John Baker	4s
Robert Woodroff	1 cottage	15d, 12d	John Shepehird	3s
Robert Bernard	1 cottage with garden	12d	William Hogeson	8s
Gilbert Bois	2 cottages, 4 acres	3s 4d ob		
Gilbert Monc	1 cottage with croft	6d		
'Litilsteuen'	1 cottage with croft	18d, 12d		
John Wodroffe	1 cottage	3d		
John Stephan	1 cottage	3d		

* Land included in the lottery system; the entry fine represents the amount to be paid for the reversionary lease of their holdings.

Sources: R. A. Lomas and A. J. Piper (eds.), *Durham Cathedral Priory Rentals, Vol. 1: Bursar's Rentals*, Surtees Society, 198 (1989); W. H. D. Longstaffe and J. Booth (eds.), *Halmota Prioratus Dunelmensis: Containing Extracts from the Halmote Court or Manor Rolls of the Prior and Convent of Durham, 1296–1384*, Surtees Society, 82 (1886), appendix. DCM/E/BA: List of Tenants, With Rents and Valuations, Temp ~ Dean Hunt (1620–38).

Elizabethan Survey, 1580			Survey ~ Dean Hunt, c. 1620–38	
Tenant	**Rent**	**Fine**	**Tenant**	**Rent**
Robert Clifton	£3 0s 2d	£15*	Robert Clifton	£3 0s 2d
Vidua Pickering	£3 0s 2d	£20*	William Law	£3 0s 2d
William Marshall	£3 0s 2d	£20*	George Clifton	£3 0s 2d
Robert Lawrence	£3 0s 2d	£16*	William Marshall	£3 0s 2d
William Lawe	£3 0s 2d	£20*	John Lawrence	£3 0s 2d
Nicholas Lawe	£3 0s 2d	£20*	John Browne	£3 0s 2d
George Davison	£3 0s 2d	£20*	Robert Johnson	£3 0s 2d
Marmaduke Grene	£3 0s 2d		Henry Webster	£3 0s 2d
Richard Whildon	£3 0s 2d	£20*	John Rawes	£3 0s 2d
William Clifton	£3 0s 2d		Richard Davison	£3 0s 2d
Marmaduke Grene	12s		John Browne	8s
John Burne	8s		Marmaduke Clifton	4s
John Busby	8s		Christopher Wilson	4s
9 cottages	30s 10d		John Browne	12s
Christopher Cotes	4s 4d		William Rawes	3s 4d
			John Busby	8s
			George Cooks	3s 4d
			George Clifton	2s
			John Meggison	3s 8d
			John Winds	4s
			John Rutligh	3s 4d
			George Clifton	3s 4d
			John Atkinson	4s 4d

cottagers, even in the late fourteenth century, who did not hold significant accumulations of agricultural land here, except for the few acres which accompanied their cottage. It is likely that some of the cottagers were family members of those who held the larger bondlands as, for example, in the 1390s when Richard Pulter held a cottage whilst William and John Pulter held bondlands. The rent book of 1495/96 shows that these men could be parents who gave over the family holding to sons and retired to a cottage with a small plot of land; for example, Robert Shoroton and Thomas Shoroton both held substantial holdings, but a John Shoroton senior and a Thomas Shoroton senior were amongst those with small rents, indicative of cottage holdings.[75]

The Shoroton and Stevenson families were still substantial landholders in the 1490s, but the Lawes, Cliftons and Whites had clearly replaced the other major families by the end of the fifteenth century. Timothy Lomas used these examples to show how several families were able to become wealthy landowners in Cowpen Bewley across the fifteenth century. William Clifton, for example, took up the lease of two messuages, two husbandlands, a cottage, six acres and a salting in 1483. His was an example of 'a family that entered the village and established themselves quickly as wealthy landowners', whereas the Shorotons had been in the village since at least 1391 and, from 'humble beginnings', went on to 'become the largest landowners in the village'.[76] At the end of the fifteenth century, therefore, the village appears to have become increasingly stratified and land concentrated amongst a small group of families, as the rent book of 1495/96 shows. However, this is a deceptive end point to the story and as Lomas notes, 'an accurate assessment of the success of continuity amongst such families awaits a detailed study of the sixteenth and seventeenth century palatinate records'.[77] This is primarily because Cowpen Bewley underwent the process of syndication later than Harton, so that it was not until 1524 that the majority of agricultural land here was leased out equally to ten individuals.[78] After this point, each tenant had an amount of land roughly comparable to each other as well as to their counterparts at Harton. Map 4 shows these holdings after enclosure of the moor to the west of the village, and also the considerable acreage of marshland to the east of the village, but once again showing that these holdings were largely intact in the eighteenth century.[79]

75 Ibid., pp. 157–9.

76 Lomas, 'Land and People in South-East Durham', pp. 161–2.

77 Ibid., p. 167.

78 In 1424, ten messuages and seventy-six acres of freehold land were recovered at Cowpen Bewley, which, if added to the original sixteen bondlands totalling 480 acres, puts the total acreage somewhere in the region of 1,000 acres. An eighteenth-century survey of the township gives the total acreage as 1,648 acres, but by this period much of the moor had been enclosed, whilst each holding had considerable pasture rights upon Cowpen marsh to the east of the village, which together accounted for the extra 600 acres of land.

79 DCM/E/9/AA/1–2: Plan and Survey of Cowpen Bewley, 1774.

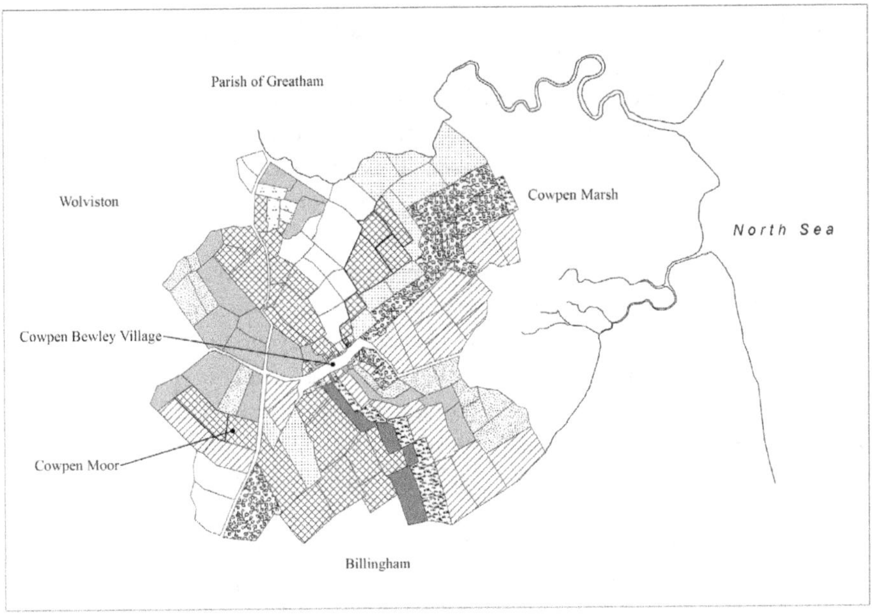

Map 4. Cowpen Bewley Township Survey Map, 1774.
Source: DCM/E/9/AA/1–2: Dean and Chapter Survey of Cowpen Bewley, 1774.

The Shorotons still survived in the 1540s, but they were the last of the families from the fourteenth-century rent books, with the newer families of Clifton and Lawe becoming the dominant landholders in the township. By the time of the Elizabethan survey in 1580 this process was complete and the Shorotons had completely disappeared, leaving the Lawes and Cliftons as the leading leaseholders in the township.[80] Again there was a proliferation of cottages, which were described by the surveyor as 'nine cottages in sundry occupations'. In the 1580 survey, nearly every holding was included in the dean and chapter's lottery system but despite these controversies, the registers of lease renewals show that there was a remarkable continuity of holdings, with almost every holding being renewed at least once, much like at Harton, even including several of the small cottages.[81] Many of these cottages were held by rela-

80 Longstaffe and Booth (eds.), *Halmota Prioratus Dunelmensis*, pp. 242–3.

81 For example, the Cliftons, Marshalls and Lawes renewed the following leases: William Clifton (1572), John Clifton (1586), Robert Clifton (1591, 1593, 1612), George Clifton (1613, 1622); William Marshall (1564), William and Lawrence Marshall (1587), Lawrence Marshall (1605); William Lawe (1575), John Lawe (1595), Nicholas Lawe (1575, 1595, 1613). Many of the smaller cottages were also renewed multiple times by the same person; for example, for a cottage with a rent of 16s, John Burn renewed his lease in 1588, 1606, 1618 and 1624. DCM, Dean and Chapter Registers, 1–15, 1541–1640.

tives of the larger tenants in the village but some were held by labourers who found work on the nearby salt pans.[82]

How did these families in the more fertile south-east of the county fare compared to their counterparts at Harton and was there a difference in the agriculture practised by these tenants? None of the leaseholders are called yeomen as some of the tenants were at Harton, with many not being given a status, and those who were all being described as husbandmen.[83] Inferring too much from this difference in status between husbandman and yeoman would be dangerous, however, as many of these Cowpen Bewley tenants possessed more household goods than their counterparts at Harton. These examples of Harton and Cowpen Bewley confirm Morrin's impression of the dean and chapter's tenants at Merrington as 'mainly of the middling sort' and those 'who were themselves the occupiers and cultivators of their farms'.[84] She found the average probate inventory before 1600 was £69.70 and between 1601 and 1650 was £189.27, again broadly comparable to the figures here for two very different townships on the dean and chapter's estate. Although families like the Cliftons may have appeared wealthy landowners in the late fifteenth century, it is clear that their descendants were not enjoying such levels of prosperity as many members of the yeomanry were in the late sixteenth and early seventeenth centuries (Table 24).[85]

Table 24. A Breakdown of the Types of Wealth in the Surviving Probate Inventories of Cowpen Bewley Tenants, 1540–1640

Testator	Date	Arable	Livestock	Household	Owed	Total	Owing
Robert Lawe	d. 1551	£31 3s	£37 1s	£15 1d	–	£83 4s 6d	-£17 10s 8d
John Clifton	d. 1587	£60	£58 2s	£21 2s	12s	£139 17s 10d	-£59 7s 8d
William Marshall	d. 1590	£45 6s	£43 5s	£29 1s	–	£115 11s	-£96 13s 1d
William Lawe	d. 1593	£54 4d	£61 1s	£25 4s	£32 2s	£183 13s 11d	-£13 15s 9d
John Lawe	d. 1603	£51 5s	£57 3s	£28 2s	£10 11s	£145 13s	-£31 6s
John Pickering	d. 1607	£71 3s	£73 6s	£34 7s	11s 5d	£227 17s 1d*	-£17 0s 10d
John Lawe	d. 1630	£165	£98 2s	£24 3d	£20 5s	306 19s 1d	-£248 3s 8d
Robert Clifton	d. 1631	£66 2s	£51 1s	£23 2s	–	£143 2s 6d	Unknown

* John Pickering's lease was valued at £45 in his inventory.

Source: DPRI/1/1551/L1/1–2; DPRI/1/1587/C6/1; DPRI/1/1590/M4/2–4; DPRI/1/1593/L2/3–4; DPRI/1/1603/L3/2; DPRI/1/1607/P8/3–4; DPRI/1/1630/L1/3–4; DPRI/1/1631/C6/2–3.

82 The salt pans in Cowpen Bewley have a long history with, for example, a Roger Barri taking on a salt pan there for which he owed 30 measures of salt per annum in 1296. Longstaffe and Booth (eds.), *Halmota Prioratus Dunelmensis*, p. 2 and p. 155.

83 DPRI/1/1551/L1/1–2; DPRI/1/1587/C6/1; DPRI/1/1590/M4/2–4; DPRI/1/1593/L2/3–4; DPRI/1/1603/L3/2; DPRI/1/1607/P8/3–4; DPRI/1/1630/L1/3–4; DPRI/1/1631/C6/2–3.

84 Morrin, 'Merrington: Land, Landlord and Tenants', p. 37 and p. 39.

85 See chapter 7 for a more in-depth discussion of the yeomanry of the region in the late sixteenth and early seventeenth centuries.

There is an even greater focus on arable agriculture in the inventories of these leaseholders from the south-eastern part of the county: two inventories described the deceased as possessing thirty-four and thirty-six acres of sown corn, showing not only the importance of arable farming but also the fact that these were tenant-farmers who were not subletting vast tracts of land at commercial rents. For example, Robert Lawe (d. 1551) possessed livestock worth £37 1s, of which the largest value came from his eight oxen worth £20, whilst he also possessed thirty-six acres of corn worth £12 and further wheat, barley, peas and hay worth £16 13s 4d.[86] John Lawe (d. 1630) was one of the few dean and chapter tenants to break this typical mould, for although he possessed the usual eight oxen, eight cows, thirty-seven sheep and five horses, he had corn worth £150 in his barn. However, he also owed considerable debts, especially to people from York, Kirby and Ripon totalling £248, amongst which he owed £35 to alderman Agar of York and £10 to alderman Hoyle of York.[87] The value of his corn was far beyond what his holding at Cowpen Bewley could have produced and it seems likely that he was involved in the grain trade in some capacity.[88]

It thus appears that the vast majority of these tenants were engaging in arable farming, with a rough parity between the value of their grain and livestock, but even this is slightly deceptive for by far the greatest value of their livestock came from their plough oxen. This belies contemporaries' common portrayal of the north as being dominated by a pastoral economy and further brings into question Levine and Wrightson's view that even in the 'intermediate foothills and the eastern lowland zone ... animal husbandry remained the mainstay of the rural economy'.[89] Certainly at Whickham, with its extensive moorlands, the pastoral sector was important, but just a few miles closer to the coast on the dean and chapter's lands at Harton there was a higher degree of arable farming, whilst there can be little doubt that grain was very much the 'mainstay' of the agricultural economy of the more fertile south-east region of the county despite the close proximity of moorland and marshland for additional pasturage. This is further confirmed for the fifteenth century by the high quantities of grain with which Durham Priory's tenants were paying their rents. In 1495/96, for example, tenants at Billingham met a significant portion of their rental obligation with 71 quarters of barley; those at Hesilden with 50 quarters of wheat, 37 quarters of barley and 16 quarters of oats; and tenants at Cowpen Bewley with 35 quarters of wheat and the same amount of salt.[90] As Barrie Dobson concluded for

86 DPRI/1/1551/L1/1–2.

87 DPRI/1/1630/L1/3–4.

88 In many ways, therefore, he is the exception to the rule, with the vast majority of the dean and chapter's tenants showing few variations from the agriculture practised by these tenants at Harton and Cowpen Bewley.

89 Levine and Wrightson, *The Making of an Industrial Society*, p. 87.

90 For more on the payment of rents in kind see, Brown, 'A Money Economy?'.

the fifteenth century, 'the countryside revealed to us by the priory accounts is one in which the plough was still very much the king.'[91]

Conclusion

The change of tenure and organisation of the cathedral's holdings across the fifteenth and early sixteenth centuries was perhaps most remarkable not because it led to the rise of a rural elite, but because it led to a general prosperity amongst most of the tenants. After the Black Death, these tenants engrossed holdings of anywhere between 50 and 150 acres of land, but it was the process of syndication and leasing which officially recognised these consolidated holdings as the permanent form of landholding on the estate. In the face of rising population levels in the sixteenth and early seventeenth centuries, these holdings were rarely fragmented or subsumed into larger leaseholds by outsiders. Although several families remained upon their holdings in each township for generations, there were few instances of a single person holding concurrent leases in a township or of significant sub-letting before the second half of the seventeenth century. Jean Morrin has shown for the Merrington area of the dean and chapter's estate that 'the vast majority of tenants, over eighty per cent, had only one farm and in the last sixty years of the sixteenth century ninety-nine per cent of the tenants lived in the township where their landholding was located.'[92] This holds true for the estate at large, with few, if any, signs that the dean and chapter's tenants entered the ranks of the gentry in this period.[93]

This group of Church leaseholders in the sixteenth century bore many resemblances to their thirteenth-century predecessors. The evolution of these tenants into husbandmen and yeomen in the sixteenth century came about through a combination of institutional changes and market opportunities rather than any significant change in mentality. The combination of high wages and low prices in the fifteenth century was not necessarily conducive to creating a large marketable surplus but when this situation was reversed in the sixteenth century their descendants benefited from the inflation of agricultural prices. However, there are remarkably few signs of any qualitative break with their predecessors or even of a slow transformation of mentalities, and French and Hoyle's description of a medieval peasant as a 'petty entrepreneur, who looked for market opportunities' is equally as apt for these Church leaseholders of the sixteenth and early seventeenth centuries as for their medieval

91 Dobson, *Durham Priory*, p. 252.

92 Morrin, 'The Transfer to Leasehold', p. 121.

93 Apart from, of course, the prebendal families settled on the estate discussed in chapter 5. See chapter 7 for a comparison with the social ambition and mobility evidenced by the neighbouring tenants on the bishop of Durham's estate.

ancestors.[94] It is far from clear that these tenants possessed qualitatively or even quantitatively more luxury household goods than their fifteenth-century ancestors might have enjoyed, nor is there any sign of specialisation for the market; many of these tenants were passively benefiting from the unearned increment caused by the high inflationary trends of the sixteenth century rather than actively exploiting the increased economic opportunities of the period.[95] In this respect the change of tenure had relatively little effect upon the continuity of families in certain villages, despite Larson's suggestion that the priory's conversion to leasehold would cost tenants in the long run by eliminating heritable rights.[96] However, these core village families did not accumulate significantly larger holdings than relative newcomers and, although there are indications that some of these older families, such as the Newtons and Pearsons of Harton, may have possessed a slightly higher standard of living than their neighbours, this was far from representing significant social stratification. This situation led to a general rise in the prosperity of the majority of the dean and chapter's leaseholders – a modest rise it must be said, but one which was shared by many in the village and which led to relatively little stratification of landownership on the estate before the Civil War. The same could not be said of the bishops' estate.

94 French and Hoyle, *Earls Colne*, p. 38.

95 John Lawe of Cowpen Bewley is the only tenant studied here to show any noticeable signs of commercial engagement beyond his holdings on the dean and chapter's estate.

96 Larson, 'Peasant Opportunities', p. 148.

7

Diverging Experiences: Yeomen and Smallholders

The divergent development of the ecclesiastical estates of Durham explored in chapters 1 and 2 had profound effects upon the tenantry of Durham more broadly and, as a result, their experiences greatly differed across the sixteenth century. By the mid-sixteenth century, all of the agricultural land owned by the dean and chapter of Durham Cathedral was leased for twenty-one years. Although the dean and chapter faced the controversy over entry fines in the 1570s, this was ultimately resolved and fines appear to have become fixed from 1626 onwards at three years' improved rental value, ensuring that entry fines would keep pace with inflation in the future. In contrast, the estate of the bishops of Durham contained a diverse mixture of tenures, from customary tenants in Weardale to tenants-at-will, copyholders, freeholders and leaseholders throughout the palatinate.[1] This brief summary fails to portray the myriad tenures which existed on the bishops' estate, with some leases running for anywhere between forty and ninety-nine years, a substantial number running for twenty-one years and, by the early seventeenth century, the rest composed of leases for three lives.[2] This chapter explores the consequences of these developments for the bishops' tenants: how far did they face different problems and potential opportunities to their counterparts on the dean and chapter's estate as a result of the differences in estate management and institutional constraints laid out in chapters 1 and 2?[3]

The Church leaseholders on the dean and chapter's estate had a relatively uniform experience across the sixteenth century, with similar holdings and living standards, but this was far from the norm across England between the fifteenth and sixteenth centuries. Indeed, it was perhaps atypical, with Outhwaite describing the 'later middle ages as a, perhaps even *the*, great era of engrossment', and Dyer has similarly suggested that rural society underwent an important restructuring in the late fourteenth and fifteenth centuries.[4] Dyer concluded that a much 'higher proportion of holdings reached thirty to sixty acres, but very large accumulations of land,

1 DUL, ASC, Survey of Durham Bishopric Estates, CCB D/1981/185000B, ff. 1–66r.

2 See chapter 2 for the complexity of the tenurial development on the estate of the bishops of Durham in the sixteenth century.

3 See chapter 6 for the comparative experience of the tenants of Durham Cathedral from the late fourteenth to the early seventeenth century.

4 Outhwaite, 'Progress and Backwardness', pp. 1–18.

containing a hundred acres or more, were quite rare'.[5] He estimated that if twelve to fifteen acres of land was the amount that could provide a family with all of the grain that it needed, then in 1280 in the East Midlands at least 42 per cent of rural households were inadequately provided for and therefore had to buy at least part of their food.[6] By comparison, in 1480 about two-thirds of rural households in the midlands had enough land to produce all of the grain for their consumption needs.

This restructured rural society came under increasing pressure as the sixteenth century progressed, primarily because of rapid population increase, with Joan Thirsk describing how 'in the sixteenth and early seventeenth centuries men made war upon the forests, moors, and fens with a zeal they had not felt for some three hundred years'.[7] For example, Swain showed how the fifty-one copyholds in the Colne manor in 1527 had become 102 by 1617, and whereas only twenty-five copyholders held less than twenty acres at the earlier date, eighty-two did so ninety years later.[8] Appleby similarly observed that the number of customary tenants doubled on the manor of Irthington between 1502 and 1611, whilst at Cumwhitton twenty-nine tenants at the earlier date had become sixty by 1603.[9] When studying the Elizabethan duchy of Cornwall, Graham Haslam found that seven of the seventeen conventionary manors showed marked increases in the number of tenants between 1570 and the first two decades of the seventeenth century. Moreover, he found that several of the copyholders had engrossed much larger holdings within some of the manors as, for example, at Bradninch where six copyholders possessed 688 acres between them out of a total of 2,377 acres of copyhold land in the manor in 1615.[10]

The sixteenth century was thus a period of diverging experiences for people lower down the social scale in rural society, with the peasant elite assimilating into the lower ranks of the gentry and the poor suffering from the decline in real wages. This can be seen in Margaret Spufford's study of Chippenham where she found an increasing stratification of holdings across the sixteenth century with the middle range of holdings of between fifteen and forty-five acres disappearing almost completely.[11] Marjorie McIntosh similarly found a high level of stratification on the manor of Havering after the 1460s when three powerful outsiders with connections in London and the court

5 Dyer, *Making a Living*, p. 294.

6 Dyer, *An Age of Transition?*, p. 175. For the picture in early sixteenth-century Norfolk, see Whittle, *Agrarian Capitalism*, pp. 178–224.

7 Thirsk, 'Farming Regions of England', p. 2.

8 J. T. Swain, 'Industry and Economy in North-East Lancashire, circa 1500–1640' (unpublished PhD thesis, University of Cambridge, 1983), figures cited in Outhwaite, 'Progress and Backwardness', p. 9.

9 Appleby, 'Agrarian Capitalism or Seigneurial Reaction?', pp. 574–94. See, for example, the experiences at Havering in McIntosh, *A Community Transformed*, p. 1.

10 Graham Haslam, 'The Elizabethan Duchy of Cornwall: An Estate in Stasis', in R. W. Hoyle (ed.), *The Estates of the English Crown, 1558–1640* (Cambridge, 1992), p. 108.

11 Margaret Spufford, *Contrasting Communities: English Villages in the Sixteenth and Seventeenth Centuries* (London, 1974), p. 69.

Table 25. Rental Value and Standard Deviation of Holdings on the Bishop of Durham's Estate in 1588

Township	Rent and Tenure of Holdings	Standard Deviation
	Easington Ward	
Shadforth	1 copyhold, 22s 7d; 11 leaseholds, 6s 8d–45s 2d; 1 at will, 3s	15.3
Sherburn	11 leaseholds, 5s–64s; 1 at will, 8s	19.6
Cassop	5 leaseholds, 50s–£5; 1 at will, 50s	23.6
Newbottle	16 copyholds, 5d–71s; 8 leaseholds, 4s–52s 4d	23.7
Bishopwearmouth	22 copyholds, 4d–£6 17s 4d; 1 leasehold, 15s 4d	34.6
Burdon	7 leaseholds, 22s–52s	9.5
Warden	Richard Bellasis holds all copyhold land, £4 13s 4d	0.0
Ryhope	19 leaseholds, 11s 8d–59s; 1 at will, 3s 4d	14.0
Houghton	26 copyholds, 3d–£6 2s 2d; 2 leaseholds, 6s 8d–40s	30.5
Morton	Richard Bellasis holds all land here by lease, £6	0.0
Tunstall	Richard Middleton holds all land here by lease, £16	0.0
	Chester Ward	
Whitburn	24 copyholds, 8d–£5	23.5
Cleadon	11 copyholds, 9s 1d–£4 16s 3d	24.1
East Boldon	14 copyholds, 6s 8d–£5 4s 6d	29.1
West Boldon	7 copyholds, 6d–£3 3s 4d; 1 leasehold, 23s 4d	18.6
Lanchester	66 copyholds, 1d–56s 4d	10.2
	Stockton Ward	
Stockton	21 copyholds, 4d–24s 1d	6.6
Hartburn	12 copyholds, 12d–26s 1d	7.3
Norton	48 copyholds, 1d–40s	9.9
Carleton	14 copyholds, 6s 6d–32s	8.5
Sedgefield	29 copyholds, 6d–53s 4d; 12 leaseholds, 10s 7d–71s 9d; 5 at will, 6d–3s	14.6
Middleham	21 copyholds, 6d–72s 6d; 9 leaseholds, 10s 10d–48s 9d; 1 at will, 12s 9d	16.2
Cornforth	2 copyholds, 4d–6s 8d; 11 leaseholds, 22s 4d–55s 10d	15.6
	Darlington Ward	
Darlington	55 copyholds, 2d–51s	11.1
Cockerton	25 copyholds, 4d–44s 9d	14.6
Blackwell	27 copyholds, 6d–£3 7s 7d	20.6
Haughton	13 copyholds, 2s–54s; 1 leasehold, 56s 8d	19.7
Whessoe	Francis Parkinson holds all copyhold land, £7 9s 2d	0.0
Byers Green	16 copyholds, 4s 4d–23s; 1 leasehold, £8	35.4
Heighington	14 copyholds, 12d–22s 2d; 15 leaseholds, 5s–52s 11d	14.1
Middridge	5 copyholds, 10s 8d–30s 8d; 11 leaseholds, 12d–53s 4d	14.8

Killerby	5 leaseholds, 30s–£4 11s; 3 at will, 2s 6d–60s	24.3
West Auckland	41 copyholds, 2d–47s 9d; 1 leasehold, 40s	9.8
Coundon	5 copyholds, 2s 3d–£3 3s 4d; 6 leaseholds, 33s 11d–52s 4d	17.8
Escomb	19 copyholds, 8d–66s 1d	15.9
Newton Cap	17 copyholds, 2d–£3 11s 6d	24.4
Lynesack	40 copyholds, 1d–15s 4d	4.4
Bishopley	8 copyholds, 4d–28s 10d	8.6
Stanhope	29 copyholds, 3d–£4 10s 3d	19.5
West Thickley	George Tonge holds all copyhold land, £12	0.0
Evenwood	32 copyholds, 2d–£4 9s; 5 leaseholds, 2s 4d–26s 8d; 5 at will, 2d–4d	14.9
Wolsingham	128 copyholds, 1d–31s 6d	5.1

Source: DUL, ASC, Survey of Durham Bishopric Estates in County Durham, April 1588, Sede Vacante, P. M. Richard Barnes, CCB D/1981/185000B, ff. 1–66r.

invested heavily in Havering land. She concluded that 'economic power and influence over religion and local government, formerly distributed among more than a hundred families of yeomen, husbandmen, and craftsmen/traders, were by 1620 concentrated into the hands of just a few gentlemen and nobles with great landed estates'.[12] As Wrightson and Levine have noted, fifteenth-century society thus gave way to a 'more marked differentiation of rich and poor, observable in terms of attitudes, education, and manners. Those at the bottom of the social scale became not simply poor, but culturally different.'[13] It was this kind of stratification which was happening in the Durham countryside more broadly, not just between the yeomanry and labourers within the same village, but also between tenants in neighbouring villages as estates and institutions played a role in creating or curtailing the opportunities available to tenants in this period.

The Stratification of Holdings on the Bishops' Estate

An important consequence of the tenurial and institutional differences between the two main ecclesiastical estates in Durham can be seen in the much greater level of stratification in the size of holdings on the estate of the bishops of Durham compared to the relative uniformity on much of the dean and chapter's estate. Whereas the majority of the dean and chapter's townships had no deviation between rents and the size of holdings within a village, there is not a single village on the bishops' estate where the same could be said except, of course, where an individual had acquired

12 Sir Thomas Cook bought up c.900 acres, Avery Cornborough acquired c.1,200 acres, and Sir Thomas Urswick gained c.500 acres. McIntosh, *A Community Transformed*, p. 1.

13 Wrightson and Levine, *Poverty and Piety*, p. 2.

all of the land. Table 25 shows this range and deviation in the tenure and rent of holdings on the bishop of Durham's estate in the 1580s, comparable to Table 19 in chapter 6 above.[14]

There was a significant degree of stratification in the rent paid and size of holdings on the estate, with some individuals able to accumulate substantial amounts of both copyhold and leasehold land. Substantial yeomen or members of the lesser gentry, like Richard Bellasis, Richard Middleton, George Tonge and Francis Parkinson, were able to acquire all of the land in several villages.[15] Even in those villages where control over land was not so concentrated, there was a distinct stratification in the size of holdings which could be extensive, especially upon the bishops' copyhold land where a small cottage holding at places like Bishopwearmouth, Houghton or Whitburn might be worth a few pence in rent, but the largest copyholds were above £5. The profile of landholding at East Boldon, for example, was significantly different from any of the dean and chapter's villages, with John Thompson holding copyhold land with a rent of £5 4s 6d, but the likes of Richard Ayre, Edward Robinson and Archibald Atkinson with smaller holdings of 30s, and William Todde and Henry Matthew paying 18s 9d for their copyhold land.

The greater opportunities for the accumulation of land provided on the estate of the bishops of Durham compared to that of the dean and chapter had important social consequences for tenants in the region. The sheriff of Durham created a list in the first half of the seventeenth century which detailed those 'freeholders and grand-jurymen who were styled gentlemen and yet did not bear arms', giving an annual valuation of their estates. This list includes 115 individuals but there is not a single dean and chapter tenant who can be positively identified amongst the names. By comparison, it includes at least ten individuals who are readily identifiable as holding considerable amounts of land from the bishops of Durham.[16] These do not appear to have been successful gentry families who swooped into villages on the bishops' estate because of the opportunities there, but were long-standing yeomen families who became increasingly socially ambitious as their material wealth improved across the course of the late sixteenth and early seventeenth centuries. This list includes the likes

14 See Table 19 in chapter 6 above for a comparable table of the dean and chapter's estate in the 1580s. To summarise that table: 18 townships experienced no deviation in the size and rent of holdings; 4 townships showed signs of some stratification; and small cottage holdings survived in a further 5 townships in the south-east of the county, p. 205.

15 This is separate from the long leases of whole manors granted out by the bishops of Durham to members of the gentry or the Crown, which would only emphasise this concentration further. See chapter 2 for more on these long leases.

16 This seventeenth-century list includes the following individuals who are identifiable as tenants on the bishops' estate: John Shepherdson of Bishopwearmouth, £160 p.a.; Richard Cornforth of Blackwell, £60 p.a.; George Clarke of Chester, £80 p.a.; John Jackson of Coatham, £150 p.a.; John Gill of Haughton, £140 p.a.; Henry Bailes of Newton Cap, £30 p.a.; Simon Lackenby of Shadforth, £100 p.a.; William Pearson of Sherburn, £100 p.a.; Anthony Shadforth of Tunstall, £160 p.a.; Francis Parkinson of Whessoe, £50 p.a. For the full list see Blair, 'Durham Armorials', pp. 156–203.

of Francis Parkinson of Whessoe who was described as a non-armorial gentleman possessing land worth £50 per annum and who held eight messuages, one cottage and thirteen oxgangs of copyhold land from the bishop of Durham at Whessoe for a rent of £7 9s 2d in the late sixteenth century.[17] Henry Bailes of Newton Cap was similarly included in this list of gentlemen holding land worth £30 per annum, one of the smallest valuations there. He acquired, and soon assigned to William Richardson, a lease of eight pasture gates in the close belonging to Bishop Auckland in 1634, whilst Joan Bailes held three copyholds in Newton Cap as the widow of James Bailes.[18]

This was, of course, not the experience of all the bishop of Durham's tenants or even the majority, but there was a demonstrable rural elite emerging on the estate who were experiencing not only financial success, but also upward social mobility. Richard Cornforth, for example, was included in the above list as a non-armorial gentleman of Blackwell, with land worth £60 per annum. The Cornforths were an important yeoman family on the bishop of Durham's estate in the Darlington region, with a William Cornforth holding copyhold land at Blackwell in 1580 with a rent of £3 7s 7d – the largest single tenement there. By the time of the parliamentary survey, a different William Cornforth held a number of messuages and cottages as well as approximately ten oxgangs of leasehold land in Blackwell, whilst Jane Cornforth held one messuage, two oxgangs and a half parcel of three oxgangs of copyhold land as the widow of Cuthbert Cornforth in Bondgate.[19] This Cuthbert Cornforth of Darlington died young in 1616 with all of his children underage. He bequeathed £70 to each of his three daughters for when they came of age, as well as making provision for his three sons, Richard, William and Thomas, from his copyhold land. Richard would go on to be styled a gentleman by the mid-seventeenth century. Even in 1616, on Cuthbert Cornforth's death, the family were clearly prospering on the bishop's estate, with a total inventory valued at £816 19s 5d, which included household goods worth approximately £57, with five silver spoons and fifty pieces of pewter; his purse, apparel and furniture valued at £35; and £478 15s 1d worth of debts from at least sixty-five named individuals.[20] Families such as the Cornforths represented a yeoman elite who prospered in the late sixteenth and early seventeenth centuries and who achieved a degree of economic and social success which neither their ancestors nor their neighbours on the dean and chapter's estate accomplished.

17 DUL, ASC, Survey of Durham Bishopric Estates, CCB D/1981/185000B.

18 Kirby (ed.), *Parliamentary Surveys*, vol. 1, pp. 74–5.

19 John Cornforth also held twenty acres of arable land and Thomas Cornforth held several copyholds in Blackwell, whilst Richard Cornforth held several parcels of copyhold land in Newton Cap. Kirby (ed.), *Parliamentary Surveys*, vol. 1, pp. 79 and 99–101.

20 DPRI/1/1616/C15/1–5.

Table 26. Newbottle Tenants in the Hatfield Survey, 1380s

Tenants	Holdings	Rent
Demesne Land		
Hugh Baynton	13 acres and 1 rood	18s 9.25d
John Wilkinson	26 acres and a half	37s 6.5d
William Tillton	25 acres	35s 5d
William Belle	10 acres	14s 2d
William Johnson	5 acres	7s 1d
William Robertson	36 acres	51s
John Syvewright	5 acres	7s 1d
William Stephanson	20 acres	29s 0.5d
William Flesschewer	49 acres and 3 roods	70s 5.75d
John Geryngh	25 acres	36s 6.5d
John Hoggeson	13 acres	18s 9.25d
Richard Saddesson	30 acres	42s 6d
Richard Shalton	23 acres	32s 11.25d
John Flech	10 acres	14s 2d
William Elisson junior	20 acres	28s 4d
John Taillour	5 acres	7s 1d
Aforesaid tenants		17d
Bondland	Each bovate contains 12 acres of land	
Hugh Baynton and William Shilton	3 cottages and 3 bovates	18s
John Wilkynson and Richard Flexhewer	3 cottages and 4 bovates	23s
John Bell	1 cottage and 1 bovate	6s
William Robynson and William Stephan	3 cottages and 3 bovates	18s
John Geryng and John Syvewright	2 cottages and 2 bovates	12s
John Rogerson	1 cottage and 2 bovates	12s
John	1 cottage and 1 bovate	6s
Richard Toddesson and Hugh Baynton	3 cottages and 3 bovates	16s
Richard Shilton and Richard Flesschewer	3 cottages and 4 bovates	18s
William Elisson	1 cottage and 1 bovate	6s
John Taillour	1 cottage and 1 bovate	6s
The aforesaid William Elisson	7 acres of land	3s 6d
William Robertson	1 cottage and 1 bovate	6s
The same tenants	1 acre of land	6d

Many tenants also held small amounts of exchequer land.

Source: W. Greenwell (ed.), *Bishop Hatfield's Survey: a Record of the Possessions of the See of Durham*, Surtees Society, 32 (1857), pp. 158–61.

Several case studies of the bishops' townships reveal the increasing disparity between the experiences of Durham tenants as a result of the differences between the two ecclesiastical estates detailed in chapters 1 and 2, as well as how this rural elite slowly emerged on the bishops' estate. The transformation of holdings, or at times the lack thereof, can be seen at Newbottle, a typical village on the bishops' estate in the Wear valley which evolved from a combination of demesne land and bondland into a village with a roughly equal distribution of copyhold and leasehold land. Table 26 shows the village in Hatfield's survey, revealing the tenure and structure of the holdings in the late fourteenth century.[21] It quickly becomes apparent that holdings were of different sizes, with tenants often holding a mix of former demesne and bondland, with the latter often forming smaller cottage holdings, although several tenants had already accumulated several of these. Even at this early date there were signs of a stratification of holdings appearing which was dissimilar to the pattern at Harton, with the likes of John Wilkinson holding twenty-six and a half acres of former demesne land and jointly holding three cottages and four bovates of land with a Richard Fleschewer. This Richard Fleschewer also jointly held another three cottages and four bovates of land alongside Richard Shilton, whilst William Fleschewer held another forty-nine acres of former demesne land. Some of these larger tenants were therefore able to accumulate holdings of between forty and fifty acres of land, usually as a combination of former demesne land and bondland. At the other end of the spectrum there were men such as John Taillour who held a cottage and a bovate of land as well as five acres of former demesne land, or John Bell who similarly held a cottage and bovate but with ten acres of former demesne land. These smaller holdings, of around twenty acres of land, would have been sufficient to provide for their families, but these tenants would have struggled to produce a significant marketable surplus compared to some of their larger neighbours. High real wages in the fifteenth century, however, meant that these differences were not overly significant because these smaller landowners could supplement their household incomes with well-paid wage labour.

By 1588 and the Elizabethan survey (Table 27), the old distinction between former demesne land and bondland had been replaced by that between leasehold and copyhold tenure, but there was no simple equation which saw demesne land become leasehold and bondland become copyhold.[22] The process of consolidation and stratification seen earlier had become much more pronounced, with several larger messuages created, half of which were leasehold and the other half copyhold, whilst there was a profusion of smaller holdings surviving as cottages whose owners appear to have had little relation to the owners of the larger, consolidated messuages. The Chiltons were clearly the leading family here by the sixteenth century, with Thomas Chilton the elder holding a copyhold messuage with a rent of 65s; Thomas Chilton

21 Greenwell (ed.), *Bishop Hatfield's Survey*, pp. 158–61.

22 See chapter 2 for the tenurial history of the estate of the bishops of Durham.

Table 27. Newbottle Tenants in the Elizabethan Survey of 1588

Tenants	Holdings	Rent
Copyholders		
Aton widow	1 messuage	57s
Surret widow	1 messuage	71s
Thomas Chilton the elder	1 messuage	65s
Thomas Chilton the younger	1 messuage	46s 8d
William Coupon	1 messuage	51s 6d
Robert Chilton	1 cottage	8s
Thomas Appleby	1 cottage	6s 8d
Henry Aton	1 cottage	8s 2d
Widow Rogerson	1 cottage	2s 4d
George Ireland	1 cottage	3s 6d
Christopher Coupon	1 cottage	3s
Margaret Hobson	1 cottage	2s 1d
Storie widow	1 cottage	6d
Stodderd widow	1 cottage	18d
Thomas Chilton the younger	1 cottage	5d
Ralph Robinson and Ralph Brough	2 closes	6s
Total		**£17 17s 4d**
Leaseholders		
George Willow	1 messuage	52s 4d
William Chilton	1 messuage	42s 6d
William Chilton	1 messuage	27s 4d
Robert Chilton	1 messuage	39s 2d
Rolland Brough	1 messuage	44s 6d
John Surret	1 cottage	4s
Christopher Coupon	1 cottage	4s
George Borrows	3 closes	20s
William Willou	Watermill	53s 4d
Total		**£18 11s 1d**
Perquisites of the Court		26s
Grand Total		**£37 14s 5d**

Contemporary rental totals provided in original survey.

Source: DUL, ASC, Survey of Durham Bishopric Estates in County Durham, April 1588, Sede Vacante, P. M. Richard Barnes, CCB D/1981/185000B, ff. 8v–9r.

the younger holding a similar messuage at a rent of 46s 8d and a cottage; whilst William Chilton held two separate leases of messuages with rents of 42s 6d and 27s 4d respectively; and a Robert Chilton held the lease of a messuage, cottage and garth for 39s 2d. The agricultural rental income of Newbottle, less the watermill and perquisites of the court there, was approximately £33, out of which the Chilton family were responsible for £11 worth of land alone: a clear sign of their dominance within the village.[23] There was also a profusion of cottagers, holding land by both copyhold and leasehold tenures, who bore no discernible relationship to those farming the larger holdings. Although some of these cottagers were widows or elderly relatives, many of these small cottagers undoubtedly earned the majority of their incomes as wage-labourers on the farms of their larger neighbours, something which appears to be noticeably absent from the dean and chapter's township of Harton.[24]

Another snapshot is afforded by the parliamentary survey in 1647, which gives a detailed picture of the village and also an opportunity to explore entry fines in some depth, although unfortunately not for leaseholds.[25] The Chiltons were still one of the leading families, having accumulated around half of the copyhold land in the village: Robert Chilton possessed a cottage, thirty-three acres of land, three oxgangs of husbandland and four of moorland for which he paid £3 6s 8d rent but only £1 as an entry fine; he also possessed further undescribed lands with a rent of £2 17s; and John Chilton held a cottage and five acres for 8s rent and 2s entry fine; with a George Chilton holding further land worth 3s 6d in rent. John Chilton and his widow Alice also held a 21-year lease of a tenement with a rent of £1 7s 5d, which was estimated to be worth £7 10s upon improvement, and another 21-year lease of a tenement with an outhouse, garth and two acres of land in every field held by £1 19s 2d rent, which was estimated upon improvement at £9. There are signs that these substantial holdings were advancing the Chiltons, for in 1575 a John Chilton, husbandman, died with an inventory valued at just £36, but by 1627 George Chilton, yeoman, died here with £266 in moveable goods, and likewise a Robert Chilton, yeoman, died with goods worth £294 15s in 1636.[26]

The prevalence of subletting in rural society during this period is very difficult to estimate, as discussed in chapter 6. The dean and chapter's tenants appear to have primarily been tenant-farmers still in the sixteenth and early seventeenth centuries and subletting does not appear to have become prevalent upon their lands until the second half of the seventeenth century, but it is entirely possible that families such as the Chiltons could profit from the stagnant rents of these copyholds by subletting

23 DUL, ASC, Survey of Durham Bishopric Estates, CCB D/1981/185000B, ff. 8v–9r.

24 Tenants at Harton (see chapter 6) undoubtedly needed to employ wage labour, but there are remarkably few cottages in the township not attached to the primary agricultural holdings, even in the eighteenth-century survey maps.

25 Kirby (ed.), *Parliamentary Surveys*, vol. 2, pp. 158–60.

26 DPRI/1/1575/C2/2; DPRI/1/1627/C4/3; DPRI/1/1636/C4/4. A seemingly different Robert Chilton died just a year later with goods similarly worth £293 6s: DPRI/1/1637/C3/3–4.

them for a more commercial rent.[27] Several of their probate inventories show quite substantial amounts of agricultural goods, suggesting that they were managing their own lands: the inventory of Robert Chilton (d. 1637) showed he possessed corn in his garth worth £43, a further £15 worth of corn on the ground, £7 worth of hay and straw, and plough and waine gear valued at £16. He also possessed the usual mixture of animals, including six oxen, five cows, two stirkes, three calves, over two dozen sheep, a horse, a mare and four swine.[28] Although this suggests that the Chiltons were working at least some of their lands, it does not preclude the possibility they were also subletting other lands. For example, a substantial proportion of George Chilton's inventory is actually made up of bonds and debts owed to him from around a dozen individuals, perhaps suggesting that he was using his property differently from the other Chiltons or that he was elderly and had retired from the daily running of the farm.[29] These larger holdings provided families like the Chiltons with opportunities either to sublet or to engage in commercial agriculture, producing a larger marketable surplus than their smaller neighbours, which in turn enabled them to purchase further lands, reinforcing their prominence in the village in a cyclical fashion.

It becomes quickly apparent that the bishops' copyhold land was radically losing its real value across the sixteenth century: the rent had not been increased since the depths of the mid-fifteenth-century recession and yet agricultural prices had increased sixfold in the intervening period. As James noted, the fines of 'the copyholders by inheritance were in some cases nominal, being less than a year's rent', whilst 'fines on leaseholds conformed to the criterion of "reasonableness", and ranged from as little as two, to as much as six years' rent'.[30] If just the rent and entry fines for copyhold land in Newbottle are taken into consideration, it is clear that the bishop was not accruing any benefit from the inflation of the period (Table 28).[31] There was, therefore, a very large divergence between rents and prices upon the bishops' copyhold land, meaning that the majority of the agricultural profits of the period were accumulated by their tenants. By comparison, tenants just a few miles away in the dean and chapter's village of Harton were paying as much as £20 as an entry fine for a 21-year lease of land at a rent of 54s 7d in the 1570s.[32] This meant that not only were tenants accruing more of the profits for their labour on the bishops' copyhold lands, but that smallholdings were also much more viable for there was less financial pressure upon them.

27 For the dean and chapter's tenants see chapter 6 above and Morrin, 'The Transfer to Leasehold', pp. 117–32.

28 DPRI/1/1637/C3/3–4.

29 DPRI/1/1627/C4/3.

30 James, *Family, Lineage and Civil Society*, p. 81.

31 Kirby (ed.), *Parliamentary Surveys*, vol. 2, pp. 158–60.

32 Ibid., pp. 158–60; Longstaffe and Booth (eds.), *Halmota Prioratus Dunelmensis*, pp. 225–6.

Table 28. Entry Fines on the Bishop's Copyhold Lands at Newbottle in the 1640s

Tenants	Annual Rent	Entry Fine
William Ranson	£1 10s 8d	15s
George Watson	1s 1d	7d
George Lilburne	£2 6s 8d	13s 4d
Richard Haswell	2s 6d	1s
Robert Ayton	8s 2d	5s
Anthony Ranson	2s 6d	1s 8d
Ann Wilson	3s	6d
Robert Chilton	£3 6s 8d	£1
John Chilton	8s	2s

Source: D. A. Kirby (ed.), *Parliamentary Surveys of the Bishopric of Durham*, vol. 2, Surtees Society, 185 (1972), pp. 158–60.

As shown in chapter 2, the composition of the bishops' estate was very diverse, and so the experience of Newbottle cannot be taken as representative of their entire estate. By comparison, Bishopwearmouth was one of the villages on the bishops' estate which was transformed from a mix of former demesne land, bondland and cottages in the late fourteenth century into entirely copyhold land, except for the windmill, fishing rights and one cottage of fifteen acres which were held by leases.[33] In the fourteenth century there was a remarkable symmetry of holdings at Bishopwearmouth: the former demesne land was held in ten-acre parcels; the bondland in parcels of one messuage and two bovates of land, each bovate containing fifteen acres of land; and the cottages held either six or twelve acres of land (Table 29). This neatness is slightly deceptive because some of these tenants had clearly accumulated land, such as William Wearmouth who held two messuages and four bovates of bondland and a further ten acres of demesne land, or Cecilia Nowell, the widow of John Nowell, who held thirty acres of demesne land with a share in another ten acres, two messuages and four bovates of bondland outright, with a further messuage and two bovates alongside Thomas Sheperdson, and a cottage with twelve acres of land.[34]

By 1588, all of the land here had been converted to copyhold tenure, and in his large study of the palatinate, the antiquarian Surtees despaired of recording all of the tenants for they 'are too numerous and their tenures too trifling to be transcribed'.[35] However, it is well worth the effort, for there is once again evidence of the accumulation of much larger holdings, with the survival of only three cottagers, two of

33 Greenwell (ed.), *Bishop Hatfield's Survey*, pp. 132–4; DUL, ASC, Survey of Durham Bishopric Estates, CCB D/1981/185000B, f. 13r; Kirby (ed.), *Parliamentary Surveys*, vol. 2, pp. 164–74.

34 Greenwell (ed.), *Bishop Hatfield's Survey*, pp. 132–4.

35 Surtees, *History of Durham*, vol. 1, pp. 224–6.

Table 29. Bishopwearmouth Tenants in the Hatfield Survey, 1380s

Tenants	Holdings	Rent
Demesne Land		
John Hobson	10 acres	18s 4d
William Gray	10 acres	18s 4d
William Wearmouth	10 acres	18s 4d
Adam Rudd and John Sunderland	10 acres	18s 4d
Cecilia wife of John Nowell	20 acres	36s 8d
Robert Robinson	10 acres	18s 4d
Robert Warden	10 acres	18s 4d
Aforesaid Cecilia Nowell	10 acres	18s 4d
Robert Parish and Thomas Sheperdson	10 acres	18s 4d
Giliana Gamell and Cecilia Nowell	10 acres	18s 4d
William Birdesman	10 acres	18s 4d
Thomas Sheperdson	10 acres	15s 8d
John Robinson	10 acres	15s 8d
Emma widow of William Robinson	10 acres	15s 8d
John Sunderland	10 acres	15s 8d
Stephan Carter	1 acre called Forland	2s
Bondland		
John Hobson	1 mess. and 2 bovates*	31s ½d and 6 bushels of oats
William Gray	1 mess. and 2 bovates	31s ½d and 6 bushels of oats
William Wearmouth	2 mess. and 4 bovates	62s 1d and 12 bushels of oats
Thomas Sheperdson and Cecilia Nowell	1 mess. and 2 bovates	31s ½d and 6 bushels of oats
John Sunderland	1 mess. and 2 bovates	31s ½d and 6 bushels of oats
Cecilia Nowell	1 mess. and 2 bovates	31s ½d and 6 bushels of oats
John Hobson and William Gray	1 mess. and 2 bovates	31s ½d and 6 bushels of oats
Robert Wardon	1 mess. and 2 bovates	31s ½d and 6 bushels of oats
Cecilia Nowell	1 mess. and 2 bovates	31s ½d and 6 bushels of oats
Mill		
Bond tenants of Wearmouth, Tunstall, Ryhope and Burdon	Mill	[blank]
Cottages		
Robert Payn	1 cottage and 12 acres	10s 4d
Idem Robert	1 cottage and 6 acres	5s 6d
Juliana Gamell	1 cottage and 12 acres	10s 4d
Thomas Shepherd	1 cottage and 12 acres	10s 4d

John Hobson	1 cottage and 6 acres	5s 6d
Thomas Marshall	1 cottage and 6 acres	5s 6d
Robert Robinson	1 cottage and 6 acres	5s 6d
Nicholas Gamell	1 cottage and 6 acres	8s 2d
Thomas Bullok	1 cottage and 12 acres	10s 4d
Cecilia Nowell	1 cottage and 12 acres	4s

* A message was a dwelling house and a bovate was a measurement of land (each bovate containing 15 acres of land in this case). Many tenants also held small amounts of Exchequer land.

Source: W. Greenwell (ed.), *Bishop Hatfield's Survey: a Record of the Possessions of the See of Durham*, Surtees Society, 32 (1857), pp. 132–4.

whom were widows and the other a tenant of one of the larger holdings (Table 30). Although the survey does not include exact details of the holdings, the rents paid are at least indicative of the general amount of land held and reveal the disparity within the village. For example, John Thompson had accumulated land with a rent of £6 17s 4d, and there were two other holdings with rents of over £4, whereas George Clarke had a holding with a rent of 6s 8d, and there were numerous tenants who held land worth around 20s. It is also clear that the Sheppsons (or Shepherdsons) had acquired substantial amounts of land: William Sheppson owned a messuage with a rent of 28s 8d; his wife a messuage with a rent of 10s 6d; John Sheppson a messuage with a rent of 64s 8d; and Richard Shepson a messuage with a rent of 63s 4d.[36]

How far were these larger tenants able to capitalise on the increase in agricultural prices during the sixteenth century? The larger holding of John Thompson, for example, enabled him to engage in agriculture on a larger scale than either his neighbours or his counterparts on the dean and chapter's estate. He possessed twenty-five acres of wheat and barley, twenty-two acres of peas and oats, as well as twelve oxen and five horses used to plough this land, sixteen cows and over fifty sheep and twenty lambs.[37] In total, John Thompson's corn and plough gear were valued at over £72, whilst his livestock was worth £116 10s – more than the majority of the dean and chapter's tenants in this period. Adam Holme's inventory on his death in 1618 reveals considerably fewer agricultural goods than John Thompson possessed, which is roughly in line with the size of their respective holdings.[38] As the largest single landholder in the village it is natural that John Thompson would also possess the largest agricultural concern, and once again shows that these tenants were often working their own lands with little evidence of subletting. For example, Adam Holme's smaller holding only enabled him to grow corn on the ground worth

36 DUL, ASC, Survey of Durham Bishopric Estates, CCB D/1981/185000B, f. 13r.

37 DPRI/1/1616/T9/2.

38 DUL, ASC, Survey of Durham Bishopric Estates, CCB D/1981/185000B, f. 13r.

Table 30. Bishopwearmouth Tenants in the Elizabethan Survey of 1588

Tenants	Holdings	Rent
Copyholders		
Robert Patteson	1 messuage	39s 8d
Thomas Hilton	1 messuage	£4 20d
Christopher Whorton and William Patteson	1 messuage	£4 6s 8d
George Gouis	1 messuage	21s
William Sheppson	1 messuage	28s 8d
William Riddell	1 messuage	26s 4d
The wife of William Sheppson	1 messuage	10s 6d
George Clarke	1 messuage	6s 8d
John Blenkinskoppe	1 messuage	21s
Adam Holme	1 messuage	42s 8d
John Sheppson	1 messuage	64s 8d
John Thompson	1 messuage	£6 17s 4d
Widow Watson	1 messuage	68s 2d
Margaret Persons	1 messuage	42s 6d
Richard Sheppson	1 messuage	63s 4d
Widow Wilkinson	1 messuage	41s 8d
Ralph Bowes, gent.	Parcel of ground	3s
John Hoote	Parcel of waste ground	12d
Christopher Whorton	Cottage	6d
Widow Chamber	Cottage	12d
Widow Colier	Cottage	12d
Philippe Hall	Waste plot	4d
Total		**£39 9s 2d**
Leaseholders		
Thomas Sparrow	Windmill	40s
Robert Patteson	Cottage with 15 acres	15s 4d
Total		**55s 4d**
Perquisites of the Court		12s
Grand Total		**£42 16s 6d**

Contemporary rental totals provided in original survey.

Source: Survey of Durham Bishopric Estates in County Durham, April 1588, Sede Vacante, P.M. Richard Barnes, DUL, ASC, CCB D/1981/185000B, ff. 13r–v.

£20, with a further £22 worth in the stack-garth. However, it was in the livestock he kept where the real discrepancies between him and Thompson appear, for he only possessed six oxen, six cows, four mares and sixty sheep; John Thompson's larger holding gave greater scope for pastoral agriculture.[39] Although Adam Holme had a smaller potential for commercial agriculture in Bishopwearmouth, this does not take into account all of his land, for his will makes it clear that he was also leasing land in Ryhope, upon which he had crops growing worth £13 6s 8d and three oxen, one mare, a waine and plough gear worth in total £15.[40] It is deceptive, therefore, to draw too many conclusions from a single village without reference to tenants' holdings outside the area, although it is perennially difficult to link such holdings without a direct reference in a document such as a will.[41]

Table 31 shows a summary of the different types of wealth found in the Bishopwearmouth tenants' probate inventories, which reveals that livestock often accounted for more of their wealth than grain. However, the most valuable livestock were always oxen and horses, which were by their very nature an extension of arable farming, being used for ploughing. It is interesting that each of these inventories totals over £200, a figure which the inventories of the dean and chapter's tenants rarely achieved, despite them sometimes including a £40–£50 valuation of their lease.[42]

Table 31. A Breakdown of the Types of Wealth in the Surviving Probate Inventories of Bishopwearmouth Tenants, 1540–1640

	Arable	Livestock	Household	Clothes	Owed	Total	Owing
William Pattinson	£86 12s	£87 18s	£25 6s	£3	£8 9s	£204 4s	-£42 12s
John Thompson	£72 19s	£116 7s	£15 2s	£4 10s	£5 1s	£217 12s 4d	–
Adam Holme	£72 1s	£96 17s	£47 4d	£5	–	£259 8s	-£16 2s
George Shepherdson	£67 7d	£90 6s	£16 5s	£4	£115 2s	£317 5s 11d	-£60 6s

Source: Durham Probate Inventories: DPRI/1/1615/P4/3; DPRI/1/1616/T9/2; DPRI/1/1618/H23/3; DPRI/1/1635/S6/1.

Were the tenants listed in Table 31 able to use these substantial holdings and agricultural pursuits to increase their standard of living? All four were described as yeomen and their net wealth was considerable, even if their household goods and clothes were sometimes modest.[43] Certainly Adam Holme possessed considerable household goods valued at £47, but unfortunately they are only summarised

39 DPRI/1/1618/H23/3.

40 DPRI/1/1618/H23/1–2.

41 To date, however, I have found little evidence of tenants holding land from both the dean and chapter of Durham Cathedral and the bishops of Durham simultaneously.

42 The total inventory values are as follows: William Pattinson (d. 1615) £204 4s; John Thompson (d. 1616) £217 12s 4d; Adam Holme (d. 1619) £259 8s; and George Shepherdson (d. 1635) £317 5s 11d.

43 DPRI/1/1615/P4/3; DPRI/1/1616/T9/2; DPRI/1/1618/H23/3; DPRI/1/1635/S6/1.

in his inventory and so cannot be explored further. One of the major differences between these larger tenants and their counterparts on the dean and chapter's estate is revealed by their probate inventories which show a diversification away from purely agricultural pursuits. For example, George Shepherdson had an eighth share in a ship worth £20 and also numerous debts owed to him, some of which were quite considerable and, judging from their surnames, appear to be from neighbours.[44] John Shepherdson also held the lease of the bishops' fishing rights in the River Wear and limestone quarries in the waste grounds at Bishopwearmouth, which included 'all lime pits and houses already digged ... with free liberty to dig and make so many lime pits and quarries within the said premises as shall please him. And also to build and erect thereupon two limehouses for laying and keeping lime in and for the persons employed about the said lime pits to live in.'[45] Applying lime or marl to agricultural lands helped raise yields by neutralising soil acidity caused by prolonged farming and leaching from heavy rainfall, with Sunderland as the 'only exporter of lime between the Humber and the Forth', long enjoying 'a virtual monopoly on this trade in north-eastern England'.[46] It was this same John Shepherdson who was one of the partners in the colliery at Harraton on the Wear, which Hatcher described as becoming a 'great colliery long before the Civil War'. In 1603 it was said there were 6,000 chaldrons of coal lying on its banks, and in 1630 it was contributing 6,000–10,000 tons annually to shipments from the Wear. A partnership involving John Shepherdson and his family was running Harraton in the early seventeenth century, which, in Hatcher's words, 'provided the driving force behind its development'.[47] These entrepreneurial activities were producing sufficient profit to be ploughed back into the land: William and John Shepherdson purchased John Shaklock's portion of Murton manor in 1624 – one of a number of manors which John, Lord Lumley, was forced to sell in order to pay off his considerable debts.[48] The Shepherdsons were thus spurring on industrial growth and agricultural innovation on a much larger scale than either their peasant ancestors or their counterparts at Harton.

The parliamentary survey of the 1640s allows for a much more detailed view of these holdings, which were still all held by copyhold tenure, except for the windmill, fishing rights and a solitary cottage. Many of the above patterns persisted, with numerous tenants holding multiple copyholds. Edward Harper, in right of Isabel his

44 John Hilton owed him £20, Christopher Shippson owed him £30, Raiph Holmes owed him £10, Christopher Pattinson owed him £10 and John Nicholson owed him £6: DPRI/1/1635/S6/1.

45 Kirby (ed.), *Parliamentary Surveys*, vol. 2, p. 173.

46 <http://www.victoriacountyhistory.ac.uk/sites/default/files/work-in-progress/lime_glass_pottery_paper.pdf> (accessed 5 June 2013).

47 Hatcher, *British Coal Industry*, p. 255.

48 See chapter 3 for the financial troubles of John, Lord Lumley. The eighth portion of Murton manor owned by Shaklock was described as containing a messuage, twenty acres of arable, twenty of meadow, thirty of pasture, fifty of furze and fifty acres of moor: Surtees, *History of Durham*, vol. 1, pp. 8–9.

wife and widow of Thomas Bryan, held three copyholds worth £4 4s 7d; Thomas Fewler and Ann his wife held five copyholds worth in total £4 19s 3d; whilst the Sheperdsons were still represented in the village by John Shipperdson the younger, who held three copyholds worth a combined total of £6, the largest rent in the village.[49] There were also increasing signs of non-agricultural tenancy here, with Richard, the brother and heir of Thomas Johnson, holding a dwelling house, hall and chamber, with a shop and moiety of some lands. A revealing entry for Thomas Fewler and his wife Ann shows the potential importance of sub-letting. They paid £4 19s 3d for their five copyholds, which included several substantial holdings, but also a third part of ten acres of land, a third part of thirty acres of former bondland, and a third part of ten acres of former demesne land 'by demise of Margaret Jarvis widow of Ralph Jarvis from St Martin the Bishop in winter for 100 years paying £6 yearly at Martinmas and Pentecost'.[50] This entry shows the substantial value of this land above the rent paid by these tenants to the bishops of Durham, for they were paying more to sublet this one piece of land than they were paying to the bishop for all of their much larger holdings in total.

These examples reveal the sheer complexity of the tenurial structure upon the estate of the bishops of Durham, with individual tenants possessing multiple holdings of disparate sizes, some of which were clearly inherited by widows and others which were divided into thirds or sublet in portions. If this is compared to the dean and chapter's holdings at Harton, it becomes clear that understanding the institutional context of a village is of paramount importance to explaining the pattern of landholding in this period, with the holdings at Harton suffering very little fragmentation, even as late as the eighteenth century. It was the lack of any uniform directive from the bishops of Durham which allowed for the steady accumulation or fragmentation of holdings upon their lands in a way which was not possible on the dean and chapter's estate after the syndication of holdings in the fifteenth century. A perfect example of the kind of accumulation and stratification of land which was possible on the bishops' estate comes from Bishop Auckland. Figure 19 shows the value in shillings of all the copyhold land found here in the 1640s. There were a multitude of people with rents worth less than 5s, some cottagers and others owing rent for small parcels of land, but there was also a group of more substantial tenants owing rents of over 20s. This example shows not only the high degree of stratification in the size of holdings but also the importance of widows in the inheritance of land and future transmission of holdings, with five of the six people with rents of over 20s being widows.[51]

49 Kirby (ed.), *Parliamentary Surveys*, vol. 2, pp. 164–74.

50 Ibid.

51 Margery Craddocke, widow of Henry Maughen, owed rents worth a total of £2 4s 2d; Ann Bayles held six copyholds by widowright which were worth £2; Isabell Hodgson held eight copyholds by widowright worth £1 2s; John Walker possessed land worth £1 8s 8d; Anne Allenson

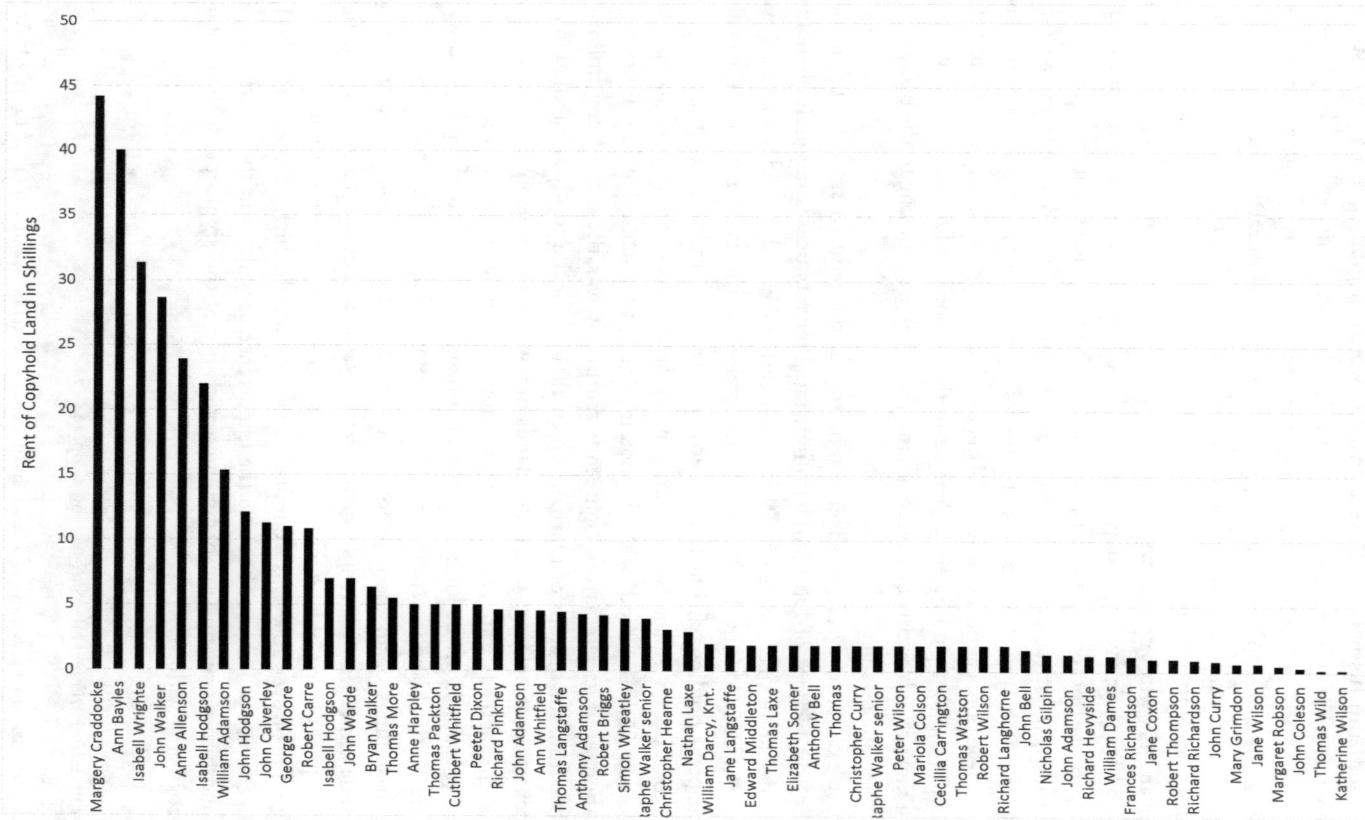

Figure 19. Total Rent in Shillings of Copyhold Land on the Manor of Auckland in the 1640s.

Source: D. A. Kirby (ed.), *Parliamentary Surveys of the Bishopric of Durham*, vol. 1, Surtees Society, 183 (1966), pp. 15–34.

Levine and Wrightson found a similar degree of stratification on the bishops' manor of Whickham in the early seventeenth century which they associated with the impact of increased coal-mining from the 1620s onwards. They described how the distribution of landholding 'underwent significant change', as the middle-range of holdings of one to three oxgangs 'which had retained their integrity up to 1600 had largely disappeared as separate units and their lands had been redistributed', creating a greater degree of stratification on the manor. There were an increasing number of very large accumulations and by 1647, there were five holdings of more 'than fifty acres, two of them falling in the eighty–hundred acres range and one being no less than 170 acres', some of which had been 'built up by families notable in 1600'.[52] This is very reminiscent of the above findings for Newbottle and Bishopwearmouth and was part of a much larger process of stratification which was happening on the bishops' estate. Indeed, the proximity of the coal trade may well have acted as an inhibiting factor in this engrossment as the middle-range of copyholders could supplement their incomes with wain carriage and thus better resist the financial pressures exerted by some of their larger neighbours. The other consequence of this process was the proliferation of tenants who held 'only a house or cottage and/or garden, garth and tiny parcels of land of less than one acre' which had swollen from twenty-six in 1600 to sixty-six by 1647.[53]

The Rise of a Yeoman Elite

Robert Brenner argued that France's stagnant agrarian growth was a result of the continuing strength of peasant landholding into the early modern period.[54] By comparison, he argued that it was disintegrating in England and, with the peasants' failure to establish essentially freehold control over the land, the landlords were able to engross, consolidate and enclose landholdings and to create large leasehold farms. More recently, however, Robert Allen has argued that the early seventeenth century marked 'the high point of peasant proprietorship' with the rise of the yeomanry who were true 'owner-occupiers', and Richard Smith has similarly noted that 'owner-occupancy reached its apogee early in the seventeenth century'.[55] This was partly

held seven copyholds by widowright worth £1 3s 11d; and lastly Isabel Wright, widow of Bryan Wright, owed rents worth £1 11s 4d. Kirby (ed.), *Parliamentary Surveys*, vol. 1, pp. 15–34.

52 Levine and Wrightson, *The Making of an Industrial Society*, pp. 137–8.

53 Ibid., pp. 137–8. This development was heavily dependent on the increasing demand for coal which provided these copyholders with the increasing opportunity for wage labour from the late sixteenth century onwards.

54 Brenner, 'Agrarian Class Structure', p. 54.

55 Allen, *Enclosure and the Yeoman*, p. 72; Richard M. Smith, 'The English Peasantry, 1250–1650', in Tom Scott (ed.), *The Peasantries of Europe from the Fourteenth to the Eighteenth Centuries* (London, 1998), p. 371.

because of the legal protection that copyholds of inheritance gave to tenants, but it was also because tenants were increasingly able to purchase freehold rights to their lands in England, especially from the second half of the sixteenth century onwards as stagnant rents provided dual opportunities: landlords in mounting financial trouble and tenants who could increasingly afford to benefit.

The increasing stratification of landholding discussed above went beyond the estate of the bishops of Durham and permeated rural society in the palatinate; indeed, the yeomanry of the county were one of the main beneficiaries of the rising prices and fixed rents which typified much of the region from the mid-sixteenth century onwards. The Radcliffes, for example, inherited the manor of Hawthorn from the Claxtons and held it until 1607 when Francis and Edward granted the whole manor and vill in several parcels to their tenants.[56] As we have seen, the financial problems of the Lumleys provided similar opportunities for their tenants to purchase land, with John, Lord Lumley, alienating Murton in eight portions to his own tenants for £341 6s 8d in 1566. In 1624, John Shaklock granted his lands here, which represented an eighth of the total manor, to William and John Shepherdson of Bishopwearmouth discussed above, comprising a messuage, twenty acres of arable, twenty of meadow, thirty of pasture, fifty of furze and fifty of moor.[57] Richard Morley, Robert and William Rickaby, Lancelot Todd and Francis and Ralph Welfoot were all described as non-armorial freeholders of Bishopton in the early seventeenth century after they had purchased portions of land from the Conyers, who had held the manor there for several centuries.[58]

These examples were not isolated incidents and show the profits that could be made in the second half of the sixteenth century as well as the potential avenues of advancement in a period of relative upheaval in the landed structure of Durham. The Hulls of Osterley were one such family 'who though apparently but very yeomanly folks, appeared at the Visitation of 1575, and were persuaded to indulge in coat armour'.[59] The Shadforths are a particularly interesting example of this yeoman elite whose success James attributed to their possession of an 'under-rented lease of the episcopal manor of Tunstall'.[60] They were in fact already on the rise before this, being one of the beneficiaries of Lord Lumley's financial troubles when Thomas

56 Surtees, *History of Durham*, vol. 1, pp. 15–17.

57 An earlier example of this is the purchase of Eppleton manor from Sir William Heron by the sitting yeoman tenant, John Todd, in a series of transactions from 1519. In Surtees' words: 'however common the transaction may now appear, this was perhaps the first instance within the bishopric, of a tenant acquiring the estate and manorial rights of his landlord': *History of Durham*, vol. 1, pp. 217–19.

58 Similarly, Thomas Hull of Stockley was alternatively described as a gentleman or a non-armorial freeholder, and benefited from the low rents on the former Neville estates, holding land worth £40 per annum in the early seventeenth century. Blair, 'Durham Armorials', pp. 156–203.

59 Surtees, *History of Durham*, vol. 2, p. 331.

60 James, *Family, Lineage and Civil Society*, p. 73.

Shadforth purchased an eighth of Murton manor in 1566. This was the same manor which the Shepherdsons of Bishopwearmouth later purchased their way into and it is hardly surprising to see this combination of improving families enclosing the whole townfield at Murton in 1640, some fifty or so years after an earlier, partial division had shown the lands to be 'better suited to pasture than tillage'.[61] George and John Shadforth also purchased the manor of Eppleton piecemeal from George Collingwood, esquire, acquiring a seventh portion in 1601 and a moiety by 1617, with his son Thomas acquiring the whole manor in 1630.[62] It was this same George Collingwood who was one of the supervisors of George Shadforth's will in 1617, as well as one of the witnesses, although a certain amount of his involvement may have been self-interest for he was recorded as being owed £900 by George Shadforth, presumably the amount outstanding for the purchase of Eppleton.[63] Furthermore, the Shadforths possessed a moiety of the vill of Whardon, which is explicitly mentioned in George Shadforth's will in 1617, out of which he expected his executors to collect £500 in the space of just ten years for the satisfaction of his daughter's filial portion: a clear sign of the profits which could be accrued in this period. Lastly, the family acquired the long lease of the episcopal manor of Tunstall from the original lessees in 1608, being now in a position where they could acquire such a valuable lease: it was thought to be worth £600 on George Shadforth's death in 1617.[64]

The Shadforths were one of many Durham yeomen who were able to make profits from commercially working their lands, taking considerable risks to purchase further lands that were used in a cyclical fashion to increase their wealth and social standing. The inventory of George Shadforth in 1617 is revealing for the amount of livestock he possessed upon his leased lands at Tunstall.[65] There were thirty-four acres of corn, with eight draught oxen, thirty-four cows, 140 sheep and a handful of horses, swine and poultry at Tunstall; and thirty acres of corn, six oxen, twenty cows, forty-one old sheep and fifty-three lambs at Murton. He was also owed considerable sums from the likes of Sir Henry Anderson and Roger Lumley.[66] By virtue of his extra hold-

61 R. I. Hodgson, 'The Progress of Enclosure in County Durham, 1550–1870', in H. S. A. Fox and R. A. Butlin (eds.), *Change in the Countryside: Essays on Rural England, 1500–1900* (London, 1979), p. 94.

62 Surtees, *History of Durham*, vol. 1, pp. 217–19.

63 DPRI/1/1617/S3/1.

64 Tunstall was leased out in two portions: one, which passed from King James I through the hands of several people before becoming John Shadforth's, was an eighty-year lease with a rent of £10 13s 4d but on improvement it was estimated at £96; the other, which was similarly an eighty-year lease, was granted to Richard Middleton who demised it to John Shadforth, had a rent of £2 13s 4d and on improvement was estimated at £24: Kirby (ed.), *Parliamentary Surveys*, p. 154.

65 The following from his inventory: DPRI/1/1617/S3/2–3.

66 Sir Henry Anderson owed him £200, Ralph Featherston owed him £100, Thomas King owed him £80, Edward Daile owed him £47 and Mr Robert Cooper of Durham owed £40, whilst he had desperate debts which included a bond owed by Roger Lumley for £64.

ings, George Shadforth was thus able to engage in commercial farming on a much larger scale than either the dean and chapter's leaseholders or many of the bishop's copyhold tenants. Indeed, the scale of his operations was not greatly dissimilar to many members of the gentry, with over £150 worth of grain and nearly £300 worth of livestock. However, it is his other possessions which reveal the primary difference between himself and his gentry neighbours: his apparel, for example, only came to £13 6s 8d, whilst the only plate or jewellery mentioned were six silver spoons worth £1 10s, with the entirety of his household goods only approaching £25. In Trevor-Roper's words, 'he had yeoman tastes, yeoman methods, yeoman habits. He did not have to keep up the port of a gentleman ... and half his prosperity was due to this saving.'[67] It was this section of society who increasingly swelled the ranks of the gentry who, as Mervyn James argued, were 'rich farmers, previously content with the traditional title of 'yeoman', [now] eager to be called gentry'.[68] This was a general phenomenon of the period, with J. T. Cliffe noting that between 1558 and 1642 'it was the yeomanry who represented the greatest source of recruitment [into the gentry] and in fact roughly half the Yorkshiremen who bought their way into the gentry in this period can be identified as yeoman farmers'.[69] As Trevor-Roper went on to comment, the rise into the gentry of successful yeomen 'seems incontestable', with yeomen farming their lands directly often able to build up properties 'worth three or four squires put together' and found 'able yearly to dispend betwixt three and five hundred pounds'.[70]

It was families like the Shadforths and Shepherdsons of the Wear valley noted above whose sons found their way to the University of Cambridge in the seventeenth century, with successive generations matriculating at Peterhouse, Trinity and Christ's Colleges.[71] The social aspiration of this burgeoning group in the English countryside during the late sixteenth century was in part predicated upon their agricultural profits, but it also acted as a motivation for further economic dynamism, especially in the north-east of England where the collapse of the Neville affinity, stagnant rents on the bishop of Durham's lands and early industrialisation provided considerable opportunities for their fulfilment. John Shadforth of Murton went on to serve as a juror in the Durham quarter sessions on at least seven occasions between 1603 and 1615, where he was described as yeoman until the session of 11 January 1615, after which he was styled gentleman.[72] It is hardly surprising to see the names of Anthony Shadforth of Tunstall and Thomas Shadforth of Eppleton included in the list of non-armorial gentlemen in the seventeenth century, with estates valued at £160 and £300 per annum respectively, as well as John Shepherdson of Bishopwearmouth

67 Trevor-Roper, *The Gentry*, p. 9.

68 James, *Family, Lineage, and Civil Society*, pp. 71–2.

69 Cliffe, *Yorkshire Gentry*, p. 19.

70 Trevor-Roper, *The Gentry*, p. 9.

71 John Venn and J. A. Venn (eds.), *Alumni Cantabrigienses* (Cambridge, 1927), p. 47 and 60.

72 Fraser (ed.), *Durham Quarter Sessions*, p. 16.

with a valuation of £160 per annum: three of the highest estimates for non-armorial freeholders in Easington ward.[73] Further indications of the increasing living standards and social aspirations of this dynamic group can be seen in the Hearth Tax of 1666, which describes Thomas Shadforth, gentleman, as owning the thirteen-hearth Eppleton Hall, whilst the next biggest house in the village similarly belonged to him with three hearths, clearly demonstrating the prominence the family achieved within the village.[74] Similarly, Mary Shadforth was taxed on a seven-hearth house at Tunstall, which was once again the largest house by a considerable margin, with fourteen non-paying households also present.[75]

Conclusion

The divergent development of the two ecclesiastical estates of Durham had long-term consequences for their tenants and resulted in quite different experiences across the fifteenth, sixteenth and early seventeenth centuries. On the estate of Durham Cathedral Priory, tenants gained holdings of roughly equal size before the process of syndication was introduced, but this process of converting to leasehold was very important in the long-term because these consolidated holdings became the standard unit of landholding on the estate. By comparison, the lack of any uniform policy on the bishops' estate meant that there was often a much larger accumulation of holdings by individuals or families. In the late fourteenth century the composition of the bishops' estate was not all that dissimilar to the priory's, with varying amounts of former demesne and bondland interspersed with freeholds and exchequer-land carved out of the waste. Although some engrossment had already occurred by the time of Hatfield's survey in 1380, this was but a precursor of what was to happen across the fifteenth and sixteenth centuries. By 1588, there were families such as the Chiltons who held around a third of all the land in Newbottle and individuals such as John Thompson who held land worth over £6 in rent, whilst at the other end of the spectrum there were groups of cottagers or smallholders with very little access to land. This was a process which Levine and Wrightson commented upon at Whickham from the 1620s onwards but which was part of a much larger polarisation of holdings upon the manors of the bishops of Durham.[76] This increasing stratification of land was reinforced in the late sixteenth and early seventeenth centuries because these larger neighbours could make substantial profits from agriculture, which led to further purchases of land and thus ensured their continued dominance of these villages.

73 Blair, 'Durham Armorials', pp. 156–203.

74 Parkinson (ed.), *County Durham Hearth Tax*, p. 55.

75 Ibid., p. 60.

76 Levine and Wrightson, *The Making of an Industrial Society*, pp. 137–8.

Peter Larson concluded for the late fourteenth century that 'the bishopric peasants clung to their concept of community, avoiding change, while many of their priory counterparts embraced the new opportunities'.[77] He went on to argue that 'on the priory estate we have what appears to be a "crisis of order" with a struggle over agriculture, rather than for moral and religious dominance, which struggle seems to have faded by 1400. Many of the tenants dwindled in consequence, becoming little more than subtenants of the syndicate members and all but disappearing from the court records ... the villages of the bishopric estate remained steady in their course.'[78] In the long term, however, the process of syndication fixed the size of holdings, whereas the lack of any change on the bishops' estate enabled the rise of a village elite over the course of the fifteenth and sixteenth centuries. The greater degree of stratification which occurred on the bishops' estate across this period led to the emergence of a group of substantial farmers who approached the gentry in terms of wealth and social standing. By the early seventeenth century, families like the Shepherdsons and Shadforths of the Wear valley formed a rural elite who accumulated capital and land, using their profits from commercial agriculture to purchase further land and to finance entrepreneurial forays into the flourishing industries of the region.

The institutional context is thus vital for understanding the living standards, social aspirations and wealth of Durham tenants in the early seventeenth century. Although the relative opportunities on the bishops' estate may have attracted more entrepreneurial tenants, it is likely that they also cultivated such an economic and social outlook amongst existing tenants, with the rise of career families amongst the gentry on the estate such as the Bellasises. Likewise, the Shepherdsons had similarly humble medieval backgrounds to the Newtons, Taillours and Pearsons of Harton, but by the early seventeenth century were amongst the wealthiest non-armorial freeholders in Easington ward, whilst the latter were still effectively tenant-farmers. Although the survival of ecclesiastical records allows developments to be seen most clearly on their lands, the situation found on the bishops' estate reflects the rise of this yeoman elite in the county more broadly. The likes of the Shadforths took their first step towards becoming freeholders at the expense of the Lumleys; the Welfoots of Bishopton benefited from the Conyers' misfortunes; and the likes of the Hulls of Stockley gained from the low rents on the former Neville estates.

Phillipp Schofield has explored the ways in which lords acted as 'filters' for exogenous factors affecting tenants in medieval England, but institutional constraints were even more significant than this, creating real structural limitations upon how tenants could, and often did, respond to the market opportunities of the late sixteenth century.[79] It was in the restructuring of rural society in the late fourteenth and fifteenth centuries that this new path dependency was created and it affected

77 Larson, *Conflict and Compromise*, pp. 237–40.

78 Ibid., p. 229.

79 Schofield, *Peasants and Community*, p. 35.

the long-term development of rural society into the early modern period. Studies of the conflict between landlords and tenants in the sixteenth and early seventeenth centuries have only served to confirm this importance of precedence and the previous history of estates with their focus on custom and tenure.[80] The divergent development of estates had long-term and wide-ranging consequences across this period, affecting not only the tenure and rent of land, but also the potential accumulation of holdings by tenants. This in turn had a significant impact upon living standards, social aspirations and ultimately upon the formation of agrarian capitalism in the sixteenth and early seventeenth centuries in England.

80 See for example, Wood, *The Politics of Social Conflict*; Hoyle, 'Tenure and the Land Market'; and the essays in Whittle (ed.), *Landlords and Tenants*.

Conclusion

Rural society in Durham was much changed by the early seventeenth century, as the lay subsidy of 1624 reveals.[1] The Nevilles had, of course, long since disappeared from the Durham countryside, whilst the Bowes were represented by Sir George Bowes of Houghton parish who was appraised at £6 and the Lumleys did not appear at all. The traditional ruling elite were still represented by Henry Hilton of Hylton castle in Monk Wearmouth parish who was appraised at £15, the highest amount in the subsidy, whilst Ralph Conyers of Sockburn was appraised at £8, but precious few of the families who had dominated Durham landed society in the early sixteenth century had survived.[2] Many of these families had gradually been replaced by the lesser gentry, families who often had claims to similarly long and impressive lineages but whose holdings until the late sixteenth century had often been relatively modest. Ralph Featherstonhaugh of Stanhope and William Bellasis of Houghton parish were both included in the group of individuals appraised at £10, whilst William Lambton and William Blakiston both feature prominently at £8 and £7 respectively. These families, 'less wealthy and less connected than the Eures and their kind' at the start of the sixteenth century, had taken full advantage of the economic, social and political opportunities of the period to emerge as some of the most important members of Durham society.[3]

The Newcastle coal merchants were also a significant group of newcomers who were appraised at £10 or higher, being represented in the lay subsidy by the likes of Henry Anderson, Thomas Liddell, Thomas Riddell and Robert Brandling. This was not a simple story of the gentrification of merchant wealth, but a complicated interaction between an affluent, socially elitist and politically astute group of Newcastle coal merchants and the surrounding countryside. This group did not flood into landed society in search of social validation and political power, but rather they sought to secure the subterranean wealth of the Durham countryside. It is not surprising, therefore, that it is in the Durham coalfield where we find the Liddells, Riddells, Brandlings, Hodgesons, Dudleys, Tempests and Coles in the 1624 subsidy, nor is it surprising that Chester ward now accounted for twenty out of the forty-six individuals appraised at £5 or over in the lay subsidy.

1 DUL, ASC, Mickleton and Spearman Manuscript 7, ff. 26–47.

2 The Conyers of Sockburn died out in the male line a decade after this lay subsidy.

3 James, *Family, Lineage and Civil Society*, p. 31.

The settlement of Newcastle coal merchants in the north of the county was but one part of the commercialisation of the Durham countryside, with established families like the Lumleys and Lambtons as well as yeomen freeholders like the Shadforths and Shepherdsons engaging in the Wear coal trade, and yeomanry throughout the region benefiting from the opportunities in supplying this burgeoning industry. The axis of wealth, power and status, which in the fifteenth and early sixteenth centuries had followed a line roughly south-west from Hylton, through Lumley, Durham, Brancepeth, Witton, Bishop Auckland, Raby, Streatlam and Barnard Castle, had been realigned to the north of the county, focused upon the coalfields just south of the Tyne and those accessible from the Wear. This can be seen most clearly in the structure of lay society in county Durham in the early seventeenth century, as shown in Table 32. Darlington and Chester wards, which had broadly similar social profiles in the early seventeenth century, were different in two notable respects. Firstly, there were considerably more non-armorial gentlemen in the former; these men were the descendants of the sixteenth-century yeomen retainers of the Nevilles, Eures and Bowes. Secondly, there were nearly twice as many individuals in Chester ward who were appraised at £5 or more in the 1624 lay subsidy, showing the wealth which was now concentrated in the north of the county and the effect the coal industry had had on Durham landed society.

Table 32. The Structure of Lay Society in County Durham in the First Half of the Seventeenth Century

Wards	Baronets	Knights	Esquires	Gentlemen	Non-armorial	Total	£5+ Lay Subsidy
Chester	1	8	12	20	27	68	20
Darlington	0	7	14	24	43	88	11
Easington	1	1	8	22	17	49	8
Stockton	0	1	3	15	26	45	7
Total	2	17	37	81	113	250	46

Source: See C. H. Hunter Blair, 'Durham Armorials of the Seventeenth Century', *AA*, 4th series, 15 (1938), pp. 156–203; DUL, ASC, Mickleton and Spearman Manuscript 7, ff. 26–47.

The works of Mervyn James and A. J. Pollard have created a narrative of economic, social and political change in the north-east of England that portrays the region as slow to recover from the fifteenth-century recession, which in turn delayed the region's emergence from the middle ages until the second half of the sixteenth century. James concluded that 1570 was a crucial turning-point in the development of the region, arguing that:

> not only the gentry, but society as a whole, was involved in this pattern of change; and particularly after 1570, when the speed at which the kaleidoscope revolved

> markedly increased. The years between the Rising of the North and the Civil War were characterised by economic and demographic growth, and by exceptionally rapid social transformation.[4]

Undoubtedly the downfall of the Nevilles played a major role in this change as it removed the single largest lay landowner in the county overnight, along with the alternative sources of patronage that the family offered in the region.

Nevertheless, James was aware that there were much more significant developments in the Durham countryside than the political downfall of the earls of Westmorland could account for, and he went on to explain that 'the fall of the Nevilles, the rise of the coal industry, [and] the changes in agriculture all made their contribution'.[5] In all of these areas, the 1570s and 1580s often proved to be vital decades of change, and nowhere more so than in the coal industry. Of course, landlords in the palatinate were aware of the financial benefits of coal mining from at least the fourteenth century onwards, whilst the Thorntons made significant inroads into the Durham countryside in order to acquire rich coal deposits in the fifteenth century. Similarly, the ecclesiastical landowners of Durham exploited their coal reserves, which if sometimes limited and on restrictive leases, were still often profitable, especially for the bishops of Durham. Despite this early interest in the coal industry, however, 'we are driven', as Hatcher concluded, 'unerringly to the 1570s and the 1580s as the turning-point. Between the later 1560s and the later 1590s shipments of coal rose fourfold', which was for the 'seasale trade alone. In the ensuing twenty-five years shipments virtually doubled again to reach an average of over 400,000 tons a year in the early 1620s.'[6] Before this period, the exploitation of coal was primarily undertaken by landowners to supplement their incomes, but from the second half of the sixteenth century onwards it became a driving force in the regional economy.

There were still other changes in the 1570s which were of crucial importance in the relationship between landlords and tenants in the region. It was in the 1570s that the dispute between the dean and chapter of Durham Cathedral and their tenants was resolved, with the Council of the North ruling in 1577 that it 'appeareth by an ancient book and register of leases ... that the lands in contention ... had been letten for years by lease' and that the tenements 'should not be holden by tenant right'.[7] Although the end result of this dispute is more ambiguous that this declaration suggests, with the tenants possessing inheritable rights over their beneficial leaseholds, it was another crucial step in recognising the changes undergone on the cathedral estate, which culminated in the rise of the Church leaseholder on its lands. By comparison, it was in the 1570s and '80s when the bishops of Durham began to

4 Ibid., p. 178.

5 Ibid., p. 178.

6 Hatcher, *British Coal Industry*, p. 78.

7 Longstaffe and Booth (eds.), *Halmota Prioratus Dunelmensis*, pp. xxxvii–xxxviii.

face some of their most difficult financial challenges, with numerous long and detrimental leases of manors and the Grand Lease granted to the Crown, whilst inflation slowly undermined the rest of their income. It was in the next few decades that the bishops set about converting almost half of their leasehold land from 21-year leases to three lives, which provided yet more problems for their successors in the first half of the seventeenth century.

The balance of landed resources within the county also underwent significant changes in the second half of the sixteenth century: not only did the Nevilles disappear, but several other landowners, including the Lumleys and the Conyers, slowly sold off portions of their estates, the former in a flurry of sales in the 1560s and '70s. Towards the end of the fifteenth century there were numerous aristocratic and knightly families with five or more manors, whilst the Nevilles, Lumleys and Bowes held around two-fifths of all lay manors in the palatinate. By the end of the sixteenth century, and primarily because of changes wrought in the second half of that century, this concentration of landownership had been greatly reduced. Conversely, there was an influx into landed society in the second half of the sixteenth century from three primary sources: Newcastle merchants, the deans and prebendaries of the new cathedral, and the prosperous yeomanry who were emerging as a significant social and economic group because of the increasing stratification of landholding across the sixteenth century.

The 1570s and '80s, therefore, formed a significant period for almost every section of landed society in Durham which shaped rural society for future generations, but many of these events had a long gestation period in the rural history of the region. Some, like the dean and chapter's dispute with their tenants, were actually the culmination of changes on the estate stretching back to the late fourteenth century, representing the official recognition of earlier tenurial change rather than a significant divergence from past practice. Likewise, the increasing financial problems that the bishops of Durham faced in the second half of the sixteenth century were as much the result of the long-term tenurial development of their estate as they were of Elizabethan intervention in the 1570s. Other changes, like the emergence of the lesser gentry, were part of an ongoing process which took several generations for yeomen families to achieve, representing the increasing opportunities created by inflation. Still other changes, like the forfeiture of the Nevilles, had a significant impact on the politics of the region by removing an important source of local patronage and power, but caused few rental or tenurial changes for their former tenants, at least until the Crown sought to make greater profits from these lands in the early seventeenth century.

The sixteenth century was, therefore, a period of upheaval and change in the palatinate of Durham, but the changes rural society underwent during the late fourteenth and fifteenth centuries had a significant influence upon these developments. In many ways, the 1370s and '80s could be advocated as similarly important decades in the transformation of England's economy and rural society. In the following generations, many gentry families alienated their manors to the knightly group of landowners within the palatinate of Durham; the revenues of the two largest landowners in the region declined by over 40 per cent; serfdom as a viable and working institution virtually collapsed; and tenants accumulated larger holdings, with low rents and greater personal freedoms.[8] The withdrawal from direct-demesne production was of paramount importance in these changes because it divorced the ownership of land from its use, a development which was to be of such significance in the sixteenth century. The responses of landowners and tenants to the problems of the late fourteenth and fifteenth centuries continued to have an importance long after the middle ages came to an end, creating a path dependency and institutional constraint upon their successors which they often found difficult to overcome. Many of the challenges of the sixteenth century have their origins in the rapid population growth of the period; in the rise of London and increasing commercialisation; and in the relationship between landlords and tenants. But the tenurial and institutional landscape which had developed during the economic problems of the late fourteenth and fifteenth centuries directly influenced how these disputes played out on manors across England, as well as the nature of their resolution.

The Durham region is important, therefore, because it shows how estates and institutions provided structural restrictions upon landowners and tenants across this period that were as real and as important as the weather, soil conditions, market opportunities, or indeed population movements.[9] For example, if we consider the village of Whickham, as Levine and Wrightson have, was the experience of these copyholders more representative of a burgeoning coal village or was it the typical experience of townships upon the bishop of Durham's estate? Placing a village or manor within the institutional context of the estate of which it was a constituent part is as important as placing it within a geological topography. The monks of Durham Cathedral Priory and the bishops of Durham faced the same demographic crisis in the fourteenth century, but how the two institutions reacted differed greatly, creating long-term structural differences between their estates which had significant consequences for their sixteenth-century counterparts. These differences in the development of their estates had profound effects upon their tenants, providing them with entirely different opportunities and challenges. There may have been differences between the two estates prior to the Black Death which affected these decisions, but it was the choices made from the late fourteenth century onwards which had long-term consequences for their divergent development and for their tenants. This insti-

8 See Bailey, *The Decline of Serfdom in Late Medieval England*, p. 307.

9 Future research into the differences between these institutional contexts will shed further light on the role they played in the development of agrarian capitalism, especially in areas of the country where estate structures were more sprawling. For example, how did monks, bishops, colleges, nobles, gentry and the Crown respond to new technologies (mills), new opportunities (towns) and changing economic conditions (withdrawal from direct-demesne agriculture and the desertion of villages)?

tutional context is vital in understanding the living standards, social aspirations and wealth of Durham tenants in the early seventeenth century, with a majority of the dean and chapter's tenants continuing as tenant-farmers at the same time as a small group of families were emerging as a yeoman elite on the bishop of Durham's estate.

It was this same path dependency which posed such problems for rentier landlords in the sixteenth century, with the likes of the Lumleys and Conyers forced to sell their ancestral estates piecemeal, often to their own sitting tenants who were increasingly benefiting from rising agricultural prices. Even when tenants held all of their land by leasehold tenure, landlords still struggled to raise rents and entry fines, as the Crown found out on the former Neville lordships of Raby and Brancepeth in the 1620s.[10] The storm over the gentry and the crisis of the aristocracy as a theoretical framework for studying this period had considerable problems, not least because historians were employing economic analyses of social groups. The high inflation and stagnant rents of the sixteenth century gave rise to a crisis, not necessarily of a social group, but of a type of landowner who struggled to benefit from the unearned increment which their tenants slowly accumulated. Rather than thinking of this problem as a crisis of the aristocracy it is more useful to conceptualise it as a crisis of rentier landlords: the problem of stagnant and unimprovable incomes had its origins in the tenurial development of their estates rather than in their social status and it is here where the answer to many of the problems rural society faced in the sixteenth century lies. Unlike in the thirteenth century when landlords were able to revert to the direct management of their lands, copyhold tenure and beneficial leaseholds gave considerable protection to their tenants in the political economy of Elizabethan England. Although there were some large lay landowners who took managerial decisions to change the tenurial structure on their lands and so increase rents, such as the ninth earl of Northumberland, it is clear that the institutional history of land was still fundamentally important in affecting their ability to do so; it is no coincidence that the one area of the Percy's estate which remained unimproved was the former monastic land at Tynemouth.[11]

The Durham region was thus in many ways different to large parts of midland and southern England: ecclesiastical and lay estates tended to be large, highly concentrated and compact in nature; the take-off of the coal industry provided investment opportunities for both landowners and merchants; and the border status of the county provided some of the impetus behind changing landlord–tenant relations. But this northern study sheds light on a range of important national economic and social debates, not least the effects that successive periods of recession and inflation had upon the evolving social structure of medieval and early modern England. It also suggests a range of questions for further research, including how far the institutional

10 TNA, Homberston Survey of 1570, E164/37, p. 13.

11 See, for example, the problems New College had in maintaining serfdom because of the previous ownership of their manor in Bailey, *The Decline of Serfdom in Late Medieval England*, p. 238.

divisions discussed here were significant in areas of the country where estates were more sprawling. Similarly, how far does an analysis of economic groups rather than social groups help to explain the changes English rural society underwent between the fifteenth and early seventeenth centuries? And how far was the gentrification of mercantile wealth part of a symbiotic relationship in this period which saw a corresponding commercialisation of gentry wealth going in reverse between two economically, socially and politically similar groups? Although demography, commercialisation and class relations were key dynamics which often combined to produce change in pre-industrial societies, there were other crucial factors which affected the outcome of these changes, one of which was the institutional constraints created by the continuing role estates played in the English countryside across the late medieval and early modern divide.

Bibliography

Unpublished Primary Sources

Durham, Durham Cathedral Muniments

DCM, Bursar's Accounts, 1400/01–1519/20
DCM, Bursar's Books, F–M
DCM, Coal Mines, 1409/10–1452/3
DCM, Dean and Chapter Registers, 1–15, 1541–1670
DCM, Dean and Prebend Accounts
DCM, Receiver's Books, 1541/2–1639/40
DCM, Receiver's Rolls, 1548/9–1604/5
DCM, Registrum Parvum IV
DCM, Transumpt of Accounts, 1571/2–1613/4
DCM/E/BA – list of tenants, with rents and valuations at the time of Dean Hunt [1620–38]
DCM/E/AA/1–2: Dean and Chapter Survey of Westoe and Harton, 1768
DCM/E/9/AA/1–2: Dean and Chapter Survey of Cowpen Bewley, 1774

Durham University Library, Archives and Special Collections

Church Commission Deposit of Durham Bishopric Estate Records:
Allerton Receiver's Accounts: CCB B/84/1–CCB B/90/124
Clerk of Mines Accounts: CCB B/79/1–CCB B/79/12
Collector's Accounts: CCB B/51/1–CCB B/67/50
Coroner's Accounts: CCB B/44/1–CCB B/50/38
Howden Receiver's Accounts: CCB B/93/1a–CCB B/101/142
Instaurer's Accounts: CCB B/81/1–CCB B/81/19
Master Forester's Accounts: CCB B/83/1–15
Receiver General's Accounts: CCB B/1/1–CCB B/12/139
Registers of Leases and Patents, 1–5, c.1530–c.1640
Survey of Durham Bishopric Estates in County Durham, April 1588, Sede Vacante, P. M. Richard Barnes: CCB D/1981/185000B, ff. 1–66r

Durham Probate Records: DPRI/1, 2, 3
Mickleton and Spearman MS 7
Microfilm Inquisitions Post Mortem: XM/film Palatinate 1

The National Archives, London

DL 44/96: Inventory of the property of Henry Neville, late Earl of Westmorland
DURH 3: Chancery Court: Cursitor's Records, Inquisitions Post Mortem
E164/37: Homberston Survey of 1570
E178/3765: Special Commission, Inquisition into the Privileges and Customs of Brancepeth Lordship
LR2/192: Survey of Crown Lands in Durham and Yorkshire, 1607

LR2/214: A Book of Fines Compounded for by Sir Henry Vane and other Commissioners, 1617–27

SC6/ELIZI/628: Accounts of the land of the Earl of Westmorland and other attainted persons

Surrey History Centre

836/1–4: Rentals and Accounts of John Lord Lumley, 1532–1608

Published Primary Sources

Batho, G. R. (ed.), *The Household Papers of Henry Percy Ninth Earl of Northumberland, 1564–1632*, Camden 3rd series, 93 (London, 1962)

Britnell, R. H. (ed.), *Durham Priory Manorial Accounts, 1277–1310*, Surtees Society, 218 (2014)

Calendar of Patent Rolls Elizabeth, v, 1569–72 (London, 1966)

Dendy, F. W. (ed.), *Extracts from the Records of the Company of Hostmen of Newcastle-upon-Tyne*, Surtees Society, 105 (1901)

Dudley, Edmund, *The Tree of Commonwealth* (ed.) D. M. Brodie (Cambridge, 1948)

'Durham Records: Cursitor's Records: Inquisitions Post Mortem', in *The Forty-Fourth Annual Report of the Deputy Keeper of the Public Records* (London, 1883), Appendix, pp. 310–542

'Durham Records: Cursitor's Records: Inquisitions Post Mortem', in *The Forty-Fifth Annual Report of the Deputy Keeper of the Public Records* (London, 1885), Appendix, pp. 153–282

Everett Green, Mary Anne, (ed.), 'Life of Mr. William Whittingham, dean of Durham', *Miscellany VI*, Camden 1st series, 104 (1871)

Fenwick, C. C. (ed.), *The Poll Taxes of 1377, 1379 and 1381*, Records of Social and Economic History, new series 27 (1998)

Foster, Joseph (ed.), *Pedigrees Recorded at the Visitations of the County Palatine of Durham Made by William Flower, Norroy King-of-Arms, in 1575, by Richard St George, Norroy King-of-Arms, in 1615, and by William Dugdale, Norroy King-of-Arms, in 1666* (London, 1887)

Fowler, J.T. (ed.), *Extracts from the Account Rolls of the Abbey or Durham*, vols. 1, 2 3, Surtees Society, 99, 100, 103 (1898, 1898, 1900)

Fraser, C. M. (ed.), *Durham Quarter Sessions Rolls, 1471–1625*, Surtees Society, 199 (1987–88)

Given-Wilson, Chris (ed.), *The Parliament Rolls of Medieval England, 1274–1504*, vol. 5 (Woodbridge, 2005)

Green, A., Parkinson, E., and Spufford, M. (eds.), *County Durham Hearth Tax Assessment Lady Day 1666*, introduced by Adrian Green (London, 2006)

Greenwell, W. (ed.), *Feodarium Prioratus Dunelmensis: A Survey of the Estates of the Prior and Convent of Durham*, Surtees Society, 58 (1871)

—— *Bishop Hatfield's Survey: A Record of the Possessions of the See of Durham*, Surtees Society, 32 (1857)

Harrison, G. B. (ed.), *Advice to his Son by Henry Percy, Ninth Earl of Northumberland, 1609* (London, 1930)

Hodgson, J. C. (ed.), *Percy Bailiffs' Rolls of the Fifteenth Century*, Surtees Society, 134 (1921)

James, M. E. (ed.), *Estate Accounts of the Earls of Northumberland, 1562–1637*, Surtees Society, 163 (1955)

Kirby, D. A. (ed.), *Parliamentary Surveys of the Bishopric of Durham*, vols 1 and 2, Surtees Society, 183, 185 (1966, 1968)

Lamond, E. (ed.), *Walter of Henley's Husbandry: Together With Anonymous Husbandry, Seneschaucie and Robert Grosseteste's Rules* (London, 1890)

Lomas, R. A. and A. J. Piper (eds.), *Durham Cathedral Priory Rentals: Bursar's Rentals*, Surtees Society, 198 (1989)

Longstaffe, W. H. D. and J. Booth (eds.), *Halmota Prioratus Dunelmensis: Containing Extracts from the Halmote Court or Manor Rolls of the Prior and Convent of Durham, 1296–1384*, Surtees Society, 82 (1886)

Milner, Edith (ed.), *Records of the Lumleys of Lumley Castle* (London, 1904)

Ornsby, G. (ed.), *The Correspondence of John Cosin D.D., Lord Bishop of Durham: Together with Other Pages Illustrative of his Life and Times*, Surtees Society, 55 (1870)

Raine, J. (ed.), *Charters of Endowment, Inventories, and Account Rolls of the Priory of Finchale*, Surtees Society, 6 (1837)

—— and W. Greenwell (eds.), *Wills and Inventories from the Registry at Durham, Parts I, II, III, IV*, Surtees Society, 2, 38, 112, 142 (1835, 1860, 1906, 1929)

Russell, J., 'The Boke of Nurture', in F. J. Furnival (ed.), *Manners and Meals in Olden Time* (London, 1868)

Stell, P. M. (ed.), *Probate Inventories of the York Diocese, 1350–1500* (York, 2006)

Strype, John, *Annals of the Reformation and Establishment of Religion, and Other Various Occurrences in the Church* (London, 1701)

Thompson, A. H. (ed.), *The Statutes of the Cathedral Church of Durham: With Other Documents Relating to its Foundation and Endowment by King Henry VIII and Queen Mary*, Surtees Society, 143 (1929)

Venn, John and Venn, J. A., (eds.), *Alumni Cantabrigienses* (Cambridge, 1927)

Welford, R. (ed.), *History of Newcastle and Gateshead*, vol. I, II, III (London, 1884–87)

—— *Men of Mark 'twixt Tyne and Tweed*, vol. 1 (London, 1895)

Willan, T. S., and E. W. Crossley (eds.), *Three Seventeenth-Century Yorkshire Surveys*, The Yorkshire Archaeological Society Record Series, 104 (1941)

Secondary Sources

Acheson, Eric, *A Gentry Community: Leicestershire in the Fifteenth Century, c.1422–c.1485* (Cambridge, 1992)

Aird, W. M., *St Cuthbert and the Normans: The Church of Durham, 1071–1153* (Woodbridge, 1998)

Alexander, Gina, 'Victim or Spendthrift? The Bishop of London and his Income in the Sixteenth Century', in E. W. Ives (ed.), *Wealth and Power in Tudor England: Essays Presented to S. T. Bindoff* (London, 1978), pp. 128–45

Alchian, Armen, 'Uncertainty, Evolution and Economic Theory', *Journal of Political Economy*, 58 (1950), pp. 211–21

Allen, M., *The Durham Mint*, British Numismatic Society Special Publication, 4 (London, 2003)

—— 'Silver Production and the Money Supply in England and Wales, 1086–c.1500', *EcHR*, 64 (2011), pp. 114–31

—— 'The Volume of the English Currency, 1158–1470', *EcHR*, 54 (2001), pp. 595–611

Allen, Robert, *Enclosure and the Yeoman: The Agricultural Development of the South Midlands, 1450–1850* (Oxford, 1992)

—— 'The Two English Agricultural Revolutions, 1450–1850', in B. M. S. Campbell and Mark Overton (eds.), *Land, Labour and Livestock: Historical Studies in European Agricultural Productivity* (Manchester, 1991), pp. 236–54

Allison, K. J., 'Flock Management in the Sixteenth and Seventeenth Centuries', *EcHR*, 11 (1958), pp. 98–112

Almond, R., and A. J. Pollard, 'The Yeomanry of Robin Hood and Social Terminology in Fifteenth-Century England', *P&P*, 170 (2001), pp. 52–77

Appleby, A. B., 'Agrarian Capitalism or Seigniorial Reaction? The North West of England, 1500–1700', *AHR*, 80 (1975), pp. 574–94

—— 'Disease or Famine? Mortality in Cumberland and Westmorland, 1580–1640', *EcHR*, 26 (1973), pp. 403–32

Arkell, Tom, 'Interpreting Probate Inventories', in T. Arkell, N. Evans and N. Goose (eds.), *When Death do us Part: Understanding and Interpreting the Probate Records of Early Modern England* (Oxford, 2000), pp. 72–102

Arthur, W. B., 'Competing Technologies, Increasing Returns, and Lock-In by Historical Events', *Economic Journal*, 99 (1989), pp. 116–31

Arvanigian, Mark, 'A County Community or the Politics of the Nation? Border Service and Baronial Influence in the Palatinate of Durham, 1377–1413', *Historical Research*, 82 (2009), pp. 41–61

Aston, T. H., and C. H. E. Philpin (eds.), *The Brenner Debate: Agrarian Class Structure and Economic Development in Pre-Industrial Europe* (Cambridge, 1987)

Aylmer, G. E., 'The Crisis of the Aristocracy, 1558–1641', *P&P*, 32 (1965), pp. 113–25

Bailey, Mark, 'The Commercialisation of the English Economy, 1086–1500', *JMH*, 24 (1998), pp. 297–311

—— *The Decline of Serfdom in Late Medieval England: From Bondage to Freedom* (Woodbridge, 2014)

—— 'Demographic Decline in Late Medieval England: Some Thoughts on Recent Research', *EcHR*, 49 (1996), pp. 1–19

—— *A Marginal Economy? East Anglian Breckland in the Later Middle Ages* (Cambridge, 2008)

—— *Medieval Suffolk: an Economic and Social History, 1200–1500* (Woodbridge, 2007)

—— 'Peasant Welfare in England, 1290–1348', *EcHR*, 51 (1998), pp. 223–51

—— 'Rural Society', in R. Horrox (ed.), *Fifteenth-Century Attitudes* (Cambridge, 1994), pp. 150–68

—— 'Villeinage in England: a Regional Case Study c.1250–1349', *EcHR*, 62 (2009), pp. 430–57

—— and S. H. Rigby (eds.), *Town and Countryside in the Age of the Black Death: Essays in Honour of John Hatcher* (Turnhout, 2012)

Barron, Caroline, 'Chivalry, Pageantry and Merchant Culture in Medieval London', in Peter Coss and Maurice Keen (eds.), *Heraldry, Pageantry and Social Display in Medieval England* (Woodbridge, 2002), pp. 219–41

—— *London in the Later Middle Ages: Government and People, 1200–1500* (Oxford, 2004)

Batho, Gordon, 'The Finances of an Elizabethan Nobleman: Henry Percy, Ninth Earl of Northumberland (1564–1632)', *EcHR*, 9 (1957), pp. 433–50

Bean, J. M. W., *The Decline of English Feudalism, 1215–1540* (Manchester, 1968)

—— *The Estates of the Percy Family, 1416–1537* (London, 1958)

—— 'Population and Economic Decline in England in the Later Middle Ages', *EcHR*, 15 (1963), pp. 423–37

Beastall, T. W., *A North Country Estate: The Lumleys and Saundersons as Landowners, 1600–1900* (London, 1974)

Beckett, J. V., 'The Peasant in England: A Case of Terminological Confusion', *AgHR*, 32 (1984), pp. 113–23

Bennett, M. J., 'A County Community: Social Cohesion among the Cheshire Gentry, 1400–25', *NH*, 8 (1973), pp. 24–44
Biddick, K., 'Medieval English Peasants and Market Involvement', *JEcH*, 45 (1985), pp. 823–31
Blair, C. H. H., 'Durham Armorials of the Seventeenth Century', *AA*, 4th series, 15 (1938), pp. 156–203
—— 'The Mayors and Lord Mayors of Newcastle upon Tyne, 1216–1940, and the Sheriffs of the County of Newcastle upon Tyne, 1399–1940', *AA*, 4th series, 18 (1940), pp. 1–64
—— 'Members of Parliament for Newcastle upon Tyne (1377–1558), for Berwick upon Tweed (1529–1558), and Morpeth (1553–1558), *AA*, 4th series, 14 (1937), pp. 22–66
—— 'The Members of Parliament for Newcastle upon Tyne, 1559–1831', *AA*, 4th series, 23 (1945), pp. 102–55
Blake, J. B., 'The Medieval Coal Trade of North-East England: Some Fourteenth Century Evidence', *NH*, 2 (1967), pp. 1–26
Blanchard, I. S. W., 'Commercial Crisis and Change: Trade and the Industrial Economy of the North-East, 1509–1532', *NH*, 8 (1973), pp. 64–86
—— 'Labour Productivity and Work Psychology in the English Mining Industry, 1400–1600', *EcHR*, 31 (1978), pp. 1–24
—— 'The Miner and the Agricultural Community in Late Medieval England', *AgHR*, 20 (1972), pp. 93–106
—— 'Population Change, Enclosure, and the Early Tudor Economy', *EcHR*, 23 (1970), pp. 427–45
—— 'Seigniorial Entrepreneurship: the Bishops of Durham and the Weardale Lead Industry, 1406–1529', *Business History*, 15 (1973), pp. 97–111
Bois, G., *The Crisis of Feudalism: Economy and Society in Eastern Normandy, c.1300–1550* (Cambridge, 1984)
Bonfield, Lloyd, et al. (eds.), *The World We Have Gained: Histories of Population and Social Structure* (Oxford, 1986).
Boserup, E., *The Conditions of Agricultural Growth: The Economics of Agrarian Change Under Population Pressure* (London, 1965)
Bowden, Peter, 'Agricultural Prices, Wages, Farm Profits and Rents', in Joan Thirsk (ed.), *Agrarian History of England and Wales, 4: 1500–1640* (Cambridge, 1967)
Bowen, J. P., and A. T. Brown (eds.), *Custom and Commercialisation in English Rural Society: Revisiting Tawney and Postan* (Hatfield, forthcoming)
Braudel, F., and F. Spooner, 'Prices in Europe from 1450 to 1750', in E. E. Rich and C. H. Wilson (eds.), *The Cambridge Economic History of Europe, IV: the Economy of Expanding Europe in the Sixteenth and Seventeenth Centuries* (Cambridge, 1967), pp. 378–486
Brenner, Robert, 'Agrarian Class Structure and Economic Development in Pre-Industrial Europe', in T. H. Aston and C. H. E. Philpin (eds.), *The Brenner Debate: Agrarian Class Structure and Economic Development in Pre-Industrial Europe* (Cambridge, 1985), pp. 10–64
Bridbury, A. R., 'The Black Death', *EcHR*, 26 (1973), pp. 577–92
—— *Economic Growth: England in the Later Middle Ages* (Westport, 1983)
Briggs, Chris, 'The Availability of Credit in the English Countryside, 1400–1480', *AgHR*, 56 (2008), pp. 1–24
—— *Credit and Village Society in Fourteenth-Century England* (Oxford, 2009)
—— 'Manorial Court Roll Inventories as Evidence for English Peasant Consumption and Living Standards, c.1270–c.1420', in A. Furio and F. Garcia-Oliver (eds.), *Pautes de Consum i Nivells de Vida al Món Rural Medieval* (Valencia, forthcoming)
—— 'Seigniorial Control of Villagers' Litigation Beyond the Manor in Later Medieval England', *HR*, 81 (2008), pp. 399–422

Britnell, R. H., *Britain and Ireland, 1050–1530: Economy and Society* (Oxford, 2004)
—— *The Closing of the Middle Ages? England, 1471–1529* (Cambridge, 1997)
—— 'The Coal Industry in the Later Middle Ages: The Bishop of Durham's Estates', in M. Bailey and S. H. Rigby (eds.), *Town and Countryside in the Age of the Black Death: Essays in Honour of John Hatcher* (Turnhout, 2012), pp. 439–72
—— *The Commercialisation of English Society, 1000–1500* (Manchester, 1997)
—— 'The English Economy and the Government, 1450–1550', in John Watts (ed.), *The End of the Middle Ages? England in the Fifteenth and Sixteenth Centuries* (Stroud, 1998), pp. 89–116
—— 'Feudal Reaction after the Black Death in the Palatinate of Durham', *P&P*, 128 (1990), pp. 28–47
—— 'The Proliferation of Markets in England, 1200–1349', *EcHR*, 34 (1981), pp. 209–21
—— and B. M. S. Campbell (eds.), *A Commercialising Economy: England 1086–c.1300* (Manchester, 1997).
—— and John Mullan, *Land and Family: Trends and Variations in the Peasant Land Market on the Winchester Bishopric Estates, 1263–1415* (Hatfield, 2010)
Broad, John, *Transforming English Rural Society: the Verneys and the Claydons, 1600–1820* (Cambridge, 2004)
Brooks, C. W., *Law Politics and Society in Early Modern England* (Cambridge, 2008)
Brown, A. T., 'Estate Management and Institutional Constraints in Pre-Industrial England: the Ecclesiastical Estates of Durham, c. 1400–1640', *EcHR*, 67 (2014), pp. 699–719
—— 'A Money Economy? Provisioning Durham Cathedral across the Dissolution, 1350–1600', in J. P. Bowen and A. T. Brown (eds.), *Custom and Commercialisation in English Rural Society: Revisiting Postan and Tawney* (Hatfield, forthcoming)
—— 'The Rise of a Rural Elite? Leaseholders on Durham Cathedral's Estates, 1540–1640', in Adrian Green and Barbara Crosbie (eds.), *The Economy and Culture of North-East England, 1500–1800* (forthcoming)
—— 'Surviving the Mid-Fifteenth-Century Recession: Durham Cathedral Priory, 1400–1520', *NH*, 47 (2010), pp. 209–31
Buckatzsch, E. J., 'The Geographical Distribution of Wealth in England, 1086–1843: An Experimental Study of Certain Tax Assessments', *EcHR*, 3 (1950), pp. 180–202
Butcher, A. F., 'Rent, Population and Economic Change in Late-Medieval Newcastle', *NH*, 14 (1978), pp. 67–77
Campbell, Bruce M. S., 'The Agrarian Problem in the Early Fourteenth Century', *P&P*, 188 (2005), pp. 3–70
—— 'Agricultural Progress in Medieval England: Some Evidence from Eastern Norfolk', *EcHR*, 36 (1983), pp. 26–46
—— 'Arable Productivity in Medieval England: Some Evidence from Norfolk', *JEcH*, 43 (1983), pp. 379–404
—— 'England: Land and People', in S. H. Rigby (ed.), *A Companion to Britain in the Later Middle Ages* (Oxford, 2003), pp. 3–25
—— *English Seigniorial Agriculture, 1250–1450* (Cambridge, 2000)
—— *Field Systems and Farming Systems in Late Medieval England* (Aldershot, 2008)
—— 'Matching Supply to Demand: Crop Production and Disposal by English Demesnes in the Century of the Black Death', *JEcH*, 57 (1997), pp. 827–58
—— 'The Population of Early Tudor England: A Re-evaluation of the 1522 Muster Returns and 1524 and 1525 Lay Subsidies', *Journal of Historical Geography*, 7 (1981), pp. 145–54
—— and Mark Overton, 'A New Perspective on Medieval and Early Modern Agriculture: Six Centuries of Norfolk Farming, c.1250–c.1850', *P&P*, 141 (1993), pp. 38–105

Cantor, N. F., *In the Wake of the Plague: The Black Death and the World it Made* (New York, 2001)

Carpenter, Christine, 'Gentry and Community in Medieval England', *Journal of British Studies*, 33 (1994), pp. 340–80

—— *Locality and Polity: A Study of Warwickshire Landed Gentry, 1401–99* (Cambridge, 1992)

Chayanov, A. V., *The Theory of Peasant Economy* (ed.) Daniel Thorner et al. (Madison, 1986)

Cipolla, C. M., *Before the Industrial Revolution: European Society and Economy, 1000–1700* (London, 1993)

Clack, Peter, 'Bishop Cosin's Survey of his Episcopal Estates', in Margot Johnson (ed.), *John Cosin: Papers Presented to a Conference to Celebrate the 400th Anniversary of his Birth* (Durham, 1997), pp. 228–36

Clark, G., 'The Cost of Capital and Medieval Agricultural Technique', *Explorations in Economic History*, 25 (1988), pp. 265–94

—— 'The Economies of Exhaustion, the Postan Thesis, and the Agricultural Revolution', *JEcH*, 52 (1992), pp. 61–84

—— 'The Long March of History: Farm Wages, Population, and Economic Growth, England 1209–1869', *EcHR*, 60 (2007), pp. 97–135

Clark, J. C. D., *Revolution and Rebellion: State and Society in England in the Seventeenth and Eighteenth Centuries* (Cambridge, 1986)

Clay, C. G. A., *Economic Expansion and Social Change: England 1500–1700*, 2 vols. (Cambridge, 1984)

—— '"The Greed of Whig Bishops"? Church Landlords and their Lessees, 1660–1760', *P&P*, 87 (1980), pp. 128–57

—— 'Landlords and Estate Management in England', in J. Thirsk (ed.), The *Agrarian History of England and Wales, 5: 1640–1750*, part 2 (Cambridge, 1985), pp. 119–251

Cliffe, J. T., *The Yorkshire Gentry from the Reformation to the Civil War* (London, 1969)

Coase, Ronald, 'The Institutional Structure of Production', *American Economic Review*, 82 (1992), pp. 713–19

—— 'The Nature of the Firm', *Economica*, 16 (1937), pp. 386–405

—— 'The Problem of Social Cost', *Journal of Law and Economics*, 3 (1960), pp. 1–44

Coleman, D. C., 'The Gentry Controversy and the Aristocracy in Crisis, 1558–1641', *History*, 51 (1966), p. 165–78

Cooper, John, 'The Counting of Manors', *EcHR*, 8 (1956), pp. 377–89

Cornwall, J., 'English Population in the Early Sixteenth Century', *EcHR*, 23 (1970), pp. 32–44

Coss, Peter, 'An Age of Deference', in Rosemary Horrox and W. M. Ormrod (eds.), *A Social History of England, 1200–1500* (Cambridge, 2006), pp. 31–73

—— 'The Formation of the English Gentry', *P&P*, 147 (1995), pp. 38–64

—— *The Foundations of Gentry Life: the Multons of Frampton and their World, 1270–1370* (Oxford, 2010)

—— *Lordship, Knighthood and Locality: A Study in English Society, c. 1180–1280* (Cambridge, 1991)

Craster, H. H. E., *A History of Northumberland, 8: The Parish of Tynemouth* (London, 1907)

Cross, Claire M., 'The Economic Problems of the See of York: Decline and Recovery in the Sixteenth Century', in Joan Thirsk (ed.), *Land, Church and People: Essays Presented to Professor H. P. R. Finberg, AgHR* Supplement (1970), pp. 64–83

Davenport, Frances Gardiner, *The Economic Development of a Norfolk Manor, 1086–1565* (Cambridge, 1906)

David, P. A., 'Clio and the Economics of QWERTY', *American Economic Review*, 75 (1985), pp. 332–7

De Vries, Jan, *The Dutch Rural Economy in the Golden Age, 1500–1700* (London, 1974)
—— 'The Industrial Revolution and the Industrious Revolution', *JEcH*, 54 (1994), pp. 249–70
—— *The Industrious Revolution: Consumer Behaviour and the Household Economy, 1650 to the Present* (Cambridge, 2008)
Dobb, Maurice, *Studies in the Development of Capitalism* (London, 1946)
Dobson, R. B., *Church and Society in the Medieval North of England* (London, 1996)
—— *Durham Priory, 1400–1450* (Cambridge, 1973)
—— 'Urban Decline in Late Medieval England', *Transactions of the Royal Historical Society*, 5th series, 27 (1977), pp. 1–22
Dodds, Ben, 'Durham Priory Tithes and the Black Death between the Tyne and Tees', *NH*, 39 (2002), pp. 5–24
—— 'Estimating Arable Output Using Durham Priory Tithe Receipts, 1341–1450', *EcHR*, 57 (2004), pp. 245–85
—— 'Output and Productivity: Common Themes and Regional Variations', in R. H. Britnell and B. Dodds (eds.), *Agriculture and Rural Society after the Black Death: Common Themes and Regional Variations* (Hatfield, 2008), pp. 73–88
—— *Peasants and Production in the Medieval North-East: The Evidence from Tithes, 1270–1536* (Woodbridge, 2007)
—— 'Peasants, Landlords and Production Between the Tyne and the Tees, 1349–1450', in C. Liddy and R. H. Britnell (eds.), *North-East England in the Later Middle Ages* (Woodbridge, 2005), pp. 173–96
—— and Elizabeth Gemmill and Phillipp Schofield, 'Durham Grain Prices, 1278–1515', *AA*, 39 (2010), pp. 307–27
—— and Christian Liddy, 'Richard Britnell: An Appreciation', in Ben Dodds and Christian Liddy (eds.), *Commercial Activity, Markets and Entrepreneurs in the Middle Ages: Essays in Honour of Richard Britnell* (Woodbridge, 2011)
Drury, Linda, 'Early settlement in Stanhope Park, Weardale, c. 1406–79', *AA*, 5th series, 4 (1976), pp. 139–49
—— 'Inventories in the Probate Records of the Diocese of Durham', *AA*, 5th series, 28 (2000), pp. 177–91
—— 'More Stout than Wise: Tenant Right in Weardale in the Tudor Period', in D. Marcombe (ed.), *The Last Principality: Politics, Religion and Society in the Bishopric of Durham, 1494–1660* (Nottingham, 1987), pp. 71–100
Du Boulay, F. R. H., 'Archbishop Cranmer and the Canterbury Temporalities', *EcHR*, 67 (1952), pp. 19–36
—— *The Lordship of Canterbury: an Essay on Medieval Society* (London, 1966)
—— 'A Rentier Economy in the Later Middle Ages: The Archbishopric of Canterbury', *EcHR*, 16 (1964), pp. 427–38
—— 'Who were Farming the English Demesnes at the End of the Middle Ages?', *EcHR*, 17 (1965), pp. 443–55
Dunsford, H. M., and S. J. Harris, 'Colonisation of the Wasteland in County Durham', *EcHR*, 56 (2003), pp. 34–56
Dyer, Christopher, *An Age of Transition? Economy and Society in England in the Later Middle Ages* (Oxford, 2005)
—— *Lords and Peasants in a Changing Society: The Estates of the Bishopric of Worcester, 680–1540* (Cambridge, 1980)
—— *Making a Living in the Middle Ages: The People of Britain, 850–1520* (London, 2002)
—— 'A Redistribution of Incomes in Fifteenth-Century England', *P&P*, 39 (1968), pp. 11–33

—— 'Rural Europe', in C. Allmand (ed.), *The New Cambridge Medieval History, Volume VII, c. 1415–1500* (Cambridge, 1998), pp. 106–20
—— *Standards of Living in the Later Middle Ages: Social Change in England, 1200–1520* (Cambridge, 1989)
—— 'A Suffolk Farmer in the Fifteenth Century', *AgHR*, 55 (2007), pp. 1–22
—— 'Were Late Medieval Villages "Self-Contained"?', in Christopher Dyer (ed.), *The Self-Contained Village? The Social History of Rural Communities, 1250–1900* (Hatfield, 2007), pp. 6–27
—— 'Were there any Capitalists in Fifteenth-Century England?', in Jennifer Kermode (ed.), *Enterprise and Individuals in Fifteenth-Century England* (Gloucester, 1991), pp. 1–24
—— and P. Coss and C. Wickham (eds.), *Rodney Hilton's Middle Ages: An Exploration of Historical Themes* (Oxford, 2007)
Eales, Jacqueline and Hopper, Andrew (eds.), *The County Community in Seventeenth-Century England and Wales* (Hatfield, 2012)
Easterly, William, *The Elusive Quest for Growth: Economists' Adventures and Misadventures in the Tropics* (Cambridge, 2001)
Eggertsson, Thrainn, *Economic Behaviour and Institutions* (Cambridge, 1990)
Ellis, Frank, *Peasant Economics: Farm Households and Agrarian Development* (Cambridge, 1988)
Epstein, S. R., 'Rodney Hilton, Marxism and the Transition from Feudalism to Capitalism', in C. Dyer, P. Coss and C. Wickham (eds.), *Rodney Hilton's Middle Ages: An Exploration of Historical Themes* (Oxford, 2007), pp. 248–269
Evans, M., *Art Collecting and Lineage in the Elizabethan Age: The Lumley Inventory and Pedigree* (London)
Everitt, A. M., *The Community of Kent and the Great Rebellion, 1640–1660* (Leicester, 1966)
—— *The Local Community and the Great Rebellion* (London, 1969)
—— 'The Peers and the Provinces', *AgHR*, 16 (1968), pp. 60–7
Faith, Rosamond, *The English Peasantry and the Growth of Lordship* (London, 1997)
—— 'Peasant Families and Inheritance Customs in Medieval England', *AgHR*, 14 (1966), pp. 77–95
Farmer, D. L., 'Marketing the Produce of the Countryside, 1200–1500', in E. Miller (ed.), *The Agrarian History of England and Wales, 3: 1350–1500* (Cambridge, 1991), pp. 324–430
—— 'Prices and Wages, 1350–1500', in E. Miller (ed.), *The Agrarian History of England and Wales, 3: 1350–1500* (Cambridge, 1991), pp. 431–525
Flinn, M. W., *Origins of the Industrial Revolution* (London, 1966)
Foster, Andrew W., 'The Struggle for Parliamentary Representation for Durham, 1600–41', in David Marcombe (ed.), *The Last Principality: Politics, Religion and Society in the Bishopric of Durham, 1494–1660* (Nottingham, 1987), pp. 176–201
Fraser, Constance M., 'The Free Court of the Priors of Durham', in C. Liddy and R. H. Britnell (eds.), *North-East England in the Later Middle Ages* (Woodbridge, 2005), pp. 111–17
French, Henry, and R. W. Hoyle, *The Character of English Rural Society: Earls Colne, 1550–1750* (Manchester, 2007)
—— and R. W. Hoyle, 'English Individualism Refuted: And Reasserted: The Land Market of Earls Colne (Essex), 1550–1750', *EcHR*, 56 (2003), pp. 595–622
Fryde, E. B., *Peasants and Landlords in Later Medieval England, c.1380–c.1525* (Stroud, 1996)
Galloway, R. L., *Annals of Coal Mining and the Coal Trade*, vol. 1 (Newton Abbot, 1882)
Garrard, Rachel P., 'English Probate Inventories and their use in Studying the Significance of the Domestic Interior, 1570–1700', in Ad van der Woude and Anton Schuurman (eds.), *Probate Inventories: A New Source for the Historical Study of Wealth, Material Culture, and Agricultural Development* (Wageningen, 1980), pp. 55–81

Gibson, W., 'The Manor of Winlaton', *AA*, 4th series, 23 (1945), pp. 8–26

Ginzburg, Carlo, *The Cheese and the Worms: the Cosmos of a Sixteenth-Century Miller* (Baltimore, 2003)

Glennie, Paul, 'In Search of Agrarian Capitalism: Manorial Land Markets and the Acquisition of Land in the Lea Valley', *Continuity and Change*, 3 (1988), pp. 11–40

Goldberg, P. J. P., *Medieval England: A Social History 1250–1550* (London, 2004)

—— 'Mortality and Economic Change in the Diocese of York, 1390–1514', *NH*, 24 (1988), pp. 38–55

—— *Women, Work and Life Cycle in a Medieval Economy: Women in York and Yorkshire, c.1300–1520* (Oxford, 1992)

Gooch, Leo, *A Complete Pattern of Nobility: John, Lord Lumley, c.1534–1609* (Sunderland, 2009)

Grassby, R., *Kinship and Capitalism: Marriage, Family, and Business in the English-Speaking World, 1580–1720* (Cambridge, 2000)

Green, Adrian, 'Houses and Landscape in Early Industrial County Durham', in T. E. Faulkner and Helen Berry (eds.), *Northern Landscapes: Representations and Realities of North-East England* (Woodbridge, 2010), pp. 125–40

—— 'Introduction', Elizabeth Parkinson (ed.), *Durham County Hearth Tax Assessment, Lady Day 1666* (London, 2006)

—— and A. J. Pollard (eds.), *Regional Identities in North-East England, 1300–2000* (Woodbridge, 2007)

Grigg, D. B., *Population Growth and Agrarian Change: An Historical Perspective* (Cambridge, 1980)

Guy, John, *Tudor England* (Oxford, 1988)

Hadcock, R. N., 'A Map of Medieval Northumberland and Durham', *AA*, 16 (1939), pp. 142–218

Hainsworth, D.A., *Stewards, Lords and People: the Estate Steward and his World in Later Stuart England* (Cambridge 1992)

Halcrow, E. M., 'The Decline of Demesne Farming on the Estates of Durham Cathedral Priory', *EcHR*, 7 (1955), pp. 345–56

—— 'The Social Position and Influence of the Priors of Durham, as Illustrated by their Correspondence', *AA*, 33 (1955), pp. 70–86

Hanawalt, B., *The Ties that Bound: Peasant Families in Medieval England* (Oxford, 1986)

Hare, J. N., 'The Bishop and the Prior: Demesne Agriculture in Medieval Hampshire', *AgHR*, 54 (2006), pp. 187–212

—— 'The Demesne Lessees of Fifteenth-Century Wiltshire', *AgHR*, 29 (1981), pp. 1–15

—— 'Growth and Recession in the Fifteenth-Century Economy: The Wiltshire Textile Industry and the Countryside', *EcHR*, 52 (1999), pp. 1–26

—— 'The Monks as Landlords: The Leasing of the Monastic Demesnes in Southern England', in C. Barron and C. Harper-Bill (eds.), *The Church in Pre-Reformation Society: Essays in Honour of F. R. H. Du Boulay* (Woodbridge, 1985), pp. 82–94

—— *A Prospering Society: Wiltshire in the Later Middle Ages* (Hatfield, 2011)

Harris, B. J., 'Landlords and Tenants in England in the Later Middle Ages: The Buckingham Estates', *P&P*, 43 (1969), pp. 146–50

Harris, S. J., 'Wastes, the Margins and the Abandonment of Land: the Bishop of Durham's Estate, 1350–1480', in C. Liddy and R. H. Britnell (eds.), *North-East England in the Later Middle Ages* (Woodbridge, 2005), pp. 197–219

Harrison, C. J., 'Grain Price Analysis and Harvest Qualities, 1465–1634', *AgHR*, 19 (1971), pp. 135–55

Harvey, Barbara, 'The Aristocratic Consumer in England in the long Thirteenth Century', in

M. Prestwich, R. H. Britnell, and R. Frame (eds.), *Thirteenth Century England VI: Proceedings of the Durham Conference 1995* (Woodbridge, 1997), pp. 17–38
——'The Leasing of the Abbot of Westminster's Demesnes in the Later Middle Ages', *EcHR*, 22 (1969), pp. 17–27
—— *Living and Dying in England, 1100–1540: the Monastic Experience* (Oxford, 1993)
—— *Westminster Abbey and its Estates in the Middle Ages* (Oxford, 1977)
Haslam, Graham, 'The Elizabethan Duchy of Cornwall: An Estate in Stasis', in R. W. Hoyle (ed.), *The Estates of the English Crown, 1558–1640* (Cambridge, 1992), pp. 88–111
Hatcher, John, 'A Diversified Economy: Later Medieval Cornwall', *EcHR*, 22 (1969), pp. 208–27
——'England in the Aftermath of the Black Death', *P&P*, 144 (1994), pp. 3–35
——'English Serfdom and Villeinage: Towards a Reassessment', *P&P*, 90 (1981), pp. 3–39
—— *English Tin Production and Trade Before 1550* (Oxford, 1973)
——'The Great Slump of the Mid-Fifteenth Century', in Richard Britnell and John Hatcher (eds.), *Progress and Problems in Medieval England: Essays in Honour of Edward Miller* (Cambridge, 1996), pp. 237–72
—— *The History of the British Coal Industry, 1: Before 1700: Towards the Age of Coal* (Oxford, 1993)
——'Mortality in the Fifteenth Century: Some New Evidence', *EcHR*, 39 (1986), pp. 19–38
—— *Plague, Population and the English Economy, 1348–1530* (London, 1977)
—— *Rural Economy and Society in the Duchy of Cornwall, 1300–1500* (Cambridge, 1970)
—— 'Unreal Wages: Long-Run Living Standards and the "Golden Age" of the Fifteenth Century', in Ben Dodds and Christian Liddy (eds.), *Commercial Activity, Markets and Entrepreneurs in the Middle Ages: Essays in Honour of Richard Britnell* (Woodbridge, 2011), pp. 1–24
—— and Mark Bailey, *Modelling the Middle Ages: the History and Theory of England's Economic Development* (Oxford, 2001)
—— and Alan Piper and David Stone, 'Monastic Mortality: Durham Priory, 1395–1529', *EcHR*, 59 (2006), pp. 667–87
Heal, Felicity, 'Archbishop Laud Revisited: Leases and Estate Management at Canterbury and Winchester before the Civil War', in Rosemary O'Day and Felicity Heal (eds.), *Princes and Paupers in the English Church, 1500–1800* (Leicester, 1981), pp. 129–51
——'The Bishops and the Act of Exchange of 1559', *HJ*, 17 (1974), pp. 227–46
—— *Of Prelates and Princes: A Study of the Economic and Social Positions of the Tudor Episcopate* (Cambridge, 1980)
——'The Tudors and Church Lands: Economic Problems of the Bishopric of Ely During the Sixteenth Century', *EcHR*, 26 (1973), pp. 198–217
—— and C. Holmes, *The Gentry in England and Wales, 1500–1700* (London, 1994)
Herlihy, D., and C. Klapisch-Zuber, *Tuscans and their Families: A Study of the Florentine Catasto of 1427* (London, 1985)
Hexter, J. H., 'Storm over the Gentry', *Encounter*, 10 (1958), pp. 22–34
Hicks, Michael (ed.), *The Fifteenth-Century Inquisitions Post Mortem: A Companion* (Woodbridge, 2012)
Hill, Christopher, *Change and Continuity in Seventeenth-Century England* (London, 1974)
—— *Economic Problems of the Church: From Archbishop Whitgift to the Long Parliament* (Oxford, 1956)
—— *The English Revolution, 1640* (London, 1940)
—— *Puritanism and Revolution: Studies in Interpretation of the English Revolution of the Seventeenth Century* (London, 1958)
Hind, A. L., *The Story of the Lambton Worm* (Durham, 1978)

Hilton, R. H., *Bond Men Made Free: Medieval Peasant Movements and the English Rising of 1381* (London, 1973)
—— *Class Conflict and the Crisis of Feudalism* (London, 1985)
—— 'The Content and Sources of English Agrarian History before 1500', *AgHR*, 3 (1955), pp. 3–19
—— *The Decline of Serfdom in Medieval England* (London, 1969)
—— *The Economic Development of Some Leicestershire Estates in the Fourteenth and Fifteenth Centuries* (London, 1947)
—— 'Medieval Market Towns and Simple Commodity Production', *P&P*, 109 (1985), pp. 3–23
—— *A Medieval Society: the West Midlands at the End of the Thirteenth Century* (Cambridge, 1966)
—— *Peasants, Knights and Heretics: Studies in Medieval English Social History* (Cambridge, 1976)
—— 'Rent and Capital Formation in Feudal Society', in R. H. Hilton (ed.), *The English Peasantry in the Later Middle Ages: The Ford Lectures for 1973* (Oxford, 1975), pp. 174–214
—— (ed.) *The Transition from Feudalism to Capitalism* (London, 1976)
Hindle, Steve, *On the Parish?: The Micro-Politics of Poor Relief in Rural England, c.1550–1750* (Oxford, 2004)
Hobsbawm, Eric, *How to Change the World: Tales of Marx and Marxism* (London, 2011)
Hodgson, R. I., 'The Progress of Enclosure in County Durham, 1550–1870', in H. S. A. Fox and R. A. Butlin (eds.), *Change in the Countryside: Essays on Rural England, 1500–1900* (London, 1979), pp. 83–102
Holderness, B. A., 'Credit in a Rural Community, 1660–1800: Some Neglected Aspects of Probate Inventories', *MH*, 3 (1975–76), pp. 94–116
—— *Pre-Industrial England: Economy and Society, 1500–1750* (London 1976)
Holford, M. L., 'Feet of Fines for the Palatinate of Durham, 1228–1457: Liberties, Law and the Local Community', *EHR*, 125 (2010), pp. 818–43
Holmes, Clive, 'The County Community in Stuart Historiography', *Journal of British Studies*, 19 (1980), pp. 54–73
Holt, J. C., *The Northerners: A Study in the Reign of King John* (Oxford, 1961)
Holt, Jennifer, 'The Financial Rewards of Winning the Battle for Secure Customary Tenure', in J. Whittle (ed.), *Landlords and Tenants in Britain, 1440–1660: Tawney's 'Agrarian Problem' Revisited* (Woodbridge, 2013), pp. 134–49
Horrox, Rosemary, 'England: Kingship and the Political Community, 1377–c.1500', in S. H. Rigby (ed.), *A Companion to Britain in the Later Middle Ages* (Oxford, 2003), pp. 224–41
—— 'Fifteenth-Century Attitudes', in R. Horrox (ed.), *Fifteenth-Century Attitudes: Perceptions of Society in Late Medieval England* (Cambridge, 1994), pp. 1–12
—— 'The Urban Gentry in the Fifteenth Century', in J. Thompson (ed.), *Towns and Townspeople in the Fifteenth Century* (Gloucester, 1988), pp. 22–44
Hoskins, W. G., *The Age of Plunder: The England of Henry VIII, 1500–1547* (London 1976)
—— 'The Elizabethan Merchants of Exeter', in S. T. Bindoff, J. Hurstfield and C. H. Williams (eds.), *Elizabethan Government and Society: Essays Presented to Sir John Neale* (London, 1961), pp. 163–87
—— *Essays in Leicestershire History* (Liverpool, 1950)
—— 'Harvest Fluctuations and English Economic History, 1480–1619', *AgHR*, 12 (1964), pp. 28–46
—— 'The Leicestershire Farmer in the Sixteenth Century', *Transactions of the Leicestershire Archaeological Society*, 22 (1942), pp. 33–94

—— *The Midland Peasant: the Economic and Social History of a Leicestershire Village* (London, 1957)
—— *Provincial England: Essays in Social and Economic History* (London, 1963)
—— 'The Rebuilding of Rural England, 1570–1640', *P&P*, 4 (1953), pp. 44–59
—— 'Regional Farming in England', *AgHR*, 2 (1954), pp. 3–11
Howell, Cicely, *Land, Family, and Inheritance in Transition: Kibworth Harcourt, 1280–1700* (Cambridge, 1983)
Hoyle, R. W., 'Faction, Feud, and Reconciliation Amongst the Northern English Nobility, 1535–1659', *History*, 84 (1999), pp. 590–613
—— 'Henry Percy, Sixth Earl of Northumberland, and the Fall of the House of Percy, 1527–1537', in George Bernard (ed.), *The Tudor Nobility* (Manchester, 1992), pp. 180–211
—— 'The Land–Family Bond in England', *P&P*, 146 (1995), pp. 151–73
—— 'Lords, Tenants, and Tenant-Right in the Sixteenth Century: Four Studies', *NH*, 20 (1984), pp. 38–63
—— *The Pilgrimage of Grace and the Politics of the 1530s* (Oxford, 2001)
—— 'Tenure and the Land Market in Early Modern England: or a Late Contribution to the Brenner Debate', *EcHR*, 43 (1990), pp. 1–20
—— 'Tenure on the Elizabethan Estates', in R. W. Hoyle (ed.), *The Estates of the English Crown, 1558–1640* (Cambridge, 1992), pp. 163–8
—— (ed.), *Custom, Improvement and Landscape in Early Modern Britain* (Farnham, 2013)
—— (ed.), *The Estates of the English Crown, 1558–1640* (Cambridge, 1992), pp. 1–58
Huizinga, Johan, *The Waning of the Middle Ages: A Study of the Forms of Life, Thought and Art in France and the Netherlands in the Fourteenth and Fifteenth Centuries* (London, 1924)
Hyams, Paul, 'The Origins of a Peasant Land Market in England', *EcHR*, 23 (1970), pp. 18–31
James, Mervyn, 'The Concept of Order and the Northern Rising of 1569', *P&P*, 60 (1973), pp. 49–83
—— *Family, Lineage, and Civil Society: A Study of Society, Politics and Mentality in the Durham Region, 1500–1640* (Oxford, 1974)
—— *A Tudor Magnate and the Tudor State: Henry, Fifth Earl of Northumberland* (York, 1966)
Kapelle, W. E., *The Norman Conquest of the North: the Region and its Transformation, 1000–1135* (London, 1979)
—— *Society, Politics and Culture: Studies in Early Modern England* (Cambridge, 1986)
Keen, Maurice, *England in the Later Middle Ages: a Political History* (London, 1973)
—— *English Society in the Later Middle Ages, 1348–1500* (London, 1990)
—— *The Origins of the English Gentleman: Heraldry, Chivalry, and Gentility in Medieval England, c.1300–1500* (Stroud, 2003)
Kermode, Jennifer, *Medieval Merchants: York, Beverley and Hull in the Later Middle Ages* (Cambridge, 1998)
—— 'Merchants, Overseas Trade, and Urban Decline: York, Beverley and Hull, c.1380–1500', *NH*, 23 (1987), pp. 51–73
Kerridge, Eric, *Agrarian Problems in the Sixteenth Century and After* (London, 1969)
—— 'The Movement of Rent, 1540–1640', *EcHR*, 6 (1953), pp. 16–34
Kershaw, I., *Bolton Priory: the Economy of a Northern Monastery, 1286–1325* (Oxford, 1973)
Kesselring, Krista, J., *The Northern Rebellion of 1569: Faith, Politics, and Protest in Elizabethan England* (Basingstoke, 2007)
Kimball, E. G., 'Commissions of the Peace for Urban Jurisdictions in England, 1327–1485', *Proceedings of the American Philosophical Society*, 121 (1977), pp. 448–74
King, Chris, 'The Interpretation of Urban Buildings: Power, Memory and Appropriation in Norwich Merchants' Houses, c. 1400–1660', *World Archaeology*, 41 (2009), pp. 471–88

Kitsikopoulos, Harry, 'Standards of Living and Capital Formation in Pre-Plague England: A Peasant Budget Model', *EcHR*, 53 (2000), pp. 237–61

Kosminsky, E. A., *Studies in the Agrarian History of England in the Thirteenth Century* (Oxford, 1956)

Kowaleski, M., 'The Commercial Dominance of a Medieval Provincial Oligarchy: Exeter in the Late Fourteenth Century', in R. Holt and G. Rosser (eds.), *The Medieval Town, 1200–1540* (London, 1990), pp. 184–216

Kussmaul, Ann, *A General View of the Rural Economy of England, 1538–1840* (Cambridge, 1990)

Langdon, J., 'Was England a Technological Backwater in the Middle Ages?', in Grenville Astill and John Langdon (eds.), *Medieval Farming and Technology: The Impact of Agricultural Change in Northwest Europe* (New York, 1997), pp. 275–92

—— and J. Masschaele, 'Commercial Activity and Population Growth in Medieval England', *P&P*, 190 (2006), pp. 35–82

Lapsley, G. T., *The County Palatine of Durham: a Study in Constitutional History* (New York, 1900)

Larson, Peter, *Conflict and Compromise in the Late Medieval Countryside, 1349–1400* (2006)

—— 'Local Law Courts in Late Medieval Durham', in C. Liddy and R. H. Britnell (eds.), *North-East England in the Later Middle Ages* (Woodbridge, 2005), pp. 97–109

—— 'Peasant Opportunities in Rural Durham: Land, Vills and Mills, 1400–1500', in B. Dodds and C. Liddy (eds.), *Commercial Activity, Markets and Entrepreneurs in the Middle Ages: Essays in Honour of Richard Britnell* (Woodbridge, 2011), pp. 141–64

—— 'Rural Transformation in Northern England: Village Communities of Durham, 1340–1400', in B. Dodds and R. H. Britnell (eds.), *Agriculture and Rural Society after the Black Death: Common Themes and Regional Variations* (Hatfield, 2008), pp. 199–216

Le Roy Ladurie, E., *Montaillou: Cathars and Catholics in a French Village, 1294–1324* (Harmondsworth, 1980)

Lee, John S., *Cambridge and its Economic Region, 1450–1560* (Hatfield, 2005)

Levine, David, and Keith Wrightson, *The Making of an Industrial Society: Whickham, 1560–1765* (Oxford, 1991)

Liddy, Christian, *The Bishopric of Durham in the Late Middle Ages: Lordship, Community and the Cult of St Cuthbert* (Woodbridge, 2008)

—— 'Land, Legend and Gentility in the Palatinate of Durham: The Pollards of Pollard Hall', in C. D. Liddy and R. H. Britnell (eds.), *North-East England in the Later Middle Ages* (Woodbridge, 2005), pp. 75–96

—— *War, Politics, and Finance in Late Medieval English Towns: Bristol, York, and the Crown, 1350–1400* (London, 2005)

—— and Steer C., 'John Lord Lumley and the Creation and Commemoration of Lineage in Early Modern England', *The Archaeological Journal*, 167 (2010), pp. 197–227

Lomas, R. A., 'The Black Death in County Durham', *JMH*, 15 (1989), pp. 127–40

—— 'Developments in Land Tenure on the Prior of Durham's Estate in the Later Middle Ages', *NH*, 13 (1977), pp. 27–43

—— *North-East England in the Middle Ages* (Edinburgh, 1992)

—— 'A Northern Farm at the End of the Middle Ages: Elvethall Manor, Durham, 1443/44–1513/14', *NH*, 18 (1982), pp. 26–53

—— 'A Priory and its Tenants', in R. H. Britnell (ed.), *Daily Life in the Middle Ages* (Stroud, 1998), pp. 103–24

—— 'The Priory of Durham and its Demesnes in the Fourteenth and Fifteenth Centuries', *EcHR*, 31 (1978), pp. 339–53

Lomas, T., 'South-East Durham: Late Fourteenth and Fifteenth Centuries', in P. D. A. Harvey (ed.), *The Peasant Land Market in Medieval England* (Oxford, 1984), pp. 252–327

Lopez, Robert, *The Commercial Revolution of the Middle Ages, 950–1350* (Englewood Cliffs, 1971)

MacCaffrey, W. T., 'England: The Crown and the New Aristocracy, 1540–1600', *P&P*, 30 (1965), pp. 52–64

MacFarlane, Alan, 'The Myth of the Peasantry: Family and Economy in a Northern Parish', in Richard Smith (ed.), *Land, Kinship, and Life-Cycle* (Cambridge, 1984), pp. 333–49

—— *The Origins of English Individualism: The Family, Property and Social Transition* (Oxford, 1978)

Maddern, P. C., 'Social Mobility', in R. Horrox and W. M. Ormrod (eds.), *A Social History of England 1200–1500* (Cambridge, 2006), pp. 113–33

Marcombe, David, 'Church Leaseholders: The Decline and Fall of a Rural Elite', in Rosemary O'Day and Felicity Heal (eds.), *Princes and Paupers in the English Church* (Leicester, 1981), pp. 255–75

—— 'A Rude and Heady People: the Local Community and the Rebellion of the Northern Earls', in D. Marcombe (ed.), *The Last Principality: Politics, Religion and Society in the Bishopric of Durham, 1494–1660* (Nottingham, 1987), pp. 117–51

Marx, Karl, *A Contribution to the Critique of Political Economy* (1859)

Masschaele, J., 'Economic Take-Off and the Rise of Markets', in Carol Lansing and Edward D. English (eds.), *A Companion to the Medieval World* (Chichester, 2009)

—— *Peasants, Merchants, and Markets: Inland Trade in Medieval England, 1150–1350* (New York, 1997)

Mate, M., 'The Farming out of Manors: a New Look at the Evidence from Canterbury Cathedral Priory', *JMH*, 9 (1983), pp. 331–43

—— 'The Indebtedness of Canterbury Cathedral Priory, 1215–95', *EcHR*, 26 (1973), pp. 183–97

—— 'Pastoral Farming in South-East England in the Fifteenth Century', *EcHR*, 40 (1987), pp. 523–36

—— 'Property Investment by Canterbury Cathedral Priory, 1250–1400', *The Journal of British Studies*, 23 (1984), pp. 1–21

Mayhew, N. J., 'Money, Supply, and the Velocity of Circulation in England, 1300–1700', *EcHR*, 48 (1995), pp. 238–57

McIntosh, Marjorie, *Autonomy and Community: The Royal Manor of Havering, 1200–1500* (Cambridge, 1986)

—— *A Community Transformed: The Manor and Liberty of Havering, 1500–1620* (Cambridge, 1991)

Milgrom, Paul, et al., 'The Role of Institutions in the Revival of Trade: the Law Merchant, Private Judges, and the Champagne Fairs', *Economics and Politics*, 2 (1990), pp. 1–23

Miller, E., 'The Elizabethan and Early Stuart Peerage', *HJ*, 9 (1966), pp. 133–44

—— 'Farming in Northern England During the Twelfth and Thirteenth Centuries', *NH*, 11 (1975), pp. 1–16

—— 'Medieval York', in P. M. Tillott (ed.), *The Victoria County History of Yorkshire: City of York* (London, 1961), pp. 25–116

Mingay, G. E., *English Landed Society in the Eighteenth Century* (London 1963)

—— 'The Size of Farms in the Eighteenth Century', *EcHR*, 14 (1962), pp. 469–88

Mitson, A., 'The Significance of Kinship Networks in the Seventeenth Century: South-West Nottinghamshire', in C. Phythian-Adams (ed.), *Societies, Cultures and Kinship, 1580–1850: Cultural Provinces in English Local History* (Leicester, 1993), pp. 24–76

Moore, John S., 'Probate Inventories: Problems and Prospects', in P. Riden (ed.), *Probate Records and the Local Community* (Gloucester, 1985)

Morrin, Jean, 'The Transfer to Leasehold on Durham Cathedral Estate, 1541–1626', in Jane Whittle (ed.), *Landlords and Tenants in Britain, 1440–1660: Tawney's Agrarian Problem Revisited* (Woodbridge, 2013), pp. 117–32

Muldrew, Craig, *The Economy of Obligation: the Culture of Credit and Social Relations in Early Modern England* (Basingstoke, 1998)

—— *Food, Energy and the Creation of Industriousness: Work and Material Culture in Agrarian England, 1550–1780* (Cambridge, 2011)

Muller, Miriam, 'A Divided Class? Peasants and Peasant Communities in Later Medieval England', in C. Dyer, P. Coss and C. Wickham (eds.), *Rodney Hilton's Middle Ages: An Exploration of Historical Themes*, Past and Present Supplement, 2 (2007), pp. 115–31

Munro, John, 'The Late Medieval Decline of English Demesne Agriculture: Demographic, Monetary and Political-Fiscal Factors', in M. Bailey and S. Rigby (eds.), *Town and Countryside in the Age of the Black Death* (Turnhout, 2012), pp. 299–350

Mussett, Patrick, *Lists of Deans and Major Canons of Durham, 1541–1900* (Durham, 1974)

Nef, J. U., *The Rise of the British Coal Industry*, 2 vols. (London, 1932)

Newman, Christine, 'Economy and Society in North-Eastern Market Towns: Darlington and Northallerton in the Later Middle Ages', in C. D. Liddy and R. H. Britnell (eds.), *North-East England in the Later Middle Ages* (Woodbridge, 2005), pp. 127–40

—— 'Employment on the Estates of the Priory of Durham, 1494–1519: the Priory as an Employer', *NH*, 36 (2000), pp. 43–58

—— *Late Medieval Northallerton: A Small Market Town and its Hinterland, 1470–1540* (Stamford, 1999)

Newton, Diana, 'The Clergy, Identity and Lay Society in the Diocese of Durham, 1561–1635', *NH*, 44 (2007), pp. 35–54

—— *North-East England, 1569–1625: Governance, Culture and Identity* (Woodbridge, 2006)

—— and A. J. Pollard (eds.), *Newcastle and Gateshead before 1700* (Chichester, 2009)

North, Douglass C., *Institutions, Institutional Change and Economic Performance* (Cambridge, 1990)

Nightingale, P., 'England and the European Depression of the Mid-Fifteenth Century', *JEEcH*, 26 (1997), pp. 631–56

—— 'Knights and Merchants: Trade, Politics and the Gentry in Late Medieval England', *P&P*, 169 (2000), pp. 36–62

—— 'Monetary Contraction and Mercantile Credit in Later Medieval England', *EcHR*, 43 (1990), pp. 560–75

—— 'The Rise and Decline of Medieval York: A Reassessment', *P&P*, 206 (2010), pp. 3–42

O'Connor, S., 'Adam Fraunceys and John Pyel: Perceptions of Status Among Merchants in Fourteenth-Century London', in D. Clayton, R. Davies and P. McNiven (eds.), *Trade, Devotion and Governance: Papers in Later Medieval History* (Stroud, 1994), pp. 17–35

O'Day, Rosemary, 'Cumulative Debt: the Bishops of Coventry and Lichfield and their Economic Problems', *MH*, 3 (1975), pp. 77–93

—— and Felicity Heal (eds.), *Princes and Paupers in the English Church, 1500–1800* (Leicester, 1981)

Ormrod, W. M. *The Reign of Edward III* (Stroud, 2000)

Outhwaite, R. B., 'Progress and Backwardness in English Agriculture, 1500–1650', *EcHR*, 39 (1986), pp. 1–18

Overton, Mark, *Agricultural Revolution in England: the Transformation of the Agrarian Economy, 1500–1850* (Cambridge, 1996)

—— 'English Probate Inventories and the Measurement of Agricultural Change', in Ad van der Woude and Anton Schuurman (eds.), *Probate Inventories: A New Source for the Historical Study of Wealth, Material Culture, and Agricultural Development* (Wageningen, 1980), pp. 205–16

—— 'Estimating Crop Yields from Probate Inventories: An Example from East Anglia, 1585–1735', *JEcH*, 39 (1979), pp. 363–78

—— et al., *Production and Consumption in English Households, 1600–1750* (London, 2004)

Page, Scott E., 'Path Dependency', *Quarterly Journal of Political Science*, 1 (2006), pp. 87–115

Palliser, David, *Medieval York, 600–1540* (Oxford, 2014)

—— 'Tawney's Century: Brave New World or Malthusian Trap?', *EcHR*, 35 (1982), pp. 339–53

Payling, Simon, *Political Society in Lancastrian England: the Greater Gentry of Nottinghamshire* (Oxford, 1991)

Phelps Brown, E. H., and S. V. Hopkins, 'Seven Centuries of Building Wages', *Economica*, 22 (1955), pp. 195–206

—— and S. V. Hopkins, 'Seven Centuries of the Prices of Consumables, Compared with Builders' Wage-Rates', *Economica*, 23 (1956), pp. 296–314

Pierson, Paul, *Politics in Time: History, Institutions and Social Analysis* (Princeton, 2004)

Pirenne, Henri, *Medieval Cities: Their Origins and the Revival of Trade* (Princeton, 1925)

Pollard, A. J., *Late Medieval England, 1399–1509* (Harlow, 2000)

—— 'The North-Eastern Economy and the Agrarian Crisis of 1438–40', *NH*, 25 (1989), pp. 88–105

—— *North-Eastern England During the Wars of the Roses: Lay Society, War, and Politics, 1450–1500* (Oxford, 1990)

—— (ed.), *The North of England in the Age of Richard III* (Stroud, 1996)

Poos, L. R., *A Rural Society After the Black Death: Essex, 1350–1525* (Cambridge, 1991)

Postan, M. M., 'The Cost of the Hundred Years War', *P&P*, 27 (1964)

—— 'The Economic Foundations of Medieval Society', in M. M. Postan, *Essays on Medieval Agriculture and General Problems of the Medieval Economy* (Cambridge, 1973), pp. 3–27

—— 'The Fifteenth Century', *EcHR*, 9 (1939), pp. 160–7

—— 'Investment in Medieval Agriculture', *EcHR*, 27 (1967), pp. 576–87

—— 'Medieval Agrarian Society in its Prime: England', in M. M. Postan (ed.), *The Cambridge Economic History of Europe, 1: The Agrarian Life of the Middle Ages* (Cambridge, 1966), pp. 548–70

—— *The Medieval Economy and Society: Economic History of Britain, 1100–1500* (London, 1972)

—— 'Money, Population and Economic Change in Late Medieval Europe', *EcHR*, 12 (1959), pp. 77–82

—— 'Some Economic Evidence of Declining Population in the Later Middle Ages', *EcHR* 2 (1950), pp. 221–46

—— 'Some Social Consequences of the Hundred Years' War', *EcHR*, 12 (1942), pp. 1–12

Prestwich, Michael, *The Three Edwards: War and State in England, 1272–1377* (London, 1980)

Puffert, Douglas J., 'Path Dependence, Network Form, and Technological Change', in Timothy W. Guinnane, William A. Sundstrom, and Warren Whatley (eds.), *History Matters: Essays on Economic Growth, Technology, and Demographic Change* (Stanford, 2004), pp. 63–94

Pugh, T. B. (ed.), *The Marcher Lordships of South Wales, 1415–1536: Select Documents* (Cardiff, 1963)

Raftis, J. A., 'Peasants and the Collapse of the Manorial Economy on some Ramsey Abbey Estates', in R. H. Britnell and J. Hatcher (eds.), *Progress and Problems in Medieval England: Essays in Honour of Edward Miller* (Cambridge, 1996), pp. 191–206

—— *Peasant Economic Development Within the English Manorial System* (Montreal, 1996)

—— *Tenure and Mobility: Studies in the Social History of the Medieval English Village* (Toronto, 1964)

Razi, Zvi, *Life, Marriage, and Death in a Medieval Parish: Economy, Society, and Demography in Halesowen, 1270–1400* (Cambridge, 1980)

—— 'The Myth of the Immutable English Family', *P&P*, 140 (1993), pp. 3–44

—— 'The Struggles Between the Abbots of Halesowen and their Tenants in the Thirteenth and Fourteenth Centuries', in T. H. Aston et al. (eds.), *Social Relations and Ideas: Essays in Honour of R. H. Hilton* (Cambridge, 1983), pp. 151–67

Reed, Michael, *Buckinghamshire Probate Inventories, 1661–1714* (Aylesbury, 1988)

—— and Wells, Roger (eds.) *Class, Conflict and Protest in the English Countryside, 1700–1880* (London, 1990)

Reid, D. S., *The Durham Crown Lordships in the Sixteenth and Seventeenth Centuries and the Aftermath* (Durham, 1990)

Reynolds, Susan, *An Introduction to the History of English Medieval Towns* (Oxford, 1977)

Richardson, R. C., *The Debate on the English Revolution Revisited* (London, 1988)

Riden, P. (ed.), *Probate Records and the Local Community* (Gloucester, 1985)

Rigby, S. H., *English Society in the Later Middle Ages: Class, Status and Gender* (Basingstoke, 1995)

—— 'English Society in the Later Middle Ages: Deference, Ambition and Conflict', in Peter Brown (ed.), *A Companion to Medieval English Literature and Culture, c.1350–c.1500* (Oxford, 2007), pp. 25–39

—— 'Historical Causation: Is One Thing More Important Than Another?', *History*, 80 (1995), pp. 227–42

—— 'Historical Materialism: Social Structure and Social Change in the Middle Ages', *Journal of Medieval and Early Modern Studies* 34 (2004), pp. 473–522

—— 'Introduction: Social Structure and Economic Change in Late Medieval England', in R. Horrox and W. M. Ormrod (eds.), *A Social History of England, 1200–1500* (Cambridge, 2006), pp. 1–30

—— 'Urban "Oligarchy" in Late Medieval England', in John A. F. Thomson (ed.), *Towns and Townspeople in the Fifteenth Century* (Gloucester, 1988), pp. 62–86

—— 'Urban Population in Late Medieval England: the Evidence of the Lay Subsidies', *EcHR*, 63 (2010), pp. 393–417

Roberts, B. K., *The Green Villages of County Durham: a Study in Historical Geography* (Durham, 1977)

Robinson, W. C., 'Money, Population and Economic Change in Late Medieval Europe', *EcHR*, 12 (1959), pp. 63–76

Rogers, J., *Six Centuries of Work and Wages: The History of English Labour* (London, 1906)

Rollason, D., and Prestwich M. (eds.), *The Battle of Neville's Cross, 1346* (Stamford, 1998)

Rosenthal, J., 'Fifteenth-Century Baronial Incomes and Richard Duke of York', *BIHR*, 37 (1964), pp. 233–9

Rowlands, M. B., *Masters and Men in the West Midlands Metalware Trades Before the Industrial Revolution* (Manchester, 1975)

Russell, Josiah C., 'Population in Europe', in Carlo M. Cipolla, (ed.), *The Fontana Economic History of Europe, I: The Middle Ages* (Glasgow, 1972)

Saul, Nigel, 'Bold as Brass: Secular Display in English Medieval Brasses', in Peter Coss and Maurice Keen (eds.), *Heraldry, Pageantry and Social Display in Medieval England* (Woodbridge, 2002)

—— *Knights and Esquires: The Gloucestershire Gentry in the Fourteenth Century* (Oxford, 1981)

Schneider, Eric, 'Prices and Production: Agricultural Supply Response in Fourteenth-Century England', *EcHR* 67 (2014), pp. 66–91

Schofield, Phillipp, 'England: the Family and the Village Community', in S. H. Rigby (ed.), *A Companion to Britain in the Later Middle Ages* (Oxford, 2003), pp. 26–46

—— *Peasants and Community in Medieval England, 1200–1500* (Basingstoke, 2003)

—— 'The Social Economy of the Medieval Village in the Early Fourteenth Century', *EcHR*, 61 (2008), pp. 38–63

—— 'Tenurial Developments and the Availability of Customary Land in a Later Medieval Community', *EcHR* 49 (1996), pp. 250–67

Sharpe, J. A., *Early Modern England: A Social History, 1550–1760* (London, 1987)

Shaw-Taylor, Leigh, 'The Rise of Agrarian Capitalism and the Decline of Family Farming in England', *EcHR*, 65 (2012), pp. 26–60

Simpson, Alan, *The Wealth of the Gentry, 1540–1660* (Cambridge, 1961)

Smith, Richard M., 'The English Peasantry, 1250–1650', in Tom Scott (ed.), *The Peasantries of Europe from the Fourteenth to the Eighteenth Centuries* (London, 1998), pp. 339–71

—— 'Human Resources', in G. Astill and A. Grant (eds.), *The Countryside of Medieval England* (Oxford, 1988), pp. 188–212

—— 'Measuring Adult Mortality in an Age of Plague: England, 1349–1540', in M. Bailey and S. H. Rigby (eds.), *Town and Countryside in the Age of the Black Death: Essays in Honour of John Hatcher* (Turnhout, 2012), pp. 43–85

—— 'Some Issues Concerning Families and their Property in Rural England, 1250–1800', in R. M. Smith (ed.), *Land, Kinship and Life-Cycle* (Cambridge, 1984), pp. 1–86

Spufford, Margaret, *Contrasting Communities: English Villages in the Sixteenth and Seventeenth Centuries* (London, 1974)

—— 'The Limitations of the Probate Inventory', in J. Chartres and D. Hey (eds.), *English Rural Society, 1500–1800: Essays in Honour of Joan Thirsk* (Cambridge, 1990), pp. 139–74

Sreenivasan, G., 'The Land-Family Bond at Earls Colne (Essex), 1550–1650', *P&P*, 131 (1991), pp. 3–37

—— 'The Land-Family Bond: A Reply', *P&P*, 146 (1995), pp. 174–87

Stephenson, M., 'Risk and Capitol Formation: Seigneurial Investment in an Age of Adversity', in M. Bailey and S. Rigby (eds.), *Town and Countryside in the Age of the Black Death: Essays in Honour of John Hatcher* (Turnhout, 2012), pp. 175–212

Stone, David, *Decision-Making in Medieval Agriculture* (Oxford, 2005)

—— 'Medieval Farm Management and Technological Mentalities: Hinderclay before the Black Death', *EcHR*, 54 (2001), pp. 612–38

Stone, Lawrence, 'The Anatomy of the Elizabethan Aristocracy', *EcHR*, 18 (1948), pp. 1–54

—— 'The Bourgeois Revolution of Seventeenth-Century England Revisited', *P&P*, 109 (1985), pp. 44–54

—— *The Causes of the English Revolution, 1529–1642* (London, 1972)

—— 'Counting Manors Again: A Reply to Mr Thompson', *EcHR*, 25 (1972), pp. 131–6

—— *The Crisis of the Aristocracy, 1558–1641* (Oxford, 1965)

—— 'The Elizabethan Aristocracy – A Restatement', *EcHR*, 4 (1952), pp. 302–21

—— 'Social Mobility in England, 1500–1700', *P&P*, 33 (1966), pp. 16–55

Storey, R. L., *Thomas Langley and the Bishopric of Durham, 1406–1437* (London, 1961)

Strong, R., *The English Icon: Elizabethan and Jacobean Portraiture* (London, 1969)

Sturges, Charles, *Cuthbert Tunstall: Churchman, Scholar, Administrator* (London, 1938)

Surtees, R., *The History and Antiquities of the County Palatine of Durham*, vols. 1–4 (1816)

Sweezy, Paul, et al., *The Transition from Feudalism to Capitalism* (London, 1954)

Tabili, Laura, *Global Migrants, Local Culture: Natives and Newcomers in Provincial England, 1841–1939* (Basingstoke, 2011)

Tawney, R. H., *The Agrarian Problem in the Sixteenth Century* (London, 1912)

—— 'The Rise of the Gentry, 1558–1640', *EcHR*, 11 (1941), pp. 1–38

—— 'The Rise of the Gentry: A Postscript', *EcHR*, 7 (1954), pp. 91–7

Taylor, Stephen and Tapsell, Grant (eds.), *The Nature of the English Revolution Revisited* (Woodbridge, 2013)

Thirsk, Joan, 'The Farming Regions of England', in J. Thirsk (ed.), *The Agrarian History of England and Wales, 4: 1500–1640* (Cambridge, 1967), pp. 1–112

Thompson, Christopher, 'The Counting of Manors Reconsidered', *EcHR*, 25 (1972), pp. 124–31

Thompson, F. M. L., *Gentrification and the Enterprise Culture: Britain, 1780–1980* (Oxford, 2001)

Threlfall-Holmes, M., *Monks and Markets: Durham Cathedral Priory, 1460–1520* (Oxford, 2005)

—— 'Newcastle Trade and Durham Priory, 1460–1520', in C. D. Liddy and R. H. Britnell (eds.), *North-East England in the Later Middle Ages* (Woodbridge, 2005), pp. 141–52

Thrupp, S., *The Merchant Class of Medieval London, 1300–1500* (Chicago, 1948)

Titow, J. Z., *English Rural Society, 1200–1350* (London, 1969)

—— 'Lost Rents, Vacant Holdings and the Contraction of Peasant Cultivation after the Black Death', *AgHR*, 42 (1994), pp. 97–114

—— 'Some Differences Between Manors and their Effects on the Condition of the Peasant in the Thirteenth Century', *AgHR*, 10 (1962), pp. 1–13

—— *Winchester Yields: a Study in Medieval Agricultural Productivity* (Cambridge, 1972)

Trevor-Roper, H. R., 'The Bishopric of Durham and the Capitalist Reformation', *Durham University Journal*, 7 (1946), pp. 45–58

—— 'The Elizabethan Aristocracy: An Anatomy Anatomized', *EcHR*, 3 (1951), pp. 279–98

—— *The Gentry, 1540–1640* (Cambridge, 1953)

Turner, Michael, 'The Demise of the Yeoman, c.1750–1940', in J. Broad (ed.), *A Common Agricultural Heritage? Revising the French and British Rural Divergence* (*AgHR* supplement series 5, 2009), pp. 83–106.

Van Bavel, B. J. P., and Zanden, J. L., 'The Jump Start of the Holland Economy During the Late-Medieval Crisis, c. 1350–c.1500', *EcHR*, 57 (2004), pp. 503–32

Warde, Paul, 'Subsistence and Sales: The Peasant Economy of Wurttemberg in the Early Sixteenth Century', *EcHR*, 59 (2006), pp. 289–319

Wareham, Andrew, *Lords and Communities in Early Medieval East Anglia* (Woodbridge, 2005)

Weatherill, Lorna, *Consumer Behaviour and Material Culture in Britain, 1660–1760* (London, 1996)

Weber, Max., *The Protestant Ethic and the Spirit of Capitalism* (London, 1930)

Whittle, Jane, *The Development of Agrarian Capitalism: Land and Labour in Norfolk, 1440–1580* (Oxford, 2000)

—— 'Individualism and the Family-Land Bond: A Reassessment of Land Transfer Patterns Among the English Peasantry, c.1270–1580', *P&P*, 160 (1998), pp. 25–63

—— 'Leasehold Tenure in England, c.1300–c.1600: its Form and Incidence', in B. van Bavel and P. R. Schofield (eds.), *The Development of Leasehold in North-Western Europe, c.1200–1600* (Turnhout, 2008), pp. 139–54

—— 'Population Mobility in Rural Norfolk among Landholders and Others, c.1440–c.1600', in Christopher Dyer (ed.), *The Self-Contained Village? The Social History of Rural Communities, 1250–1900* (Hatfield, 2007), pp. 28–45

—— 'Tenure and Landholding in England, 1440–1580: A Crucial Period for the Develop-

ment of Agrarian Capitalism?', in Bas van Bavel and Peter Hoppenbrouwers (eds.), *Landholding and Land Transfer in the North Seas Area* (Turnhout, 2004), pp. 237–49
—— (ed.), *Landlords and Tenants in Britain, 1440–1660: Tawney's 'Agrarian Problem' Revisited* (Woodbridge, 2013)
Williams, Lorelei, and Sally Thompson (eds.), *Marlborough Probate Inventories, 1591–1775* (Chippenham, 2007)
Williamson, Oliver E., *The Economic Institutions of Capitalism* (New York, 1985)
Wilson, R. G., *Gentlemen Merchants: the Merchant Community in Leeds, 1700–1830* (Manchester, 1971)
Winchester, A. J. L., *Landscape and Society in Medieval Cumbria* (Edinburgh, 1987)
Withington, Philip, *The Politics of Commonwealth: Citizens and Freemen in Early Modern England* (Cambridge, 2005)
—— 'Two Renaissances: Urban Political Culture in Post-Reformation England Reconsidered', *HJ*, 44 (2001), pp. 239–67
Wolf, Eric, *Peasants* (Englewood Cliffs, NJ, 1966)
Wood, Andy, *The Memory of the People: Custom and Popular Senses of the Past in Early Modern England* (Cambridge, 2013)
—— *The Politics of Social Conflict: the Peak Country, 1520–1770* (Cambridge, 2000)
Woodward, Donald, *Men at Work: Labourers and Building Craftsmen in the Towns of Northern England, 1450–1750* (Cambridge, 1995)
—— 'Wage Rates and Living Standards in Pre-Industrial England', *P&P*, 91 (1981), pp. 28–45
Woolf, Stuart, 'The Aristocracy in Transition: A Continental Comparison', *EcHR*, 23 (1970), pp. 520–31
Wright, Susan, *The Derbyshire Gentry in the Fifteenth Century* (Derby, 1983)
Wrightson, Keith, *Earthly Necessities: Economic Lives in Early Modern Britain, 1470–1750* (New Haven, 2000)
—— *English Society, 1580–1680* (London, 1982)
—— 'Kinship in an English Village: Terling, Essex, 1500–1700', in Richard Smith (ed.), *Land, Kinship and Life-Cycle* (Cambridge, 1984), pp. 313–32
—— *Ralph Tailor's Summer: A Scrivener, his City and the Plague* (London, 2011)
—— '"That Lamentable Time": Catastrophe and Community in the Great Newcastle Plague of 1636', in D. Newton and A. J. Pollard (eds.), *Newcastle and Gateshead Before 1700* (Chichester, 2009), pp. 241–64
—— and David Levine, *Poverty and Piety in an English Village: Terling, 1525–1700* (Oxford, 1995)
Wrigley, E. A., 'Urban Growth and Agricultural Change: England and the Continent in the Early Modern Period', *JIH*, 15 (1985), pp. 683–728
—— and R. S. Davies, J. E. Oeppen and R. S. Schofield, *English Population History from Family Reconstitution, 1580–1837* (Cambridge, 1997)
—— and R. S. Schofield, *The Population History of England, 1541–1871: A Reconstruction* (London, 1981)
Yates, Margaret, 'Change and Continuities in Rural Society from the Later Middle Ages to the Sixteenth Century: The Contribution of West Berkshire', *EcHR*, 52 (1999), pp. 617–37
—— *Town and Countryside in Western Berkshire, c.1327–c.1600: Social and Economic Change* (Woodbridge, 2007)
Young, Charles R., *The Making of the Neville Family, 1166–1400* (Woodbridge, 1996)
Youngs, Deborah, 'Estate Management, Investment and the Gentleman Landlord in Later Medieval England', *HR*, 73 (2000), pp. 124–41

—— 'Servants and Labourers on a Late Medieval Demesne: The Case of Newton, Cheshire, 1498–1520', *AgHR*, 47 (1999), pp. 145–60

Zell, Michael, *Industry in the Countryside: Wealden Society in the Sixteenth Century* (Cambridge, 1994)

Unpublished Doctoral Theses

Barnett, C. M., 'Memorials and Commemoration in the Parish Churches of Late Medieval York' (York, 1997)

Boniface, Jonathan Paul, 'The Durham Gentry: Social Stability and Change in the Palatinate of Durham, c.1286–1346' (Durham, 2006)

Brown, John, 'Lead Production on the North-East Periphery: A Study of the Bowes Family Estate, c.1550–1771' (Durham, 2010)

Dodds, Ben, 'Tithe and Agrarian Output Between the Tyne and Tees, 1350–1450' (Durham, 2002)

Fisher, E. J., 'Some Yorkshire Estates of the Percys, 1450–1650' (Leeds, 1954)

Hamilton, D. E., 'Social Networks, Families and Neighbourhoods: Brancepeth Parish in the Seventeenth Century' (Durham, 2000)

Horton, Peter Henry, 'The Administrative, Social and Economic Structure of the Durham Bishopric Estates', 1500–1640 (Durham, 1975)

Lomas, Richard, 'Durham Cathedral Priory as a Landowner and a Landlord, 1290–1540' (Durham, 1973)

Lomas, Timothy, 'Land and People in South-East Durham in the Later Middle Ages' (Teesside, 1976)

Marcombe, David, 'The Dean and Chapter of Durham, 1558–1603' (Durham, 1973)

Morrin, Jean, 'Merrington: Land, Landlord and Tenants, 1541–1840: A Study of the Estate of the Dean and Chapter of Durham' (Durham, 1997)

Newman, Christine M., 'The Bowes of Streatlam, County Durham: A Study of the Politics and Religion of a Sixteenth Century Northern Gentry Family' (York, 1991)

Index

www.ingramcontent.com/pod-product-compliance
Lightning Source LLC
LaVergne TN
LVHW011820200926
848484LV00005B/1257

* 9 7 8 1 7 8 3 2 7 0 7 5 0 *